# Between Jew & Arab

David N. Myers
*Between Jew and Arab: The Lost Voice of Simon Rawidowicz*

Sara Bender
*The Jews of Białystock during World War II and the Holocaust*

Nili Scharf Gold
*Yehuda Amichai: The Making of Israel's National Poet*

Hans Jonas
*Memoirs*

Itamar Rabinovich and Jehuda Reinharz, editors
*Israel in the Middle East: Documents and Readings on Society, Politics, and
Foreign Relations, Pre-1948 to the Present*

Christian Wiese
*The Life and Thought of Hans Jonas: Jewish Dimensions*

Eugene R. Sheppard
*Leo Strauss and the Politics of Exile: The Making of a Political Philosopher*

Samuel Moyn
*A Holocaust Controversy: The Treblinka Affair in Postwar France*

Margalit Shilo
*Princess or Prisoner? Jewish Women in Jerusalem, 1840–1914*

Haim Be'er
*Feathers*

Immanuel Etkes
*The Besht: Magician, Mystic, and Leader*

DAVID N. MYERS

# BETWEEN JEW & ARAB

## THE LOST VOICE OF SIMON RAWIDOWICZ

BRANDEIS UNIVERSITY PRESS

WALTHAM, MASSACHUSETTS

*Published by University Press of New England*

*Hanover and London*

Brandeis University Press
Published by University Press of New England,
One Court Street, Lebanon, NH 03766
www.upne.com

© 2008 by Brandeis University Press
First Brandeis University Press paperback edition 2010
Printed in the United States of America 5 4 3 2 1
ISBN for the paperback edition: 978-1-58465-854-2

This book was published with the generous
support of the Lucius N. Littauer Foundation.

LIBRARY OF CONGRESS CATALOGING-IN-PUBLICATION DATA
Myers, David N.
    Between Jew and Arab : the lost voice of Simon Rawidowicz / David N. Myers. —
1st ed.
        p. cm. — (The Tauber Institute for the study of European Jewry series)
    Includes bibliographical references and index.
    ISBN 978-1-58465-736-1 (cloth : alk. paper)
    1. Rawidowicz, Simon, 1897-1957—Criticism and interpretation. 2. Rawidowicz,
Simon, 1897-1957. 3. Zionists—Biography. 4. Israel—Emigration and immigration.
5. Emigration and immigration—Moral and ethical aspects. 6. Arab-Israeli
conflict. I. Title.
    DS151.R375M94 2008
    320.54095694092—dc22
    [B]                                                                    2008037291

*Cover illustration:* Reuven Rubin, *Sheikh Munis*, 1924, oil on canvas, courtesy Rubin
Museum, Tel Aviv. See page 303 for additional illustration credits.

University Press of New England is a member of the Green Press Initiative. The paper
used in this book meets their minimum requirement for recycled paper.

To ARNOLD J. BAND
Teacher, Colleague, Friend

# CONTENTS

# ILLUSTRATIONS

# Between Jew & Arab

# INTRODUCTION

*Unless there is very careful steering it is upon the Arab rock
that the Zionist ship may be wrecked.*

—Herbert Samuel to Chaim Weizmann, 1921[1]

I

In the seemingly ceaseless struggle between Jews and Arabs over the land
known alternately as Erets Yisrael and Palestine, few notions inspire as
much passion and radical divergence as "the right of return." Most Jews regard as historically mandated the return of the Jewish people to the Land
of Israel after millennia of dispersion; a fair number of them (and, for that
matter, of Christians as well) consider this act to be divinely ordained. Accordingly, the long-desired realization of the dream of return, as embodied
in Israel's Declaration of Independence (1948) and Law of Return (1950),
has been seen by Jews as an event of monumental significance—and, especially after the Holocaust, of essential restorative justice.[2]

Conversely, Palestinians regard the displacement of some three-quarters
of a million of their people in the wartime hostilities of 1948 as the *Nakba*
(the Catastrophe), for which "return" is the most just and obvious remedy.[3]
Whether or not millions of Palestinians would return to their or their ancestors' homes in the current State of Israel, if afforded the right, is unclear. Palestinian pollster Khalil Shikaki asserted in the summer of 2003
that while "almost all (Palestinian) refugees viewed the right of return as
sacred," he estimated that "only 10 percent of the refugees surveyed want
to exercise the right of return in Israel."[4]

Shikaki's methods and conclusions quickly came under attack, primarily from fellow Palestinians who insisted that he was deeply mistaken
about their willingness to surrender the right of return.[5] In fact, Shikaki
was attacked at a news conference announcing the results of his survey in
Ramallah in July 2003. The reception accorded him gives a fair indication of
the extraordinary contention that the issue engenders among Palestinians.

And to be sure, if there are different opinions among Palestinians on the question, the gap is far wider between Jews and Arabs. Whereas the renowned Palestinian intellectual Edward Said declared some years ago that there was "a universal Palestinian demand heard all over the globe for the right of return," Israel Prime Minister Ehud Olmert reiterated the long-standing position of his predecessors when he asserted in an interview from May 2007: "I'll never accept a solution that is based on (the refugees') return to Israel, any number."[6] These competing notions undergird the towering walls that separate Zionist and Palestinian nationalism, as well as the competing Israeli and Palestinian historical narratives and public discourse.

For much of the past six decades, these narratives have been almost entirely exclusive of one another. Each side has tended to see its claim to the land not only as superior to, but exclusive of, the other's. Moreover, each side has seen the other as the chief aggressor in the struggle over the land—and, accordingly, justified its own behavior in the name of self-defense and national honor. For Palestinians, the Zionists were and remain colonial usurpers who succeeded in 1948 in their plan to supplant the native inhabitants of the land. For Jews, the Arabs were and remain unrelentingly hostile to the Zionist aspiration of creating a Jewish state. This hostility necessitated a steadfast and unwavering military effort that reached its successful climax in the War of Independence. These competing perspectives have become ritualized in commemorative days: Independence Day for Israelis, marking the declaration of the state on 5 Iyar (according to the Hebrew calendar); and more recently, Nakba Day for Palestinians, usually on 15 May (the date of the Arab states' declaration of war on the new Jewish state), but in some places held to coincide with Israel's Independence Day. This ritualization of historical memory reinforces the attitude of many advocates on both sides of the divide that to acknowledge in any way the validity of the other's claim to the land is tantamount to national betrayal.

The protagonist of this book, Simon Rawidowicz (1897–1957), did not subscribe to this belief. Neither a Palestinian nor an Israeli, Rawidowicz was a Jewish thinker, ideologue, and scholar who followed a long and meandering career path from his native Eastern Europe to Germany and England before arriving in the United States at the age of fifty-one. A few years after coming to American shores, Rawidowicz joined the faculty of the newly founded Brandeis University as a professor of Jewish thought. It was

while at Brandeis that he arrived at the conclusion that the most compelling moral and political challenge facing Jews after 1948 was the resolution of the "Arab Question," the term he used to refer to the status of Arabs
resident in the new State of Israel, as well as to the Arab refugees who left
Palestine in 1948. Rawidowicz issued a plea to address the Arab Question,
culminating in the bold call to repatriate Arab refugees, in a chapter-length
coda to his lengthy Hebrew tome, *Bavel vi-Yerushalayim* (Babylon and Jerusalem). He worked on the large book, along with the small chapter, over
the course of the early to mid-1950s and completed the overall project in
the year of his death, 1957. It is his controversial and far-reaching proposal to redirect the course of the nascent State of Israel—as well as of Jewish political discourse—by confronting the Arab Question that stands at
the center of our concerns here.

Rawidowicz came to his views on the Arab Question rather late—only
after 1948—and not out of strident anti-Zionism. He was, in fact, a staunch
Jewish nationalist who, from his youth, supported the Zionist attempt to
resettle Palestine. Where he departed from more conventional Zionists
was in believing that a vibrant Jewish center in Palestine was a necessary
but not sufficient condition for a flourishing Jewish nation. Such a flourishing also required a vibrant Diaspora community that both stood on its
own and worked in close partnership with the center based in the Land of
Israel. Rawidowicz sought to counter the view that "the Diaspora cannot
survive and be creative" unless it develop a dependent relationship on the
new State of Israel.[7] On the contrary, he believed that the Diaspora experience of the Jews had much to teach Zionists and the State of Israel about
the nature of relations between a ruling majority and a minority in its
midst. The assumption of sovereignty by the Jews in 1948 demanded humane treatment of the new state's Arab minority, much as Jews in the Diaspora had demanded the right to such treatment in the countries of their
residence. Moreover, sovereignty placed a weighty responsibility on the
State of Israel's leaders to address the status of hundreds of thousands of
Palestinian Arab refugees. To make this point, Rawidowicz claimed, was
not starry-eyed utopianism. Rather, the refusal to acknowledge the refugee
problem was a dangerous exercise in self-delusion.

A good part of the intrigue in our story stems from the fact that the
chapter in which Rawidowicz presented his views, entitled "Between Jew
and Arab," never made its way into print, dwelling in obscurity for decades.

Indeed, this thirty-three-page essay, which was intended for publication in *Bavel vi-Yerushalayim,* is presented in full—in English translation—for the first time here.

It is not only the chapter's inimitable Hebrew style that catches our attention. It is also that the subject matter both follows and deviates from Rawidowicz's traditional concerns. From the very beginnings of his professional career in Berlin in the late 1920s, he sought to understand, improve, and provide a theoretical foundation for the status of the Jews as a national minority in the Diaspora. After 1948 his concerns shifted to the status of the Arab national minority in the new Jewish state and the refugees beyond. This new focus on the Arab Question would seem to be a mirror reflection of the central place of the Jewish Question in Rawidowicz's thought. At the same time, the subject matter of the unpublished chapter departs from the familiar themes ( for example, the need for a vibrant Diaspora Hebrew culture or a single Jewish nation with two centers) that recur in the large body of Hebrew writing that Rawidowicz assembled over three decades. This departure highlights the extraordinary nature of his foray into terrain that he had pledged never to enter: namely, Israeli foreign policy and the Arab Question. It may also help explain why he or someone close to him ultimately decided to leave the chapter in a desk drawer rather than publish it.

Of course, the main reason one might have chosen to suppress this chapter was its call for the repatriation of refugees, an explosive suggestion in the Jewish world in the mid-1950s when the State of Israel faced the persistent hostility of its Arab neighbors. That said, the taboo that has often surrounded the refugee question in Israeli and Jewish circles was not universally present. During and immediately after the 1948 war, Israeli policymakers, journalists, authors, and intellectuals discussed various aspects of the refugee question, including the prospect of a partial return of Palestinian Arabs to the new State of Israel. To be sure, this discussion usually took place *sotto voce* or at the margins of Israeli political discourse. Over the course of the early 1950s, as the new state labored to confront its manifold problems ( for example, security, immigration, economy), discussion of the refugees became even more muted, yielding to a posture of silence that has obtained until quite recently.[8]

Among those Jews who contemplated a return of refugees in the aftermath of 1948, Simon Rawidowicz was one of the most distinctive and impassioned. For him, the refugee question was a matter of political urgency for the new state, as well as of compassion for the well-being of the displaced. But it was perhaps above all an important test of Jewish morality. The creation of the State of Israel in 1948, Rawidowicz affirmed, marked an epochal turning point in the history of the Jews. It augured new prospects for the renewal of the Jewish nation, both in the homeland and abroad. But the ascent to political power by Jews also posed major challenges. Rawidowicz approached this new development not as a pacifist opposed to the use of force, but as a skeptic wary of the misuse of power. Would the sensitivity that Jews had cultivated and internalized over centuries of existence as a national minority in the Diaspora vanish? Would they adopt the ways of the Gentiles—an especially unappealing prospect in the wake of the Holocaust—when relating to the new national minority in their midst? In raising these questions in "Between Jew and Arab," Rawidowicz revealed his own unreconstructed vision of Jewish exceptionalism. He often framed this posture in the language of classical Jewish sources and personalities, such as when he cast the Jews as the biblical Jacob and the Gentile nations as Esau.

Rawidowicz's concern was not only that Jacob would come to act like his coarser older brother Esau, but that Esau would enthusiastically welcome Jacob's descent into the world of internecine tribal struggle. More to the point, he feared that the behavior of the Jews vis-à-vis Palestinians Arabs would evince a knowing wink from the Western powers, as if to signal satisfaction that the Jews at long last had come to understand the true—which is to say, amoral—nature of the world. Such a signal would spell profound damage to the ethical integrity and reputation of the Jews, an unfortunate though not unexpected consequence of the advent of Jewish political sovereignty.

As in the case of the Arab refugee question, a small circle of Jewish intellectuals had hesitations about the celebratory spirit that attended the creation of the State of Israel.[9] It is interesting, though perhaps not surprising, that Rawidowicz, the Eastern European Jew, was in regular touch with none of them. This cohort, which included Hannah Arendt, Martin Buber, Hans Kohn, Judah Magnes, and Akiva Ernst Simon, was predominantly German by language and culture, and possessed a somewhat different political sensibility. Whereas the Germans (and the American of German origin, Magnes) wondered whether a Jewish state—as distinct from a binational state or a confederation—was the optimal political arrangement for Palestine, Rawidowicz never articulated any preferred alternative to the State of Israel (as a Jewish state). He did, however, share the anxiety of these thinkers that "normalization"—the long-standing Zionist goal to grant the Jews a state like other nations—might bring out the basest of instincts in the Jewish people.

To be sure, debate about the virtues of normalization has not ceased sixty years after the State of Israel was established. A number of recent Jewish thinkers (for example, Yoram Hazony, Michael Oren, and Ruth Wisse) continue to advocate normalization, in the form of state power, as the necessary corrective to the tortuous path followed by Jews in the Diaspora prior to 1948.[10] They tend to regard Jewish critics of normalization—past and present—as beset by delusions and posing a danger to their own people. Rawidowicz would surely have merited designation as such had he published his chapter. But it is important to emphasize that his criticism did not amount to a renunciation of Zionism. Rather, it was related to his long-held desire to resist one particular tendency in Zionist thought: that strain which favored diminishing or "negating" the Diaspora. Rawidowicz repeatedly declared throughout his long career of scholarly and public activity that the Diaspora was a center of Jewish national life unto itself and need not be subservient to the Jewish center in the Land of Israel. It was this proposition that stood at the core of his capstone work, *Bavel vi-Yerushalayim,* whose title evoked the two historic centers of Jewish national life from antiquity.

Following the creation of the State of Israel, Rawidowicz feared that the negationist strand of Zionism would gain considerable force and upend the balance between Diaspora and Zion. He was especially dismayed by the rise of "cruel Zionism" (*ha-Tsiyonut ha-akhzarit*), a term invoked in the 1940s by a Zionist activist, Avraham Sharon (né Schwadron), to advocate intentional disregard for the fate of Diaspora Jewry in order to marshal all available resources for the Jewish community in Palestine.[11] Ultimately, the consequences of such a "cruel Zionism," Rawidowicz feared, would fall not only upon the Diaspora. They would also be—indeed, already had been—visited upon the Arabs, now that the Jews had gained an upper hand in the battle over Palestine. In the course of analyzing this process, Rawidowicz came to believe that the problem that must now occupy world Jewry—as an urgent moral and political necessity—was the fate of the Palestinian Arabs.

Rawidowicz's assessment of the Arab Question parallels that of a Jewish figure whom he held in the highest esteem: the Israeli author, S. Yizhar (né Yizhar Smilansky, 1916–2006). In 1949, Yizhar published a well-known short story, "Hirbet Hiz'ah," that described the expulsion of local Palestinian Arabs by a rather callous and indifferent group of Jewish soldiers during the War of Independence. As we shall later see, the story generated a considerable amount of acclaim and controversy. For Rawidowicz, Yizhar's boldness reflected a moral courage that was unique among Labor Zionists of Eastern European origin—who, unlike the above-mentioned German Jews, had abandoned by 1948 the rhetoric of brotherhood and peaceful coexistence with Arabs they had earlier favored.[12] Throughout his life, Yizhar continued to advocate those values, all the while remaining a committed Zionist who served six terms in the Israeli parliament as a member of the ruling Mapai party.

Of particular relevance are Yizhar's words delivered at a memorial tribute to Martin Buber in 1990. Although he never had a chance to see Rawidowicz's chapter "Between Jew and Arab" (and most probably never knew of its author's views), there is a striking affinity in perspective between the two. At the Buber tribute, Yizhar was no longer addressing the events of 1948, as he had in "Hirbet Hiz'ah," but rather the aftermath of the 1967 Six-Day War. He called for an end to Israel's occupation of the West Bank and Gaza Strip, not the least on ethical grounds, which he described as "the primary consideration, the strongest, and in the final analysis, the most decisive." He then proceeded to evoke the spirit and letter of Rawidowicz's "Between Jew and Arab": "The Palestinian Question is not an Arab Question, but entirely a Jewish Question. . . . It is a question for the Jews and a question for Judaism. And instead of continuing to run away from it, one must stop and turn to face it, turn and look at it directly."[13]

The passage of forty years created a different historical context in which to voice moral concerns. Advocating repatriation of refugees in the early 1990s would have pushed Yizhar well beyond the bounds of legitimacy within Israeli political culture. Once acutely mindful of the wound of expulsion, Yizhar now declared that "our task as Jews and as Zionists is to put an end to our existence as conquerors of another people."[14] In this sense, the similarity of language between Yizhar and Rawidowicz belies the important differences between them as well: not only the distinct versions of the Arab Question framed by the experience of 1948 and then again of

1967, but the fact that Rawidowicz was far more radical, marginal, and, ultimately, silent than Yizhar.

If silent in his day, why recall the buried legacy of Simon Rawidowicz? Was not Yizhar the more tempered and realistic moral voice? Did he not understand better the harsh realities of the Middle East that so readily undo hopes of reconciliation? It is easy to imagine critics of Rawidowicz describing his call for repatriation as naïve, or even worse, suicidal for the Jewish state. They would point out that the twentieth century witnessed many population exchanges, transfers, and refugee crises involving tens of millions of people. Reflecting this kind of realist stance, the scholar and Revisionist Zionist Joseph Schechtman, who might well have been a critic of Rawidowicz, declared at the outset of one of his lengthy studies on population exchanges that he was "in favor of the transfer of ethnic groups as a solution to those nationality problems which have proved to be insoluble in any other way." In his more focused study, *The Arab Refugee Problem* (1952), he continued by asserting that never before "has repatriation proved a solution to the problems which arose from these movements of population."[15] Other potential critics of Rawidowicz, one might speculate, would point out that the "right of return" was not granted, or even demanded, in many of these cases—and thus should not be accorded to the Palestinians.[16]

In fact, Rawidowicz's call for repatriation did not rest on a detailed analysis of international law nor of the logistical or political risks it would pose to the State of Israel. The force of his chapter did not lie then in its practicality, but rather in its unusual attention to the quandary that Rawidowicz designated as the "plight of the refugees." His text stands out for its ability to reach over the political and rhetorical chasm that separates Jews and Arabs in the matter of their shared homeland. It gave powerful voice to what has been so disputed in the violent decades since the establishment of the State of Israel: not only that the two sides have legitimate claims to Palestine, but that the dispossession of hundreds of thousands of Palestinians in 1948, even as the result of a military conflict that the Jews did not initiate, represented a deep wound both for the displaced and for those who came in their place.

This sense of wound may well remain as true today as before. For the Palestinians, the wound is a festering and open one, exacerbated by the malign neglect of Arab countries, their own ineffectual and self-serving political leaders, and Israel's ongoing occupation of the West Bank. The wound has become an organizing principle of Palestinian national identity, breeding a state of suspended reality among the exiled, brooding resentment in refugee camps, and at times murderous behavior. For many Palestinians, the principle of return is the only acceptable salve to the indignity of having been uprooted from their dwellings, property, and homeland in the midst of the 1948 war. They assert that the principle is rooted in international law (for example, U.N. Resolution 194), but add that it is a "sacred" right that cannot be surrendered or modified in any way.[17] All too often, the professed sanctity of the Palestinian right of return allows for no recognition of competing rights, particularly, of the internationally recognized right of Jews to national self-determination in Palestine (U.N. Resolution 181). Thus, the normal political, diplomatic, or legal work of adjudicating between competing claims falls victim to the uncompromising assertion of absolute right.[18]

Meanwhile, for the Jews, the wound of the refugees is a lingering blemish whose denial bespeaks a dangerous opacity. We recall that the Jewish side was prepared to accept the partition of Palestine proposed by the United Nations on 29 November 1947 and did not initiate hostilities with the Arab side, either in the wake of the Partition Plan or in the immediate aftermath of the declaration of the State of Israel. In fact, many Jews in Palestine believed that they were facing a war of extermination (an especially terrifying prospect given the recent memory of the Holocaust). That said, there is clear evidence that Jewish and Israeli forces engaged in the expulsion of thousands, and likely hundreds of thousands, of Palestinian Arabs from the country.[19] We also know that some Israeli government officials were more than happy to be rid of these hostile (or theoretically hostile) residents in order to proceed with the goal of stabilizing the new Jewish state. In fact, there were those who referred to the flight of Arabs, either by force or choice, in the recurrent messianic language of the day: as a "miracle."[20] Moreover, the new Israeli government often undertook to erase traces of the physical presence of Arabs in parts of Palestine that fell under the jurisdiction of the State of Israel, a process chronicled by Meron Benvenisti in *Sacred Landscape*. This effort was intended not only to "Judaize" the new state, but to set firmly in place the image of the mythic Hebrew reclaiming his land. One consequence was that reminders of Palestinian Arab dispossession were largely repressed from the early 1950s, soon to be supplanted in Israeli public consciousness by an even larger wound: the searing tale of Jewish victimization in the Holocaust.[21]

The contiguity of these open (Palestinian) and closed (Israeli) wounds stemming from the refugee crisis of 1948 adds an important psychological dimension to the conflict.[22] It is not the ambition of this book either to heal these wounds or to provide a definitive answer to what is an immensely complicated question. It is to suggest that Israel-Palestine is a crossroad of overlapping, competing, and multiple truths, of parallel historical experiences but for one detail: the vectors of change move in opposite directions—from homeland to exile in the case of the Palestinians, and from exile to homeland in the case of the Jews.[23] The price of acknowledging the multiplicity of historical truths or the legitimacy of the other's narrative has often been perceived to be too high to pay. Undoubtedly, there are those on both sides who are capable of pushing past the psychological barriers and stale rhetoric to acknowledge the other. But often times, such individuals seem to have an audience of little more than one.[24]

It is in that tradition of isolated and solitary thinkers that we locate Simon Rawidowicz, who at one point in his life assumed the pseudonym "Lonely Man." Given that his views on the Arab Question did not exert any influence on others, it remains for us to explain further why his position deserves to be rescued from silence.

The first set of reasons derives from Rawidowicz's distinctive stance as a passionate, empathic, and yet agitated critic of his own people. Neither content to swim in the current of popular opinion nor ignore it altogether, Rawidowicz felt an obligation to voice his views on matters affecting the Jewish commonweal. At times, these views took him well beyond the mainstream, even making him seem what he desperately sought to avoid being: a dreamy utopian. That he refused to surrender his commitment to write in the Hebrew language while remaining in the Diaspora—and hence detached himself from the natural audience of Hebrew readers in Palestine (as well as the much larger English-reading audience in the United States and elsewhere)—did little to discourage this image.

And yet, we would be missing the force of Rawidowicz's plea and position by continuing to neglect him. He was a probing critic of Zionism without being anti-Zionist. His impulse to afflict the comfortable from among his own compatriots was an act of devotion to "Israel," the transnational Jewish people. This devotion was itself consciously grounded in *ahavat*

*Yisrael,* love of the Jewish people. It is this quality that Gershom Scholem famously accused Hannah Arendt of lacking in 1963, in the aftermath of her reportage on the Eichmann trial. Arendt responded by affirming that "I have never in my life 'loved' any people or collective. . . . I indeed love 'only' my friends and the only kind of love I know of and believe in is the love of persons."[25]

In contrast to Arendt (and other Jewish critics of Zionism), Simon Rawidowicz resembled earlier, nineteenth-century nationalists, who were proudly capable of loving their people. But he was also willing to adopt a sharp tone of rebuke toward his people—and more specifically, toward the Zionist project—even if it compelled him to become a "lonely man" of conscience. He knew well the ancient tradition into which he stepped. Like the prophets Amos and Jeremiah, he beseeched his people to retain a measure of humility in its behavior and to acknowledge, when necessary, its errant ways. His call became increasingly urgent at the point when he recognized that the millennial fulfillment of the Jews' dream of renewed sovereignty coincided with—indeed, contributed to—the "catastrophe" of Palestinian Arab dispossession.

Rawidowicz's *cri de coeur,* born of love and moral indignation, was not heard in this period, or later. Even if it had seen the light of day, it is highly doubtful that it would have changed public attitudes in the State of Israel toward the Palestinian refugee question. A mix of fear, shame, indifference, and plain ignorance largely consigned this question to the recesses of Israeli collective memory. Misinformation and denial regarding Palestinian refugees have been even more pronounced in the Diaspora, where the organized Jewish community prides itself on standing in lockstep with the government of the State of Israel and defending it from reproach by external critics.[26] Rawidowicz lamented the fact that the Diaspora Jewish press was less open and self-critical than the press in the State of Israel itself. We should note that this tendency is not restricted to the journalistic sphere, and surely not to the Jewish case; diaspora communities in general are often more conformist (and conservative) in their politics than the public—and at times, the government—back in the homeland.[27] Well aware of this tendency, Rawidowicz may have elected to remain silent over the refugee question rather than face the wrath of his fellow Jews in America.

We cannot be altogether certain about the circumstances in which his chapter was suppressed. What is clear is that conformity was and remains a prominent value among Diaspora supporters of the State of Israel. It is also clear that we know a good deal more about the circumstances in which the actual plight unfolded, indeed, far more than Rawidowicz and other concerned Jews in the late 1940s and early 1950s could have known. This greater awareness is due largely to the work of the so-called New Historians, a group of Israeli scholars who began to comb newly opened archives in Israel more than two decades ago and, as a result of their discoveries, challenge historical myths that had accompanied the State of Israel from its birth in 1948. One of the key findings of these historians was that the Palestinian refugee problem did not arise solely as a result of voluntary flight in the midst of wartime. Rather, the Jewish/Israeli side was responsible for the forced removal of a significant portion of the Arab population from Palestine in 1948. While many Israelis today continue to deny or ignore this claim, a growing number, including the scholar who most systematically unearthed evidence of the removal—Benny Morris— affirm that expulsions by Jewish forces took place. But Morris, and some who follow in his wake, have come to occupy a middle position between denial and acknowledgment of responsibility. That is, they no longer adhere to the mythic view of the past, but they do resist redress for the Palestinians, maintaining that expulsions were necessary and justified in the midst of a pitched battle for national survival.[28]

Other Israelis are more remorseful. Shlomo Ben-Ami, historian and former Israeli foreign minister during the late phases of the Oslo peace process, wrote recently, in a summary of the events of 1948, "of an Arab community in a state of terror facing a ruthless Israeli army whose path to victory was paved not only by its exploits against the regular Arab armies, but also by the intimidation, and at times atrocities and massacres, it perpetrated against the civilian Arab community."[29] A similar recognition prompted the renowned Israeli author, Amos Oz, to declare in a recent opinion piece: "The time has come to acknowledge openly that Israelis had a part in the catastrophe of the Palestinian refugees. We do not bear sole responsibility, and we are not solely to blame, but our hands are not clean."[30]

Despite this recognition, neither Oz nor Ben-Ami favor granting Palestinians the unlimited right to return to their or their forebears' old homes in what is now the State of Israel. Indeed, Ben-Ami offers a view of the refugee problem that, while empathic, is preeminently pragmatic: "On *moral* grounds, one could of course convincingly defend the case for the repatriation of refugees. But this was out of the question in a *historical* and *political* context, where a clash existed between an emergent Jewish state and its defeated enemies."[31]

One could well imagine such a response by an Israeli politician in dismissing the claims of Simon Rawidowicz. And yet, it is important to add that Ben-Ami and the Israeli side in the Camp David peace talks brokered by President Clinton were apparently willing to consider a modest version of the Palestinian right of return: not the full return of all refugees to pre-1967 Israel, but, among other features, a right of return to a new state of Palestine (including some swaths of Israeli land that would be swapped), a limited number of returnees to Israel proper, and compensation for those who chose not to return (in accordance with U.N. Resolution 194).[32] In this regard, it is germane to mention the various proposals that have been advanced by Palestinians and Israelis, politicians and academics, to solve the refugee question as part of a larger peace settlement.[33] These include the Beilin–Abu Mazen document of October 31, 1995, and the 2003 Geneva Accord, which provides a detailed elaboration of the principles laid out in the Clinton Parameters.[34]

It is far from certain whether these proposals, and their call for a modified right of return, will ever succeed in regaining political and diplomatic traction. Nor is it clear that the Israeli government would ever agree to issue an acknowledgment of responsibility for the refugee problem à la Amos Oz—or that partial acknowledgment would suffice for the Palestinians. If, in fact, no such acknowledgment and acceptance ensue, it remains an open question whether Palestinians will ever heal the wound of 1948, at least enough to recognize in meaningful fashion the right of Jews to a safe and stable collective existence. A leading Palestinian intellectual and observer, Sari Nusseibeh, has recently warned: "by denying all responsibility, besides being historically absurd to the point of craziness, you will guarantee eternal antagonism—a never-ending search for revenge."[35]

Fifty years before Nusseibeh, Simon Rawidowicz arrived at a similar conclusion, insisting that the refusal to address the "plight of the refugees" would be an ongoing thorn in the side of the State of Israel. Rereading his unpublished chapter today, in the midst of the current (and perennial) impasse between Israelis and Palestinians, is hardly a panacea to all of the conflict's ills. But it is a bracing call to historical cognizance and responsibility regarding a key feature of the Arab Question that has routinely been ignored or dismissed as baseless by Jews.

There is a second reason, apart from the distinctiveness of his message, that we are prompted to recover the lost voice of Rawidowicz here. In general, he has escaped serious and sustained scholarly attention. The limited scholarship that is dedicated to him has dealt very briefly, if at all, with his concern for refugees. The most systematic treatment of Rawidowicz and his thought comes from his son, the historian Benjamin Ravid. Ravid has written a pair of detailed studies on the life and thought of his father, drawn from a large trove of correspondence with family members and leading Jewish literary and cultural activists, as well as from Rawidowicz's published work. The first incarnation, a lengthy introduction to a volume of Rawidowicz's writings in Hebrew, makes no mention of "Between Jew and Arab." A shorter version of Ravid's biographical essay introduces a collection of his father's essays translated into English. There Ravid produced a one-page synopsis of the chapter in question, concluding that Rawidowicz himself chose not to publish it after consulting with the man in Paris responsible for printing *Bavel vi-Yerushalayim*.[36]

An even briefer reference to the issue appears in Avraham Greenbaum's short study of the London-based Ararat Publishing Society, of which Rawidowicz was a founder. In a personal recollection, Greenbaum remembers Rawidowicz telling him that he had decided to suppress his views on the Arab Question so as not to draw attention away from other matters of greater importance to him (for example, the relationship between the State of Israel and the Diaspora).

Neither Ravid nor Greenbaum was primarily interested in Rawidowicz's unpublished chapter, but rather in shedding light on his interrelated goals of creating a vibrant Hebrew culture in the Diaspora and advancing the idea of a dual-centered Jewish nationalism (based in the Diaspora and in the Land of Israel). Indeed, it is this set of ideas—and especially Rawidowicz's critique of the hegemonic instinct of the Zionist movement toward the Diaspora—that has managed to attract the fleeting attention of Israeli scholars (for example, Yosef Gorny and Ehud Luz), as well as the scrutiny of Gordon Tucker in a short book review.[37]

The most extensive analysis of Rawidowicz to date apart from Benjamin Ravid's is provided by Noam Pianko in his fine 2004 dissertation. Pianko examines Rawidowicz alongside the better-known Horace Kallen, Mordechai

Kaplan, and Hans Kohn in an effort to trace the contours of nonstatist forms of Jewish nationalism. This inquiry into Diaspora nationalism reminds us that, although it ultimately emerged triumphant, Zionism was hardly alone among Jewish nationalist ideologies that competed in a crowded marketplace of ideas in the early (and to a lesser extent, mid-) twentieth century. Even more germane for us, the dissertation devotes several pages to Rawidowicz's chapter on the Arab Question. Alone among those who have written about the chapter, Pianko grasps that Rawidowicz's engagement with the Arab Question did not stand in isolation, but was part and parcel of his broader political thought. It would be inaccurate to describe this thought as a fully developed or systematic political theory; indeed, the sprawling *Bavel vi-Yerushalayim* often has a haphazard feel to it, mixing the historical and contemporary, the philosophical and the impressionistic, the familiar and the novel.

Nonetheless, Pianko is right to note that Rawidowicz succeeded in stitching the threads of his political thinking together in interesting ways. Thus, he advanced a conception of Jewish nationalism that "would apply to both Jews in their own political state and those who would continue to live as a distinct minority population within other political entities." Pianko follows the logic of the argument by pointing out that, for Rawidowicz, "Diaspora Jewish nationalism would lose its ability to advocate a more tolerant attitude towards minority cultural, ethnic or religious orientation if its own political homeland denied the rights of its Arab minorities."[38]

This insight returns us to a key feature of Rawidowicz's engagement with the Arab Question. To a great extent, it was the historical example of the Jews, a national minority dispersed throughout the world prior to 1948, that prompted his concern for Palestinian Arabs: both for those who lived as a minority in the State of Israel and for those who dwelt as refugees beyond its borders (and whose fate Rawidowicz regarded as two pieces of a single puzzle). Not only did he hope that Jews would exhibit political and cultural sensitivity toward other national minorities based on their past experience. He also feared that if Jews did not manifest such sensitivity as a majority in their homeland, they would be that much less likely to be treated well as a minority in the Diaspora. The Arab Question became then, for Rawidowicz, a mirror through which to reflect on Jewish power, sovereignty, and national minority rights as he set out to write *Bavel vi-Yerushalayim*.

The central axis around which Rawidowicz's analysis revolved was 1948: the year in which the State of Israel was established and the year that altered the course and narrative of Jewish history. He affirmed the right of Jews to a place under the sun, but was concerned that 1948 had unleashed a torrent of uncontrollable forces. In particular, he feared that Jews had become, in the words of the Proverbs, "the servant who has come to reign" (Proverbs 30:21–22). Hannah Arendt, for her part, described this phenomenon as "the tendency, only too common in history, to play the oppressor as soon as one is liberated."[39] Rawidowicz's great trepidation was that the new political power accorded Jews in their state would dull the ethical sensors that had guided and preserved them throughout history. The result, he feared, would be a most Pyrrhic victory.

## II

Telling the story of Simon Rawidowicz and his chapter here marks a certain degree of closure. For more than two decades, from the time I can first remember reading him, Rawidowicz has exerted a kind of hypnotic hold on me. His thinking, especially (but not exclusively) about a dual-centered Jewish nation, was so intuitive, original, and yet forgotten that I vowed to explore his life and work in greater detail at some point. Over the years, in the midst of other research projects that have diverted my attention, I have dipped into Rawidowicz's world, penning a few articles or delivering a few lectures on him. The allure to do more has been great, and regularly stimulated my visits to the wonderful trove of archival sources—manuscripts, organizational materials, and letters to every important Jew of the twentieth century (or so it seems)—that dwells in the basement of Rawidowicz's son, Benjamin Ravid, in Newton, Massachusetts. Ben Ravid is the custodian not only of this remarkable trove, but of his father's memory as well. He has been an exceptionally gracious and welcoming host to the world of his father, allowing me and other scholars unfettered access to the materials in the basement. To the lucky visitor to Newton, Ben also offers a wealth of anecdotes that only a child can tell of his father, as well as contextual insights that only a fine historian can offer up. It has been a real pleasure to get to know Ben over the years that I have been making pilgrimages to his basement. Without his constant assistance and encouragement, this book would not have been possible.

Notwithstanding Ben's generosity, this book signals a failing of sorts. I had once harbored the hope of writing a full-fledged biography of Simon Rawidowicz, one that relies even more fully on the archival treasures in Newton to piece together his life and work. The book at hand is not that full-length biography. Nor is it an analysis of his rich thought or scholarly production. Those books still remain to be written.

Rather, the present volume focuses on a much smaller aspect of his oeuvre. Initially conceived as an article-length introduction to his chapter, it has grown in size, and thus represents something of a hybrid between a brief preface and a full biography. One can certainly make the argument that the subject matter of his chapter provides an illuminating vista from which to reflect on the guiding principles that animate his thinking. But, truth be told, the fact that this book focuses on Rawidowicz's attention to the Arab Question stems as much as anything from a more personal reason: my own growing awareness of and unease over the relations between Jews and Arabs in Israel/Palestine. Like Rawidowicz, I have become unsettled by the intoxicating effects of political power and sovereignty on the Jews. And like him, I recognize that the absence of such power has had even more devastating effects on the Jews (though its presence does not, alas, guarantee Jewish survival in the future). Facing that conundrum, Rawidowicz sought to forge a path that permitted both unvarnished criticism of his people and a profound sense of *ahavat Yisrael*.[40] For much of his career, he spoke openly and without apology, undaunted by the prospect of being attacked for his views. Rawidowicz was aware that his words in "Between Jew and Arab" would elicit stiff opposition from fellow Jews, especially in the Diaspora where the need to uphold the image of a noble and invincible Israel is often stronger than in Israel itself. And yet, at the point of publishing his most trenchant and provocative challenge to his people, words failed him.

Despite (or perhaps because of) this mysterious end to the story, I am drawn to Rawidowicz's project of self-criticism, which enabled him to see that a major—if not *the* major—measure of Zionism's success would be its treatment of the Arab Question. It is possible that in reclaiming his self-critical voice, we are violating Rawidowicz's own judgment that his forgotten text should rest in peace, never to upset the audience for which it had been intended. While we cannot be sure about this, the ongoing salience of the issues he raises, and the novelty of his perspective, make a compelling case for recovering and translating his text—all the more so in light of the inability of most Israeli Jews and Palestinian Arabs to escape their own self-affirming narratives. This is not to say that Rawidowicz's call for the repatriation of hundreds of thousands of Palestinian refugees is practicable in the current political climate. But his intuition that the State of Israel must address the deep wound of Palestinian dispossession strikes us as painful, yet legitimate and healthy. So too was his intuition that the sovereign Jewish state has the power, responsibility, and, though not always evident, self-interest to *initiate* a resolution to the wound of 1948.

At the end of the day, it is for the reader to decide whether Rawidowicz's idiosyncratic views have relevance to the pressing issues of today. It is also for the reader to determine whether I have managed to strike an appropriate balance between empathy and distance. In dealing with such a charged issue as the Israeli-Palestinian conflict, some say, it is preferable to avoid overinvestment and passion. But dispassion in this matter is well-nigh impossible. In fact, what seems the best antidote to political and historiographical small-mindedness is an empathic perspective that acknowledges the worth of both Arab and Jewish ambitions as distinct from the usual practice of privileging one set of claims over another.[41] This book, though surely not it alone, takes a step in that direction by excavating a text that frames the Palestinian refugee problem not only as an Arab question, but as a Jewish one as well.

### III

The final task of this introduction is to offer a brief roadmap to the book, which is divided into two main sections: "The Jewish Question" and "The Arab Question." At the end of these two sections is a full English translation of Rawidowicz's chapter "Between Jew and Arab," undertaken in collaboration with Arnold J. Band. An epilogue follows and concluding the volume is a collection of appendixes, including a timeline, highlighting historical events to which Rawidowicz made reference or of which he would have been aware, and several official Israeli and international legal documents, most of which are mentioned in his chapter.

Part I of this book introduces us to the peripatetic life, iconoclastic thought, and intellectual development of Simon Rawidowicz. Relying on a wide range of published and archival sources, it traces the career of a confirmed advocate of Jewish cultural nationalism who, for a mix of personal and ideological reasons, chose to live his entire life in the Diaspora. As we follow his manifold scholarly and public activities, we shall begin to see his distinctive vision of a Jewish cultural nation take root. We shall also notice his evolving interest in the legal and political discourse of national minority rights, as well as the significant rethinking that 1948, the year of Israeli independence, caused in his intellectual and political worldview. Ultimately, this part aims to provide a clear and textured understanding of what Rawidowicz referred to as "she'elat Yisrael," the Jewish Question.

Those less interested in Rawidowicz's biography and view of Jewish politics can turn directly to part II, which concentrates on his audacious chapter, "Between Jew and Arab." This part analyzes the structure, content, and context of the chapter, paying particular attention to Rawidowicz's calls for an end to discrimination against Arab citizens of Israel, on one hand, and for the repatriation of those refugees who left Palestine in 1948, on the other. It also seeks to place these calls within the context of Israeli attitudes toward the refugee question in the early 1950s. Throughout this part, we gain a clearer sight of the competing vectors that made up Rawidowicz's complex character: his deep Jewish pathos and decided rejection of received Jewish communal wisdom, as well as his political prescience and conscious disengagement from the drama of Jewish history unfolding in his day.

# PART I | THE JEWISH QUESTION

In 1957, Simon Rawidowicz (fig. 1) could look back on his sixty years with a newfound sense of fulfillment and purpose. After a peripatetic career as a Jewish scholar writing in Hebrew in the Diaspora, Rawidowicz joined the fledgling faculty of Brandeis University in 1951. Very quickly, he established himself as a central presence on the Waltham campus, earning wide praise and admiration among administrators, colleagues, and students alike. Brandeis was precisely the kind of vibrant Jewish university of which he had dreamt and which he had advocated for years.

The year 1957 was also when Rawidowicz neared completion of the *summa summarum* of his life's work, *Bavel vi-Yerushalayim* (Babylon and Jerusalem).[1] After decades of research, thinking, and ideological refinement—followed by five years of writing (1951–55)—Rawidowicz was on the brink of publishing a nine-hundred-page Hebrew text that gave full

Fig. 1. Simon Rawidowicz (1897–1957).

We thank you very much for your expression of
sympathy on the passing of our dear husband and
father, Simon Rawidowicz.

ESTHER E. RAWIDOWICZ

BENJAMIN C. I. RAVID

Waltham, Mass.
October, 1957

תודתנו מקרב לב נתונה בזה לכו' על השתתפותו
באבלנו הכבד בהלקה מאתנו בעלי ואבי היקר,
שמעון ז"ל

אסתר ראבידוביץ

בנימין חיים יצחק ראביד

ולתאם, מאסס.
תשרי, תשי"ח

Fig. 2. Thank-you note from Esther Rawidowicz (wife) and Benjamin Ravid (son) to
condolence callers.

expression to his distinctive vision of Jewish nationalism.[2] This vision rested on the claim that there had been throughout Jewish history, and should continue to be in the future, two main centers of Jewish national life and culture: one in the Land of Israel (symbolically designated Jerusalem) and the other in the Diaspora (Babylon).

As fate would have it, Rawidowicz did not live to see the publication of the two volumes of *Bavel vi-Yerushalayim*. He died on 20 July 1957, index cards with him in hospital and page proofs at home in Waltham (fig. 2).[3] The two volumes were published a bit later in 1958 (although with a 1957 imprint) by the Hebrew publishing house, Ararat, that Rawidowicz and a number of collaborators had established in England fifteen years earlier.

If there is a certain poignancy in the fact that Rawidowicz did not live to see the book's publication, there is also an element of mystery. At some point in the preparation of *Bavel vi-Yerushalayim*, a decision was made to withhold from publication a chapter that Rawidowicz had been working on throughout the early and mid-1950s. The rest of the book engaged Rawidowicz's usual concerns: the origins and development of the Jewish nation over millennia, the relations between the main centers of Jewish culture in the Diaspora and the Land of Israel, and, as of 1948, the impact of the creation of the State of Israel on the Jewish world. As we have seen in the introduction, the suppressed chapter departed from these concerns to address the fate of the Arab population of Palestine during the 1948 war and thereafter. Rawidowicz argued in this chapter that the great triumph of the Jews—the assumption of statehood in their ancestral homeland—spelled disaster for the Arabs. In the first place, he sought to demonstrate that the Arabs who remained within the borders of the new state—156,000 in 1949—were subject to unacceptable discrimination by the Knesset, the legislative body of the Jewish state. Even more dramatically, Rawidowicz argued that it was the responsibility of the State of Israel to attend to the plight of hundreds of thousands of Arabs displaced during the hostilities that ensued in Palestine from late 1947 through the armistice agreements of 1949.[4]

Accustomed to the charge of being an anti-Zionist,[5] Rawidowicz proceeded with the drafting of his chapter, placing at its center the argument that the Arab Question had become the most compelling Jewish Question of the day. We shall address this most unlikely of equations in part II; now, however, we turn to the literary mystery of why the chapter "Between Jew and Arab" never made it into the published version of *Bavel vi-Yerusha-layim,* and in fact, has not seen the light of day until now.

### The Disappearing Chapter: A Case of Self-Censorship?

Rawidowicz entitled the thirty-three-page Hebrew text that has been translated here "Ben 'Ever le-'Arav."[6] We have rendered this title "Between Jew and Arab," though a more literal reading would be "Between Hebrew and Arab." This title clues us in to the unusual qualities of Rawidowicz's highly idiosyncratic Hebrew. In typical fashion, he eschewed the modern noun forms for Jew (*yehudi*) and Arab (either *'aravi* or *'arvi*), choosing instead terms reminiscent of the classicizing style that entered the Hebrew language in the late eighteenth-century *Haskalah* (Jewish Enlightenment) and continued through the late nineteenth-century era of national literary and linguistic revival.[7]

There is indeed an intentionally archaic quality to Rawidowicz's Hebrew. At once elegant and stilted, it followed many byways of the ancient tongue, incorporating a wide range of biblical, mishnaic, and medieval rabbinic allusions. It was a style better read than spoken, a function of the fact, we might surmise, that Rawidowicz lived in his own, somewhat isolated, diasporic world of Hebrew letters rather than in a dynamic Hebrew-speaking environment.

Rawidowicz wrote the bulk of the chapter in question in his new home of Waltham sometime between 1951 and 1953. We can assume this dating because he relates in a footnote that much of the text was completed two years before the infamous episode at Kibya in October 1953, when scores of Palestinian civilians were killed in a retaliatory strike by the Israel Defense Forces following a terrorist attack in the town of Yehud.[8] We know that Rawidowicz continued to work on the chapter after the Kibya episode, because he relates in another note that he largely completed it two years before the conference of nonaligned African and Asian countries held in Bandung, Indonesia, on 18–25 April 1955.[9] The fact that he mentioned Bandung indicates that he was still at work on the chapter, if only in slight measure, at the time of the conference.

In fact, we have in our possession an envelope sent to Rawidowicz's printer in Paris and labeled "'Ever ve-'arav" (Hebrew and Arab) that is dated 15 April 1955, three days before the opening of the Bandung conference

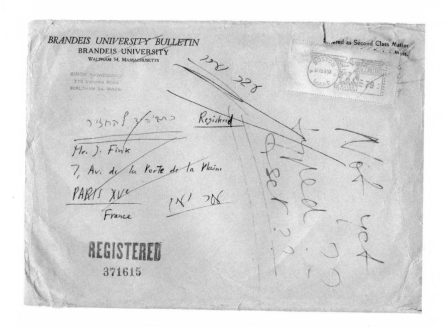

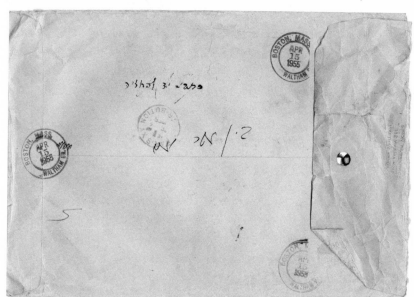

Fig. 3. Envelope from Rawidowicz to Jacob Fink in Paris indicating that the manuscript of "Jew and Arab" should be returned.

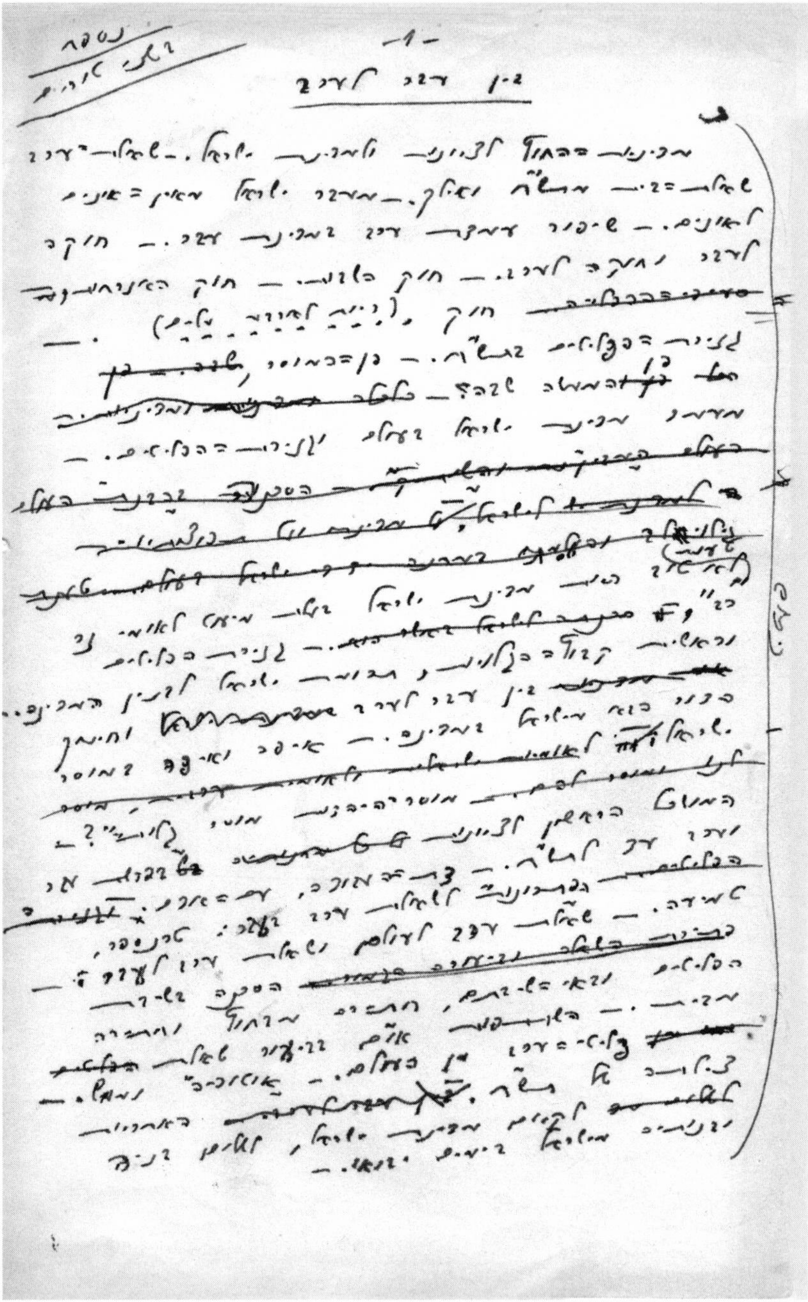

Fig. 4. First page of the handwritten text of "Between Jew and Arab."

(see fig. 3). The envelope likely contained a typed version of the handwritten text, both of which have been preserved (figs. 4 and 5). The page proofs of "Between Jew and Arab" that were produced in Paris made their way back to Waltham sometime between the late spring of 1955 and Rawidowicz's death in the summer of 1957.[10] This brief itinerary begs the

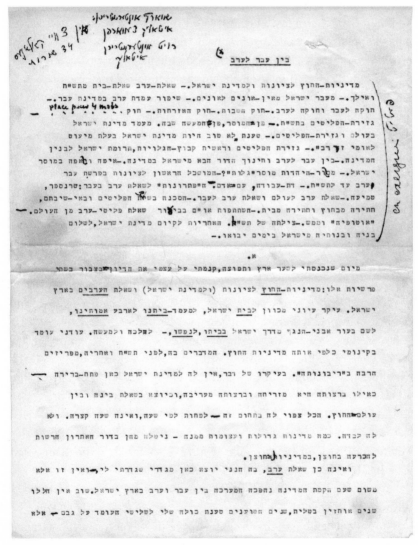

Fig. 5. First page of the typed text of "Between Jew and Arab" with editorial instructions in multiple languages.

question of why Rawidowicz sent his Hebrew manuscript to Paris, of all places, to be published.

Paris, it turns out, was a minor center of Hebrew publishing, where Rawidowicz had had his Hebrew work printed for the better part of a decade. Israel would have been a far more obvious place to send a Hebrew-language manuscript to be printed, with the United States a distant second. The Ararat Publishing Society, which Rawidowicz cofounded with two Jewish businessmen from Germany, Alexander and Benzion Margulies, and which published *Bavel vi-Yerushalayim,* considered these two venues. But the cost of Hebrew printing in the United States was too high, and the material conditions in Israel a bit too unreliable in the immediate pre- and post-state era. Indeed, when the Ararat Society did make use of a Jerusalem printer on one occasion, it was compelled to send along its own supply of paper, as there was only a limited amount of paper available in Israel until 1955.[11]

At the outset of its existence in 1943, the Ararat Society availed itself of a printer in London named Israel Narodiczky, who was the publisher for a host of Anglo-Jewish organizations and individuals.[12] Following Narodiczky's death in 1945, Ararat turned a year later to Jacob Fink (1894–1955), a Ukrainian-born engineer who had become a Zionist and Hebrew cultural activist in Paris. It was Fink who oversaw the printing of Ararat's largely Hebrew list until his death in the fall of 1955.[13] His efforts earned him a warm homage at the end of the introduction to *Bavel vi-Yerushalayim.* Rawidowicz recalled that Fink had been utterly disengaged from Hebrew culture and literature for two decades before his "return"—an act stimulated by the appearance of Rawidowicz's Hebrew-language journal, *Metsudah,* in London. Rawidowicz further acknowledged that he and Fink had differences of opinion, presumably over the nature of Zionism.[14] Nonetheless, Fink became a contributor to *Metsudah,* as well as its printer. In reciprocal fashion, Rawidowicz appeared in the pages of Fink's short-lived Hebrew journal in Paris, *Shevivim,* praising the journal as a latter-day Noah's ark that kept Hebrew culture alive in the wake of the deluge that was the Holocaust.[15] Indeed, Rawidowicz saw Jacob Fink as a partner in the noble but Sisyphean task of encouraging the spread of Hebrew throughout the Jewish world, especially outside of the Land of Israel.

The acknowledgment that he and Fink held different views gestures alluringly toward a solution to our literary mystery. Could it be the case, as Benjamin Ravid has proposed, that Rawidowicz's comrade-in-arms in

Diaspora Hebrew letters persuaded him to suppress "Between Jew and Arab?"[16] If so, Fink did not have that much time to offer his criticism of the text. He received the manuscript in April 1955 and wrote Rawidowicz in September of that year, less than two months before his death, to say that he had not yet had a chance to read the chapter.[17]

We also have the opinion of Avraham Greenbaum, author of a short volume on the history of the Ararat publishing house. Greenbaum reports that Rawidowicz decided "to keep to himself his opinion that the Arab refugees should be allowed to return [to the State of Israel] in order not to distract attention from what, in his eyes, was the main issue." The main issue, according to Greenbaum, was Rawidowicz's insistence that the name "Israel" could not and should not be applied to the territorially demarcated State of Israel.[18] Rather, Israel—or the Hebrew *Yisrael*—was the term that designated the Jewish people in the grandest global sense, spread over time and space.[19]

This terminological issue was the subject of an intense burst of correspondence in 1954–55 between Rawidowicz and David Ben-Gurion, who was between tenures as Israel's prime minister. We shall return later to the subject of this exchange, which suggests that Rawidowicz's thoughts were taken seriously by at least one prominent Jewish leader. For now, our concern remains the text of "Between Jew and Arab," the proofs of which were sent to Rawidowicz from Paris.[20] The version Rawidowicz received back (and that remains extant) was in need of a good bit of editorial work, containing typographical errors, jumbled words, and incomplete or garbled sentences.

Notwithstanding these defects, the chapter is arresting. It bristles with the outrage of the Israelite prophets, as Rawidowicz insisted that the moral balance of the new State of Israel hinged on "the plight of the refugees," those who fled or were expelled in the midst of the hostilities of 1948. And yet, the chapter is more than the jeremiad of a frustrated academic. It is informed by, and attentive to, the geopolitical situation of the State of Israel, as well as to legal and social developments within the fledgling country. Few Jews of the day, either in the State of Israel or the Diaspora, followed as carefully as Rawidowicz the wide stream of Israeli newspapers, magazines, and journals. In addition to what was available to him in Boston-area libraries, he received by mail regular packets of article clippings from his brother Avraham Ravid in Tel Aviv. Sitting thousands of miles away, he was consumed by this welter of material, along with the pressing moral and political questions facing the State of Israel.

To a certain extent, Rawidowicz was a victim of his own unique brand of Jewish nationalism. His commitment to the ideal of a genuine *shutafut* (partnership) between Jerusalem and Babylon meant that, in physical and psychological terms, nowhere was truly home. Ideology and psychology had become intimately entwined. In a revealing letter to his brother Avraham from 1948, Rawidowicz wrote: "Over the course of time, I have lost the desire to settle in this place or that, in any specific place. I live beyond time and space."[21]

In all likelihood, it is this sense of isolation that prompted Rawidowicz to adopt some years earlier his nom de plume: Ish Boded (lonely, or solitary, man). Avraham Greenbaum suggests that this pen name was more situational than characterological, owing to Rawidowicz's lonely existence as an Hebraist in Leeds, England, after leaving London to assume a university post there in 1941.[22] Here the term is understood otherwise, as an internalized measure of Rawidowicz's own cultural, political, and emotional— not just geographic—isolation. This is not to deny that Rawidowicz often found his way to a rich circle of friends, colleagues, and admirers whether in Berlin, London, Chicago, or Waltham. In each of those places, he led a full and active life, stimulating interest in Hebrew and Jewish culture, and gaining respect for his erudition and affability. And in each of those places, his home was open to a steady stream of visitors, who came to discuss matters scholarly and ideological in a convivial setting presided over by his wife, Esther. That said, Rawidowicz's distinctive interests and ideas, as well as his peripatetic life path, reinforced his own sense of uniqueness and, by extension, isolation.

It may well be these qualities that lent Rawidowicz his prescience. Accustomed to swimming against the current of Jewish national politics (and dwelling, by his own account, "beyond time and space"), he challenged conventional ways of thinking. While other Jews reveled in the triumph of Zionism, Rawidowicz decried the onset of Jewish hubris. While other Jews ignored the condition of Palestinian Arabs inside and outside of the new state, Rawidowicz believed this condition was a yardstick of Jewish moral rectitude.[23]

Of course, Rawidowicz's concerns were not unique to him. The international community had begun to take an active interest in the fate of Palestinian Arab refugees already in the midst—and certainly toward the end—of hostilities between Israel and her Arab neighbors. Significantly, the United Nations General Assembly issued Resolution 194 on 11 December 1948 stating that "the refugees wishing to return to their homes and live at peace with their neighbours should be permitted to do so at the earliest practicable date, and that compensation should be paid for the property of those choosing not to return and for loss of or damage to property."[24] Since that time, the refugee issue has remained a central concern, particularly in the Arab and Muslim worlds. And yet, the State of Israel has largely refused to discuss it. This refusal stems, in part, from the fact that Israel has found itself alone in the midst of a hostile region, locked in a state of war with its neighbors. Its own sense of fragility took root in the midst of its fight for independence, in the immediate aftermath of the Holocaust, when many Jews feared expulsions themselves and a proportionately large number of Israelis (6,000) died in the war. The resulting sense of siege has led to widespread anxiety among Israelis that revisiting the charged history of 1948 might lend credence to calls for the right of return for Palestinian refugees or their descendants; such a right, many Israelis have feared, would entail the end of the Jewish state by tipping the demographic balance decisively in favor of the Arab population.

Perhaps Simon Rawidowicz came to this conclusion himself after he wrote his chapter "Between Jew and Arab." Perhaps he was nudged toward this conclusion by Jacob Fink, who urged him to avoid the risk to his reputation and toss the page proofs of "Between Jew and Arab" into the garbage. Or perhaps Rawidowicz made a calculated tactical decision based on the recognition that his main goal in life—to forge a genuine partnership between the Diaspora and the Land of Israel—would be buried under the weight of controversy. He hinted in this direction when he noted at the end of his chapter (sec. XVII) that he often discussed the Arab Question with fellow Jews, and was concerned that his perspective on the matter might "suffice to disqualify the entire project of 'Babylon and Jerusalem.'" We shall explore some additional evidence in part II, but unfortunately, a definitive resolution to the mystery of the chapter's suppression remains elusive.

## The "Lonely Man" of Hebrew Letters

"Between Jew and Arab" came at the end of a long and varied career. Rawidowicz not only passed through a good number of physical and intellectual

stations in his life; he engaged in substantive conversation and correspondence with many major Jewish political, cultural, and religious leaders of the twentieth century—from Chaim Nahman Bialik to David
Ben-Gurion to Rabbi Joseph Soloveitchik. Moreover, he was at once a keen
student of Jewish thought and an original thinker and exponent of Jewish
nationalism. Consequently, it is somewhat surprising that Rawidowicz's
renown was limited in its day and has diminished a good deal since. His
name has not entered the pantheon of luminaries of modern Jewish scholarship and thought alongside such contemporaries as Abraham Joshua
Heschel, Saul Lieberman, and Gershom Scholem. In fact, he is less known
today than other Brandeis colleagues of the same era such as Nahum Glatzer and Alexander Altmann.[25]

It is interesting to speculate about his relative lack of renown. First, Rawidowicz's peripatetic existence, which took him from his native Grayewo
to Białystok and then in succession to Berlin, London, Leeds, and Chicago,
prevented him from gaining a solid institutional base from which to dis-
seminate his views in any concerted fashion. Had he lived longer, it is con-
ceivable that Brandeis, which deeply satisfied his ideal of a Jewish university,
would have offered such a foundation. But he died an early death, before
the full effects of the stability afforded by Brandeis could be felt.

Second, the fact that he quite consciously blended scholarship and ideological pronouncements left him dangling between the purist poles of either domain of activity. The Harvard sociologist Daniel Bell famously noted
that there was "at the end of the fifties . . . a disconcerting caesura," a growing divide between ideas and action—and by extension, between research-
focused scholars and intellectuals intent on yoking thought to deed. This
new division of labor led Bell to declare "the end of ideology."[26] Rawidowicz had come of age in an earlier era, replete with ideological energy and
contestation, and he unapologetically fashioned himself as both a scholar
and an ideologue for whom historical and philosophical ideas were prods
to action. This dual identity was an important feature of his *Bavel vi-
Yerushalayim,* as well as of scores of articles and essays up to his death in
1957.

Such a blurring of scholarly and ideological lines posed a challenge to
the antiquarian ideal of *Wissenschaft des Judentums* (the Science of Judaism), whose nineteenth-century practitioners often spoke of the supreme
importance of a pure scholarly endeavor. Owing to this influence, many

modern Jewish scholars often regarded explicit "descent" into issues of contemporary concern à la Rawidowicz as an abdication of the true scholarly vocation. On the other hand, Rawidowicz wrote in a literary style and with a conceptual arsenal that made his writing less accessible to the large popular audience that he hoped to attract.

A third reason for Rawidowicz's relative neglect was the idiosyncrasy of his ideological vision. It was not simply that he advocated two centers of Jewish national life (and thus alienated advocates of either). It was that he believed that Hebrew was and must continue to be the language of Jewish national life—in New York and London, as well as in Tel Aviv and Jerusalem. This claim, which stimulated his efforts to establish a World Hebrew Union, proved to be a rather significant miscalculation, although, in other respects, Rawidowicz was far more cognizant of uncomfortable realities than were more mainstream Jewish and Zionist thinkers.

Those who know to read Rawidowicz today are often struck by the originality of his mind. A number of his essays—"Israel: An Ever-Dying People" and "On Interpretatio," to name two prominent examples—are minor classics, admired by a devoted cadre of cognoscenti for their acuity and erudition. Moreover, a small number of serious students of Jewish thought find his studies of Saadya Gaon, Moses Mendelssohn, and especially Maimonides and Nachman Krochmal to be significant.[27] Perhaps an even smaller number regard *Bavel vi-Yerushalayim* as a compelling and underappreciated work that merits far more attention than it has received. The fact that the book was printed only once—and only fragments were translated into English—made it unavailable to a wider audience of Diaspora Jews. Meanwhile, in the State of Israel, the book has failed to gain a large audience of Hebrew readers, for whom the book's style and content are rather alien.

Nonetheless, discerning minds did recognize Rawidowicz's talents. Brandeis' founding president, Abram Sachar, relates that he was once invited to the White House by President Lyndon Johnson for a reception in honor of Israeli President Zalman Shazar. When introduced to Sachar, Shazar declared: "Brandeis—that's where Rawidowicz was," and then proceeded to hold up the receiving line "to explain to President Johnson what a seminal scholar Rawidowicz was!"[28] Some years earlier, Shazar insisted that, notwithstanding his political disagreements with Rawidowicz, the latter should be recognized as "one of the founders of the organized Hebrew movement" whose memory must be perpetuated.[29] This opinion was shared by Israeli Prime Minister David Ben-Gurion, who lauded Rawidowicz not only for his wide-ranging knowledge, but for his passion for everything Jewish and Hebrew" (see fig. 6).[30] For his part, Nahum Glatzer offered a powerful encomium to his Brandeis colleague ten years after his death, calling him "a link in the long series of lonely men, who, amid ruins, affirmed the idea of Israel, men who, in the midst of a burning Jerusalem, saw the vision of a new Jerusalem."[31]

The image of the solitary prophet that emerges from Glatzer's recollection comports with Rawidowicz's self-description as an "Ish Boded" (lonely man). It also leads us to conclude that Rawidowicz imagined his life's work in much the same vein that two of his Jewish heroes imagined theirs: the twelfth-century Moses Maimonides and the nineteenth-century Nahman

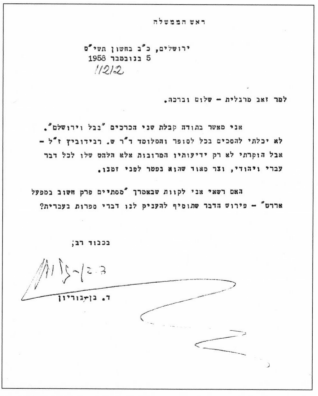

Fig. 6. Letter of Prime Minister David Ben-Gurion from 5 November 1958 to William (Zev) Margolies expressing sadness over the death of Rawidowicz.

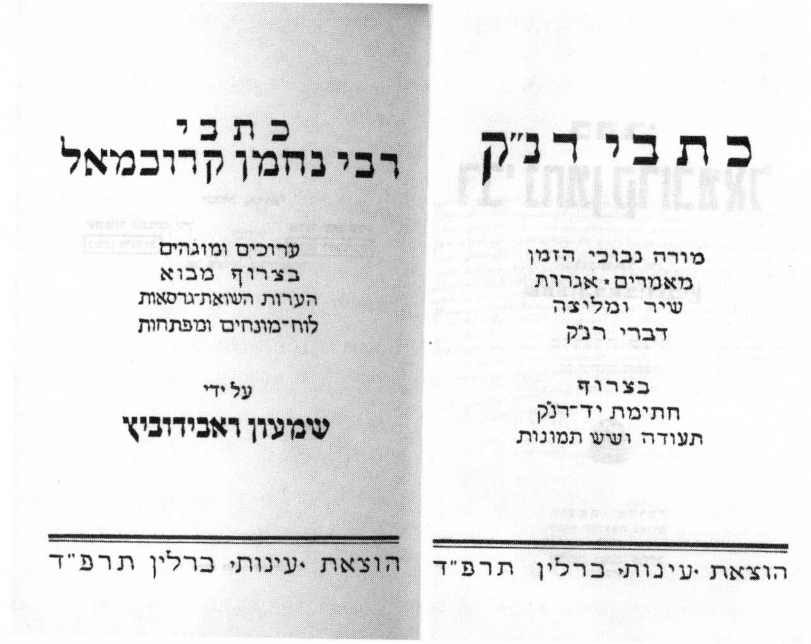

כתב י
רבי נחמן קרוכמאל

ערוכים ומוגהים
בצרוף מבוא
הערות השואת־גרסאות
לוח־מונחים ומפתחות

על ידי
שמעון ראבידוביץ

הוצאת ·עינות· ברלין תרפ"ד

כתב י רנ"ק

מורה נבוכי הזמן
מאמרים · אגרות
שיר ומליצה
דברי רנ"ק

בצרוף
חתימת יד־רנ"ק
תעודה ושש תמונות

הוצאת ·עינות· ברלין תרפ"ד

Fig. 7. Title page of one of Rawidowicz's early Hebrew publications from Berlin, *Kitve RaNaK* (1924).

Krochmal. These two great scholars saw confusion among Jews of their day and responded by writing for the perplexed. Simon Rawidowicz, as a young scholar working in Berlin, researched these two figures extensively. In 1924, he produced a critical edition of Krochmal's *More nevukhe ha-zeman* (Guide for the Perplexed of the Time) that remains valuable to this day (fig. 7).[32] He also devoted a good deal of research to Maimonides through the 1920s and 1930s, especially on the *Guide for the Perplexed* and the philosophical introduction (*Sefer ha-mada'*) to the great legal code, *Mishneh Torah*.[33] Not only did Rawidowicz feel a strong sense of identification with the two guides for the perplexed of their time, but he also may well have seen *Bavel vi-Yerushalayim* as a guide for the perplexed of his own time, a call to those who, while transfixed on short-term political goals (for example, statehood), neglected the larger struggle for the soul of the Jewish nation. And yet, self-styled prophecy rarely wins a wide audience, especially if announced in the 1950s in Waltham, Massachusetts, in the Hebrew language—and not just in Hebrew, but in a Hebrew style more attentive to classical rabbinic phrasing than to modern Israeli neologisms.

## From Grayewo to Berlin

As noted in the introduction, our best source of information on Rawido-wicz is the work of his son, the historian Benjamin Ravid, who has written a series of excellent sketches that draw on published materials and unpublished letters.[34] Ravid makes clear that any serious study of Rawidowicz must commence by discussing the formative environment of Grayewo, where he was born on 2 February 1897. Grayewo is a town located about sixty kilometers northwest of Białystok in northeastern Poland (see fig. 8). Although reference to it in Polish sources extends back to the fifteenth century, the town did not boast, as a Hebrew writer who spent time there observed, "one of the ancient Jewish communities in Poland, noted for its long and glorious chain of tradition."[35] By the standards of Jewish history, Grayewo was relatively new. Only eighty-three Jews dwelt in the town in 1765. Following the final Partition of Poland in 1795, theł fell under tsarist Russian control. Some 197 Jews lived there in 1827, accounting for nearly 40 percent of the population. Seventy years later, 4,336 Jews lived in Grajewo, and in 1921, under Polish sovereignty, there were 2,384 Jews, who constituted 39 percent of the entire town.[36]

The rapid growth of the Jewish community in Grayewo had much to do with the town's emergence as a regional commercial center, especially after a new railway line connecting it to Białystok and Brest-Litovsk opened in 1873–74.[37] The rail line forged new trade routes between Russia and eastern Prussia, the border of which was a mere four kilometers from Grayewo. The advent of rail service also promoted economic and, particularly, industrial development within Grayewo, attracting new settlers and commerce to the town.

In fact, the bustling nature of Grayewo's commercial life encouraged more than the exchange of goods and capital. There was also a noticeable trade in cultures: Polish and Lithuanian (native to the region), German (from nearby Prussia), and Russian (the imperial power of the area). The Jews of the town, conditioned to geographic, social, and cultural mobility, proved particularly adept at moving across borders, cultures, and languages.

It was to this bustling commercial and cultural ambience that Chaim Yitzhak Rawidowicz, Simon's father, came in 1883 (see fig. 9). Raised in Tykocin and trained in the yeshivot of Łomża, Mir, and Volozhin, Chaim Yitzhak made a living in Grayewo as a purveyor of leather and mushrooms.

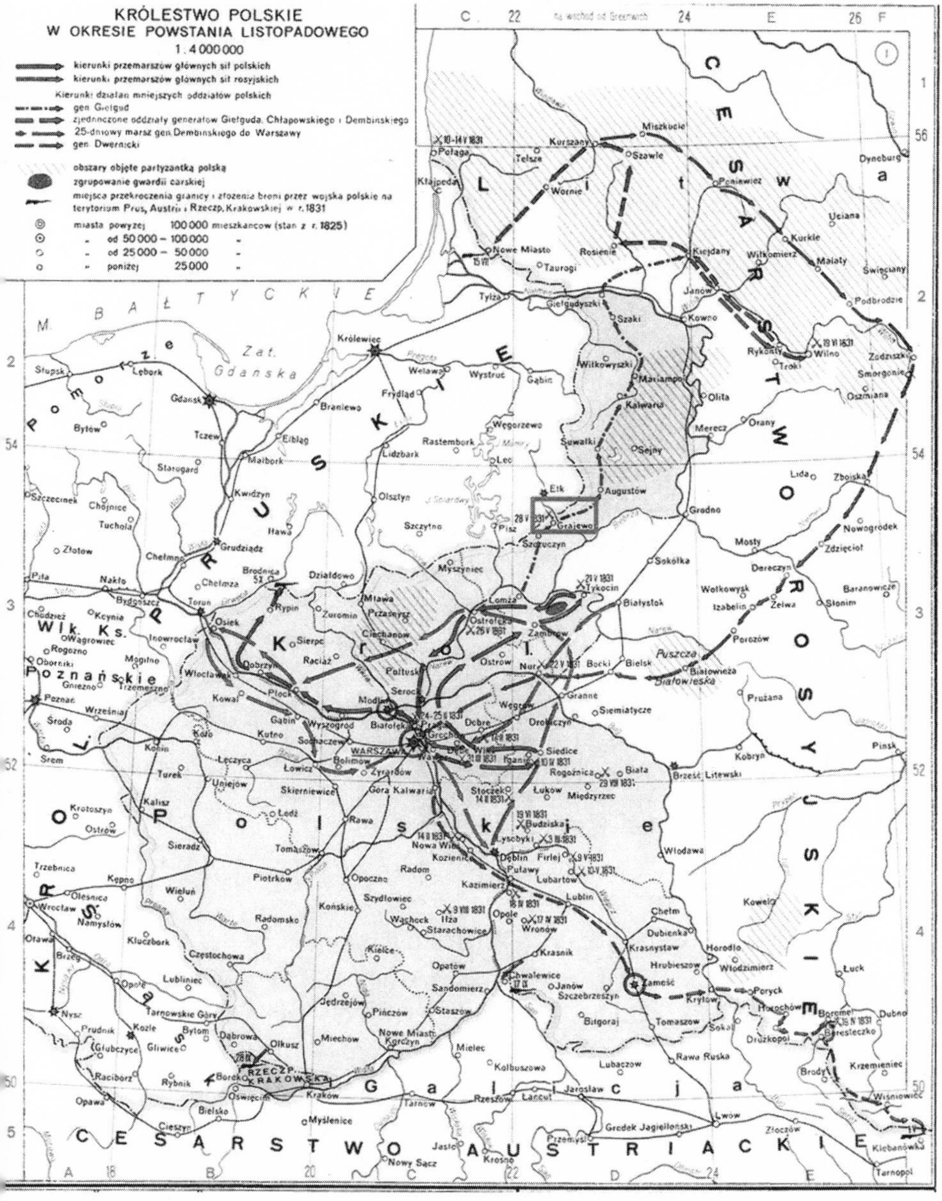
KRÓLESTWO POLSKIE
W OKRESIE POWSTANIA LISTOPADOWEGO
1 : 4 000 000
kierunki przemarszów głównych sił polskich
kierunki przemarszów głównych sił rosyjskich
Kierunki działań mniejszych oddziałów polskich
gen. Gielgud
zjednoczone oddziały generałów Giełguda, Chłapowskiego i Dembińskiego
25-dniowy marsz gen. Dembińskiego do Warszawy
gen. Dwernicki
obszary objęte partyzantką polską
zgrupowanie gwardii carskiej
miejsca przekroczenia granicy i złożenia broni przez wojska polskie na terytorium Prus, Austrii i Rzeczp. Krakowskiej w r. 1831
miasta powyżej 100 000 mieszkańców (stan z r. 1825)
od 50 000 – 100 000
od 25 000 – 50 000
poniżej 25 000
M. BAŁTYCKIE
Zat. Gdańska
PRUSKIE
CESARSTWO ROSYJSKIE
CESARSTWO AUSTRIACKIE
Litwa
Królestwo Polskie
Galicja
Wlk. Ks. Poznańskie
RZECZP. KRAKOWSKA
Królewiec
Gdańsk
Ełk
Grajewo
Augustów
Suwałki
Łomża
Warszawa
Lublin
Kraków
Wilno
Kowno
Grodno
Białystok
Poznań
Wrocław
Lwów

Fig. 8. Map of Poland with Rawidowicz's birthplace, Grayewo, highlighted.

Fig. 9. Chaim Yitzhak Rawidowicz (1863?–1936), father of Simon.

But his great passion in life was Torah study, to which he devoted himself at any free moment, particularly in the wee hours of the morning. He even received the keys to the local study hall so that he could commence learning before dawn, particularly with his elder sons, Ya'akov and Simon.[38]

Chaim Yitzhak Rawidowicz was hardly alone in his passion for Torah study. Not only was a majority of the town's residents Jewish; the Jewish population was itself quite observant, of whom the largest portion belonged to the Lithuanian *mitnagdic* tradition renowned for its intellectual and ritual rigor. Meanwhile, two houses of prayer (*shtiblekh*) served the town's small population of Hasidim, the erstwhile rivals of the Mitnagdim. It was, at least in part, the presence of these different strands of religious orthodoxy—which together constituted the vast majority of the town's

Jews—that prompted Simon Rawidowicz to note: "Jewish life in Grayewo was a totality . . . extending from 'when thou liest down [to] when thou risest up.'"[39]

There were also newer currents of Jewish culture that added to the sense of a Jewish "totality." Especially notable in the case of the Rawidowicz family was a trio of interlacing trends that emerged out of the nineteenth-century *Haskalah* in Eastern Europe: the revival of the Hebrew language, Jewish settlement in the Land of Israel, and Zionism. Unlike most Jewish residents of Grayewo, Chaim Rawidowicz was swept up by all of these currents. For example, he insisted on speaking Hebrew to his children on the Sabbath, in contrast to traditionalists who regarded such an act as a profanation of the holy tongue. And he was actively involved in supporting Jewish settlement in the Land of Israel from the early 1890s, culminating in his selection as a delegate to the Seventh Zionist Congress in 1905 in which the British offer to settle Jews in East Africa was formally rejected.[40] Within his own community of Grayewo, Chaim Rawidowicz's unofficial status as "head of the Zionists" placed him in a minority position.[41]

The Jewish causes that Rawidowicz père valued—Torah study, Zionism, and Hebrew—were transmitted to his seven sons and daughters. Simon was the fourth child born to Chaim Yitzhak and Chana Batya in 1896. He proved to be a gifted student whom his father saw as an ideal candidate for the rabbinate. But Simon was not destined to fulfill this dream. As a young teen, he studied regularly under his father's tutelage, and then in various yeshivot, including those of Rabbi Y. Y. Reines in Lida and Rabbi M. A. Amiel (later of Tel Aviv).[42] He was more attracted, however, to the new strains of Jewish culture that had begun to penetrate Grayewo. Rawidowicz penned his first Hebrew story, "Shene achim," shortly after his return to Grayewo from Lida in 1911. He sent the piece to the Zionist journal, *Ha-Olam,* which returned the manuscript to him without comment. Earlier, while in Lida, he had asked his father to send him a copy of this journal, but his father admonished him to focus more on his Talmud studies.

This suggests to us that Rawidowicz's ardor for Hebrew surpassed even that of his Hebraist father. Indeed, love of Hebrew would become a cornerstone, perhaps the foundation, of his vision of a Jewish national culture. From an early age, the ability to render the ancient tongue into a modern language was a point of pride. Rawidowicz once recounted the great delight that he experienced as a young man in Grayewo when he paid with his own money to undergo a physical examination with a doctor who spoke

Hebrew (even though he had no ailment).[43] Curiously, he related this experience not in his beloved Hebrew, but in Yiddish—Hebrew's sworn rival in the fierce Jewish "language battle" of the early twentieth century.[44] How are we to understand this choice of language, given Rawidowicz's unequivocal preference for Hebrew as the medium of Jewish culture and communication? We might surmise that it is a reflection of Rawidowicz's formative upbringing in Grayewo, an environment in which he learned to converse, write, and lecture in both Yiddish and Hebrew.

Perhaps we are overreading this Yiddish retrospective on the delights of speaking Hebrew. It came, after all, in the Yiddish-language memorial book (1950) for Grayewo, whose Jewish community was destroyed by the Nazi assault. Rawidowicz must have felt compelled to honor the language of his forebears on such an occasion. On the other hand, we do know that, as a young man, Rawidowicz delivered stirring speeches on behalf of Hebrew— in Yiddish![45] Moreover, he served as an editor of Yiddish journals and publications at various points in his life, periodically returning to Yiddish oratory and scholarship later in his career. He also had a collection of his writings published posthumously in Yiddish in 1962. As early as 1937, Rawidowicz noted that his aim was "to create understanding and a *modus vivendi* between Yiddish and Hebrew."[46]

This ambition complicates a bit the image of Simon Rawidowicz as an unyielding Hebrew purist. It is also reminds us that it was not always easy to mark out boundary lines in the swirling struggles over Jewish collective identity that engulfed turn-of-the-century Eastern Europe. The battle lines were not simply between Mitnagdim and Hasidim, or between religious traditionalists and enlightened modernizers. Major urban centers like Odessa, Vilna, and Warsaw—and, for that matter, countless small towns like Grayewo—were arenas of ideological contest in which Hebraists battled Yiddishists, Zionists were pitted against Diasporists, and advocates of *aliyah* (immigration to Palestine) squared off against advocates of *doikeyt* (the ideological commitment to "hereness," that is, to fortifying Jewish life in the Diaspora), not to mention the intense infighting within each of these groups. It would not be inaccurate to describe this tension-filled environment as a golden age of ideological, and particularly nationalist, ferment.

One of the most intriguing characteristics of the era was the central place of culture in Jewish life. Culture was no longer understood, as in previous eras, as an instrument to achieve enlightenment or emancipation. Rather, it was appreciated as an end in and of itself, as the heart and soul of the Jewish nation. Indeed, if we might be permitted to modify Heine's (and later George Steiner's) well-known aphorism, culture became, for many Jewish nationalists, the "portable homeland of the Jewish people." It is not surprising then that Jewish journals, organizations, and schools bearing the name "culture" (e.g., *Kultura* or *Tarbut*) arose in the early decades of the twentieth century. What is surprising is that declared political enemies—for example, Yiddishists and Zionists—shared a commitment to the idea that culture was the most treasured property, embodying the cherished *Volksgeist* of the Jewish nation. This commitment translated into support for Jewish cultural institutions of various kinds in the Diaspora (which the Zionists might have been expected to, but did not always, oppose). A comprehensive study of this phenomenon—of a Jewish cultural nationalism spanning the ideological spectrum—still remains to be written.[47]

To understand Simon Rawidowicz, one must recognize two important historical-biographical qualities: first, he came of age in the teeming marketplace of ideas that characterized fin de siècle Eastern Europe; and second, the development of Jewish national culture was his main life objective. In his teen years, the closely linked pillars of Hebrew and Zionism anchored his emerging sense of that culture. He attended to both in Grayewo, but even more intensively after his family moved to Białystok in 1914. The move to the larger, heavily Jewish city was prompted by the outbreak of the First World War, which brought an end to some four decades of economic growth and prosperity in Grayewo. Białystok had itself been in the throes of tumult for nearly a decade, following the violent pogrom that broke out there in June 1906 that led to the death of seventy Jews. From the turn of the century, the city had also been a cauldron of Jewish political activity, especially among the socialist working class. This political activity, in a time of instability, aroused claims of disloyalty that could and did turn into lethal anti-Jewish action.

Claims of Jewish disloyalty were quite common during the First World War, as Jews in Eastern and Central Europe attempted to navigate among the competing combatants—and not merely the principals (Russia and Germany), but also smaller national groups like the Poles and the Ukrainians. In 1915, Białystok came under German control, when the Central Powers undertook a major offensive that led to considerable territorial

Fig. 10. Rawidowicz with a group of students in a Hebrew course, Białystok (20 May 1919).

conquest in Eastern Europe. The resulting German occupation of Białystok led not to a worsening, but rather to an amelioration, of conditions for Jews. In particular, Jewish culture and language were less restricted than they had been under Russian control.

It was in Białystok that Simon Rawidowicz was exposed to a richly multicultural setting, as well as to the efforts of national minorities (variously Poles, Germans, Russians, Ukrainians, as well as Jews) to preserve their physical and cultural well-being in the face of indifferent or hostile hosts. Białystok was an incubator of diverse ideological strains, and Rawidowicz developed a new degree of maturity, in addition to a host of organizational and oratorical skills, in this ambience. Along with a friend, he initiated a Hebrew-language course for adults that became "a center for cultural and Zionist activity." As a teacher, Rawidowicz was remembered with great enthusiasm by one of his students who recalled, forty years later, that "we sat enchanted and saw come alive before us the idea of a 'man floating in the celestial heavens.'"[48] A picture from this era reveals the broad-faced Rawidowicz, smartly attired in a suit, surrounded by his students whom he sought to guide down the path of Hebrew culture (see fig. 10). Meanwhile, Rawidowicz himself was drawn further into Zionist circles in Białystok, particularly into the Tse'ire Tsiyon, a youth movement made up of socialist and nonsocialist Zionists (fig. 11).

Already at this stage, Rawidowicz was intent on placing culture at the forefront of his Zionist activity. At a regional Zionist conference in 1918, he was invited to give a lecture on Jewish cultural activities; he proposed the creation of a fund to support an expansion of such activities that was accepted by the conference participants.[49] Subsequently, a number of new Jewish schools were established out of this culture fund.[50]

The nexus between Zionism and culture of course summons up the memory of Ahad Ha-am (1856–1927), the renowned Hebrew author and advocate of the Land of Israel as the main site of Jewish cultural vibrancy. Rawidowicz, who read and drew inspiration from Ahad Ha-am as a young man, shared a number of key tenets with the Hebrew essayist, ranging from their views on the primacy of culture in the national project to their concerns over Zionist attitudes to Palestinian Arabs. And yet, he would come to reject out of hand Ahad Ha-am's prescription that the Land of

Fig. 11. A young Rawidowicz (with moustache) in the company of friends.

Israel must become the primary "spiritual center" of the Jewish people, radiating rays of vitality to second-order Jewish communities in the Diaspora. For Rawidowicz, the prospect of a vibrant Jewish—and specifically *Hebrew*—culture required a relationship of equals, both in terms of professed ideology and financial investment, between the Diaspora and Palestine.[51]

While the seeds of Rawidowicz's views were sown in Białystok during the First World War, they blossomed more fully in Berlin, where he moved in 1919. When we think today of the vibrant cultural ambience of Weimar Berlin, we tend to call to mind its extraordinary cohort of German-Jewish intellectuals: Buber, Rosenzweig, Benjamin, Scholem, Bloch, and Strauss, among others. In fact, Berlin also became an important center of settlement for Eastern European Jews, tens of thousands of whom came in the last years of the war and in its immediate aftermath. By extension, Berlin was home to a substantial amount of cultural activity and publishing in both Yiddish and Hebrew. In fact, the city was not merely one among many centers of Hebrew culture in this period, but rather, as Michael Brenner asserts, "*the* center between 1920 and 1924."[52]

## Hebrew Culture in Berlin

It was not initially the allures of Hebrew and Yiddish culture that attracted Simon Rawidowicz to Berlin in June of 1919. Rawidowicz joined other young Eastern European Jews in search of higher education: both to avoid long-standing restrictions in their native countries and to escape the chaotic postwar situation in Eastern Europe (for example, the upheaval of the Russian Revolution and the anti-Jewish pogroms in Ukraine and Belorussia). Without the requisite German gymnasium education, foreign students—in this case, Jews from Eastern Europe—were required to pass an external exam to gain admission to university.

Rawidowicz undertook studies for the *Abitur* at the Realgymnsium zu Berlin-Reinickendorf and entered the Friedrich-Wilhelms University of Berlin in the winter semester of 1921–22 (see fig. 12).[53] Similar to a number of other notable Jewish figures from Eastern Europe, perhaps most prominently, Joseph B. Soloveitchik and Abraham Joshua Heschel, Rawidowicz decided to embark upon the study of philosophy in Berlin. It is worthwhile to consider briefly the allure of this field for these traditional Jews from Eastern Europe. Philosophy, it would seem, was an ideal medium

## Lebenslauf.

Ich wurde am 22. 2. 1893 zu Bialystock als Sohn des Isaak R., jetzt Landwirt in Merchawjah (Palästina) und seiner Ehefrau Hanna geb. Rembelinker, geboren. Nachdem ich mehrere Jahre hindurch die Cheder-Schule, dann die höhere Talmudschule (Jeschiwah) besucht hatte, wandte ich mich dem allgemeinen Studium zu. Während des Krieges war ich in meiner Vaterstadt als Lehrer für Alt- und Neuhebräisch wie auch für jüdische Literatur und Wissenschaftsgeschichte am dortigen Lehrerseminar tätig, und wandte mich daneben der literarischen Tätigkeit zu. Im Juni 1919 kam ich nach Berlin. Im September 1921 bestand ich als Extraner die Reifeprüfung am Realgymnasium zu Berlin-Reinickendorf. In Berlin setzte ich dann. meine literarisch-wissenschaftliche Tätigkeit in hebräischer Sprache fort. Abgesehen von einigen Einzel-Abhandlungen erschienen von mir zwei wissenschaftliche text-kritische Ausgaben, nebst größeren Einleitungen, Noten u. a.: 1) Eines Maimonidischen Textes. 2) Der gesamten Werke des Historikers und Philosophen N. Krochmal. Beide Werke sind im Verlag „Ajanoth", Berlin erschienen.

Seit dem Wintersemester 1921/22 studierte ich an der Philosophischen Fakultät der Friedrich Wilhelms Universität zu Berlin. Mein Hauptstudium war der Philosophie, allgemeinen Geschichte mit besonderer Berücksichtigung der russischen Geschichte bei Herrn Prof. Dr. K. Stählin und den semitischen Sprachen bei Herrn Prof. Dr. E. Mittwoch gewidmet. Es ist mir ein Bedürfnis, Herrn Geh. Rat Prof. Dr. Heinrich Maier für die mir erwiesene Unterstützung bei meiner Arbeit und für seine Vorlesungen und Seminarübungen meinen herzlichsten Dank auszusprechen. Ebenfalls bin ich Herrn Prof. Dr. Max Dessoir zu Dank verpflichtet. Herrn Privatdozent Dr. David Baumgardt, der mich auf Feuerbach hingewiesen und mir auch beim weiteren Verlauf der Arbeit freundlich zur Seite gestanden hat, schulde ich besonderen Dank.

Fig. 12. "Lebenslauf"—brief autobiographical statement required for acceptance of dissertation with incorrect year and place of birth.

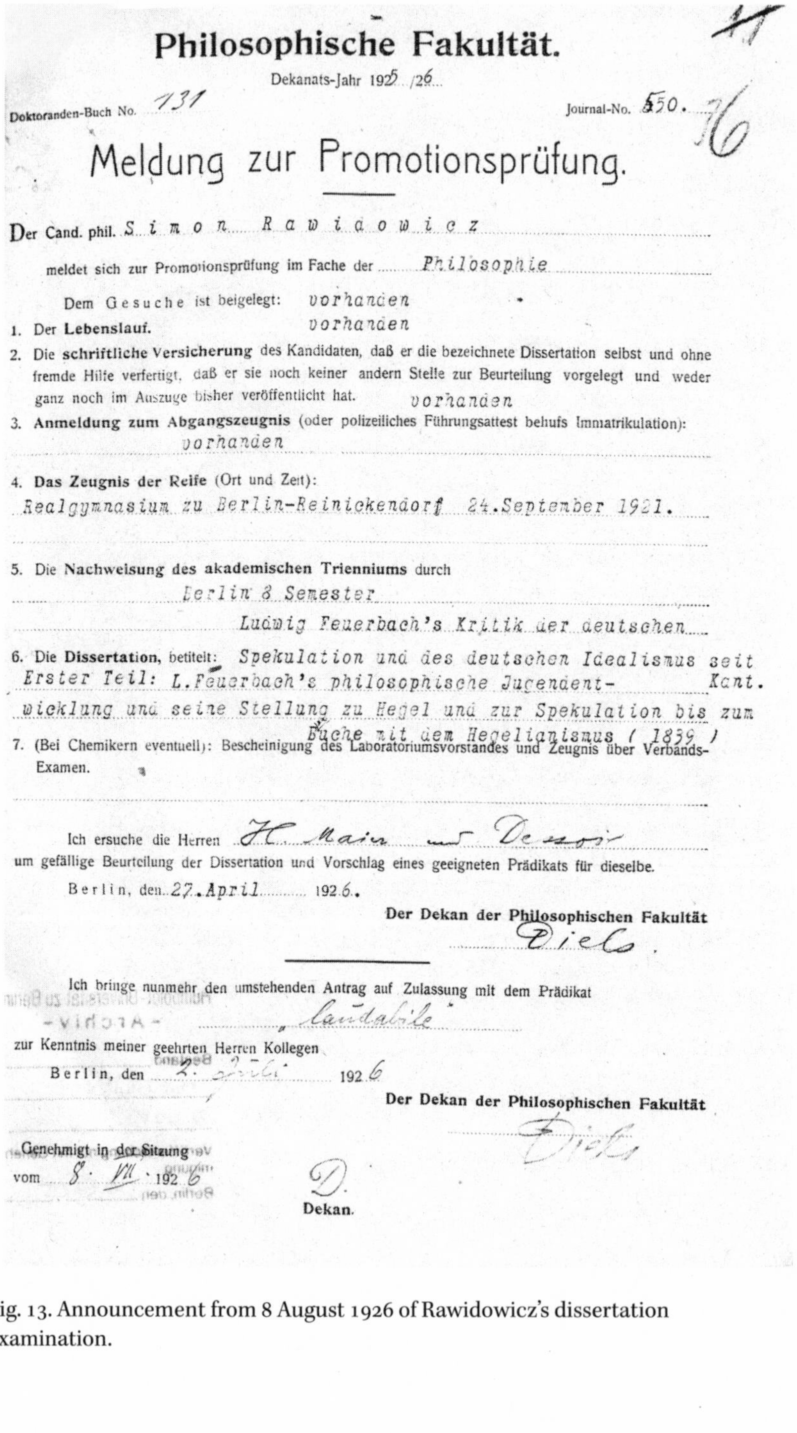

# Philosophische Fakultät.

Dekanats-Jahr 192*5* /2*6*

Doktoranden-Buch No. *131*

Journal-No. *550*.

## Meldung zur Promotionsprüfung.

Der Cand. phil. S i m o n   R a w i d o w i c z

meldet sich zur Promotionsprüfung im Fache der *Philosophie*

Dem G e s u c h e ist beigelegt: *vorhanden*

1. Der Lebenslauf. *vorhanden*
2. Die **schriftliche Versicherung** des Kandidaten, daß er die bezeichnete Dissertation selbst und ohne fremde Hilfe verfertigt, daß er sie noch keiner andern Stelle zur Beurteilung vorgelegt und weder ganz noch im Auszuge bisher veröffentlicht hat. *vorhanden*
3. **Anmeldung zum Abgangszeugnis** (oder polizeiliches Führungsattest behufs Immatrikulation): *vorhanden*
4. **Das Zeugnis der Reife** (Ort und Zeit): *Realgymnasium zu Berlin-Reinickendorf 24.September 1921.*
5. Die Nachweisung des akademischen Trienniums durch *Berlin 8 Semester*
6. Die **Dissertation**, betitelt: *Ludwig Feuerbach's Kritik der deutschen Spekulation und des deutschen Idealismus seit Kant. Erster Teil: L.Feuerbach's philosophische Jugendentwicklung und seine Stellung zu Hegel und zur Spekulation bis zum Buche mit dem Hegelianismus ( 1839 )*
7. (Bei Chemikern eventuell): Bescheinigung des Laboratoriumsvorstandes und Zeugnis über Verbands-Examen.

Ich ersuche die Herren *H. Maier und Dessoir*
um gefällige Beurteilung der Dissertation und Vorschlag eines geeigneten Prädikats für dieselbe.

B e r l i n, den *27.April* 192*6*.

Der Dekan der Philosophischen Fakultät

*Diels*.

Ich bringe nunmehr den umstehenden Antrag auf Zulassung mit dem Prädikat *"laudabile"*
zur Kenntnis meiner geehrten Herren Kollegen

B e r l i n, den *2. Juli* 192*6*

Der Dekan der Philosophischen Fakultät

*Diels*

Genehmigt in der Sitzung
vom *8. VII* 192*6*

*D*

Dekan.

Fig. 13. Announcement from 8 August 1926 of Rawidowicz's dissertation examination.

through which to mediate between their traditional religious worldview and the new intellectual sensibilities of the West that they had encountered and embraced.[54] All three were supervised in their studies by two mainstays of philosophical study in Berlin, the Jewish neo-Kantian scholar of aesthetics, Max Dessoir, and the logician and classicist, Heinrich Maier.[55]

In addition to working with Dessoir and Maier, Rawidowicz also studied with the well-known Jewish Orientalist, Eugen Mittwoch; the historian of Russia, Karl Stählin; and the young Jewish philosopher, David Baumgardt. Rawidowicz credits Baumgardt with drawing his attention to the Young Hegelian philosopher, Ludwig Feuerbach (1802–72), who became the subject of his doctoral research (see fig. 13).[56] The dissertation that Rawidowicz completed in 1926 (and for which he was "promoted" in the following year; see fig. 14) was an intellectual history of Feuerbach's early thought, focusing in particular on the impact of his engagement with G. W. F. Hegel, whom Feuerbach met in Berlin in 1824.

We should recall that as Rawidowicz proceeded with his university studies, he remained active in a variety of Hebrew literary and publishing activities in Berlin, including writing a long introduction to Nachman Krochmal's *More nevukhe ha-zeman*. One of the key suppositions that Rawidowicz sought to investigate, and would ultimately challenge, was the claim that Krochmal was a Hegelian.[57] In the very same period, he was engaged in his dissertation research on the nature of Feuerbach's debt to Hegel. The common interest in Hegel—and his relationship to Feuerbach and Krochmal—revealed the overlapping, yet distinct, intellectual circles (for example, German idealist and Jewish Enlightenment) that Rawidowicz was studying in this Berlin phase.

One wonders whether Rawidowicz, now at a remove from Grajewo and his traditional upbringing, felt a sense of identification with Feuerbach, who, to the consternation of his father a century earlier, had moved away from his erstwhile theological studies to become a sharp critic of Christianity and religion in general. Rawidowicz, in the midst of his own ferment, moved away from the personal ritual practice of his father's home. But he never became a sharp critic of Jewish Orthodoxy. Nor, for that matter, did he find an analogue to Feuerbach's claim that just as "there was no Christian medicine or mathematics, so there was no Christian philosophy."[58] That is, he believed that there *was* a Jewish philosophy, a rich tradition of

**Ludwig Feuerbachs
philosophische Jugendentwicklung
und seine Stellung zu Hegel
bis 1839.**

Inaugural-Dissertation
zur
Erlangung der Doktorwürde

Genehmigt von der Philosophischen Fakultät
Der Friedrich-Wilhelms Universität zu Berlin

Vorgelegt von
**Simon Rawidowicz.**

Tag der Promotion: 27. Mai 1927.

Fig. 14. Announcement of Rawidowicz's *Promotion* on 27 May 1927 for his dissertation on Feuerbach.

Jewish thought and interpretation that spanned millennia. More broadly, he belonged to a generation of young Jewish intellectuals and activists who believed that there was a Jewish literature, music, art, and theater—all part of an age-old and evolving Jewish culture that stood at the brink of rejuvenation in the age of nationalism.

In Berlin, Rawidowicz made his way to an exceptionally lively circle of Jewish scholars, thinkers, and activists, mainly from Eastern Europe, that included the historian Simon Dubnow, the writer Shaul Tchernichovsky, the philosopher Jacob Klatzkin, and the Hebrew poet Chaim Nahman Bialik.[59] The arrival of Bialik in Berlin in 1921 was greeted, Rawidowicz noted, almost as a religious happening: "as an event on the order of a festive holiday, an elevation of the soul."[60]

Rawidowicz had admired Bialik from his youth, taught his poetry in Bi-ałystok, and now came to develop a close relationship with him in Berlin based on their shared passion for Hebrew language, literature, and culture. The older Bialik became a mentor to Rawidowicz, and the two met and corresponded frequently. And yet, in the fractious and ideologically charged world in which they dwelt, Bialik and Rawidowicz did not always see eye to eye. To wit, the twenty-six-year-old Rawidowicz founded in the same year in which he started his graduate studies—1922—a small He-brew publishing firm, Ayanot, that put out more than a dozen Hebrew ti-tles over the next three years, including his study of Maimonides' *Sefer ha-mada* (1922) and his edition of Krochmal's writings, *Kitve RaNaK* (1924). As Rawidowicz records in his journal, Bialik, whom one might have expected to be thrilled at the prospect, opposed the establishment of Aya-not. He, after all, was editor-in-chief of a competing Hebrew publishing firm, Devir, and at one point asked Rawidowicz to close down Ayanot and take over Devir.[61]

Ayanot and Devir were not the only Hebrew publishing houses in Ber-lin. A number of others, including the renowned Stybel firm from Warsaw, made their home in Berlin. The pull was, first and foremost, the large as-sembly of Eastern European Jewish intellectuals in Berlin, who were the natural readers (and authors) of Hebrew books. Another, rather counter-intuitive, factor was the staggering inflation that afflicted Germany, espe-cially in 1923, when the mark was reduced to less than a trillionth of its former value. The cheap cost of publishing attracted those able to pay with foreign currency. As a result, this period marked the peak of the flourish-ing of Hebrew, as well as of Yiddish, letters in Berlin.[62] Already by 1924, the efflorescence began to dim, ironically because of a stabilized economy. In that year, Bialik left Germany for Palestine, as did the great Hebrew au-thor, S. Y. Agnon.

Rawidowicz himself went to Palestine in the following year. His father and five of his siblings had already immigrated there, acting upon their lifelong Zionist creed. Despite his professed desire to join them and partic-ipate in the vibrant Hebrew culture of the Land of Israel, Rawidowicz did not settle there. In a letter to his brother Avraham in Tel Aviv in 1925, he wrote what might well have been an epitaph for the rest of his life by invok-ing God's expulsion of Cain in Genesis 4:12: "A fugitive and a wanderer shalt thou be in the earth. You will perforce emigrate to the Diaspora, for you will not strike roots in Palestine. You will always have next to you a ticket for travel and a wanderer's staff."[63]

This intuition—that despite his love of Hebrew culture and a solid Zionist background, he would not make his home in Palestine—points to a powerful and lifelong ambivalence in Rawidowicz. He struggled to balance his desire to inhabit a living Hebrew culture with the desire to effect a genuine partnership between Babylon and Jerusalem. As a practical matter, Rawidowicz could not yet abandon his philosophical studies in Berlin for the newly created Hebrew University in Jerusalem, which did not have a scholar of Jewish or general European philosophy on staff in 1925 (nor, for that matter, did the Hebrew University offer degrees of any sort to students at this time).[64]

And yet, Rawidowicz maintained an active interest in an academic position at the Hebrew University after earning his Ph.D. from Berlin. Such a position would, first of all, provide a measure of economic stability to Rawidowicz, who worked at various part-time jobs in Berlin—editor, researcher, and librarian, among others—in order to make ends meet.[65] Rawidowicz also tried to make the case to friends and potential supporters in the late 1920s and early 1930s that Jerusalem suited him on intellectual and cultural grounds. We gain a glimpse of this effort in a series of missives to the conservative Zionist thinker, writer, and Hebrew University professor Joseph Klausner in which Rawidowicz makes quite clear his interest in a proposed job in Jewish philosophy. In one of the first of these letters from 1928, Rawidowicz reports that the noted Berlin rabbi and scholar, Leo Baeck, had proposed his name to the university's board for this job.[66] Subsequent letters from 1930 to 1931 reveal a far more plaintive tone. Rawidowicz pleads with Klausner to take up his candidacy with Hebrew University chancellor, Judah L. Magnes, as well as with professors of the university's Institute for Jewish Studies. In one of these letters from 4 February 1931, Rawidowicz issues what amounts to a directive to Klausner: "After it becomes clear that Prof. Guttmann will not settle in Palestine, the gentleman [that is, Klausner] must propose my candidacy. He should speak of the matter with the University Council, and we will see how the matter ends up."[67]

The "Prof. Guttmann" in question was Julius Guttmann, the doyen of scholars of Jewish philosophy in Berlin and the director of the Akademie für die Wissenschaft des Judentums, a leading center of Jewish scholarship where Rawidowicz was employed as a researcher and editor (for the bicentennial edition of Moses Mendelssohn's writings). Guttmann was the preferred candidate of the Jerusalem faculty throughout most of its discussions about the job; he satisfied the ideal of scholarly respectability so important to the new university. The chief question was whether Guttmann, who neither spoke Hebrew well nor was an especially ardent Zionist, would agree to come to Palestine. As a result, other candidates were mentioned in institute faculty meetings, including Rawidowicz, his fellow Akademie researcher Leo Strauss, Zvi Diesendruck, Avraham Tsifroni, and Max Wiener. Rawidowicz did his best in letters to Klausner to assert both his superior qualifications and his ideological affinity with the university. "Is there no place in this university," he asked in 1930, "for young Hebrew scholars who come from within?" How could it be, he continued, that the Hebrew University would invite a scholar like Guttmann who did not know Hebrew?[68] Rawidowicz posed similar questions to Klausner about Strauss, another German-Jewish candidate who did not command spoken Hebrew.[69]

Rawidowicz sensed that he was at an ironic disadvantage both because he was born in Eastern Europe and was a devoted Hebrew activist and author. It is the case that many faculty associated with the Hebrew University at this nascent stage conceived of it as a bastion of proper German scholarship.[70] According to this standard, a figure such as Julius Guttmann, the flag-bearer of *Wissenschaft des Judentums* in his day, would be valued more than Rawidowicz, who divided his labors between scholarship and ideological advocacy. However, it is not true, as Rawidowicz suspected, that his path was thwarted by the steadfast resistance of one particularly significant institute faculty member, Gershom Scholem.[71] Scholem was in fact committed to Julius Guttmann's candidacy from the first until Guttmann's arrival in Jerusalem in 1934; but so too were other members of the institute's faculty, *including* Rawidowicz's putative ally, Joseph Klausner.[72] In short, we may conclude that Rawidowicz was never a frontline contender for a position that he considered, at least in this period, to be rightly his.[73]

Meanwhile, Rawidowicz kept Klausner informed of a number of other teaching prospects that did or might come his way. He mentioned discussions over an offer to teach Jewish philosophy at the Hebrew Union College in Cincinnati, whose president, Julian Morgenstern, had been in touch with him from 1926 to 1928.[74] He also noted that he was offered a position teaching Jewish philosophy at the new institute for Jewish studies in Warsaw under the leadership of Moses Schorr.[75] When he later mentioned this offer to Judah Magnes in 1930, he hastened to add that "if the opportunity to teach philosophy at the University in Jerusalem came to me, I would accept it with great pleasure."[76] Around the same time, Rawidowicz was also being considered for *Privatdozentur* in philosophy at the University of Berlin. Following the publication of his thesis on Feuerbach in 1931, Rawidowicz reported to Klausner that his doctoral adviser Heinrich Maier was interested in advancing his cause within the university. Rawidowicz was not optimistic about this prospect given the rising tide of antisemitism in German academic circles in 1931 (which even infected, Rawidowicz suggests, Maier himself).[77] But the very fact that he would be considered for a position (even as an unsalaried *Privatdozent*) in Berlin, the world's capital of philosophical study, compounded his bewilderment over his failure to make headway in Jerusalem.

We have dwelt on Rawidowicz's largely unrequited interest in the Hebrew University because it helps us to understand better his frame of mind and motivations at a crucial time in his life. On one level, he had earned the imprimatur of the German university for his philosophical research. On another level, he had devoted the better part of the 1920s to working on behalf of a vibrant Hebrew culture, not only through his work at the Ayanot publishing house, but also as coeditor of the journal *Ha-tekufah* and as one of the founders of the Hebrew cultural house, the Bet ha-'am ha-'ivri.[78] At the very time that he was prodding Klausner and others about his fate at the Hebrew University, he was busily preparing for the first conference of an international organization for Hebrew culture, the Brit 'Ivrit 'Olamit, that he helped to create. To be sure, the desire to garner an appointment in Jerusalem casts his efforts for a Diaspora Hebrew culture in a rather unusual light. Two weeks before the opening of the Brit conference in 1931, Rawidowicz confided to Klausner that his energies were waning: "This is my last attempt to do something for the revival of Hebrew in the Diaspora. If I come to the recognition that the Hebrew public does not want to organize itself, that this public does not want to carry the burden of our culture in the Diaspora, then I will be forced to abandon that public altogether."[79]

We might attribute this sentiment to the normal trepidation one feels before undertaking a major new initiative. But even after the conference, as Rawidowicz took steps to solidify the Brit, he indicated to Klausner that the time had come "to put an end to my wandering." In the fall of 1933, Rawidowicz went to Palestine a second time to explore the possibility of moving there. Writing shortly thereafter from London, he declared to Klausner that "during my time there, it became clear to me that my place, after all, is in Erets Yisrael."[80]

Needless to say, Adolf Hitler's ascent to power in 1933 made refuge from Berlin both highly desirable and advisable. Rawidowicz's apparent interest in settling in Palestine stood in sharp contrast to the letter to his brother from 1925 in which he admitted that he may not be able to "strike roots in Palestine." It also poses an interesting juxtaposition to Rawidowicz's declaration from fifteen years later that "I have lost the desire to settle . . . in any specific place."[81] No doubt, the fact that Rawidowicz did not receive an offer from the Hebrew University in 1933—or any other serious offer of employment in Palestine—was the source of frustration, weariness, and even desperation.[82] The interesting question is whether this frustration, and the subsequent physical wandering, became for Rawidowicz a kind of metaphysical state that he grew to accept and even mold into the persona of a self-conscious "lonely man." Perhaps more to the point, did this frustration fuel the formation of his dual-centered vision of Jewish nationalism, as against the monocentric approach of Zionism?

On one hand, it seems likely that Rawidowicz's lack of acceptance by the scholarly and literary establishments in Palestine played a substantial role in his remaining in the Diaspora. It would be hard to imagine otherwise for a scholarly activist so singularly committed to the Hebrew language. On the other hand, we should not fail to recall that his ideological worldview had taken shape well in advance of the painful experience with the university in Jerusalem. Even as a young committed Zionist, Rawidowicz was uncertain about his comrades' disparagement of the Diaspora.[83] Later, toward the end of the 1920s, he sharpened his critique of Ahad Ha-'am's notion of a single spiritual center for the Jewish nation. It may well be that his unsuccessful attempts to find a home in Palestine solidified this critique, but clear traces of it were present and articulated before 1933.

Indeed, it was in Weimar Berlin that Simon Rawidowicz crystallized his thinking around the goal of preserving and enriching Jewish life in the Diaspora—as long as there was a significant Jewish presence to warrant it. Berlin proved to be fertile ground for this sensibility, in part because it dwelt among other active diasporist agendas. The city was home to a substantial

Yiddish intelligentsia that supported as many as seventeen Yiddish journals, as well as the publication of hundreds of Yiddish-language books.[84] In fact, it was in Berlin that the first institutional steps were taken in 1925 to create the great center of Yiddish scholarship, YIVO, which arose in the same period as—and in competition with—the Zionist-inspired Hebrew University in Jerusalem.

Berlin was also home, as we noted, to the prominent Jewish historian and diasporist thinker, Simon Dubnow (1860–1941). Rawidowicz got to know him initially through Ayanot, which published Dubnow's edition of the records of the Jewish council in the Grand Duchy of Lithuania, *Pinkas medinat Lita*; the two went on to develop a close relationship through ten years of acquaintance in Berlin (1923–33).[85] Dubnow's well-known notion of shifting centers of Diaspora influence was a theoretical pillar of his ten-volume *Weltgeschichte des jüdischen Volkes* published in Berlin between 1925 and 1929. It was also an influential doctrine in the debates among early twentieth-century Jewish nationalists in Europe, and served as the foundation for Dubnow's political party in Russia, the Folkspartay, which advocated national cultural autonomy for the world's largest concentration of Jews in Eastern Europe. Moreover, the impact of Dubnow's diasporist views extended beyond his native Eastern Europe. We see traces of his perspective in the name and work of the Jüdische Volkspartei, a coalition party of Germans and Eastern Europeans within the German-Jewish community that was committed to advancing the interests of "Jews as a national minority that autonomously determines its cultural activities."[86]

While notable as a reflection of the migration of Eastern European political ideas to Berlin, the Volkspartei is perhaps even more interesting to us because of an intriguing family connection. Among the founders of the Volkspartei was Alfred Klee, the father of Esther Klee, whom Simon Rawidowicz met in 1921 and married five years later (figs. 15 and 16). Klee was also active in the Jewish Colonial Association (ICA), the organization of the "Territorialists" whose raison d'être was to ameliorate the conditions of, and find refuge for, Jews in any available land.

Despite his involvement in organizations committed to Jewish life in the Diaspora, Alfred Klee was also an active Zionist who frequently spoke on behalf of the movement and counted Theodor Herzl and Max Nordau as personal friends. As a German Zionist of the first generation, Klee did not conceive of his commitment to Zionism as inconsistent with his

Fig. 15. Esther Klee Rawidowicz (1900–1980), wife of Simon Rawidowicz.

support for social and cultural work in the Diaspora. Indeed, there were more than a few Zionists such as Klee who rejected the principle of "negating the Exile" and saw Jewish life outside of Palestine less as a permanent state of exile than as a venue replete with creative possibilities.

In this regard, Simon Rawidowicz was quite similar to his father-in-law, continually traversing the border between Zionism and diasporism. To take a further biographical step, we might say that the evolution of his

Fig. 16. Marriage of Esther Klee and Simon Rawidowicz (1926).

distinctive version of Jewish nationalism was an ongoing—indeed, life-long—effort to negotiate between two inspirations and ideological foils, Ahad Ha-am and Simon Dubnow. Both emphasized the importance of a national mission that preserved and nurtured Jewish culture, though they advocated different sites—the Land of Israel and the Diaspora—as the main locus of that mission.[87] Like his two elders, Rawidowicz's vision of Jewish nationalism was anchored by the primacy of Jewish culture. But rather than choose one venue over the other, he settled on his distinctive idea of two centers.

As we have seen, at various points in time, such as when he sought a position at the Hebrew University, Rawidowicz harbored doubts about the viability of Jewish culture in the Diaspora, especially one that revolved around the Hebrew language. Yet, from his time in Berlin until his last days in Waltham, he continued to agitate for recognition of a Jewish nation rooted in "Babylon and Jerusalem." A particularly significant moment came at the opening conference of the World Hebrew Union (Brit 'Ivrit 'Olamit) in June 1931 (fig. 17). Lacking any of the doubt he privately expressed a few weeks before, Rawidowicz gave an address to the conference, "Organizing the Hebrew Diaspora," that spelled out a number of core principles anchoring his subsequent thought. The question at hand, he proclaimed, was not simply the fate of Hebrew language. It was the fate of "Israel," the Jewish people at large.[88]

Indeed, the Land of Israel was not the only home of "Israel." Taking direct aim at Ahad Ha-am's notion of Erets Yisrael as "the spiritual center" of the Jewish people, he argued that "wherever there is a living Jewish community, there is a living center of Jewish creativity. The Land of Israel should not fear these centers of creativity; rather, it requires them."[89]

Rawidowicz's language of "centers of creativity" marked a substantial revision of Ahad Ha-am's notion of "imitation" as a means of cultural enrichment.[90] As Rawidowicz saw it, Ahad Ha-am fundamentally misunderstood the nature of Jewish cultural life, especially in the Diaspora. Jewish culture did not come about through "imitation" of Gentile culture (not even from the more benign "competitive" version of imitation that Ahad Ha-am distinguished from the self-negating form). Rather, Rawidowicz held to a different, we might say, more insular, view predicated not on cultural interaction between Jews and Gentiles, but on the inner cultural forces of the Jews themselves. Thus, he proclaimed that "the life that we

# ישיבת הפתיחה

הכנסיה העברית נפתחה ביום א', ו' תמוז תרצ"א
(21 ביוני 1931), בעשר וחצי בבקר, באולמי
"בית העם העברי" ֟בברלין, רחוב קורפירסטנדם 61

ד"ר שמעון ראבידוביץ פותח את הכנסיה בנאום זה:

כנסיה נכבדה, גבירותי ורבותי!

אנו מתכנסים בכנסיה זו בשעה קשה, הן בארץ ישראל והן בגולה.
בנין ארץ ישראל נתקל במכשולים גדולים, ואנו מתפללים על כך שיעלה
ביד הקונגרס הציוני הקרוב להסירם מדרך בניננו. גם שאלת היהודים והיהדות
לובשת פרובלמטיות חריפה ומבהילה. במדינה זו שאנו מתכנסים בה לבשה
שנאת ישראל צורה גסה ומעליבה, קדרו שמי היהדות במזרח ובמערב,
בתפוצות ובארץ. שבעתים קשה מצב החנוך העברי בגולה, מוסדות החנוך
בליטא, בפולניה וברומניה כורעים תחת סבל לא ישוער. ובשעה קשה זו ֟אנו
מתכנסים לטכס עצה על גורלה ועתידה של התנועה העברית בגולה. אם
יהיה מי שיאמר: בעת »הרת עולם« זו אתם מצטמצמים בנקודתכם האחת,
נאמר לו: צמצום זה צורך קיומנו הוא. תנועה אחת יש בעולם, שבה לא
פגע כמעט המשבר העולמי – היא התנועה העברית בגולה. ומשום מה?

Fig. 17. Opening page of published version of Rawidowicz's address at the first
conference of the Brit 'Ivrit 'Olamit (World Hebrew Union) in Berlin on 21 June 1931.

live is the life that we create for ourselves; if we do not create, we do not live."[91] The key to this creativity, he reiterated, lay not primarily in the relationship between a host society and its Jewish minority, but rather in the "partnership" between Babylon and Jerusalem: "Just as Diaspora Jewry cannot solve the problem of Judaism alone, neither can the Land of Israel solve, today or in the foreseeable future, the question of a complete Jewish culture." "The two," Rawidowicz asserted in borrowing from a well-known Mishnah, "are clinging to the same garment." He continued: "The material from which they are made is the same, and their soul is the same."[92]

As we shall see, Rawidowicz would later employ the metaphor of "two clinging to the same garment" to refer to the struggle between Jews and Arabs over Palestine. Already in 1931, though, Rawidowicz had fixed on the language that would course throughout *Bavel vi-Yerushalayim*. Thus, the idea of a "partnership" (*shutafut*) between the two main centers of Jewish life figured prominently in his Berlin address. This relationship required, he continued, respect for the cultural creations produced in both centers: "This Union [the World Hebrew Union] must emphasize the idea that Babylon cannot remain without its Talmud as long as Israel (i.e., the Jewish people) is located in Babylon; as long as Babylon is part of the Jewish world, then Israel must study not only the Jerusalem Talmud but the Babylonian Talmud.... Do not leave Babylon without its Talmud."[93] Shorn of his recent insecurity, Rawidowicz was now prepared to fight on behalf of Hebrew culture and to affirm the existence of the Diaspora. In this sense, he felt it important to keep the Union independent of the World Zionist Organization in order to serve as the representative voice of "the Hebrew nation in the Diaspora."[94]

At the same time, Rawidowicz was intent on affirming his Zionist credentials. As he told the delegates in Berlin in 1931, "my Zionism is no less than those who discharge their obligations by 'negating the Diaspora' or reciting 'kaddish' [the mourner's prayer] for Diaspora Jewry."[95] In attempting to explain his position, Rawidowicz relied on a prestigious, if rather surprising, example: Albert Einstein. Without mentioning the great scientist by name, Rawidowicz asserted that his own form of Jewish cultural nationalism was grounded in "a theory of relativity," as distinct from "a theory of the Absolute." He explained that this theory of *relativity* did not entail a retreat into *relativism*. It did mean, however, that one could no longer analyze a complex condition in simple-minded or monistic fashion. According to Rawidowicz's oft-repeated formula, "the Jewish Question had one solution that was in fact two: one relative to the building up of Jewish life in Palestine and the other relative to Jewish life in the Diaspora."[96]

This attempt to craft an applied theory of relativity did not win over many Zionists, whose sights were set on Palestine. Nor did Rawidowicz develop a large following among his natural allies, the devotees of Hebrew. In the lively ambience of Weimar Berlin in the early 1920s, one could have dreamt of a vibrant global Hebrew culture in which the Diaspora was a full partner. It was in this ambience, as Bialik put it in 1923, that "relatives who had been separated by force"—Eastern European and German Jews— "happened onto the same inn."[97] But by the first years of the 1930s, the bold spirit of innovation—and the vision of a rich Jewish culture—in Weimar had waned. Leading Hebrew luminaries such as Bialik and Agnon had left for Erets Yisrael years earlier, convinced that only there could Hebrew have a meaningful future. Meanwhile, massive economic and political instability in the mid- to late 1920s severely disabled the Weimar cultural experiment.

Observers looking on from the *Yishuv,* the Jewish community in Palestine, expressed perplexity at the Berlin conference of the World Hebrew Union. The editors of the journal of the Hebrew writers' association, *Moznayim,* agreed to publish Rawidowicz's conference address. And yet, before the second of two installments of Rawidowicz's lecture, one of the coeditors, the Hebrew author Fishel Lachover, took pointed aim at Rawidowicz's ideas. Diaspora Jews have only a "superficial knowledge" of developments in Palestine, and impose upon the country "abstract theories" at the expense of a more realistic perspective.[98] So as to leave no doubt, Lachover then attacked a key claim of Rawidowicz mentioned above. "We are of the view," he declared, "that the greatest creation of the Diaspora, the 'Babylonian Talmud,' found its spiritual center in the creativity of the Land [of Israel], and is but the periphery of this center, a kind of commentary to the core text." He proceeded to echo Ahad Ha-am's doubts that Hebrew culture could survive as a creative force in the Diaspora without the spiritual vitality of Palestine. Perhaps the final blow in Lachover's editorial, consistent with its generally dismissive tone, was his praise for the delegates of the Berlin conference who knew to distinguish between constructive practical steps and the overarching theory of "Dr. Rabinowicz" (instead of Rawidowicz).[99]

This insult from the heart of the Hebrew literary establishment must have wounded Rawidowicz, just as he was pressing friends and colleagues in Jerusalem to secure him a position at the Hebrew University. But even as he contemplated leaving the Diaspora, he pushed on with his agenda. In the wake of the 1931 conference, he was chosen to lead the central committee of the Union and began formulating plans for a World Hebrew Congress. Not long after, he sensed that his key role in the work of the Union was being erased from memory, as "other people are coming and asserting their paternity."[100] In fact, the problem was far more serious than determining who deserved credit for conceiving the Union. The real issue was that the moment of hope for a World Hebrew Union had passed. Just as Zionism had definitively moved from its European laboratory to Palestine, so, too, the critical mass of Hebrew speakers, and with them the Hebrew culture movement, had definitively settled in Erets Yisrael.

Simon Rawidowicz's virtue was perhaps also his vice: namely, his stubborn refusal to surrender hope in a viable and robust Diaspora community that dwelt as a national minority outside of the ancestral homeland. In this belief, he could draw theoretical support not only from Simon Dubnow and other Jewish diasporists, but also from a longer tradition of "autonomists" extending back to the late nineteenth century. The Austrian social theorist Karl Renner attempted at the turn of the nineteenth century to articulate a vision of a multiethnic state that recognized discrete cultural and linguistic groups as national corporations (*Körperschaften*).[101] Renner insisted, in a curious adumbration of the later Rawidowicz, that his far-reaching proposals were "the least utopian" of available political options, especially for tottering multinational empires. Incidentally, neither Renner nor his fellow Austrian theorist of autonomism, Otto Bauer, believed that Jews qualified as a national corporation possessed of its own personality. Nonetheless, as Roni Gechtman has skillfully shown, a number of early twentieth-century Jewish political activists in Eastern Europe, especially those associated with the Yiddish socialist-nationalist party, the Bund, adapted Renner and Bauer to their cause. That is, they advocated a kind of national-cultural autonomy that depended on state recognition and subvention, but not territorial sovereignty.[102]

The various streams of Jewish nationalists, including the autonomists, were shaken to the core by the Kishinev pogroms (1903), in which the physical vulnerability of Jews was baldly exposed. This vulnerability became even more apparent in the immediate aftermath of the First World War. Not only were new states being carved out of eviscerated empires, but Jews, especially in Ukraine, faced new targeted threats exceeding even those that had been directed at them in the Great War itself. Advocates for the defense of the Jews, who included staunch nationalists from Eastern Europe and antinationalist communal leaders from the West (France, England, and the United States), looked to the Paris Peace Conference and the Treaty of Versailles in 1919 as the opportunity to set in place lasting safeguards for physical, religious, and cultural protection.[103] Strong pressure was placed, especially by President Woodrow Wilson, to insert into the founding Covenant of the new League of Nations clauses guaranteeing to "all racial or national minorities . . . exactly the same treatment and security . . . that is accorded to the racial or national majority."[104] When these clauses failed to be enshrined in the Covenant, advocates of Jewish rights turned their attention to the Minorities Treaties of the newly emerging East Central and Southern European states. Clauses were actually incorporated into the treaties of new states (for example, Poland, Lithuania, Greece, Romania, Albania, Greece, Yugoslavia, and Iraq) that called for the rights of minorities to speak their own language, establish religious, educational, and welfare institutions under their own control, and receive proportional state funding for educational instruction. Despite their inclusion in the treaties, these principles were rarely implemented. As one authoritative account declared: "Violations of treaty obligations never ceased; the foundations of the Versailles system began to be undermined even before the peace treaties had been signed."[105]

With the rapid unraveling of the "Versailles system" and, with it, the once-grand promise of international recognition of national minority rights, the argument in favor of Diaspora autonomism essentially ran out of steam. It is true that the Soviet Union established a Jewish Autonomous Region in Birobidzhan in 1928. And it is also true that the Bund remained a central player in the communal politics of Jewish Poland up to 1939, but this centrality owed less to its vision of Jewish cultural autonomy than to its committed fight against the rising tide of antisemitism. Indeed, a combination of factors—resurgent ethnic nationalism in East Central Europe, the changing attitude of the Soviet Union to its Jewish minority, and above all, the specter of Nazism—snuffed out much hope in the 1930s for a robust "national extraterritorial autonomy" (which, Ezra Mendelsohn recalls, had once been "championed by all the modern Jewish parties").[106]

There were still calls in the period, of course, for protection of Jews as a beleaguered national minority; it was this cause, after all, that led to the creation of the World Jewish Congress in 1936.[107] Simon Rawidowicz, for his part, would stay on theme in support of a broader view of Jewish collective rights than mere physical protection; he would continue to advocate, in the midst of the darkening clouds over Europe, for a vibrant Jewish cultural presence in the Diaspora. What made his mission even more Sisyphean than it already was was his choice of language. While Yiddish was spoken by millions in Europe (and celebrated as the leading national language by Diaspora autonomists), it was Hebrew, spoken by a small minority of Diaspora Jews, that served as the unifying agent in Rawidowicz's vision.

Notwithstanding these ongoing allegiances to Hebrew and the Diaspora, Rawidowicz must have sensed in the early 1930s that the tide of current events was sweeping away the pillars of his vision. In the throes of uncertainty, he went, as we noted, for a second time to the heartland of Hebrew culture, Palestine. He arrived in the late summer of 1933, meeting with family, friends, and colleagues and delivering a lecture at the Hebrew University. He returned to Europe without a job offer several months later and, having decided to leave Germany behind, made his way to an even less significant center of Hebrew culture than Berlin: London. At the time, he was of the belief that his tenure in England would be brief; he wrote his father that "from London, the path to Jerusalem is short."[108] He also admitted to Joseph Klausner in late 1933: "I have not yet discovered the secret and greatness of the 'Babylon' in which we live. I have no desire whatsoever to integrate here in London."[109]

One can only speculate what life would have been like for Rawidowicz had he found employment and moved to Palestine. To be sure, he would have found a large and active Hebrew-speaking public. And he would have been able to devote more time to his research on Maimonides and Krochmal. But what was perhaps his main life mission—fostering a dynamic Hebrew culture in Zion *and* in the Diaspora—would have had very limited resonance. Far more urgent tasks remained for the Zionist enterprise such as fortifying the economic, political, and military foundation of the Yishuv, or attending to the growth of local Hebrew culture in Palestine. Few Jews there had the inclination or patience to devote themselves to

Hebrew culture in the Diaspora. It was the mission of Simon Rawidowicz, newly settled in London, to continue to pursue that objective.

### "The Last Pillar of Hebrew Literature in Europe"

Upon arrival in London, Rawidowicz found that the quest for regular employment remained elusive there as well. As a refugee scholar from Germany, he was invited to give a series of lectures on Maimonides at Jews' College, the main rabbinical seminary of London (fig. 18). He also was called upon to serve as an outside examiner in philosophy for students at the college.[110] In addition, Rawidowicz was a part-time instructor at the School of Oriental Studies (later SOAS) in London from the beginning of the academic year in fall 1934. While Rawidowicz forged close relations at both institutions, he landed a full-time job at neither.

The annual reports from the School of Oriental Studies (fig. 19) suggest that Rawidowicz, although only a part-time instructor, was one of the most prolific lecturers and writers on the staff.[111] He wrote extensively in the field of Jewish thought, with particular emphasis on the work of Saadya Gaon, Maimonides, and Moses Mendelssohn. True to form, Rawidowicz paired his research and teaching at Jews' College and SOAS with a busy schedule of lecturing and writing on behalf of Hebrew culture. He served as head of the executive of the Brit 'Ivrit 'Olamit, whose work was soon incorporated into the local branch of the Hebrew cultural organization, the Tarbuth Association (fig. 20) that operated under the auspices of the English Zionist Federation.[112] Rawidowicz, the tireless advocate of Hebrew, took pride in 1938 that it was now possible "to undertake wide-ranging and important Hebrew cultural activities" in the city. In fact, he noted in a report from that year that the Tarbut Association sponsored more than sixty events in the preceding year, many of which featured him as main speaker.[113]

Rawidowicz was also a frequent speaker for other Jewish organizations throughout England, offering single lectures and longer courses in English, Hebrew, and even Yiddish (fig. 21). In the absence of a regular teaching position, this lecturing became a source of much-needed remuneration. So too was his writing for Jewish journals in London, including the *Jewish Chronicle,* the *Zionist Review,* and the Hebrew weekly, *Ha-'olam,* published by the World Zionist Organization.

Minutes of the Emergency Meeting of the Council held at Jews'
College on the 31st July 1933.

-----------------------------------

Present: Mr. S. Japhet (in Chair), Dr. Buchler, Mr. Arthur
Blok, Sir Robert Waley Cohen, Dr. S. Daiches, Dr.
Duschinsky, Mr. Max Falk, Dayan Dr. A. Feldman,
Mr. Augustus Kahn, Mr. E. D. Lowy, Mr. Percy
Schwarzschild, Rev. J. F. Stern, Mr. J. Wassermann.

-----------------------------------

Apologies for non-attendance were received from Dr. W. M.
Feldman, Dr. R. N. Salaman and Mr.Wilfred Samuel.

The Chairman explained that two Professors from Germany,
Dr. Heinemann and Dr. Rawidowicz, had reason to expect a subsidy
from the Academic Assistance Council if they could state that they
had some occupation.   These Professors had therefore offered
their services without cost to the College.   He felt sure that
the Council, anxious to help their co-religionists, would avail
themselves of this opportunity.   The President of the College
was in favour of the proposed step.

After some remarks by Dr. Buchler, Mr. Augustus Kahn,
Dr. Daiches, and Sir Robert Waley Cohen, the following resolution,
proposed by Sir Robert Waley Cohen and seconded by the Rev.
J. F. Stern was unanimously adopted:-

> "That the President, Chairman and Principal of the College
> be authorised to add to the Staff of Jews' College for a
> period of one year Dr. Heinemann and Dr. Rawidowicz and
> other men of high academic achievement provided that they
> are willing to give Lectures at the College, and on the
> understanding that attendance at the Lectures should be
> optional to the students."

The Chairman stated that it was understood that these
appointments would involve no financial responsibility to the
College.

The Council gave permission for the use of the College
Canteen for German Refugee Students.   24/10.33

-----------------------------------

Fig. 18. Minutes of a meeting at Jews' College on 31 July 1933 in which Rawidowicz is
discussed as a possible lecturer.

30     ANNUAL REPORT

DR. B. HEIMANN . . . "Comment interpréter les termes philosophiques hindous." ("Synthesis," Paris, 1936.)
"The Absorbent Power of Hindu Religions." (Journ. Soc. Study. Relig., 1936.)
Reviews in J.R.A.S.; Int. Review of Missions and Bibl. Bouddhique, Paris.

MR. S. HILLELSON . . . Sudan Arabic Texts with translation and glossary.

PROF. A. LLOYD JAMES . . "The Spoken Word." (Journal of the English Association.)
Review: Maître Phonétique.

MR. V. MINORSKY . . . "Raiy, Rām-Hurmuz, Rūs, Rūyān" in Ency. of Islam.
Reviews in B.S.O.S., J.R.A.S., Journal Asiatique.

MR. C. S. K. PATHY . . Review of the Trade of India in the Fairplay Annual, Dec., 1935.

DR. S. RAWIDOWICZ . . "Knowledge of God. A Study in Philosophy of Religion."(Landau-Book, Jerusalem, 1936.)
"Maimonides' Guide for the Perplexed." (Haolam, London; Haarets, Tel-Aviv, 1935.)
Moses Mendelssohn. (Gaster-Jubilee-Book, 1936.)
The 150th Anniversary of Mendelssohn's death. (Davar, Tel-Aviv, 1936.)
Studies in Jewish Philosophy of the 18th century. (Haolam, London, 1935-36.)
The Idea of "Shelihut". (Haolam, Jerusalem; Baderech, Warsaw, 1936.)
On the Diaspora. (Moznajim, Tel-Aviv, 1936.)

ANNUAL REPORT     31

Articles on Problems of Hebrew Literature and Philosophy. (Haolam, London-Jersualem; Baderech; Warsaw; Hadoar, New York; Barkai, Johannesburg, South Africa.)

PROF. SIR E. DENISON ROSS . "Thomas Sherley's Discours of the Turks." (Campden Series.)

MR. C. A. RYLANDS . . Reviews in B.S.O.S. and J.R.A.S.

DR. WALTER SIMON . . "Die Rekonstruktion des archaischen Chinesisch." (Asia Major.)
Reviews in "Orientalistischen Literaturzeitung".

DR. W. STEDE . . . . Reviews in J.R.A.S., "Orientalistische Literaturzeitung," "Religion". (Journal of the S.P.S.R.)

DR. J. A. STEWART . . "Introduction to Colloquial Burmese." (In the press.)

DR. A. S. TRITTON . . Reviews in B.S.O.S., J.R.A.S., J.R.C.A.S.

DR. A. N. TUCKER . . . Articles, etc. "African Alphabets and the Telegraph Problem." (Bantu Studies, March, 1936.)
Gramophone course in Zulu pronunciation and verb tone system. (For Department Library.)

PROF. R. L. TURNER . . Sanskrit a-kseti and Pali acchati in Modern Indo-Aryan: B.S.O.S., VIII, 793-812.
Linguistica: B.S.O.S., VIII, 201-227; other reviews in B.S.O.S., J.R.A.S., Times Lit. Sup.
Collaborated with Dr. H. W. Bailey in editing Indian and Iranian Studies presented to Sir George Grierson (B.S.O.S., VIII, 2 and 3.)

DR. I. C. WARD . . . An Introduction to the Ibo Language.
English in Nigeria III. (Nigerian Teacher.)

Fig. 19. Annual report of the activities of affiliated lecturers (including Rawidowicz) of the School of Oriental Studies (later SOAS) in London.

It was in the last journal that Rawidowicz published a stream of essays on the theme of "affirming the Diaspora" (as one of the first of these articles was entitled).[114] Zionism erred in focusing on Jewish life in Palestine to the exclusion of the Diaspora. The result was to divide the Jewish nation. To prevent this danger, Rawidowicz sounded a familiar theme: "It is one and the same nation that it is creating its own homeland and defending the walls of its existence in the Diaspora."[115] In imagining the relationship between the two centers, Rawidowicz averred that "the idea of a partnership (that I have been discussing for ten years) can be visualized in the form of an ellipse with two foci on which the entirety of the ellipse must of necessity stand: and this is Israel."

Rawidowicz's oft-invoked image of an ellipse, in which the sum of the distance from any point on it to two foci is constant, meant to convey the

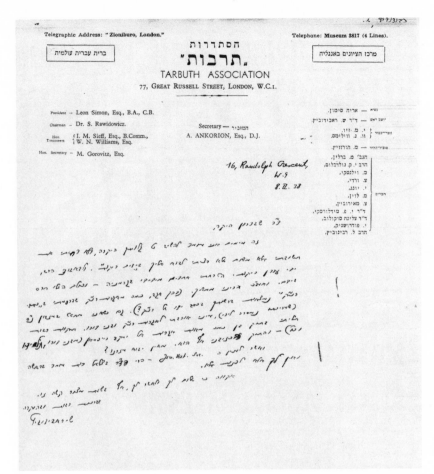

Fig. 20. Letter of Rawidowicz from 8 February 1938 to Avraham Schwadron (Sharon) on stationery of the Tarbuth Association in London, successor to the Brit ʿIvrit ʿOlamit. Rawidowicz Archives.

idea that the two centers of Jewish national culture were both indispensable foundations of a single Jewish nation. The relationship between them was fluid, but each focal point had to be supported institutionally and materially in order to assure a healthy Jewish nation. If the World Zionist Organization was not up to the task of serving the "national" needs of Diaspora Jewry, Rawidowicz wrote, then a new federation of Jewish communities should be created.[116]

It is surprising, to say the least, that views such as these would be welcome in the pages of *Ha-ʿolam*, the journal of the Zionist movement. Part

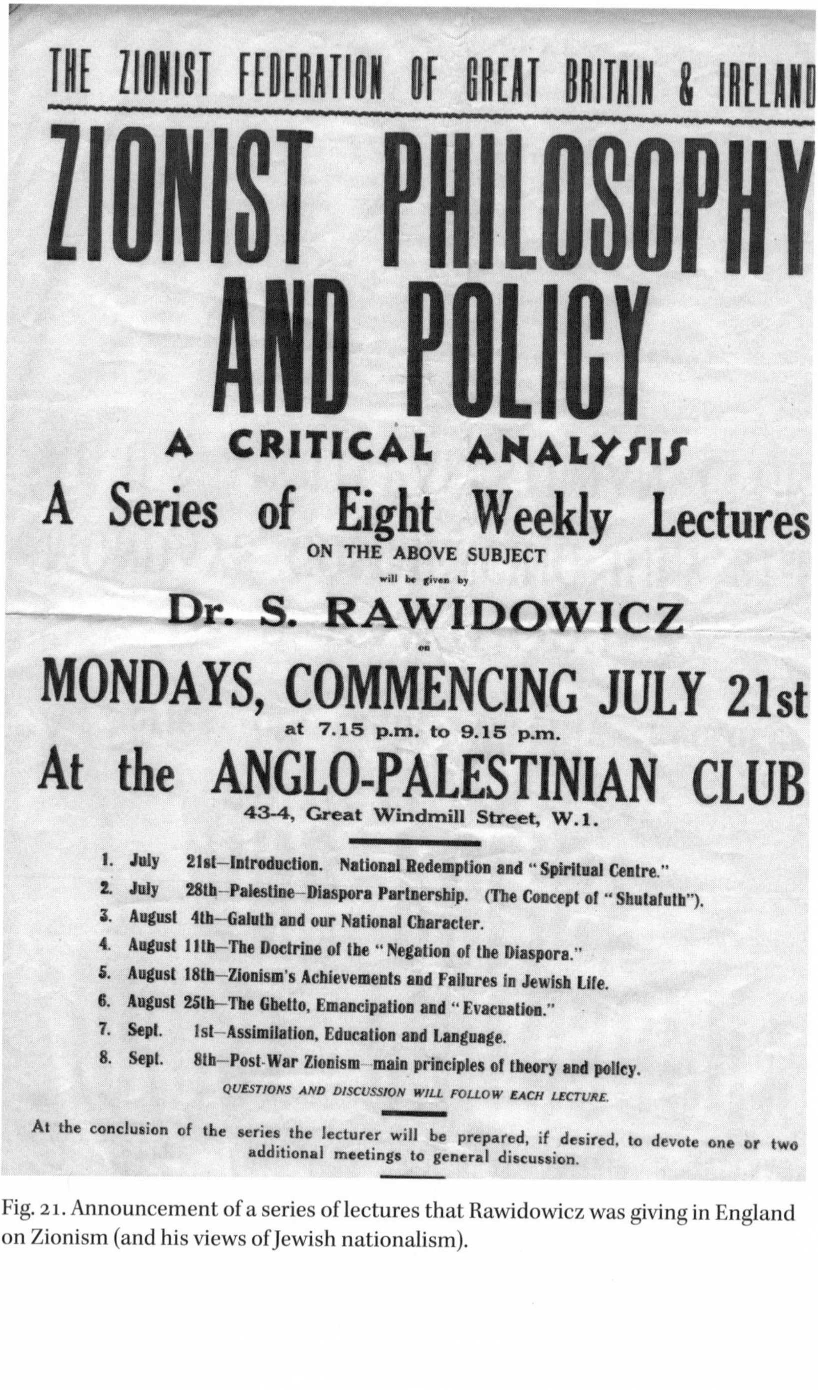

THE ZIONIST FEDERATION OF GREAT BRITAIN & IRELAND

# ZIONIST PHILOSOPHY AND POLICY

## A CRITICAL ANALYSIS

A Series of Eight Weekly Lectures

ON THE ABOVE SUBJECT

will be given by

## Dr. S. RAWIDOWICZ

on

## MONDAYS, COMMENCING JULY 21st

at 7.15 p.m. to 9.15 p.m.

## At the ANGLO-PALESTINIAN CLUB

43-4, Great Windmill Street, W.1.

1. July 21st—Introduction. National Redemption and "Spiritual Centre."
2. July 28th—Palestine–Diaspora Partnership. (The Concept of "Shutafuth").
3. August 4th—Galuth and our National Character.
4. August 11th—The Doctrine of the "Negation of the Diaspora."
5. August 18th—Zionism's Achievements and Failures in Jewish Life.
6. August 25th—The Ghetto, Emancipation and "Evacuation."
7. Sept. 1st—Assimilation, Education and Language.
8. Sept. 8th—Post-War Zionism—main principles of theory and policy.

QUESTIONS AND DISCUSSION WILL FOLLOW EACH LECTURE.

At the conclusion of the series the lecturer will be prepared, if desired, to devote one or two additional meetings to general discussion.

Fig. 21. Announcement of a series of lectures that Rawidowicz was giving in England on Zionism (and his views of Jewish nationalism).

of the reason may have had to do with Rawidowicz's steadfast allegiance to Hebrew culture, which was often and easily assumed to be equivalent to support for Zionism. But perhaps the more important reason was Rawidowicz's long-standing relationship with the editor of *Ha-ʿolam,* Moshe Kleinmann, whom he assisted and even temporarily replaced in 1936 when Kleinmann moved from London to Palestine. There was talk at the time that Rawidowicz might be invited to join Kleinmann, but in the end, he was not. He remained in the Diaspora, persisting in his commitment to Hebrew culture.

Indeed, as the clouds darkened over European Jewry, Rawidowicz's sense of mission intensified; centuries of literary productivity in the Hebrew language, he feared, were coming to a close. It was no longer the threat of assimilation or Zionism's disdain for the Diaspora, but Nazism's assault on Jewish life and culture. Necessarily, this threat preoccupied Rawidowicz in much of his writing from the outbreak of the Second World War. In 1940, he inaugurated, with the financial support of the German-born English Zionist leader, Oskar Phillip, a Hebrew monthly entitled *Yalkut* to serve as a supplement to the *Zionist Review* of the English Zionist Federation. Rawidowicz opened the first number of the journal with the following warning: "The destruction [*hurban*] of 1939/40, which threatens to reach the British Isles, may the Guardian of Israel protect them, is also the destruction of the last pillars of Hebrew literature in Europe."[117] In subsequent issues, Rawidowicz argued that England had a unique task, to serve as the "fortress" of freedom for Jews in Europe. Concomitantly, it was incumbent upon Jews in England (and the broader Anglophone world) to safeguard and enrich the precious national treasure of Hebrew. This effort did not require spurning English culture or language, as Rawidowicz elaborated via an intriguing comparison:

> The Welsh, even after hundreds of years of coexistence with the English, intermarriage, wandering, and uprooting (although on their land, which is "one land" with the English), preserved and continue to preserve their language. The wealth of English literature does not require an uprooting or weakening of their desire to have their own vehicle of expression. Except for some extreme fanatics who refuse to speak English in a court of law, most speak and understand English without giving up the Welsh language.[118]

Rawidowicz urged the Jews of England to follow suit by creating "a Hebrew-speaking world" alongside their Anglophonic one. Such a call, echoing similar ones he had made earlier in Berlin, was destined to move very few, perhaps no more than a hundred or so committed Hebraists that he estimated to be in London.[119] Not surprisingly, it was in this dark period that Rawidowicz's literary alter ego, Ish Boded, was born, hinting at the solitary state of the advocate of Hebrew culture writing as the last vestiges of that culture in Europe were being extinguished.[120]

### "The Right to be Different"

Rawidowicz's loneliness was compounded by his move to Leeds in 1941, which took him a step further away from the more vibrant (though, to his mind, still lacking) Jewish community of London. But the move did have a salutary side; his appointment in that year as lecturer in medieval and modern Hebrew in the Department of Semitic Languages at the University of Leeds brought to an end Rawidowicz's long quest for a permanent university position and provided him with a stable source of income.[121] His colleague from London, the renowned scholar of Arabic H. A. R. Gibb, warmly congratulated him: "I am so glad that you are to be established at Leeds, and the university there is to be congratulated on securing you for the lectureship. After the long and difficult days which you have had to go through, you have earned the right to a secured position and a steadier horizon."[122] Rawidowicz's position, which was funded by the Jewish industrialist and philanthropist in Leeds, Montague Burton, was originally conceived of as an assistant lectureship. But in light of his "high qualifications and standing," Rawidowicz was hired at Leeds at the level of lecturer.[123] At the university, he continued to research and publish, mainly in Hebrew, on two of his main scholarly interests, Maimonides and Nachman Krochmal. He earned a reputation as an active and well-appreciated member of the faculty, and served as head of the department from 1946 to 1948. One of his colleagues, the Rev. Dr. John Bowman, described Rawidowicz in an obituary as "both a great and good scholar and a great and good man."

This comment points to a rather mystifiying feature in Rawidowicz's biography. For an iconoclastic thinker and ideologue, he seemed to have few personal enemies. And for a self-described "solitary man," he seemed to have a rich social life. His relationship with his wife, Esther Klee, was close and supportive. Notwithstanding her own professional aspirations (a Ph.D in biology from Berlin), she followed him on his wandering life course, always

creating a hospitable ambience for the many guests who visited the Rawidowicz home. He earned the respect of colleagues in the academy in England ( for example, Bowman and Gibb), as he had in Germany and would in
America. He impressed Jewish leaders of varying stripes, from Orthodox rabbis (Yehezkel Abramsky and Joseph Hertz) to the Zionist officials at 77 Great
Russell Street in London. But he felt most at home among fellow supporters
of Hebrew culture in London, figures such as Shlomo Auerbach, Joseph
Heller, and Alexander and Benzion Margulies. These men tended to be less
critical of Zionism than he. But it was Rawidowicz who crafted for them a vision and vocation on behalf of Hebrew culture in England.

One of those who shared in the enterprise was a London Jew named
Bernard Lewis, the future scholar of Islam, who established a group of
young Hebrew speakers in London called "Dovre 'Ivrit" (literally, "Hebrew
speakers"). Lewis recalls Rawidowicz as an inspiration to the group, as well
as a man of great erudition, deep curiosity, and charming and sardonic
wit.[124] Following their first meeting, the two developed a warm friendship.
In fact, Rawidowicz stayed at Lewis's apartment when he visited London
after leaving for Leeds in 1941. Moreover, he recruited Lewis to write an article for another Hebrew journal that he edited, *Metsudah*. Alluringly, this
article, which offered a wide-ranging historical synthesis of Muslim-Jewish
relations up to the early modern period, was entitled "'Ever ve-'arav" (Hebrew and Arab)—a title nearly identical to that of the chapter we shall discuss in the latter half of this book.

Lewis also contributed to another Hebrew journal that appeared in
England in 1944 known as *Melilah*. The two journals shared a number of
writers including Samuel Krauss, I. D. Markon, Arthur Marmorstein, Nathan Morris, Cecil Roth, and Isadore Wartski. *Melilah*, for its part, was
published under the auspices of the University of Manchester, where the
editors, Edward Robertson and Meir Wallenstein, were members of the
Semitics Department. In his opening editor's note, Robertson observed,
with a bit of exaggeration, that there was at present "a great and growing
eagerness to bring to life again the Hebrew tongue." And he added that
"through the enthusiasm of Dr. Rawidowicz, an outlet for Hebrew literature in Hebrew has been provided in his periodical *Yalqut* [sic], later con-
verted into *Metsudah*."[125]

While he was correct in pointing to Rawidowicz's leading role in Hebraist circles in England, it is not accurate to see *Metsudah* as the direct

heir of *Yalkut.* The latter was an organ of the English Zionist movement. The former, which first appeared in February 1943, was not. Rather, it was printed by the independent Ararat publishing house.

The name "Ararat" evoked the sense of crisis that Rawidowicz and his comrades felt at the time. Ararat was the mountain top where, according to the Bible, Noah's ark came to rest after the floodwaters had receded (Genesis 8:4); it was also a symbolic place of refuge from a terrifying storm. The latter-day Ararat Publishing Society was to provide a safe haven for Hebrew language and culture in the face of the terrifying storm of Nazism.[126] Ironically, London had become Ararat: "the last city in Europe," Rawidowicz observed, "where it is possible to publish in the Holy Language."[127]

From this new Ararat, Rawidowicz aimed to erect a fortress—a *metsudah*—in defense of Hebrew. The term recurs throughout his writing in this period. In the first issue of *Metsudah,* for example, Rawidowicz wrote of the combined force of Great Britain and the United States as "a fortress that is a bastion of strength" in the battle against Hitler. He also expressed the explicit hope that the new journal would serve as a "fortress" of strength and encouragement in trying times.[128]

This aspiration was somewhat undercut by Rawidowicz's plaintive tone. Both he and his alter ego, Ish Boded, frequently inveighed against the deficiencies of the contemporary Jewish world, taking aim at a familiar target: the "fatal Zionist tradition of 'negation of the Diaspora.'" To the extent that Zionism could be of assistance to Jews in Europe, it was not in demanding their mass migration to Palestine, but rather in ameliorating their present condition and preparing for "the revival of European Jewry in the future days to come."[129]

Rawidowicz did not reserve his criticism only for the Zionists. Writing as Ish Boded, he found fault with those English Jews who offered no credible alternative either to Zionism or to synagogue-based Judaism. He included in this indictment his putative allies: "Neither the national-Hebrew camp nor the circles of socialists and Yiddishists within Anglo Jewry, both of which are powerless and ineffective, are engaged in their own educational projects. Neither labors to mold the image of the coming generation." Ish Boded expected more from these groups: "Don't English Jews have the obligation of Jewish citizenship incumbent upon them, full citizenship in the House of Israel both in England and beyond, in the Land of Israel and in the Diaspora."[130]

As he had earlier in *Yalkut,* Rawidowicz (writing as Ish Boded) again looked to the experience of the Welsh. While "no less 'British' than Anglo Jews," the Welsh "did not surrender their language" or literature—even though they failed to produce "a single author who can stand at the feet of the most minor biblical authors."[131] Quite by contrast, the Jews, authors of literature of world significance, quaked with fear over the charge of dual loyalty and, consequently, chose to abandon their cultural heritage in England and elsewhere: "Who but the Jews, the people of the book, have become illiterate strangers?"[132]

The idea that the Jews of England had abdicated "the obligation of Jewish citizenship incumbent upon them" reminds us that Simon Rawidowicz had not surrendered the idea of a single Jewish nation with both a territorial center and a substantial extraterritorial presence. He was not altogether alone in this view. Even though the promise of national minority rights at Versailles was, to a large extent, stillborn, the Nazi assault on European Jews once again exposed the vulnerability of the Jewish minority. Duly mindful of this, Hannah Arendt argued vigorously for the creation of a Jewish army in Palestine. "The defense of Palestine," she wrote in November 1941, "is part of the struggle for the freedom of the Jewish people." A month later, she further clarified that "the solution to the Jewish question is not to be found in one country, not even in Palestine."[133] Indeed, her thinking in this period focused on the ideal of a Jewish presence in Palestine alongside the right of Jews in Europe to be part of a commonwealth of nations in which "we could be recognized as a nation and be represented in a European parliament." Arendt's sense of personal identification with the fate of the Jews was noticeably strong here—and in some tension with her later refutation of the principle of "ahavat Yisrael." Those Jews who seek to escape their fate by converting are, in her unforgiving formulation, "virtual traitors."[134]

In similar fashion, anguish over the Nazi assault on European Jewry weighed heavily on Simon Rawidowicz, and figured in his editorial choices at *Metsudah.* We see this quite graphically in the dedication page with which he opened the second issue in 1943.[135] The upper portion of this page featured a striking visual image of resistance drawn by London-based artist Walter Hertz: a picture of an arm holding a gun imposed upon an open book, with destroyed dwellings in the background ( fig. 22). The lower portion consisted of an encomium that evoked the traditional memorial prayer, "El Maleh Rahamim":

מאות אלפי ישראל ·
אנשים ונשים וטף ·
פליטת סופרינו שומרי משמרת
תרבותנו · מקדשי־השם וישראל
בגימאות פולניה ·
שמתו מות קדושים וטהורים ·
בידי חיל היטלר ידים וטמאים·
בארצת אידיפה השבויה ·
בשנות הי"ש — תש"ד.


ארץ אל תכסי דמם


אם נשכחכם
קדושי תש"ש – תש"ד...

Fig. 22. Ode to martyrs of Nazism in *Metsudah* 2 (1943).

To the memory
Of the hundreds of thousands of Jews,
Men, women, and children
Remnant of our great authors and guardians of our culture,
Martyrs of God and Israel in the ghettoes of Poland,
Who died a holy and pure death,
By the evil and dirty hands of Hitler's army,
In the countries of occupied Europe
From the years 1939 to 1944.

O Earth, do not cover their blood.

If we forget thee, martyrs of 5700–5704 (1939–1944)...[136]

Immediately after this dedication, Rawidowicz directed his criticism in a familiar, but curious direction: Zionism. Although Zionists claimed Palestine by "right" and not "sufferance," they denied Diaspora Jews the same right to a national existence outside of the homeland.[137] It was the unique merit of the socialist Bund, with which Rawidowicz did not normally sympathize, to insist on this right to a full national life in the Diaspora. The Zionists, for their part, had abandoned this right and, by extension, their Jewish brethren in Europe—all in keeping with the principle of "negating the Diaspora."[138]

The criticism of Zionism would continue throughout the remaining five numbers of *Metsudah,* which were published somewhat irregularly in three volumes (as 3–4, 5–6, and 7) from 1945 to 1954. Indeed, the crisis precipitated by Nazism had the effect of deepening Rawidowicz's disappointment over Zionism's failings. At the same time, it pushed him to a new, and to a great extent, more mature phase of theorizing his view of Jewish nationalism. Prior to this point, his chief concern was to forge a third path between Zionism and Diasporism according to the terms of reference of Jewish nationalism. At this moment though, Rawidowicz felt compelled to lay a foundation for Jewish collective existence by engaging the terms of reference of Western political theory.

The first of his efforts in this vein was a long essay, written in the fall of 1944, entitled "Unconditional Survival." Rawidowicz opened by noting that "the Second World War of the twentieth century did not make many waves on political thought, and the few waves that it did make do not address in any way the magnitude of the destruction that the war brought upon the world."[139] He then went on to propose what he regarded as an innovation in rights discourse that was urgently needed in the postwar world. He recalled that Franklin D. Roosevelt had enunciated four freedoms in his 1941 State of the Union address: freedom of speech, freedom of religion, freedom from want, and freedom from fear. Rawidowicz added to this list a fifth, which he called "the source of all freedom, the right of the individual and group to be different: *libertas differendi.*"[140] Not surprisingly, his main interest in articulating this fifth freedom was the right of the *group* to be different. It was this point that enabled him to articulate a companion principle: that in a world full of difference, the Jews were first among equals. "Israel," Rawidowicz announced, is "the most different in the world."[141] No other group, he argued, had survived for so long by "dwelling alone" (Numbers 23:9), preserving its own religion, culture, and language in the midst of hosts who often reacted negatively to Jewish difference.

In forging his theory of *libertas differendi,* Rawidowicz attempted to avoid two extremes: a totalitarian nationalism, of which Nazism was the most obvious example, and the far lesser, but oft-concealed peril of Western liberalism. In the first case, Rawidowicz believed that the Second World War "has taught us that a certain diminution of the sovereignty of states, large and small, a delimiting of their authority, is more likely to bring about the blessing of peace to the world—and to the Jews—than an intensification of nationalism." On the other hand, liberalism, with its constant focus on the rights of the individual, possesses the potential to undermine the right to *group* difference. The reassertion of liberal values in a postwar world should not come at the expense of recognizing the right to cultural differences among groups, particularly national minorities without states of their own. In fact, Rawidowicz believed that "the United Nations must fully and completely recognize the right to be different, insert it in every peace treaty between one country and another, and root it in the constitution of every state." Evoking the legacy of Versailles, he continued by demanding that every nation-state permit "a system of education for every national or linguistic group" in its midst.[142]

Rawidowicz remained on this theme in the next issue of *Metsudah* (numbers 5 and 6 combined), which was published in 1948. The opening article, a book-length essay of 153 pages, was entitled "Toward Destruction or Revival?" Rawidowicz began writing the article in the last months of the war, and completed it in late October 1946. Despite the dramatic course of events since that time, particularly the passage of United Nations Resolution 181 on 29 November 1947 calling for the partition of Palestine into "Independent Arab and Jewish States," Rawidowicz left his long article unchanged. His primary concern remained the affirmation of the right to group difference. In a revealing footnote, he confessed:

> I am not among those who pray for the return of the crown of European-American liberalism to its glory. I doubt whether liberalism has the wherewithal to repair the total devastation of society and the world. The world needs a new political-social movement that can guarantee the freedom of individual and society—together and completely. This cannot be merely a formal legal freedom, but material and economic so that it not fail to overcome the obstacles that wiped out earlier movements for freedom.[143]

Rawidowicz hoped that, in the aftermath of the war, a more durable framework for national minority rights would emerge. This expectation was shared in a companion article written by a colleague in London, Ya'akov Fleischer, in the same *Metsudah*. Fleischer detailed the failure of the international community to set in place safeguards for national minorities following the First World War. The initial promise of Versailles, he argued, was dashed when signatory states blithely refused to implement the minority rights clauses not long after the Paris Peace Conference concluded.[144] Now after the Second World War, Fleisher argued, another peace conference was held in Paris (July–October 1946), once again to resolve outstanding territorial disputes, recognize new national borders, and assure the rights of minorities. He was disappointed to discover that "the names 'Jew' and "Jews' do not appear in a single peace treaty" emerging out of Paris. The moral of the story was that the international community, following the two world wars and the failure of two Paris conferences, must finally own up to its obligation to protect the national minority rights of Jews and establish a viable mechanism for implementation.[145]

Rawidowicz shared Fleischer's disappointment over the failure to provide such protection. But apart from his earlier call on the United Nations and individual states to enshrine the "right to be different," he did not outline any specific steps that should be taken to provide guarantees to the Jews. Instead, he retreated to his familiar position that a solution to the "Jewish Question" did not lie solely with the creation of a Jewish state. In fact, in a short editorial in *Metsudah* that was written just after the United Nations' decision to partition Palestine, he pointed to some potential difficulties. He wondered whether a new Jewish state would be able to provide a stable economic and political foundation for Jews and manage to live peaceably with its neighbors. Ever present was his fear that Zionism in its statist form would ignore "the question of Israel in the Diaspora (which) is the question of the overwhelming majority of Jews." As momentum built toward the creation of a Jewish state, the well-being of the Diaspora might well be forgotten. At that point, Rawidowicz surmised: "the gulf between a 'state people' (that sees itself as redeemed and capable of standing on its own) and a 'Diaspora people' (that will not have the right of citizenship and all that is bound up with it in this state—such that its rights will be fewer than those of the Arab, Christian, or other minority that dwells within its borders) will widen greatly."[146]

This concern was the logical extension of Rawidowicz's long-standing attempt to distinguish between a statist form of nationalism grounded in territory and a nonstatist nationalism grounded in a common culture. While Rawidowicz may have been right in seeing the decisive triumph of the former over the latter, he was wrong in at least one regard in his *Metsudah* editorial. With the enactment in 1950 of the Law of Return by Israel's parliament, the Knesset, Jews from all over the world were granted the opportunity to gain rights of citizenship in the State of Israel that were equal and often superior to those of Arabs who were native to Palestine. In fact, Rawidowicz would soon become keenly aware that Arab citizens were subject to discriminatory legislation by the Knesset in the early years of the state. But in late 1947 the state had not yet been created, and Rawidowicz's attention had not yet turned to the "Arab Question."

That said, although he did not make an explicit connection yet, Rawidowicz's focus on the status of national minority rights and the dangers of a state-based nationalism—so evident in his *Metsudah* essays during the 1940s—remained constant as he shifted his gaze from the Jewish Question to the Arab Question in "Between Jew and Arab." In fact, as we follow the development of his thought, the two cases stand as mirror images. Both Diaspora Jews and Palestinian Arabs were national minorities that posed different kinds of obstacles to a Zionist movement intent on building a Jewish state. Both were deemed extraneous and even hostile to this statist agenda. Indeed, we cannot make sense of Rawidowicz's sensitivity to the plight of Arab refugees and the status of Arab citizens in Israel in isolation from his concern for Jews as a ravaged national minority.

## "What's in a Name?" The Question of "Israel" after 1948

Before making his way to the Arab Question, Rawidowicz had to reckon with the monumental new chapter in the history of the Jews that began in 1948. The creation of the State of Israel in that year triggered a mix of new and old sentiments, expectations and anxieties, in Rawidowicz. But the year 1948 also marked a major change in his personal life. After a lifetime in Europe, and fifteen years of relative tranquillity in England, Rawidowicz moved to the United States.

Initially, he was invited to teach for a half-year at the College of Jewish Studies in Chicago in the second semester of 1948. This institution was one of a handful of Jewish colleges around the country—others were located in Boston, Baltimore, Cleveland, and Philadelphia—whose mission was to provide Jewish teacher training, Hebrew instruction, adult education, and, significantly, employment to Jewish scholars at a time when few other opportunities existed. Given the fact that he was head of the department at a large university in England, we can assume that it was not the prestige of a small Jewish college in Chicago that attracted Rawidowicz. Rather, it was the opportunity to experience Jewish life in the United States. And in this regard, he was not disappointed. The match between Chicago and Rawidowicz proved to be felicitous. In Rawidowicz, the College of Jewish Studies found a first-rate scholar who attracted and left a deep imprint on students in his lectures and seminars on Jewish history and philosophy. In Chicago (and at the college), Rawidowicz found a bustling Jewish community that included, to his satisfaction, a respectable number of Jews who were "faithful to Hebrew culture."[147]

Upon later reflection, Rawidowicz came to see Jewish communal existence in his previous home, England, from a rather critical perspective: "When the sun set on the German diaspora following Hitler's revolution, it did not rise in the British Isles." He noted that a long series of distinguished visitors, extending back to the twelfth-century Abraham ibn Ezra, had spent time in England, but a vibrant native Jewish culture never arose. Not even the presence of the international Zionist movement and its institutions in London succeeded in invigorating English Jewry.[148]

By contrast, America, though of far more recent vintage, brimmed with energy and hope for a Jewish future. To a great extent, it was this realization that prompted him to write to the vice-chancellor of Leeds University on

Chicago Jewish Archives
Spertus Institute of Jewish Studies
618 South Michigan Avenue
Chicago, Ill. 60605

*A Good New Year!*

# ALON

| VOL. 17, NO. 1 | TISHRI, 5709 | OCTOBER, 1948 |

## COLLEGE LAUNCHES ITS 24th ACADEMIC SEASON !

DR. SIMON RAWIDOWICZ

RABBI SIDNEY J. JACOBS

### MORE THAN 45 COURSES IN MANY DEPARTMENTS OFFERED; ACCREDITED BY OTHER SCHOOLS

With the Convocation exercises on September 26, The College of Jewish Studies has opened its 24th academic season in the Departments of Advanced Hebrew Studies, Training of Hebrew and Sunday School Teachers and of Jewish Youth and Adult Education. More than 45 courses in Hebrew, Bible, Religion, Talmud, History, Literature, Philosophy, Sociology and Education are being offered during the academic year 1948-49.

In addition to the courses offered afternoons and evenings, The College conducts classes in Graduate Studies on Tuesday, Thursday and Friday mornings. The following Graduate Courses are being given the Autumn Quarter: History and Methods of Education; Jewish Sects, Hassidism, Ghetto Life and Folklore; Modern Jewish Philosophy; Liturgy and Ethical Ideas, and Midrash.

The Preparatory Department for high school juniors and seniors conducts classes in Hebrew, Jewish History, Bible and Jewish Literature and a variety of extra-curricular activities of a Jewish social and cultural nature.

The Women's Institute, organized in co-operation with Chicago Senior Hadassah in response to the demand of Jewish women who are unable to attend evening classes, will start its Thursday morning classes in November, with courses in Hebrew Language and "The Rise of Modern Israel."

### DR. RAWIDOWICZ JOINS PERMANENT FACULTY; RABBI JACOBS IS NAMED REGISTRAR

With the announcement of opening of the academic year at The College of Jewish Studies came word from Dr. Samuel M. Blumenfield, its President, of two appointments.

Rabbi Sidney J. Jacobs has been named Registrar of The College. Rabbi Jacobs has served as Director of Activities and Instructor in Jewish History since June, 1946, when he became the first alumnus (Class of 1937) to join the Faculty and administrative staff. A graduate of the Jewish Institute of Religion, founded by Dr. Stephen S. Wise, Rabbi Jacobs is Secretary of the Chicago Rabbinical Association.

Dr. Simon Rawidowicz, distinguished Jewish scholar and editor, has joined the Faculty of The College with the rank of Professor of Jewish Philosophy and will serve as Chairman of the Department of Graduate Studies, it was announced by Dr. Blumenfield. A native of Grayewo, Russian Poland, Dr. Rawidowicz lived for many years in Berlin, where he published a textbook edition of Maimonides' *Sefer Hamadda*, a monograph on Mordecai Zeeb Feierberg (1923), and an extensive treatise on Nachman Krochmal, whose writings he edited (with Commentary, 1924). His writings include also Ludwig Feuerbach und die deutsche Philosophie

Philosophie (Hebrew, 1930), and Knowledge of God (English, 1936).

From 1927 to 1930, Professor Rawidowicz was one of the Editors of the Hebrew periodical, Hatekufah, in Berlin, and in 1932 and 1933 Librarian of the Jewish Community of Berlin. He was founder and head of the Central Hebrew Organization, B'rith Ivrith Olamith (1931-33).

In 1943, Dr. Rawidowicz was appointed to the newly-created chair of Modern Hebrew Language and Literature at the University of Leeds, England, and also edited Yalkut, the only Hebrew monthly in Europe.

In January of this year, Dr. Rawidowicz came to Chicago as Visiting Professor of Jewish Philosophy at The College. This past summer he returned to England and has now returned for permanent residence, bringing with him Mrs.

The College fosters study and activity in the Jewish arts through the following media: liturgic, folk and art songs in Hebrew, Yiddish and English taught during assembly periods; choral work, in co-operation with the Halevi Choral Society on Wednesday evenings; lectures on the history and development of Jewish art; study groups and workshops in Jewish artcraft on Monday nights; plays and dramatic programs of Jewish content presented by the Pargod Dramatic Society on Wednesday evenings; Jewish and Palestinian folk-dancing sessions on Monday evenings.

The College awards to graduates from the Department of Advanced Hebrew Studies the degrees of Bachelor and Master of Hebrew Literature, and diplomas to graduates of other departments. Many colleges and universities in Chicago and throughout the country grant credit for academic work pursued at The College of Jewish Studies.

### MANNY FEIGIN IN ISRAEL

Emanuel Feigin, who was graduated in 1944 from the Department of Advanced Hebrew Studies, arrived in Tel Aviv on Sunday, June 27, to study at the School of Public Service of the Jewish Agency and the Republic of Israel. Son of Dr. Samuel I. Feigin, Professor of Bible at The College of Jewish Studies, and Mrs. Feigin, Manny received his M.A. degree from the University of Chicago in June for his thesis on the Va'ad Leumi, National Council of Palestine

Fig. 23. Announcement of Rawidowicz's appointment in 1948 to the College of Jewish Studies in Chicago in the college newsletter, "Alon."

June 12, 1948 to inform him that he had received an offer to teach full-time at the College of Jewish Studies and that he intended to accept it ( fig. 23).[149]

For all of his enthusiasm for Chicago, Rawidowicz was enervated by the cumulative toll of his journeying from Berlin to London to Leeds to the United States over the course of fifteen years. It was not only the physical dislocation; it was also his constant swimming against the political and linguistic current, along with recurrent health problems (most significantly, a heart condition that would ultimately prove fatal). A short while after leaving Leeds for Chicago, Rawidowicz wrote to his brother that he felt himself in a peculiar state of exile. We recall this sentiment from earlier, but can now situate it more fully in the context of his life journey: "Over the years, my heart has lost the desire to settle in this place or that, in a specific place. I live beyond time and space. If only I could find a quiet corner for some study and to complete a few projects. I fear that I will find it neither here nor in the State of Israel. It doesn't exist for me."[150]

To understand Rawidowicz, one must recognize that such doubts constantly plagued him. And yet, he never ceased to pursue goals large and small. Rawidowicz often coupled—we might say, combated—his loneliness with the laying of grandiose plans. On the eve of his departure for the United States, he issued a call in *Metsudah,* in the guise of Ish Boded, for a major postwar enterprise: the creation of a "European Talmud" that would capture the intellectual breadth and vibrancy of what was once the most populous Jewish community in the world. This sweeping project should draw on "each and every Jewish thinker of Eastern European origin who knew Judaism from home, in the language of the home, in its innermost chambers, indeed, who drank from its well in the original and not in translation." In contemplating this undertaking, Rawidowicz posed a sharp question that still echoes in contemporary debates in the Jewish community: "What do memorials, tombstones, monuments, museums, and documentary repositories do for us?" Whereas some were committed to commemorating the death or persecution of European Jews, he held out hope that the past glories of European Jewish culture not only would be remembered, but would serve as a stimulus to renewed cultural activity.[151]

The proposal for a "European Talmud" revealed both the strengths and weaknesses of Rawidowicz as a thinker. As he imagined it, a new Talmud could become the cornerstone of a strong and self-confident Diaspora Jewish world. But the grandness of this concept was matched by a dearth of specificity, both in content and form. Rawidowicz gave little indication of what should be in the new Talmud or how it should be composed. Similarly, his clarion call for a new "movement for Babylon and Jerusalem" never developed from the level of a slogan to a deliberate plan to build an institutional framework that would house a true partnership between the

Diaspora and the new State of Israel. Nor, for that matter, did his insistence that the West respect the *libertas differendi* of the Jews ever yield a concrete blueprint for national minority rights in a post–World War II world.

In this sense, Rawidowicz failed to give his life project the requisite theoretical foundation and practical direction to generate momentum or gain adherents. One could imagine America as Rawidowicz's new Babylon, a venue in which his thinking about a dual-centered Jewish nation could be advanced. But such was not the case: America inspired no major revision or elaboration of his worldview, which remained rooted in an earlier, twentieth-century European mold of Jewish nationalism.

Still, at least one treasured ideal of Rawidowicz's did reach fruition in America. In a *Metsudah* article from 1948, Rawidowicz expressed his support for the establishment of a major Jewish university in the Diaspora (in New York, in fact), an institution that would hark back to the great rabbinic academies of Sura and Pumbeditha in late antique Babylonia. Why, he asked in response to a speech given by Chaim Weizmann, should Jerusalem be the only home of "a Jewish university ... with a Hebrew spirit?"[152] Little did Rawidowicz know at the time that he would soon make his way to such an institution in the Diaspora.

Two years after arriving in the United States, he was approached by Abram Sachar, president of the fledgling Brandeis University in Waltham, Massachusetts, and invited to join the faculty there. Rawidowicz had been content and productive in Chicago at the College of Jewish Studies.[153] But the temptation of Brandeis was too great to resist. That new institution's twin commitments to academic excellence *and* the centrality of Jewish learning came as close to his ideal of a Jewish university "infused with a Hebrew spirit" as anything he had experienced previously. Rawidowicz accepted Sachar's offer and, after a final year in Chicago, assumed his new position in Waltham in 1951 (fig. 24).

He took to the new institution with gusto, playing a leading role in establishing the graduate (1953) and then undergraduate programs (1956) of Brandeis' Department of Near Eastern and Judaic Studies (NEJS). His seminars on Jewish thought (in Hebrew) quickly became a rigorous rite of passage for aspiring scholars. Likewise, NEJS quickly became a major center of Jewish studies, with other fine European-born scholars such as Nahum Glatzer and later Alexander Altmann also joining as core faculty members.

Fig. 24. Rawidowicz (*left*) at Brandeis with Philip W. Lown (*center*), philanthropist and Brandeis donor, and Abram L. Sachar (*right*), founding president of Brandeis University.

Newly ensconced at Brandeis, Rawidowicz continued to address his long-standing ideological concerns. For example, his ruminations on the impact of the creation of the State of Israel on the "Jewish Question" animated the seventh and final volume of *Metsudah,* published in 1954 and entitled "After 1948." He welcomed to the pages of the journal the president of the State of Israel at the time, Yitzhak Ben-Zvi, who contributed a short article on contemporary followers of Shabtai Zevi. Rawidowicz offered "praise to that state whose president sets aside time for Torah—and who participates in a Hebrew journal that is published 'at the end of the West.'"[154]

But Rawidowicz's long lead article, "Israel," struck a different chord, resonating with his past critique of Zionism and foreshadowing what would come in *Bavel vi-Yerushalayim.* The first and most important issue he addressed was the very appellation of the new state:

> There are those who say: there is no problem at all. They find support in Shakespeare, who asked: What's in a name? And there are those who say that the severity of the problem has passed. Reality—or history—has determined

(the name): Israel. . . . The claims of the former and those of the latter only prove the point that the name "Israel" for a state in Palestine comforts them. . . . But I declare in public: the same name has disturbed my peace from the outset.[155]

Why, he wondered, does the Jewish community in Palestine arrogate to itself the right to decide the name of the new state? If the new state aimed to be Jewish in the broadest sense, then it should share the responsibility for determining its name with Jews throughout the world. Rawidowicz did not believe that the state—which he here referred to rather dismissively as "the partition-state of 1948," hinting both at its trumped nature and recent vintage—could or should call itself, formally or colloquially, "Israel." Rather, the Jewish people the world over deserved that name.

We should note that the question of the new entity's name was the subject of debate within the leadership of the Zionist movement shortly before the state was established on 14 May 1948. A committee of the Provisional Government was charged with the mission of exploring various names, including "Zion." Ironically, opponents of that name worried about imposing such a partisan appellation upon Arab residents of the state, who could hardly be expected to be Zionists. "Israel" was deemed less objectionable to their ears, although Mordechai Nissan points out in an article on the subject that the name Israel was not "any less Jewish than 'Zion.'"[156]

David Ben-Gurion, as leader of the Provisional Government, decided that the name of the new state should be "Israel." As we have noted, Simon Rawidowicz took exception. His concern, as he outlined in an impassioned exchange with Ben-Gurion in 1954–55 (during the latter's brief retirement from government service), had nothing to do with the sensitivities of Arabs.[157] Rather, it had to do with the true historical valence of the term "Israel." To tie that name to a political state, Rawidowicz wrote in *Metsudah*, would be to undermine "the purity and integrity of a millennia-old tradition, a framework of thoughts and feelings hidden in the depths of the soul of the nation."[158]

Ben-Gurion, for his part, disagreed sharply if respectfully. He attacked a core proposition of Rawidowicz's:

> I deny the uniformity (not the unity) of the Jews in the *Golah* (Diaspora) and in the Land. The Jew in the *Golah*, even a Jew like you who lives an entirely Jewish life, is not able to be a complete Jew, and no Jewish community in the *Golah*

is able to live a complete Jewish life. Only in the State of Israel is a full Jewish
life possible. Only here will a Jewish culture worthy of that name flourish.[159]

As on previous occasions, Rawidowicz argued that a Jewish culture worthy of its name could—and must—flourish in the Diaspora, as it had in
the past. The very impulse to circumscribe Jewish identity to the physical
borders of the State of Israel almost by definition risked chauvinism. With
growing trepidation, Rawidowicz noticed that some, including Ben-
Gurion, were giving voice to the hope of expanding the borders of the state
beyond the 1949 armistice lines—to the point of reviving the Revisionist
Zionist goal of a Jewish state on both banks of the Jordan River.[160]

Closely linked to this territorial appetite, Rawidowicz identified an
ethos of militarism that was propelling the state down an errant path.[161] "If
the State of Israel," Ish Boded asked toward the end of the seventh *Metsudah,* "had no gun salute in honor of its presidents, would it lose much?"
What sense did it make, he wondered, to have an enfeebled old dignitary
board a ship, only to be rattled by a booming cannon? "Where is the
strength demonstrated here? Where is the spirit of Israel here?"[162]

These questions, while validating some of his fears about Zionism,
brought Rawidowicz little succor. Many fellow Jews heralded the sight of
the bronzed, gun-toting Sabra soldier; he, by contrast, lamented the triumph of precisely that which he had warned against: a "cruel Zionism"
that had little concern for or connection to Jews who lived outside of the
homeland. Meanwhile, the Israeli soldier and his newly discovered power
had replaced, as far as Rawidowicz could see, the Jewish author and his
pen as the embodiment of the Jewish spirit. Raison d'état had become the
Jewish raison d'être.

The effects of this development would be felt not only by Jews, but Arabs
as well. As we have seen, Rawidowicz was chiefly consumed by "the question of Israel"—and demonstrated few signs of interest in or empathy for
Arabs—over the course of his career. In fact, one of the reasons that he opposed the name "Israel" for the state was because he found it utterly incon-
gruous that an Arab citizen of the state could be labeled an Israeli, but a
Jew living in London or New York could not.[163]

Nonetheless, by the early 1950s (when Rawidowicz wrote his article "Israel" and edited the final *Metsudah* that appeared in 1954), he had begun
to apply the logic of his thinking to the status of Palestinian Arabs in Israel
and beyond. He obviously had this status in mind when he placed just after

his opening article an essay by the sociologist Aryeh Tartakower that dealt with the nature of democracy in the State of Israel. Tartakower devoted a section near the end of his article to the question of the Arab minority in Israel; some of its turns of phrase and arguments would make their way to Rawidowicz's "Between Jew and Arab."

Tartakower asserted that the methods used by regimes, particularly those in modern Europe, to deal with national minorities—ranging from forced assimilation to physical violence—were absolutely unacceptable. He wondered whether, if a neighboring country were willing, it might be "possible to rid ourselves of the [Arab] minority through peaceful means—for example, by a population exchange." But assuming that this could and would not occur, he asserted that "there is no alternative but to view its members as citizens equal to the rest, and to give them the possibility of preserving their language and culture so that they not become half-*conversos.*"[164]

Akin to Rawidowicz and Ya'akov Fleischer, Tartakower was mindful of the inability or unwillingness of previous governments to safeguard the rights of national minorities, especially in the immediate aftermath of the First World War. "There are few greater failures in modern history," he wrote, "than this failure to protect minorities."[165] Meanwhile, he claimed—a bit flippantly—that the question had largely disappeared in contemporary Europe, owing to the fact that national minorities were killed, expelled, or assimilated during and after the Second World War.[166] However, the problem, he insisted, was very much alive in the State of Israel, where the native Arab population had been displaced as the majority by the Jews in 1948. As a result, Jews now had an obligation—what Tartakower called a "duty of the heart living in the soul of the nation from antiquity"—to provide for the "well-being of the stranger in our midst and not to discriminate between him and us." Significantly, this did not mean instituting a new regime of individual rights *at the expense* of group rights; to do so might eviscerate the discrete linguistic and cultural properties of the Arab minority within the state. And that would not only be a great loss for the Arabs, but a signal failure for the State of Israel.[167]

Tartakower's stance is worth mentioning because it both adumbrates and provides a foundation for Simon Rawidowicz's own mix of moral and pragmatic considerations in addressing the Arab Question. Like Tartakower, Rawidowicz remembered well the failed history of national minority rights in Europe after the First World War (and during and after the

Second), with the Jews as major victims. Like Tartakower, he was firmly committed to preserving the cultural and linguistic distinctiveness of national minorities, especially the Jews. And like Tartakower, he believed that the logic of such a principled commitment mandated that the State of Israel extend equal rights and respect to the Arab national minority in its midst. To fail to do so would be to succumb to the very policies and practices that had rendered the Jews one of the most vulnerable and persecuted group in history.

Ever cognizant of this history, Simon Rawidowicz penned a chapter-length brief, full of perspicacity and indignation, and far more extensive than Tartakower's discussion of the Arab national minority. It is this brief that will occupy us in the next part.

# PART II | THE ARAB QUESTION

*The narrow line of justice runs between the Scylla of blind
revenge and the Charybdis of impotent cowardice.*
                    —Hannah Arendt, 14 August 1942[1]

"Between Jew and Arab" was planned as an appendix to Rawidowicz's
massive *Bavel vi-Yerushalayim*. From the time that he arrived at Brandeis in 1951, he began to consolidate his thoughts on the Jewish past and future that had been germinating since the late 1920s into a single book.[2] The English subtitle of *Bavel vi-Yerushalayim,* "Toward a Philosophy of Israel's Wholeness," gives a fair indication of the sweep of Rawidowicz's vision, as well as of his characteristic nomenclature for the Jewish people.

In reflecting on this book, we must recall the distinct, though related, domains of Rawidowicz's life at Brandeis. He was busy establishing a graduate program in Jewish studies that would assume a position of prominence in the American academy. He was also an active and well-respected figure beyond his home department of Near Eastern and Judaic studies, participating in various intellectual and institutional initiatives that helped give shape to the young Brandeis campus. Moreover, he was at work publishing scholarly studies, mainly in Hebrew, on medieval and modern Jewish thinkers (for example, Saadya Gaon, Judah Ha-Levi, Maimonides, and Nachman Krochmal).

At the same time, Rawidowicz was writing the nine-hundred-page text of *Bavel vi-Yerushalayim.* Unlike his more narrow scholarly studies, this text was not intended for a small circle of academic researchers. Rather, its target audience was a wider, if somewhat mythic, learned laity that not only could read Hebrew fluently, but was open to viewpoints well out of the Jewish mainstream.

---

Section numbers in parentheses refer to the translated English version (presented in this volume) of "Between Jew and Arab."

As we have noted, Rawidowicz never held hard and fast to a boundary line between scholarly and ideological writing. In fact, in introducing *Bavel vi-Yerushalayim,* he consciously challenged the distinction between historical scholarship and contemporary reflection, between work dedicated solely to the past and work born of the present. He noted, in a gloss on Leopold von Ranke's famous call to understand the past "wie es eigentlich gewesen" (usually translated as "as it actually happened"), that the scholar is a product of and informed by his own time. Thus, one should not prefer "static research, frozen and already molded" over research focused on dynamic change.[3] A scholarly endeavor worth its weight must mix historical and present-day concerns.

We gain here a glimpse of Rawidowicz's penchant for traversing borders in the name of overcoming seeming opposites. Perhaps the most obvious example of this impulse was his unflagging interest in the well-being of both Babylon and Jerusalem, not of one to the exclusion of the other. This interest was more than a matter of geographic focus. It was a methodological, even epistemological, stance. As Rawidowicz elaborated in the introduction: "A Babylon-Jerusalem approach in Jewish scholarship is not simply a matter of place and time, of connecting one place to another or one time period to another time period, but rather a matter of meaning, content, and form. It requires a vantage point that embraces the wholeness of Israel, both inside and out."[4]

Rawidowicz's tendency to break down established boundaries was evident beyond his distinctive focus on Babylon and Jerusalem or his desire to efface the boundary between the vocations of the scholar and the public intellectual. It was present as well in his constant pairing of moral and political considerations. Mindful of the danger of being branded a dreamy utopian, Rawidowicz endeavored to balance what he saw as the unique ethical charge of "Israel" with a utilitarian impulse to justify that which was in the best interests of the Jewish people. This mix of considerations was especially evident in "Between Jew and Arab."

The aim of this part of the book is to uncover and analyze Rawidowicz's provocative unpublished chapter. We begin by situating it in the charged era of 1948, marked by the restoration of political sovereignty—and accompanied by great joy for many Jews, though also considerable trepidation for Simon Rawidowicz. After exploring the reasons for Rawidowicz's restraint about 1948, we turn to his claim that the Jewish Question and Arab Question were inextricably entwined, now that a previously oppressed national minority had come to control an erstwhile majority. We follow his growing alarm at the treatment of Arab residents in the State of Israel and his close attention to political and legislative acts taken in the early 1950s. We then devote the remainder of this chapter to the subject that occupied most of Rawidowicz's own attention in "Between Jew and Arab": the fate of the Palestinian Arab refugees of 1948, for whom he proposed a sweeping and bold solution rooted in his distinctive moral and political worldview—repatriation to the State of Israel.

### "A Third 'Bayit'"

The eclectic, and at times self-consciously dialectical, method of *Bavel vi-Yerushalayim* belongs to a lost genre of writing. Unrestrained by disciplinary boundaries or the taint of subjectivity, this massive book recalls, in scope and mission, works by two other leading Jewish thinkers that were written in the midst of Rawidowicz's own intellectual fermentation: Yehezkel Kaufmann's *Golah ve-nekhar* (Exile and alienation [1929–30]) and Mordechai Kaplan's *Judaism as a Civilization* (1934). Kaufmann, the wide-ranging biblical scholar, used a historical-sociological approach to demonstrate that the threat of assimilation in the Diaspora could best be blunted by the Zionist-led return to Palestine. For his part, Kaplan, the American rabbi, undertook a lengthy historical and terminological survey that yielded the idea of a Jewish civilization, all in the name of commencing "the reconstruction of American-Jewish life" (as the subtitle of his book read).

Kaplan shared an affinity with Rawidowicz, believing that the creation of the State of Israel was not a panacea to the Jewish Question; he asserted in 1949 that its emergence "has raised more problems for us Jews than it has solved."[5] Nonetheless, it is not ideological consonance that links Rawidowicz to Kaplan, nor for that matter to Kaufmann. Rather, it was their shared willingness to combine historical descriptions of Judaism and the Jewish people with philosophical meditations and contemporary reflections on the Jewish condition. All three undertook monumental projects, animated by the conviction that engagement with the past was an essential precondition to understanding—and guiding action in—the present. Ra-widowicz grasped that this blend of methods and perspectives was char-acteristic of earlier eras: for example, the first decades of the twentieth century when he began to formulate his ideas. It was less characteristic of the time in which he wrote *Bavel vi-Yerushalayim,* that period in which Da-niel Bell noticed that ideas had become the tools of professional scholars much more than of public intellectuals or political activists. Straining to ward off "the end of ideology," Rawidowicz urged the renewal of an ener-getic and combative literary enterprise, what he called in Hebrew a *sifrut lohemet.* He lamented that "Hebrew literature in our day seriously lacks a creative polemical spirit. It has no manuals of battle, a battle for Israel."[6]

Rawidowicz's own tome, *Bavel vi-Yerushalayim,* started off with a typi-cally idiosyncratic intellectual history. Described as a chapter in "the phi-losophy of the history of Israel," the 110-page section (part I) bore a num-ber of telling titles. The title page to the section was called "Sha'ar ha-bayit," which we can translate literally as "the gate to the house"—indeed, a gate to the edifice of Babylon and Jerusalem. An alternative translation, focused on the Hebrew word *bayit,* relates to another title that Rawidowicz gave this section at the top of the first page of the text: "Al parashat batim." This alternative refers unmistakably and polemically to the title of Ahad Ha-am's collected essays (1913), *Al parashat derakhim* (At a crossroad). Rawi-dowicz's play on Ahad Ha-am yields "On the Matter of *Batim,*" and thereby begs the key question of what is meant by the Hebrew word *bayit* or its plural form, *batim.*

Although it commonly connotes "house" or "home," the word is also used to designate the First and Second Temples in Jerusalem (known in Hebrew as the *bayit rishon* and *bayit sheni* respectively). The term is, on one hand, a physical-spatial referent, identifying the actual buildings that contained the Holy Temples. On the other, the term refers to the time pe-riods in Jewish history covered by the existence of the respective temples.[7]

Rawidowicz made ample use in *Bavel vi-Yerushalayim* of the Hebrew terms *bayit rishon* and *bayit sheni,* but not to refer to a physical edifice of any sort. Rather, the two *batim* referred to distinct and competing phases of Jewish national-cultural activity.[8] Because of this, it makes sense to re-tain the Hebrew *bayit* over the less fitting English "temple" or "house."

The first *bayit,* in Rawidowicz's lexicon, was marked by a "primitive" bib-lical outlook, anchored by the desire to uproot the reigning myths of ancient Near Eastern culture and replace them with a new myth. The prevailing interpretive mode in this system of Jewish life was a rather simpleminded explication.[9] By contrast, the second *bayit*, for which Rawidowicz expressed admiration and indeed a clear preference, embodied a new degree of conceptual sophistication in Jewish culture that he associated with the evolving Oral Law (as distinct from the fixed Written Law). It signaled the triumph of the cognitive over the sensory, of reason over myth, and particularly of a creative and original interpretive process over unimaginative explication.[10] The spirit of the second *bayit* was rooted in the Jews' collective creativity, now liberated from adherence to a single building or text and, to a great extent, unfolding in the Diaspora. In this way, Rawidowicz upended the conventional view of the Second Temple by using its Hebrew name to refer not to the period from 520 BCE up to the destruction of the second Holy Temple, but rather to the lengthy era of rabbinic culture that continued long after the building's demise in 70 CE.

At the end of this first section, Rawidowicz introduced the notion of a third *bayit*, a term traditionally used to denote the anticipated Third Temple that would arise in the time of the Messiah. True to his unusual cast of thought, Rawidowicz suggested that a third *bayit* had arisen in his own day—indeed, in the year 1948 with the creation of the State of Israel. But he was loath to ascribe to this development any trace of divine intervention, and regarded with suspicion the specter of messianism invoked in this period, including by secular politicians such as David Ben-Gurion.[11] Rawidowicz harbored the anxiety that 1948 would not herald a new age of national renewal, but instead would entail a violation of "the first commandment of a people from its origins to the end of days"; that is, the abandonment of its own culture for the world beyond. Translated into other terms, he feared that the creation of the state might encourage a process of normalization—as in Theodor Herzl's desire to overcome the Jews' "abnormal" Diaspora existence—that would dissolve the cultural distinctiveness of the Jews.[12]

It was between the poles of dangerous messianic expectation and the prospect of collective Jewish assimilation that the creation of the State of Israel stood in Rawidowicz's thinking. He entitled the nearly four-hundred-page second section of *Bavel vi-Yerushalayim* "Sha'ar TaShaH" (The Chapter of 1948) indicating the centrality of that year in Jewish history.[13] Many of the units in this section were based on previously published reflections on the problem of an anti-Diaspora Zionism, written over the course of a quarter century (but especially those that appeared in *Metsudah*). Thus, the reader familiar with Rawidowicz's earlier writings will find a good deal of repetition regarding the need to preserve a vital relationship "between Israel and Israel," as he often described the relationship between Jews in the State of Israel and those outside of it.

But there was clearly a new urgency in Rawidowicz's voice after 1948. At the time of the state's establishment, the overwhelming majority of world Jewry still lived in the Diaspora—slightly less than 11 million out of 11.5 million Jews. And yet, the creation of the state had not only introduced a dangerous messianic idiom into Jewish public discourse; it had emboldened its leaders to assert themselves as the guardians of the fate of all Jews. Rawidowicz of course rejected this self-assertion and continued to insist on the equal partnership of Jerusalem and Babylon.[14]

Rawidowicz was no more content with the leadership of Diaspora Jewry. In general, Diaspora Zionists had little sense of mission or ambition to play an active role in the collective Jewish fate. To complicate matters further, non-Zionist Jews, including the leaders of major Jewish organizations, often operated with a diluted notion of Jewish identity that was tethered to a rather weak religious affiliation. Rawidowicz was withering in criticizing this sort of leadership, which he saw as "the reign of assimilationism, a status quo regime of wealthy bosses."[15]

Nonetheless, it was the prospect of rupture between Babylon and Jerusalem that most unsettled Rawidowicz. He struggled to stem the tide of expectations that 1948 would transform collective Jewish existence. He asked pointedly at the outset of the final chapter of part II, "1948: Does it mark a new era?" His response was telling:

> At present, it does not have the ability to dismantle the era that preceded it. If it is to establish itself in the future as a year that commenced a new and decisive period for the entire nation—only a prophet can know. 1948 captured a new-old battleground in the war of the mighty among Israel, the war between homeland and Diaspora; and it did so right at the outset. It cast off the restraint surrounding the messiah; indeed, it raised anew the question of the messianic dream, but without answering it.... It opened a door to the ingathering of exiles, but this closed just as quickly. Those who laid the foundation for the turning point that began in 1948 did not stand the test in terms of the alliance among (Jewish) brethren. They and their supporters in the Diaspora still have not grasped the imperative of eliminating the movement

that brought Israel to the gates of 1948—this in order to create a new national movement that will be able to capitalize upon 1948 in the Land of Israel and the still present Diaspora as one.[16]

This paragraph encapsulates much of Rawidowicz's anxiety about the new rhetoric—and actual conditions on the ground—in the wake of the creation of the State of Israel. From messianism to assimilation, from outright disregard to paternalistic control over the Diaspora, the new state exposed, perhaps even induced, an array of dangers that could disable the Jewish national body. Rawidowicz must have felt himself a truly "lonely man" at this moment, not unlike Ahad Ha'am, who described himself as a mourner at a wedding feast while sitting at the First Zionist Congress in Basel in 1897. As we have suggested at various points, he found little common cause with anti-Zionist Jewish critics of the State of Israel, who denied the national character of the Jews or the need for a vibrant Jewish center in "Jerusalem" alongside "Babylon."[17]

As noted in the introduction, it would seem natural for Rawidowicz to count as allies the Central European Zionists who had formed the core of the Brit Shalom movement and long advocated a binational arrangement in which governance over Palestine would be shared by Jews and Arabs. Following the demise of Brit Shalom in 1933, a number of these intellectuals continued to support the ideal of binationalism through a series of succeeding organizations including Kedma Mizraha, the League for Arab-Jewish Rapprochement, and, finally, the Ihud Association.[18] Understandably, 1948 posed a serious challenge to the worldview of these figures and organizations. A Jewish state was now a fait accompli, thereby ending their dream of a binational arrangement. This new recognition, for example, informed the Hebrew University philosopher, Shmuel Hugo Bergmann. In March 1950, Bergmann wrote to the new organ of Ihud, *Ner,* to suggest that it was time to surrender the oppositional stance that had characterized the Jewish binationalists hitherto and return to the fold, taking pride in and responsibility for the Zionist movement and the new state.[19] Bergmann's colleague in Jerusalem, Martin Buber, adopted a different tack in a pair of articles in 1949–50. In one devoted to the theme "Should the Ihud Accept the Decree of History?" Buber argued that the success of Zionism should not be measured either by the numbers of Jewish immigrants who come to Israel nor even by the newly earned independence of the State of Israel. Rather, it was to be realized through the regeneration of the Jewish nation (as distinct from the Jewish state), living in harmony with its neighbors. For Buber, "the verse 'Zion shall be redeemed in justice' (Isaiah 1:27) is not simply a poetic phrase . . . but a prophecy of truth."[20] Buber reaffirmed the relevance of reclaiming the prophetic imperative in a second article, "The Children of Amos," that appeared in the opening issue of *Ner*. There, he asserted that the ethos of the prophets must guide the Jewish nation "to establish justice both among its various parts—individuals and groups—and in its relations with other nations, for the sake of its salvation and the salvation of humanity in the making."[21]

Buber and the *Ner* group were among those Jews who feared that the State of Israel would abandon—indeed, had already begun to abandon—this age-old Jewish imperative. At a great remove from this Jerusalem circle, Simon Rawidowicz sat in Waltham, formulating similar thoughts and addressing similar issues, though with no apparent contact. Among the many Jewish thinkers whom he mentioned, Buber's name did not arise. Likewise, among the many Israeli journals and newspapers that he read, *Ner* seems not to be among them.[22]

In fact, there were key differences between Rawidowicz and Buber. The former never advocated binationalism and was not especially interested in the task of rejuvenating the Jewish religion. Moreover, while both critiqued Zionism, they did so from their distinct vantage points in the Diaspora and State of Israel respectively. Unlike Buber, who chose to make his life in what he regarded as the site of Jewish spiritual renewal, the land of Israel, Rawidowicz never relented in his commitment to the logic of "Babylon and Jerusalem." He reaffirmed this in a forum in New York in 1949 in which Israel's new ambassador to the United States, Eliahu Elath (né Epstein), also participated. There he argued that the idea of a genuine partnership between the two cultural centers was valid "when 94 percent of all Jews live in the Diaspora, but it will apply equally when that percentage will be 50 or 40."[23]

In today's world, in which there is relative demographic parity between the two centers of Jews (and yet growing signs of alienation and misunderstanding between them), Rawidowicz's call for a *shutafut,* a close and substantive partnership between Israel and Diaspora, seems as relevant as ever.[24] So, too, his belief in a single transnational Jewish nation, while gesturing to a past era of nationalist discourse, also anticipates contemporary discussions about the relationship between homeland and diaspora in the age of globalization.[25]

This prescient quality in Rawidowicz is perhaps no clearer than in "Between Jew and Arab," the unpublished chapter of *Bavel vi-Yerushalayim*. From the notation at the top of the first page, it appears to have been intended as appendix I. a. to the second volume of *Bavel vi-Yerushalayim*. This volume, which constitutes part III of the book, contains a series of fourteen essays, the first four of which offer observations on the state of modern Hebrew literature.[26] The latter ten essays provide elaboration on various points that Rawidowicz discussed at length in the section on 1948.

Nowhere in these fourteen chapters does Rawidowicz engage the Arab Question. But there can be no doubt that he was deeply preoccupied by it at the time of writing *Bavel vi-Yerushalayim* in the early to mid-1950s. Although Rawidowicz relates in "Between Jew and Arab" that he was largely finished with the chapter in 1953, he continued to work on it through 1955. It was in April of that year that he sent a parcel with the manuscript to his Parisian printer, Jacob Fink. Fink writes back on 5 September 1955—a mere seven weeks before his death—that he has not yet had a chance to copy-edit the piece. Presumably, he either did so in the following weeks or the task was left to another editor at the printing shop on 232, rue de Charenton in Paris.[27]

It seems likely that Rawidowicz was still considering publishing the chapter in mid-1956. In May of that year, he wrote his brother Avraham in Tel Aviv, responding to various observations and criticisms that Avraham had made after reading a draft of *Bavel vi-Yerushalayim*. Rawidowicz acknowledged, apparently in response, that it was not easy to write on the question of the "Arab and Jew." But he emphasized that "it is necessary to eliminate the problem of the refugees." Yes, it was a dangerous proposition to contemplate their return, he averred. But "are not thousands of refugees outside [of the State of Israel] also dangerous?"[28] This letter suggests to us that Rawidowicz had encountered criticism on the chapter, presumably from his brother among others, but had not yet pulled the piece from *Bavel vi-Yerushalayim*. Rawidowicz explicitly acknowledges this criticism in one, and only one, place in "Between Jew and Arab" in which he recalled that his views on the Arab Question were known and might turn readers against the idea of a robust partnership between "Babylon and Jerusalem." Clearly then, Rawidowicz was engaged in conversation with at least a small number of Jews about the Arab Question up through 1956. Why at that point might he have decided to withhold the chapter?

We can only speculate, but it is worth noting that tensions were growing in that year between Israel and Egypt, leading up to the outbreak of
the Suez War in late October 1956. Egyptian President Gamel Abdul Nas-
ser's threatening words and actions (including the blockade of the Straits
of Tiran and nationalization of the Suez Canal) may have amplified Rawidowicz's own reservations about voicing sharply critical views of the State of
Israel. Among other effects, Rawidowicz might well have sensed that voicing criticism, such as he did in "Between Jew and Arab," would alienate fellow Jews in a moment of crisis—and defeat his larger goal.²⁹

### "When a Servant Comes to Reign"

Written in his typically rich and allusive Hebrew style, "Between Jew and
Arab" adhered to the form of other chapters in *Bavel vi-Yerushalayim*. It
contained a summary of topics at the top of the first page (twenty-five in
this case), and was divided into seventeen sections of several pages each.
It bore a particular resemblance to one of the last chapters of the second
volume (part III) of *Bavel vi-Yerushalayim*. In that chapter entitled "Illusions," Rawidowicz began the discussion with a formulation similar to that
found at the outset of "Between Jew and Arab." In the former case, he wrote:
"From the day that I developed my own opinions, I made a vow not to use
the word 'goy' as a description of someone who is not a member of the
Covenant [that is, who is not a Jew]."³⁰

Meanwhile, he opened "Between Jew and Arab" with the following
claim: "From the day that I first broached the subject of Israel and Diaspora, I made a vow not to discuss publicly two issues: the foreign policy
of the Zionist movement and [of the State of Israel], and the Arab question in Erets Yisrael. In both cases, he employed a most uncommon Hebrew verb (from the root קום) to indicate his commitment to avoid the
word or subjects in question. In the latter case, however, he now felt compelled, in light of circumstances, to abandon his earlier vow and address
the Arab Question, which actually consisted of two entwined issues: (1) the
status of Arab residents in the new State of Israel and (2) the status of
Arabs refugees who exited the boundaries of what had become the State
of Israel.

The catalyst for Rawidowicz's equation of the Jewish Question and the
Arab Question was his view that, after 1948, "the nature of the battle

between Jew and Arab in the Land of Israel has been transformed" (sec. 1). Resorting to a familiar rabbinic image, he elaborated: "This is no longer about 'two people holding on to a garment,' both of whom claim to the master watching over them that the garment is all theirs. Rather, one has grabbed hold of it, dominates, and leads, while the other is lead. The first rules as a decisive majority, as a nation-state. The other is dominated as a minority. And domination is in the hands of 'Israel'" (sec. 1).

In the Mishnah (Baba Metzia 1:1), the remedy in a case in which two parties lay claim to the same object is equitable division. But that principle, Rawidowicz suggested, was not upheld in the recent battle between Jews and Arabs over Palestine. Driven by the Zionist injunction to overcome their centuries of powerlessness, the Jews had assumed power and, in the process, displaced the Arabs. This did not mean that sovereignty was an illegitimate goal. Rather, Rawidowicz believed, in paraphrasing the Book of Proverbs, that the risk was great when the "servant has come to reign."[31]

Rawidowicz was not the first modern Jew to use this phrase in describing the relations between Jews and Arabs in Palestine. It surfaces at the margins of Zionist discourse, when critical voices periodically questioned the behavior of Jews as they aspired to and then acquired political power. Rawidowicz's perennial intellectual inspiration and foil, Ahad Ha-am, used the expression in his essay, "Truth from Erets Yisrael," written after his trip to Palestine in 1891. Far from departing the homeland in a state of euphoria, the future prophet of Cultural Zionism was demoralized and depressed by what he saw of his fellow Jews, including their attitude toward the local Arab population. Ahad Ha-'am enjoined them to learn from both past and present experience:

> how much we must be cautious in our conduct toward a gentile people in whose midst who now live, how we must walk together with that people in love and honor and, needless to say, in justice and righteousness. And what do our brothers in Erets Yisra'el do? Exactly the opposite! They were slaves in Exile, and suddenly they find themselves in a state of unrestrained freedom, a wild freedom that can be found only in a country like Turkey. This sudden change has planted in their hearts a tendency toward despotism, as always happens "*when a servant comes to reign.*"[32]

Ahad Ha'am here was referring to the Jewish settlers of the First Aliyah, the first wave of modern Jewish immigrants who began to move to Palestine in 1882. Seeking to establish self-sufficient agricultural communities, the settlers frequently resorted to hiring Arab workers, who were cheaper and more readily available than Jewish workers. This arrangement set up a dynamic of labor dependence that the succeeding wave of Jewish immigrants, the Second Aliyah, vowed to eliminate. But it also introduced a colonial dimension to the relationship between Jews and Arabs in Palestine whereby the latter assumed a position of economic and cultural superiority vis-à-vis the latter. Ahad Ha-am took aim at this stance, condemning the widespread perception that "Arabs are all wild desert beasts, a people resembling a donkey, who neither see nor understand what is going on around them."[33]

This imagery had later iterations in the Yishuv. Fifteen years after Ahad Ha-am's first report, another Zionist in Palestine, Yitzhak Epstein, felt compelled to dispel the widely held impression among Jews that Arabs were uncivilized and lazy. On the contrary, Epstein argued in 1907, the Arabs are a "great nation, possessed of physical and intellectual terms." As a result, he warned against the tendency to "suppress the national character of our neighbors."[34]

Epstein belonged to a small group of early twentieth-century Zionists (including Nissim Malul, R. Binyomin, and Joseph Lurie) who have been called "integrationists" by historian Yosef Gorny. Integrationists tended to highlight the neighborly or even familial relations between Jews and Arabs and/or advocated for economic and social cooperation between the two communities in Palestine. Some of the integrationists (for example, R. Binyomin, Epstein, and Lurie) would later join forces with newly arrived Central European Jews in the mid-1920s to found Brit Shalom and work for cooperation and binational power–sharing between Jews and Arabs in Palestine.[35]

Although the idea of binationalism stood at the edge of Zionist politics, the broader principle of cooperation between Jews and Arabs, especially in the economic realm, was part of the self-identity of the Socialist Zionists who came as part of the Second Aliyah from Eastern Europe beginning in 1906. None other than David Ben-Gurion stressed the importance of a shared class consciousness when he called in 1921 for "friendly relations between Jewish workers and the Arab working masses on the basis of joint economic, political and cultural activity." He advanced specific proposals for parallel Jewish and Arab labor unions to act in concert, as well as for Jews and Arabs to maintain autonomy over their respective "cultural, economic, and social affairs."[36] Over time, as enmity between Arabs and Jews in Palestine deepened, Ben-Gurion's commitment to cooperation with Arabs, not unlike his commitment to socialist values, gave way to the single-minded goal of creating a state with a Jewish majority in Palestine.[37] A chastening moment came in 1929, the year in which disturbances broke out at the Western Wall that triggered murderous Arab attacks against Jews in Jerusalem and Hebron. Responding to the still conciliatory stance of Brit Shalom, Ben-Gurion gave voice to what would become a recurrent theme: Palestine did not have equal value to Jews and Arabs. In contrast to that of the Jews, "(t)he economic, cultural, and administrative existence of the Arab nation does not depend on Erets Yisrael."[38] Rather, it was spread over a wide array of countries throughout Asia. Jews, he countered, had only Erets Yisrael as their homeland, which belonged to them by historical right.[39]

Still, Ben-Gurion, in the early 1930s, continued to hold out some hope of dialogue with Palestinian Arabs that could lead to a power-sharing arrangement; he even sought out the young Palestinian lawyer, Musa Alami, as a potential negotiating partner with this goal in mind.[40] However, by the time of the Arab revolt of 1936, the earlier spirit of cooperation had almost entirely faded among Labor Zionists of Ben-Gurion's stripe.[41] There remained a minority strand among Eastern European socialist Zionists that clung to the ideals of a shared Jewish-Arab class struggle and of binationalism throughout the 1930s and 1940s. This group was associated with the Ha-Shomer Ha-Tsa'ir movement, whose members populated the collective settlements of the Kibbutz Artsi union. In 1948, Hashomer Ha-Tsa'ir joined forces with Ahdut Ha-Avodah and Po'ale Tsiyon to form the Mapam political party. Meanwhile, the more mainstream "constructivist" socialists led by Ben-Gurion remained in the dominant Mapai party (founded in 1930).

This digression into Yishuv politics is not unconnected to Rawidowicz and his attention to the Arab Question. It is not merely that some of those who made up the new Mapam party were long-standing supporters of binationalism; some of the new party's members were also distinctly concerned about the fate of Arabs in 1948. Although reconciled to a Jewish rather than a binational state, Mapam leaders such as Meir Ya'ari, Moshe Sneh, Yaakov Hazan, and Aharon Cohen expressed serious misgivings in party councils, memoranda, and newspapers about (1) the manner in which Palestinian Arabs left their homes (that is, via expulsions) in the midst of the 1948 war; and (2) the refusal of the new Israeli state to consider *seriously* the return of the refugees.[42]

Meanwhile, Ben-Gurion's Mapai party was much less open to these questions; according to Benny Morris, it "almost never discussed" them. An important exception was the debate that ensued in late July 1948 following the flight of tens of thousands of Arabs from the cities of Ramle and Lod (Lydda) on 12–13 July. On the occasion of that debate, at which Ben-Gurion was present, dissonant and irate voices rose up to question the morality of acts of expulsion and looting allegedly undertaken by Jewish forces. Perhaps most poignant—and resonant to us—was the view of veteran activist Shmuel Yavne'eli, who declared that Jews, who themselves "were persecuted and expelled, slaughtered and destroyed," had now become like "servants who have come to reign."[43]

Yavne'eli's statement reveals that there were Jews in the newly established State of Israel—indeed, passionate Zionists—who feared that the transition from powerlessness to power would be treacherous and compromising, especially as it affected Arabs. A small cohort of Israeli journalists, authors, and scholars in the late 1940s and early 1950s took it upon itself to address the difficult questions of how, when, and why the Palestinian Arab refugee problem developed. Unlike the government and army "Arab experts" recently studied by Haya Sasportas-Bambaji and Gil Eyal, this disparate group refused to accept the narrative of total Arab culpability for the flight of Palestinians.[44] Writing in Hebrew journals such as *Ner* (Ihud), *Kol ha-'am* (Communist), and *'Al ha-mishmar* (Mapam), they openly discussed the expulsions by Jewish forces of Palestinian Arabs from their homes. For example, Mapam leader Meir Ya'ari took note in *'Al ha-mishmar* in late July 1948 of the recollection of some comrades who said: "We did not expel them [the Arabs]. They left of their own accord." He countered that while "it is true that hundreds of thousands fled, they did not always do so of their own accord."[45] We also notice in this period discussion of whether and under what conditions the refugees should be permitted to return to their homes. Two days after Ya'ari's remarks, Alexander Prag wrote in *'Al ha-mishmar:* "The vast majority of the villagers did not collaborate with the invaders [that is, the invading Arab armies], and we should accept these residents back into our state as citizens with full rights."[46]

Moreover, the Ihud journal *Ner*, from its opening issue in February 1950, was filled with reports of expulsion, displacement, and discrimination against Arabs. *Ner*'s editor, Rabbi Binyomin, used the journal to challenge Israeli society to assume responsibility for the expulsion of Arab residents and to accept their right of return to the State of Israel.[47] In this context, we notice in an early issue of *Ner* the familiar phrase, "a servant who has come to reign," along with the famous dictum associated with the first-century sage Hillel: "That which is hateful to you, do not do unto your neighbor."[48] This kind of religiously infused reflection on the virtue of the Jewish path characterized the perspective of *Ner*'s contributors, prominent figures in the Ihud Association such as Martin Buber, Ernst Simon, Meir Plessner, and Rabbi Binyomin himself.

Unlike other leading members of Ihud, Rabbi Binyomin was not a *yekke*, a German Jew, but rather an Eastern European Jew for whom traditional Jewish learning and the Hebrew language came naturally. In this regard, he and Simon Rawidowicz were alike. The two men were fellow travelers in the byways of Hebrew culture, promoting its growth through their prolific writing and editing. Both developed deep concerns about the State of Israel's treatment of Arabs, regarding it as a pressing moral matter. And both drew often from the font of classical Jewish sources—as when they compared the triumphant Zionists after 1948 to "a servant who has come to reign."

That said, the two had long-standing differences of opinion over how necessary or valid Jewish life in the Diaspora was. Some fifteen years earlier, Rabbi Binyomin sharply criticized Rawidowicz's 1934 essay "Kiyum ha-tefutsah" (Affirming the Diaspora), arguing that "the duty is not to strengthen the walls of the Diaspora, but to destroy its foundation, to prepare for its liquidation while there is still time."[49] Rawidowicz, meanwhile, responded to Rabbi Binyomin that "it was sinful to suppress the will to live of . . . the masses in the Diaspora."[50]

Whether or not there was lingering animosity from a bygone era, Rawidowicz barely mentioned Rabbi Binyomin, a natural ally, in "Between Jew and Arab." When he did recall the name of the Ihud Association, of which Rabbi Binyomin was a key member, he did so by noting that it was not only this group or, for that matter, Arabs in the State of Israel, who opposed discriminatory legislation by the Knesset against Arabs. He was implying that both groups, unlike more mainstream Jewish voices, were marginal in their views and limited in their impact.

At various points in his chapter, Rawidowicz sought to tack away from the political margins toward the center. For example, he averred that the Jewish side was not solely, even principally, to blame for the hostilities with the Arabs. "Of course, one cannot escape the fact," Rawidowicz stated without qualification, "that the Arab countries attacked the State of Israel in 1948, and that the decisive majority of Arabs in the State—one can even say all—prayed for the victory of the attackers" (sec. II). But that, he added, was not the central issue. Nor, for that matter, was it the question of what caused the flight of Palestinian Arabs:

> It matters little whether they left because their Arab brothers and British friends incited them to do so by promising them a quick return to a Palestine in which there would be no State of Israel, or whether they fled out of fear of the Jews (and the Deir Yassin massacre, for example, certainly could have frightened the Arabs of that country), or out of the chaos of war which uproots people from their place of residence and sweeps them beyond the borders, or out of political naïveté and "technical" ignorance (it is told that a night rain storm once drove the Arabs from their homes in Safed, and they believed that it was a "secret weapon" of the Jews that triggered the storm). (sec. v)

This passage signals to us that Rawidowicz's preoccupation with the Arab Question was not informed by what he called "Arab-Oriental romanticism." Rawidowicz did not count himself among "those who bestow glory on the Arabs either in the past or the present." (sec. XVI). There were a number of Jewish scholars, intellectuals, and public officials in Palestine—including S. D. Goitein, L. A. Mayer, Judah Magnes, and Yitzhak Ben-Zvi—who were either great admirers of Islamic and Arab culture and/or believers in the prospect of a historic reconciliation between East and West in the Land of Israel. Rawidowicz was not among them. His motivation in writing "Between Jew and Arab" was much less reverence, compassion, and respect for Arabs than fear for the moral decline of the Jews (and the political consequences of such a decline for Diaspora Jewry).

To be sure, it was not only relatively ignored Jewish intellectuals such as Rawidowicz or Rabbi Binyomin—or opposition Mapam party members—who looked on with concern at the refugee question in the first years of the State of Israel. Debate over the refugees reached the highest levels of government as well. As Benny Morris and others have shown, Prime Minister Ben-Gurion, Foreign Minister Moshe Sharett (né Shertok), and a host of other ministers and advisers were intent on developing policy on the refugee problem in the late spring and summer of 1948, as the military tide was turning decisively in Israel's favor—and the pace of flight in general, and of expulsions in particular, was picking up.[51] One of the government's experts on Arab affairs, the Syrian-born diplomat Eliahu Sasson, who was then serving as director of the Middle East Department of the Israeli Foreign Ministry, suggested in mid-August that it might be politically prudent to consider "the return of a small part of them [that is, the refugees], 40 to 50 thousand, over a long period." Sasson's opinion was quickly drowned out by a chorus of government officials who at a meeting of 18 August determined that the State of Israel should not permit the return of any refugees.[52] This judgment was made in the face of growing pressure on Israel from the United Nations and the United States to make the kind of concession that Sasson was proposing. One of the most vocal advocates of this pressure, the United Nations' mediator for Palestine, Count Folke Bernadotte, issued a report on 16 September, the day before being assassinated by Jewish terrorists, in which he reiterated his belief in the principle of the right of return for Palestinian refugees. Recognizing the likely opposition of the Israeli government, however, his report requested that "without prejudice to the question of the ultimate right of all Arab refugees to return to their homes in Jewish-controlled Palestine if they desire, the principle be accepted that, from among those who may desire to so [sic], a limited number, to be determined in consultation with the Mediator, and especially those formerly living in Jaffa and Haifa, be permitted to return to their homes as from 15 August."[53]

Bernadotte's proposal was hardly received with open arms in Israel. The government, nonetheless, had to play a delicate balancing act between its internal resolve to reject the return of any refugees and the desire to project the appearance of being open and reasonable in the diplomatic sphere. Thus, a week before Bernadotte's report was issued, Moshe Sharett communicated to the chief American diplomat in Israel, James McDonald, that Israel was willing "to consider the return of individual refugees now, and the return of part of the refugees after the war, on condition that most of the refugees would be settled in Arab countries with our help."[54]

We shall return at the end of this chapter to the question of the Israeli government's willingness to consider a return of refugees in 1948–49. For now, it is important to bear in mind that the refugee question was raised, and not infrequently, both in closed government settings and in the press in Israel during and immediately after the war in 1948. Not surprisingly, this era of relative openness did not last long. Anita Shapira observes, in a rich discussion of the immediate postwar cultural climate, that "the expulsion [of Palestinian Arabs], which at the beginning of the 1950s had been acknowledged as an obvious fact of the war, was now transformed into a virtual 'state secret'—of course, with many 'confidants.'"[55] With a few notable exceptions, this "state secret" was preserved in Israeli and Jewish collective memory from the early 1950s until the 1980s. In that later period, the group of scholars known as the New Historians (including Benny Morris, Ilan Pappé, Tom Segev, and Avi Shlaim) began to make use of newly available archival sources and novel guiding principles to question long-standing assumptions about the Jewish-Arab conflict over Palestine, including the relative size and strength of the competing forces, the extent of British animosity to the Zionist side, the existence and number of Palestinian refugees, and the reasons for their flight.

There are a number of important and oft-overlooked scholars whose work adumbrates some of the key issues raised by the New Historians. One was the American political scientist Don Peretz, whose 1954 Columbia dissertation—published in 1958 as *Israel and the Palestine Arabs*—offered a careful and judicious analysis of the stages of development in Israeli, Arab, American, and international thinking about the Palestinian refugee problem. Peretz traces the shift in the late 1940s and early 1950s from a first phase of discussions focused on the repatriation of refugees to a second phase focused on their resettlement in Arab countries, as well as on the prospect of compensation from Israel. Moreover, Peretz provides, through his extensive review of Israeli newspapers, parliamentary proceedings, and government documents, an especially insightful perspective on the range of Israeli attitudes toward the refugees in the early 1950s.[56]

Another important anticipation of later research was the work of the Iraqi-born Israeli scholar, Rony Gabbay, who wrote a doctoral dissertation in 1959 that examined at great length the genesis and unfolding of the Arab refugee problem. Akin to the later New Historians, Gabbay wrote his study in English and beyond the environs of Israel (in his case, Paris), which perhaps afforded him a greater sense of liberty in reaching his conclusions. In fact, his intention was not to issue a writ of indictment against the State of Israel. Gabbay felt that the onus of responsibility for initiating the conflict between Jews and Arabs in Palestine lay squarely with the latter side.

But in his detailed analysis (based on government documents, interviews, and newspaper accounts), he noticed a shift both in the tide of the war and the tactics employed by the Israeli side in the late spring and summer of 1948. From that point forward, one could notice "the great use by the Jews of psychological warfare" against Palestinian Arabs, as well as the fact that "reluctant Arabs were forced to flee into Arab country [*sic*]."[57] Gabbay added that following the evacuation of Arab villages, "looting and pillaging of Arab properties, and the commandeering of goats, sheep and mules by the Israelis were not uncommon features."[58]

Curiously, Gabbay's discussion left few traces on Israeli scholarship and public recollection.[59] The research of the New Historians in the late 1980s and 1990s—for example, Benny Morris's study of the Palestinian refugee problem—was seen as both new and corrosive of the fabric of Israeli collective memory.[60] Earlier and quite frontal discussions of the refugees were largely forgotten as Israeli public memory repressed the role of Jewish and Israeli forces in expelling thousands of refugees, ridding the landscape of traces of their presence, and denying them any prospect of return. Flickers of the refugee question flared up on rare occasions. For example, in the wake of Israel's wars in 1956 and 1967, the conquest of new territory with large Arab populations both awakened some public awareness of the presence of refugees in the newly occupied land and prompted extensive, though secret, government debates about what to do with them.[61] There were other brief moments of recognition in Israel in the 1960s and 1970s, as Anita Shapira traces in her discussion of the reception of S. Yizhar's short story "Hirbet Hizʿah" (to be discussed later).[62] Nonetheless, it is fair to say that "the plight of the refugees" became a largely taboo subject in Israeli public discourse and polite conversations alike from the early to mid-1950s. The reasons relate to a complex of factors that together mandated repression—apart, that is, from the natural passage of time. First, there was a pervasive (and not ungrounded) sense among Israelis that the Arab side was not only unrelenting in its opposition to a Jewish state, but had initiated the 1948 war and thereby had brought on its own defeat. Israel's just rewards, according to this logic, meant not only reclaiming title to the ancestral homeland, but asserting actual property rights over land previously held by Arabs consistent with the common-law principle of adverse possession. The accompanying belief in their own virtue did not allow Israelis much emotional room for sympathy for the displaced

Palestinians—especially as they grew more temporally and spatially detached. Nor, for that matter, did the very real struggles they faced to achieve economic and military stability in the 1950s incline Israelis to dwell on the fate of their enemies—especially considering that the face of Israeli society was constantly being remade as a result of major waves of Jewish immigration. The new *'olim*—those from devastated Europe and from Arab countries in the early 1950s, as well as those from the former Soviet Union in the 1970s and 1990s—came to Israel with their own economic concerns and cultural norms, and without a particularly strong inclination or incentive to take up the cause of displaced Palestinians.

There is another factor that strikes me as potentially important in explaining the evaporation of public awareness and discussion of the Arab refugees. As the new state took rise, its leaders, especially Ben-Gurion, sought to set in place a collective memory that rested on Israel's position both as the center of Jewish life and as the logical culmination of Jewish history. In this emerging narrative, the State of Israel was not only the antidote to the vulnerability of Jewish life in exile, but also the custodian of the accounts of woe and persecution that had befallen the Jews prior to the advent of statehood. The greatest of the tales of Jewish woe and persecution was, of course, the Holocaust, which now became an important pillar of Israeli collective memory. Tom Segev has described in *The Seventh Million* how new rituals (Yom Ha-Shoah) and institutions (Yad Vashem) were created in the early to mid-1950s to commemorate the Shoah, whose occurrence affirmed to many Israelis—and certainly to their political leaders—that a Jewish state was an absolute precondition to Jewish survival.[63] The new moral calculus that accompanied this commemorative moment did not allow for a competing, even if less devastating, narrative—that of the Palestinians in the Nakba. As a result, the story of Palestinian dispossession, fragmentary as it was to begin with in Israel just after the 1948 war, was pushed further in to the recesses of collective memory by the story of Jewish victimization in the Holocaust. In part, this dismissal owed to a rather natural human instinct: Israeli Jews proved far more able and committed to recalling the trauma of their own family than that of their nemesis—all the more so with a trauma on the previously unimaginable scale of the Holocaust. But in part, this process was also the function of a rather deliberate strategy by Israeli political leaders to shape the boundaries of the national memory, a strategy that was pursued throughout the

1950s and reached a peak in the planning and implementation of the Eichmann trial in 1961. Not only were the capture and trial of Adolf Eichmann intended to demonstrate that the State of Israel had boldly reversed the course of an unrelentingly lachrymose Jewish history once and for all. They also provided an opportunity, as Ben-Gurion declared in a December 1960 interview, "to ferret out other Nazis—for example, the connection between the Nazis and some Arab rulers."[64] The link Ben-Gurion drew here was not new, but belonged, as Idith Zertal has shown, to a longer pattern of equating Nazis and Arabs that predated the establishment of the State of Israel. Zertal notes that Ben-Gurion made use of this equation to justify various state objectives, such as accepting reparations from Germany in the early 1950s or developing a nuclear bomb.[65] We might add that the equation of Nazis and Arabs, which has been echoed by assorted Israeli public officials since Ben-Gurion, would seem to leave little emotional, rhetorical, or political space for a serious reckoning with Palestinian dispossession.

## "By Right, Not Sufferance"

As in so many other ways, Simon Rawidowicz departed from his fellow Jews in focusing on the painful consequences of the Arab Question. His fears were triggered by the first legislative steps of the State of Israel in the early 1950s. The Knesset enacted a number of laws that, to his mind, were clearly directed against the remnant of the Arab population—estimated at 156,000 in 1949—that remained in the country after the hostilities of 1948.[66] Such discrimination was intolerable: "The Arabs dwell in the State of Israel by right, not sufferance" (sec. II).

This formulation has its own distinct pedigree relevant to our story. In 1922, a young Winston Churchill, serving then as British secretary of state for the colonies, upheld and refined the British commitment to Zionism as spelled out in the Balfour Declaration of 1917. While he labored to point out that the British government did not favor "a wholly Jewish Palestine," Churchill did declare in his White Paper that "it is essential that it [that is, the Jewish people] should know that it is in Palestine as *of right and not on the sufferance*" (emphasis mine).[67]

Of course, this assertion of Jewish rights to Palestine was central to Zionist thought (including to the Brit Shalom circles that spoke of the "historical right" of the Jews to Palestine). Rawidowicz, for his part, made use of the "right, not sufferance" language more often in the context of Jews in the Diaspora than of Jews in Palestine mainly by arguing that Diaspora Jews, and not Jews in Palestine, dwelt where they dwelt by right, not sufferance. He had long insisted that Diaspora Jews be treated as a cultural collective with physical protection and dignity afforded them by their host countries. On the basis of his defense of this collective right, he now urged that the Arabs of Israel be treated "just like any minority in the world, including a Jewish minority which dwells where it dwells by right, not sufferance" (sec. II).

Rawidowicz was hardly alone in insisting on full and equal rights for Arabs in the State of Israel. A long line of individuals and organizations, Jewish and Arab, have analyzed and called for an end to discrimination against Arabs in Israel,[68] including two prominent Israeli Jewish intellectuals who authored powerful accounts of the relationship between Palestinian Arabs and the State of Israel: Meron Benvenisti, the former deputy mayor of Jerusalem, and David Grossman, a leading Israeli writer. Benvenisti's *Sacred Landscape* (2000) chronicles in detail the conscious effort by the new State of Israel to erase traces of a large and vibrant Arab community in pre-state Palestine. The book opens by discussing the efforts of state officials to draw up new maps that replaced Arabic place names with Hebrew ones. Benvenisti then moves on to argue that Israeli actions in June–July 1948 "came dangerously close to fitting the definition of 'ethnic cleansing'" and chronicles the disappearance of four hundred Arab villages and the reclamation of 4.5 million dunams of Arab land by the State of Israel.[69] Benvenisti's book, which concludes with a chapter that raises the prospect of Israeli acknowledgment of "historical injustices" committed against Palestinians, is significant because it comes from a veteran Israeli public official with deep ties to the land and extensive experience in issues of land and natural resource management.

Meanwhile, David Grossman agitates in *Sleeping on a Wire* (1991) for a similar kind of historical reckoning, drawing on his credibility not as a public official or scholar, but as a keen observer of Israeli and Palestinian life. Concerned in general by the state's dismissive attitude toward Arabs, Grossman is particularly vexed by the status of the *nokhehim nifkadim,* those Palestinian Arab residents of the State of Israel known in Orwellian language as "present absentees" (or, in the language of international law, as IDPs, internally displaced persons). This designation refers to those who exist in a kind of legal limbo either because their places of residence were never officially registered or because they did not squeeze through the narrow window of time afforded by the state to register as legal residents. Grossman traces the difficult struggles that the "present absentees" wage to reclaim their confiscated property or return to their native (often destroyed) villages.[70]

These struggles invariably lead to the question of the nature of citizenship for the "present absentees"—and Palestinian Arabs, more generally—in the State of Israel. On the one hand, the state's Proclamation of Independence called for "full and equal citizenship . . . and due representation" for Arabs.[71] On the other hand, the state's self-definition as a Jewish state, along with its leaders' unquestionable preference for a singularly Jewish society, created a distinct brand of citizenship for the Arabs. Shira Robinson demonstrates in a recent study that the very granting of citizenship to Arab residents and Jewish immigrants in the 1950s was differential, with a much more complicated and time-consuming process required of the former. Her careful archival work points to a category of citizenship for Arabs in Israel that was inclusive, in a formal sense, and yet exclusive, given the difficulties involved in procuring it—and the large number of people who were ineligible to receive it (that is, the former Arab residents of Palestine who had taken flight beyond Israel's borders).[72]

What complicated this notion of citizenship even further was the fact that the areas of greatest Arab population density in Israel were, from the establishment of the state in 1948 until 1966, subject to military rather than civilian authority. The omnipresent control of a military regime over Arab areas, justified according to "emergency regulations" rooted in British Mandatory times, seems to exemplify Carl Schmitt's well-known observation that the legitimacy of the modern state rests upon its ability to initiate a state of emergency.[73] In the case of Arabs in Israel, the presence of the military government invariably rendered their rights of citizenship less than full—not only by distinguishing them from the rest of the population under civilian control, but by closely regulating travel (and hence economic, social, and political activity) through the required use of permits for movement outside of one's home district.[74]

Scholars have noted that the friction in Israeli collective identity between two competing conceptions, a particularist, Jewish-centered "ethnonational peoplehood" and a more universal "civic citizenship," reaches the point of greatest tension in the status of Palestinian Israelis.[75] This tension was apparent shortly after the State of Israel was established to an assortment of intellectuals, journalists, party activists, and even government officials (including Martin Buber, Mapam activist Aharon Cohen, Communist Party leader Meir Vilner, Rabbi Binyomin, cabinet minister Bechor Shetreet, and Eliahu Sasson), most of whom had also manifested awareness and concern for the refugees. In a variety of different settings, ranging from *Ner* and *'Al ha-mishmar* to government meetings, they gave voice to their discomfort at (and sought redress for) the gap between the rhetoric of equal citizenship and the actual status of Palestinian Arabs in Israel.[76]

Simon Rawidowicz was well-informed about the public discussions regarding Arabs in Israel. In addition to a regular diet of Israeli newspapers and journals, he read the published proceedings of Israel's parliament, *Divre ha-Keneset.* There he noticed with interest, for example, that there was little protest among Arabs in Israel against the Law of Return, which was unanimously approved by the Knesset on 5 July 1950. This law laid out the special status of Jews in the State of Israel, proclaiming that "every Jew has the right to come to this country as an *'oleh'*; that is, as a new immigrant with full rights to settle in the state and became a citizen.[77]

It was not the Law of Return, however, but the Nationality Law—passed by the Knesset on 1 April 1952—that aroused Rawidowicz's grave concern. The Knesset debate over the passage of the law was stormy, and exposed sharply divergent visions of the State of Israel among the parliamentarians. For example, the Communist deputy, Meir Vilner, proclaimed that "it is better to call this Law, instead of the Nationality Law, the Law of Denial of Nationality to Arab Residents." In response, Minister of the Interior Hayim Moshe Shapira insisted that there was complete equality between Jews and Arabs in the state. If conditions were so bad, Shapira asked, why did former residents keep attempting to steal back across the border into Israel? In fact, he answered, the status of Arabs has never been so good as in the State of Israel in 1952.[78]

What was actually at stake in the Nationality Law? While the law conferred automatic national status upon all new Jewish immigrants, it established a series of conditions in Section 3 aimed at those residents who did not qualify as *'olim;* that is to say, Arab residents of the new state. Accordingly, they were eligible for citizenship if, and only if, all of the following conditions were met:

1. They were subjects of Mandatory Palestine before the establishment of the State;

2. They were formally registered with the State as of 4 Adar 5712 (1 March 1952), pursuant to the Registration of Inhabitants Ordinance (1949);

3. They were inhabitants of the State of Israel on the day that the Nationality Law came into effect (14 July 1952);

4. They were in Israel continuously from the establishment of the State (May 15, 1948) to the day on which the Nationality Law took effect.[79]

The force of these clauses of the Nationality Law was twofold. First, they paved different legal paths toward Israeli citizenship for Jews and Arabs. Second, they effectively limited the number of Arabs eligible for citizenship by removing from consideration those who were displaced by the war of 1948 and either were unable to register with the state between 1948 and 1952 or sought to return to their homes from beyond the state's borders. This latter group, primarily consisting of those who had fled to a neighboring country during the hostilities (Lebanon, Jordan, Egypt, or Gaza), were known in Israeli parlance as "infiltrators" (*mistanenim*). In all likelihood, a large majority of them were not intent on doing harm to the State of Israel, but rather were trying to cross the border in order to retrieve items from their homes, reunite with family members, or return to their native villages.[80] And yet, the threat posed by a smaller group of "infiltrators" with terroristic inclinations, alongside the state's apparent desire to thin the ranks of Arab citizens in its midst, provided the rationale for clause 3 of the Nationality Law.

Simon Rawidowicz took direct aim at this law. "Morality itself," he wrote, "protests against these discriminatory clauses." Israel was a signatory, he observed, to the United Nations Charter and its Universal Declaration of Human Rights (1948) which guaranteed free and equal treatment to members of ethnic minorities.[81] He was familiar with the claims of advocates of the Nationality Law, who argued on both classic Zionist and national security grounds. But he countered that

> neither the ingathering of the exiles nor the security needs of the State require these discriminatory clauses. Even if one were to argue that they were required, they would not trump the obligation of the State of Israel toward

the Arab minority in its midst. Discrimination is discrimination, even when it serves the security needs of a state.

A state, especially one that claimed to embody Jewish values, needed to ground its power in a firm ethical foundation. Rawidowicz looked on with skepticism at the assertions of some representatives of the State of Israel that the Nationality Law was "the most 'liberal' of Nationality Laws in the world" (sec. III). He was more persuaded by "legal specialists of our own (that is, Jews) who . . . want to defend the government but cannot hide their concerns" (sec. III). He especially favored the analysis of an Israeli scholar, Yehoshua Freudenheim, who authored one of the first major systematic studies of the nascent Israeli political system in 1953 (with a second edition in 1956). Freudenheim rejected the claim that the Nationality Law was "a clear case of racial discrimination." He did believe, however, that "it is difficult to claim that the legal arrangement (in the Nationality Law) is very successful or that solutions that better fit both the problem and the demand for justice, and are less likely to mar our reputation in the wide world, are beyond the realm of possibility."[82]

Rawidowicz quoted Freudenheim at length, endorsing his view that the Nationality Law "remands the minority to the mercy of the authorities and does not grant it any rights" (sec. III). What made this predicament especially distressing to Rawidowicz was that the law aroused no significant and vocal public protest. He was particularly dismayed by the silence of the Jewish press in the Diaspora, which took little note of the Nationality Law. This silence violated not only Rawidowicz's sense of ethical responsibility but, equally so, his ideal of an equal "partnership" between the two centers of the Jewish nation. Presaging more recent and recurrent arguments about the legitimacy of criticism from Jews outside of Israel, he insisted that a confident and self-respecting Diaspora should not abdicate its responsibility for the well-being and moral standing of the Jewish people to the governing organs of the State of Israel, as it had in passing over the Nationality Law in silence.[83] To do so was to cast a blind eye toward discrimination against Arabs, as well as to surrender any say in the determination of citizenship in the Jewish state.

This latter point was memorialized in the agreement reached by David Ben-Gurion and Jacob Blaustein, president of the American Jewish Committee in 1950. In their efforts to clarify the nature of relations between the new state and the largest Jewish community in the world, the two leaders set in place a number of key principles: first, "the State of Israel speaks only on behalf of its citizens and in no way presumes to represent or speak in the name of Jews who are citizens of any other country"; and second, "the Jews of the United States, as community and individuals, have no political attachment to Israel." Rawidowicz undertook a substantial critique of the agreement in *Bavel vi-Yerushalayim,* depicting Blaustein and the American Jewish Committee as assimilationists who were ill-suited to serve in positions of communal leadership, and even less suited to define the relationship between the Diaspora and the State of Israel.[84] More significant, he found artificial the division of allegiances and responsibilities outlined in the agreement, which had the effect of segregating, not unifying, diverse communities of Jews who together constituted, in his lexicon, "Israel." Members of this global nation not only had the right, but the obligation, to express their views on matters affecting its welfare. In this respect, Rawidowicz was disappointed that Diaspora Jewry and its press did not weigh in on the issues of moral and political significance raised in the State of Israel's Nationality Law. At work was a culture of conformism in which critical or dissenting voices were stifled—and which, Rawidowicz lamented, "brands as an outcast anyone who doesn't answer 'amen' to the abundance of propaganda that regurgitates old tales" (sec. IV).

To a great extent, the situation was different in the state itself, where there was not the same need to combat the accusation of dual loyalty or overcompensate for the guilt of not living in the homeland. This difference, incidentally, is a typical diaspora-homeland dynamic that has obtained up to the present—and often prompts, in the Jewish, as well as Cuban, Armenian or Hindu cases, a more conservative or conformist sensibility in diaspora communities. Aware of this tendency, Rawidowicz looked on with appreciation at the willingness of Israeli newspapers and journals to print a wide range of opinions. "Blessed is the press in that country," he affirmed, "that does not lock its gates to these [that is, critical] voices." And yet, in light of this general tendency, he was disappointed that the Nationality Law did not generate more opposition in the State of Israel itself. He was even more vexed by the fact that among the few Israeli critics of this law were those who attributed the discriminatory clauses of the Nationality Law to the "*Galut* [exilic] complexes" of the Jews (sec. III). According to this logic, the history of persecution endured by Jews in the Diaspora led or enabled Zionist immigrants to direct their wrath against others.

In response, Rawidowicz thundered: "No Jewish minority in the Diaspora would dream of discriminating in this fashion." Indeed, "at what point" he asked with indignation, "do we learn from the victim how to victimize?" (sec. III). The clear, if unstated, answer was: *at the point of assuming sovereignty.* It was then that the Jews adopted a different code of ethical behavior than the one that had accompanied them throughout their long Diaspora journey. Rawidowicz would later intimate that the roots of this new code in fact extended back into the early decades of the Zionist experience in Palestine. But 1948 was unmistakably the turning point, the caesura that commanded so much of his attention—some four hundred pages—in *Bavel vi-Yerushalayim.*

Rawidowicz's critique of "Statism"—the idea that sovereignty fulfilled the Zionist dream—presented a striking contrast to Ben-Gurion's growing emphasis on the central political and social function of the state (as expressed in the notion of *mamlakhtiyut*).[85] At the core of the divide between Statism and its Jewish critics (including Buber, Arendt, Rawidowicz) was the status of Arabs. Ben-Gurion's dominant Mapai party focused its energies on the demands of state-building: establishing a stable economic and military foundation, absorbing millions of new Jewish immigrants, and forging a coherent political ideology around the notion of a Jewish state. Almost by definition, the party exhibited much less interest in and sympathy for the status and treatment of Palestinian Arabs in and outside of Israel. By contrast, those Israeli Jews who were keenly attuned to the claims of the Arab minority in Israel and the refugees beyond were often drawn from the ranks of Mapam, Maki (the Israeli Communist Party), and the Ihud. The Nationality Law of 1952 was an ominous signal to this loose assembly of the state's evolving discriminatory practices.

So too Simon Rawidowicz in America could barely conceal his dismay over this law. In similar fashion, he took grave exception to the Land Acquisition (Validation of Acts and Compensation) Law passed by the Knesset a year later on 10 March 1953 (sec. IV). It was this law that enabled the state to claim for itself land that was not currently in the possession of its owners "for purposes of essential development, settlement or security."[86] Together with the earlier Absentees' Property Law (1950), it gave the state wide latitude to deny tens of thousands of Arabs who had been displaced from their homes by the war and yet remained in Israel—the so-called present absentees—access to their property.[87] The effect was quite dramatic upon Arab property holdings, entailing the expropriation of millions of dunams of land. As David Kretzmer argued in his 1990 book, *The Legal Status of the Arabs in Israel:* "The issue of land expropriation is possibly the most painful in the relationship between the Arabs in Israel and the Jewish state."[88]

Rawidowicz, for his part, saw the state's appropriation of Arab land—and its subsequent leasing of it to Jews, including in large quantities to "both religious and socialist kibbutzim"—as a moral blemish.[89] There was a time, he maintained, when the Zionist movement attempted to "redeem Zion with justice" (Isaiah 1:27) (sec. IV). But after 1948, he asserted, the movement had entered a new era: "as a state, as a government that breaches boundaries without anyone raising a voice." Full of prophetic indignation, he declared that "it is forbidden for the Jewish people to adopt the laws of the Gentiles and expropriate the property of an enemy or combatant who was vanquished on the battlefield." This kind of behavior was morally objectionable on its own terms, but also dangerous given the fact that Jews were little more than "a weak and poor people, weak and poor even with the crown of statehood on its head" (sec. IV).

Rawidowicz's critical attitude toward the state (or more accurately, toward the State as the *telos* of Jewish history) went hand in hand with his concern for the effects of political power on morality. One could well point out that it was easy for him to be high-minded in probing the moral limits of state power from the confines of his study in Waltham. But Rawidowicz's calculus throughout "Between Jew and Arab" was never purely moral. He always mixed the demand for ethical integrity with more self-interested reflections on the physical well-being of Jews the world over. Would the state's actions invite a powerful response from its neighbors? Would its adverse treatment of the Arab national minority harm the members of the Jewish nation scattered throughout the Diaspora?

As befitted his one-time literary alter ego, Rawidowicz felt himself a "lonely man" in asking these questions. He had much reason for isolation and pessimism in "Between Jew and Arab," given the fact that there was hardly a groundswell of concern for the Arab Question. Nonetheless, he did believe that pressure from a variety of circles—Israeli Jews, Arabs in Israel, or regional and international players—might one day lead to change. "Rest assured," he vowed, "the State of Israel, its government, and the Jews within it, will ultimately rectify any wrong within its borders, either by choice or coercion" (sec. IV).

### "Miracle" or "Valley of Death"

This trace of sanguinity, if we could call it that, did not vanquish the anxiety that consumed Rawidowicz throughout much of "Between Jew and Arab." He expressed fear that the State of Israel and its citizens would suffer a fate far worse than that they had imposed on others. At the same time, he worried that the most difficult component of the Arab Question—even more problematic than discrimination against Arab residents of Israel—would never be resolved. This component was the "plight of the refugees" (*gezerat ha-pelitim*) in Rawidowicz's distinctive phrasing.[90] Everything that he had discussed previously paled in comparison to "one major act of discrimination: the denial of repatriation that was imposed upon the Arabs who left Palestine—or took flight from it" (sec. IV). He continued: "Nothing stands before me—before Israel and the entire world—except this simple fact: hundreds of thousands of Arabs, man, woman, and child, left this country, and the State of Israel will not permit them to return to their homes and settle on their land, the land of their fathers, and of their father's fathers. From 1948 on, I have spent much time thinking about this fact, from all angles, and to the best of my ability. But it is impossible for me to come to terms with it in any way, shape, or form" (sec. V).

Rawidowicz's efforts to think through the consequences of the refugee problem took up the better part of "Between Jew and Arab." By chapter's end, he had called into question two entwined propositions that had surfaced in the emerging collective memory of the State of Israel: (1) that the flight of Arab refugees was the appropriate concern of the international community and the Arab world, but not of the State of Israel; and (2) that repatriation of the refugees was diametrically opposed to its best interests.

Very few Jews in the early 1950s dared to write a text of such length, passion, and focus on the Arab refugees. Rawidowicz was prompted to act when he heard "Jewish leaders, ministers of the State of Israel, Zionist writers and even non-Zionists offer fulsome praise to the miracle, indeed, to the greatest of all miracles to happen to Israel (in their words), the fact that six, seven, or eight hundred thousand residents of Palestine . . . became refugees."[91] To take one notable example, Chaim Weizmann, the state's first president and an early advocate of peaceful relations between Arabs and Jews, is said to have referred in a conversation with

U.S. Ambassador James McDonald to the flight of Palestinian Arabs as "the miraculous simplification of Israel's tasks."[92]

While some have argued that this goal, to be effected via "transfer," was a long-standing objective of Zionism,[93] Rawidowicz seemed dubious about the existence of such a premeditated plan to expel and deny reentry to the Arabs of Palestine. "If," he asked, "one had said to David Ben-Gurion, Chaim Weizmann, Yitzhak Ben-Zvi, and their friends before 1948 that they were soon to stand as the leaders of a State of Israel that did not permit Arab refugees—men, women, and children—to return to their possessions, and thus *uprooted* them and rendered them homeless—would they not see in this claim a contemptible libel of the haters of Israel and Zion who aimed to desecrate the name of Israel and besmirch Zionism in the world?" (sec. XIII). Had they not repeatedly spoken of the "path of *peace and honor,* whose guiding principle is total equality rooted in a single law for Jew and Arab in a future state of Palestine?" (sec. XIII). Rawidowicz observed that the language of "brotherhood between Jew and Arab" issued with particular frequency from the mouths of the socialist Labor Zionists.

But he also noticed a disturbing gap between rhetoric and deed, and not just in the aftermath of 1948. Decades earlier, the revered "prophet of the religion of labor," A. D. Gordon (1856–1922) spoke of the "cosmic universal" relations between Jews and Arabs. (sec. XIII). Rawidowicz wondered whether this celestial language could be reconciled with the vision and deeds of Zionism in his own day. He was not at all certain how Gordon would have reacted to the fact that Jews lived in "expropriated and conquered homes" after 1948. Would he have "blurted out like his friends and disciples at Degania, Nahalal, and elsewhere that 'we have no stain on our hands, we are righteous and have not sinned?'" (sec. XIII).

Rawidowicz did not answer directly. But one senses in "Between Jew and Arab" a tension between two views of the history of Zionism—one that saw an intoxicating self-assurance and moral satisfaction take rise in 1948, and a second that regarded these qualities as more deeply rooted in the Zionist past. Frequently, Rawidowicz fixated on 1948 as a dramatic rupture in Jewish history beyond which a once-moral movement lost its innocence. At other times, he seemed to believe that this innocence vanished at a much earlier stage, when Zionism asserted its primacy vis-à-vis both Diaspora Jewish and Arab foes. The reader of Rawidowicz is left unclear about which of these two views he favored, as well as when he believed that the gap between Zionist rhetoric and deed had become an unbridgeable chasm.

What is beyond dispute is that 1948 created a new sense of moral urgency for Rawidowicz. It is at that point that he began to turn his attention to the Arab Question. It is also at that point that he felt intense surprise and disappointment at Zionists of a socialist stripe for their abdication of moral responsibility by failing to address this question. He held up as a sterling counterexample a person mentioned at various points in this book, the Hebrew author, S. Yizhar. Rawidowicz described Yizhar as "the one writer who salvaged the honor of our Hebrew literature in the State of Israel when he protested in his stories ("Sipur Hirbet Hizʿah" and "Hashavui") the injustice done to the Arabs" (sec. XI). As we have noted, these two stories created a great deal of attention and controversy when first published in Israel in 1949.[94]

What struck Rawidowicz and thousands of other readers was that, while fictional, these stories contained highly realistic accounts of the expulsion of Palestinian Arabs by Israeli soldiers in 1948—and perhaps even more compelling, descriptions of the soldiers' mix of cruelty and indifference to the suffering of the expelled Arabs. The narrator of "Hirbet Hizʿah" belongs to a unit entrusted with the task of removing the elderly, women, and children who had not already fled from the fictional village of Hirbet Hizʿah. He harbors qualms about this assignment, to which he gives periodic voice to his fellow soldiers. But they dismiss him through a variety of arguments, including claims that the Arabs are not worth the concern ("they are animals") or that they would slaughter the Jews if given the chance. Moreover, he hears the following from his commander, Moishe: "You listen to what I'm going to tell you. New immigrants will come, you hear, to Hirbet what-ever-it's-called, they will take the land, and they will work it. And it will be just fine here."[95] Constrained by his own timidity, the narrator can only wonder to himself: "Who will ever recall that there was once a Hirbet Hizʿah where we expelled (others) and that we inherited? We came, we shot, we burned, we blew up, we pushed, we drove out, we exiled. . . . What the hell are we doing in this place?" The resulting distress of the narrator occasioned an unvarnished anger that must have stunned Yizhar's readers: "Colonizers, my guts screamed out. A lie, my guts screamed out. Hirbet Hizʿah is not ours."[96]

What adds particular force to the voice of Yizhar's narrator is that the author, as Anita Shapira has pointed out, was not a predictable critic. He was born and raised in Palestine into an agricultural family wedded to the ideals of Socialist Zionism.[97] His great-uncle, Moshe Smilansky (1874–1953), was a well-known veteran of the First Aliyah, committed in word and deed to Jewish settlement of the Land of Israel. The older Smilansky (his nephew's given name, we recall, was Yizhar Smilansky) had come to believe that the exclusive insistence of subsequent Zionist settlers on "Hebrew labor" in Jewish settlements—to the exclusion of Arabs—was misguided. Consequently, he become a vocal advocate of Arab-Jewish coexistence, as well as the author of sympathetic, if highly romanticized, stories about Arabs in Palestine.

Rawidowicz was drawn to what he saw as the humane Zionism of the Smilanskys, Moshe and Yizhar, and contrasted it to the more callous version prevalent among other Labor Zionists. Indeed, he juxtaposed the perspective of Moshe Smilansky to that of a member of another well-known family of Jewish settlers in the Yishuv, Shmuel Dayan (father of Israeli general and politician Moshe Dayan). Accordingly, Dayan, who was a founder of the early cooperative settlement of Nahalal, based his vision of Zionism and the newly created State of Israel on the early Socialist Zionist doctrines of "the conquest of labor, the conquest of the land, and Hebrew labor"[98] (sec. XII). These doctrines were, for Dayan and many others, the foundation of the struggle to create a Jewish national society in the Land of Israel. The obstacles to this goal were the Arabs of Palestine; thus their flight in 1948 was hardly cause for tears or hand-wringing. On the contrary, Rawidowicz quoted at length Dayan's sharply worded rejoinder to the progressive American Zionist leader, Hayim Greenberg, who had expressed concern over the status of Palestinian Arabs in 1948:

> Did we commit a wrong to the Arabs by taking their land, homes, and all their possessions? *Arabs as individuals surely suffered, but the Jewish people committed no wrong to the Arab people.* They waged a war against us, sought to throw us into the sea. We defended our lives, fought, and won. . . . We acted like a man who is drowning and does everything in his power to save himself. *We pushed the Arabs from their homes to their neighbors and brothers by race,* and saved ourselves.[99]

It is this perspective that Rawidowicz would associate with "cruel Zionism," the term invoked by Avraham Sharon in 1943. "Cruel Zionism," we recall, originally referred to the impulse to gain distance from, and even sever ties with, Diaspora Jewry in order to realize the Zionist dream in Palestine.

But the concept was also translated into a more local idiom by Sharon and other Zionists in Palestine, for whom the "exodus of Arabs" was an essential condition of the realization of Zionism.[100] Sharon advocated this position in a pamphlet from 1949 entitled "Chauvinistic Remarks Regarding the Matter of the Arabs," insisting that "our enemies of old"—the Arabs—remain "the enemies of today and tomorrow." Accordingly, Jews should feel little sympathy for or guilt over those Palestinian Arabs who fled in 1948. Even an event such as the massacre at Deir Yassin, which Sharon admitted was worthy of condemnation, had a salutary outcome: it hastened the flight of Arabs from Palestine, and thus facilitated the task of creating a Jewish state.[101] Sharon was not content to recognize the value of past flight alone. Both in "Chauvinistic Remarks" and in another essay that Rawidowicz quoted ("Diplomatic Remarks of a Non-Diplomat"), he expressed support for the idea that those Palestinian Arabs who remained within the current State of Israel should be encouraged to leave the country. Conversely, he took sharp aim at those Jews who opposed his views, the weak-kneed "moralizers" (*musarnikim*) who were unwilling to subscribe to his view of power politics.[102]

Although not mentioned by name, Rawidowicz would easily qualify as one of the moralizers. So too would Moshe Smilansky, whose version of Zionism, Rawidowicz felt, looked beyond the exclusive demands and travails of the Jews. Smilansky was able to discern a pronounced and unsettling rhetorical difference when Zionists spoke about their own and the Arabs' attachment to Palestine: the former believed that "they are national heroes worthy of the world's support, whereas the Arabs who return to their property after two or three years of exile are infiltrators, whose blood it is not forbidden (to spill)" (sec. XII).

Rawidowicz observed a similar rhetorical distinction among his fellow Jews: whereas Arabs are "backward 'Asiatics,'" Jews are "men of vision, heralds of a national renaissance that has great value for the entire human race" (sec. XII). It was the ability to pierce through such sweeping stereotypes, and indeed engage in a healthy measure of self-criticism, that earned his appreciation for Moshe Smilansky—and even more so for Smilansky's nephew, S. Yizhar. With brutal candor, Yizhar challenged the self-righteous pretense of fellow Zionists. He attacked the faulty values and "phony education" that, he believed, Zionist leaders had foisted on the Jewish youth of Palestine (sec. XI). Rawidowicz quoted at length a conversation that Yizhar conducted with Zionist youth after the 1948 war. "They planted deep in the heart of everyone," Yizhar said of Zionist leaders, "that there is place for two peoples in this country—that one does not need to push the other out." And yet now they tell us that "there is no room for Arabs in this country. They are not trustworthy, they can be a fifth column during wartime. This country is indeed only for Jews, since the Jew has no other place in the world other than this country."[103]

This rhetorical shift reflected something deeper, Yizhar asserted: "a psychic wound and a breach of faith by those same leaders who spoke in such a way and in those political parties that changed their flag." Rawidowicz pointed to Yizhar's critique as an antidote to the duplicitous "new national morality" whose adepts ranged from the extreme pole of Avraham Sharon to the more centrist circles of Mapai activists. "When they [the Arabs] commit an outrage," Rawidowicz echoed, "it cries out to heaven." But when Jews commit a crime against Arabs, "it becomes an imperative that cannot be avoided. And if there is something about it that might assist our national revival, then that is well and good, and should be praised a hundred times every day" (sec. XII).

It was precisely this kind of instrumental logic that led some Jews to regard the flight of the Arab refugees as a "miracle." Nothing could be more misguided, Rawidowicz declared. Far from a miracle, it was indeed "a trap for Israel . . . a snare that history has set for us, and we have fallen into it" (sec. V). As painful as the "plight of the refugees" was to the Palestinians, it was also a terrible curse for the Jews. It marked, he observed with reference to a famous image from the Psalms, their descent into the "valley of the shadow of death" (Psalms 23:4) (sec. VI).

This stark biblical image reflected Rawidowicz's unwavering conviction that the events of 1948 had exacted a very heavy price from the Jews. The one-time "servant who came to reign" had assumed not only political sovereignty, but with it, the moral order of the nations. As an unabashed, even chauvinistic, believer in the ethical superiority of Israel, Rawidowicz could barely contain his disappointment. For the first time in two millennia, he claimed in rather exaggerated fashion, the haters of Israel had grounds to complain about the behavior of the Jews.[104] Even more worrisome was the fact that the Gentile world had come to "understand" the Jews, by virtue of their shared morality:

"The world understands"—this is what is terrifying. This world understood
. . . what Hitler did in Germany, Czechoslovakia, and later in Poland and in
Europe. Many around the world "understood" his deeds against us. Understood and understands—every evil under the sun. If the same world that accepted Hitler and his ilk, appeased him, made friendship and non-aggression
treaties with him, now understands the State of Israel when it locks its gates
to the refugees—this is a bad sign for it, indeed for us.

Rawidowicz continued by reframing this new understanding in the language of the biblical brothers, Jacob and Esau, who in rabbinic lore sym-
bolize Jews and Christians respectively:

Jacob was "not understandable" to Esau his whole life. In this very "lack of
understanding" lurks one of the sources of his hatred for Jacob. When Esau
does not comprehend the language of Jacob—"have no fear, O Jacob my servant" (Jeremiah 46:28). But when Esau begins to comprehend the language
of Jacob, woe unto Jacob. . . . I fear that from 1948 onward, Esau has been defiling Jacob through this "understanding"—the two have become alike. The
twins are no longer struggling with one another. . . .

At present, it appears—so it seems—that Esau understands Jacob's deed.
And when it will no longer be worth his while to understand it, he will not
understand it. He will surely say: I don't understand. He will demand a full accounting. Will the state of the Jews and the Jewish people be able to provide
such an accounting, to be exonerated? Perhaps one day Esau and Ishmael
[that is, Christians and Muslims] will join forces in a single union to repay
Jacob for the act that he committed in 1948. And when the avengers are given
the authority to avenge, will they know any limit?[105]

Rawidowicz was fearful of the consequences of this new "understanding" on multiple levels, though we might divide his concerns into two
broad and overlapping categories. As always, he feared its *ethical* effects.
Israel's "descent" into the moral universe of the Gentiles grated against
Rawidowicz's sense of Jewish ethical exceptionalism. It is noteworthy that
another important critic of Israeli policy at the time—the scientist and
philosopher, Yeshayahu Leibowitz—questioned whether there was such a
thing as a Jewish, as opposed to universal, morality. In reflecting on the
notorious Kibya episode of October 1953 (in which sixty Jordanian villagers were killed by Israeli forces in a reprisal raid following an Arab terrorist attack that killed a Jewish mother and her two children in Yehud), Leibowitz placed the blame for the actions of Jewish soldiers not on a failure of
"Jewish morality," but on the misapplication of the Jewish religion, and particularly the core notion of holiness, to the Zionist project. "For the sake of

that which is holy," Leibowitz warned in terms that echo powerfully today, "man is capable of acting without any restraint." The dangerous conflation of the sacred and profane, he asserted, was anchored in the famously euphemistic reference to "the Rock of Israel" (*tsur Yisra'el*) in Israel's Proclamation of Independence.[106] And it was this conflation, he implied, that empowered Jewish soldiers to act with impunity in Kibya.

Perhaps counterintuitively, it was not the Orthodox Leibowitz but rather the non-Orthodox Rawidowicz who believed that a specifically Jewish morality was violated in instances such as Kibya. "Jacob," he lamented, had fallen precipitously from the lofty moral plateau that Jews had inhabited for centuries as a national minority.[107] A different national character was emerging, that of "a man who conquers and subdues, thus not like the Jewish morality of which the Jewish people has been proud from its inception" (sec. XII).

Rawidowicz was not only arguing that Jews had neglected the moral values that had long guided them; he seemed to be implying that morality flourishes in conditions of powerlessness. The flip side of this proposition was that political power conduces all too frequently to amorality—or worse.[108] While evincing serious and repeated concern about this prospect, Rawidowicz strained to demonstrate that he was not a naïve romantic, concerned only with the fate of the Arabs and not his own people. Thus, alongside his moral remonstrations, he offered, as in the earlier case of Israel's Arab residents, a series of pragmatic political and economic arguments intended to redress the refugee problem.

The elimination of hundreds of thousands of Arab residents from Palestine in 1948 was, to his mind, hardly an economic boon. The early years of the new State of Israel were trying ones. "Reserves of food, fuel, and foreign currency," one historian noted, "were down to zero." The new state's government quickly sponsored an austerity program, as well as a Ministry of Supply and Rationing, to provide a measure of control over the economy, to stimulate growth, and, above all, to allocate the available resources to a rapidly growing, immigrant-driven population.[109] Presaging an argument heard today about the economic utility of immigrants in Western societies, Rawidowicz argued that the "rates of food and agricultural production would be much improved if the Arabs were able to return and perform their work" (sec. VI). He noted that the Arab farmers who had remained within the boundaries of the state after 1948 suffered fewer shortages than

Jewish farmers. Whether or not returning refugees would, in fact, increase rates of productivity or offset the added resource drain is a question that cannot be answered definitively. Rawidowicz, with little expertise in the matter and without any specific details about the number or ultimate destination of the refugees within Israel, was inclined to think that they would.[110]

It is interesting to juxtapose Rawidowicz's views of the potential economic benefits of repatriation of Palestinian Arabs to the potential social costs of immigration of Jews from Arab countries. At one point in "Between Jew and Arab," he noted that the void left by the Arabs of Palestine had "created an opening to the East" that was being filled by the hundreds of thousands of Jews (estimated at 850,000) who left their native Middle Eastern countries, often under duress, after 1948 (sec. x). Of course, this was neither the first nor the last time that the fates of these two groups were connected. Today, parallels between the two are often made by individuals and groups who represent Jews from Arab lands and demand recognition as (and compensation for being) refugees.[111]

Already in the aftermath of the 1948 war, various diplomatic representatives from Israel, Iraq, and Britain raised the prospect that, as part of an overall peace settlement, the Arab flight from Palestine and the flight of Jews from Arab lands to the State of Israel be deemed a population exchange.[112] Rawidowicz had his own distinctive opinion on the question. The arrival of large numbers of Jews via the "opening to the East" was not necessarily a positive development. It "placed upon the State an unbearable burden and forced its policy in a number of economic and political directions that were not beneficial" (sec. x). Indeed, it is quite clear that the rate of annual immigration to Israel between 1948 and 1951, reaching a staggering 22 percent, placed heavy burdens on the state in terms of housing, employment, and the provision of social services. But it is also the case that the Israeli economy grew at a blistering pace throughout the 1950s and 1960s.[113] What is striking here is Rawidowicz's apparent assumption that repatriated Arabs would bring economic benefit to the state, while Jewish immigrants would be a burden on the system.

Beyond this somewhat unproven economic supposition—and notwithstanding his profession that he did not distinguish between Jews based on country of origin—Rawidowicz betrayed a strong Eurocentric bias. One of the effects of the "opening to the East," he asserted, was the closing of the gates of aliyah to the West—that is, to Ashkenazic Jews whom "the State of Israel so desperately needed" (sec. x).[114] The chain reaction he was describing—the Palestinian exodus that created an opening to Jews from Arab countries had in turn discouraged immigration from Western Jews—pushed to the fore his clear belief in the superiority of European Jews over Middle Eastern Jews. It also set in relief his lack of empathy for the latter, whose predicament seemed to be of little concern to him. This is surprising not only in light of his preoccupation with the "plight of the [Palestinian] refugees," but also because of his oft-professed commitment to the ideal of a single, transnational "Israel" whose members were found the world over—in the East, as well as the West.

Rawidowicz's curious Orientalist logic exposed some of the flaws in his thinking about the practical consequences of the flight of Palestinians. He marshaled no evidence for the claim that Western Jews shied away from immigrating in larger numbers to the State of Israel because of the resettlement there of large numbers of Middle Eastern Jews. In fact, there were many other reasons—physical distance, ideological disinterest, comfort level at home, and the rough-hewn nature of fledgling Israeli society—that explain equally well, if not better, the dearth of Jewish immigration from the West (apart, that is, from the hundreds of thousands of Holocaust survivors from Europe who *did* immigrate). [115]

Also questionable is Rawidowicz's assertion about the impact of the refugee question on Jewish philanthropy to the new state. He feared that as members of liberal democratic societies, Western Jews might be inclined to insist that "the closing of the gates of the state to Arab refugees is an 'undemocratic' act, and tramples on the principles of individual and collective freedom and rights" that they presumably hold dear (sec. x). As a result, wealthy Jewish donors would be scared away from investing in Israel, and a potentially large source of economic support for the state would disappear.

Judging by the magnitude of Diaspora philanthropic giving to Israel, Rawidowicz's concern that the refugee question might have a chilling effect was off-base. Organizations such as United Jewish Communities (and the former United Jewish Appeal), the Jewish National Fund, and the State of Israel Bonds have raised billions of dollars from Diaspora Jews since the creation of the State of Israel; American Jews alone sent nearly a half-billion dollars in the first five years of the new state.[116] In fact, a deeply embedded culture of giving to Israel has taken root in the Diaspora. While it is possible that some prospective donors failed to give because of the "plight of the refugees," it seems far likelier that the opposite was true. That is, Jewish donors from abroad were and remain largely unaffected by the "plight of the refugees"; some, in fact, are motivated to give precisely *because* of the perceived danger that Israel's Arab foes represent (including the refugees, whom they often fear as a potential "demographic time bomb").

Rawidowicz was on firmer ground in claiming that the boycott imposed by the Arab countries—presumably, he meant that of the newly founded Arab League in 1945 regarding Jewish products from Palestine—would grow more burdensome with time unless the refugee problem was resolved. He speculated that if "the refugees were permitted to return home [the boycott] would surely weaken considerably, and eventually disappear altogether" (sec. VI). He continued by venturing that the refugees could serve as a bridge, both economic and political, between Israel and her Arab neighbors.

Indeed, it is in the sphere of politics that Rawidowicz saw the greatest potential fallout from the "plight of the refugees." Unlike most Israeli politicians and diplomats, he insisted that the refugees were "the source of all obstacles to the foreign policy of the State of Israel" (sec. VI). It is interesting to recall that the government was struggling in the spring of 1948 to formulate a fixed policy on the refugees. As late as 28 May 1948, the Israeli radio station in Jerusalem, Kol Yerushalayim, broadcast a message that "not only were we willing to allow [the refugees] to return to their places, but we would even pay reparations [ for damage] in certain cases." Such signals must have led U.N. mediator Count Bernadotte to declare, as he did at that time, that the refugee problem was "perhaps the most amenable to solution among the elements which made up the Arab-Israeli conflict."[117]

Nonetheless, the attack by Arab armies on Israel on 15 May 1948, compounded by the increased pace of expulsions and flight after April, prompted a series of policy deliberations among Israeli officials that culminated in a much clearer position by summer.[118] The gist of this policy was that the State of Israel would not countenance a discussion about the return of the Arab refugees so long as hostilities were under way. This proposition went hand in hand with the related position, often invoked in the various multilateral negotiations involving Israel and the Arab countries, that Israel would address the refugee problem only as part of a general peace settlement.[119]

Herein would lie a key source of diplomatic contention at the multilateral talks in Lausanne in the spring and summer of 1949 conducted through the mediation of the United Nations' Palestine Conciliation Commission. The main Arab parties to the conflict (Egypt, Lebanon, Jordan, and Syria) insisted that the refugee problem was the essential point of departure for, and repatriation the key to, an overall settlement (although there is ample reason to doubt the sincerity of their concern for the Palestinian plight).[120] By contrast, the State of Israel publicly rejected the right of return for refugees at an early stage of negotiation, arguing, as Ben-Gurion said in 1949, that "the key to peace in the Middle East [was] not a solution to the refugee problem, but vice versa: the key to solving the refugee problem [was] peace."[121]

Nonetheless, the government of Israel found itself in something of a bind and felt compelled to adopt a posture of "constructed ambiguity" toward the refugees.[122] Intense political pressure, including increasing impatience from President Truman over Israel's languid pace in dealing with the refugees, required that at least lip service be paid to the idea of repatriation.[123] The view of the international community had been clearly set forth as of 11 December 1948, when the United Nations General Assembly passed Resolution 194. The oft-invoked eleventh clause of this resolution affirmed that "the refugees wishing to return to their homes and live at peace with their neighbours should be permitted to do so at the earliest practicable date, and that compensation should be paid for the property of those choosing not to return and for loss of or damage to property which, under principles of international law or in equity, should be made good by the Governments or authorities responsible."[124]

The State of Israel could not altogether dismiss this resolution. To do so was to incur the growing wrath of the United States, as well as that of the broader international community—and at a time when Israel was seeking admission to the United Nations as a member-state (granted on 11 May 1949).[125] Seeking to alleviate this pressure, Israeli officials entertained a pair of schemes in the spring and summer of 1949 that would entail a limited version of return for Palestinian Arab refugees. The first of these, the "Gaza Plan," was an Israeli proposal from April 1949 to absorb the Gaza Strip, which included a substantial number of refugees (more than 200,000 according to American estimates). This plan never succeeded in enticing policymakers in Egypt, which controlled the Strip; they could ill afford the appearance of ceding territory to Israel.[126] Shortly after the Gaza Plan began to lose steam, and under the persistent pressure of the United States, Israeli officials floated a proposal known as the "100,000 Offer." The plan faced intense criticism at home (including within the ruling Mapai party), prompting Foreign Minister Moshe Sharett, the government's point person on the "Offer," to clarify that only 65,000–70,000 new returnees would be permitted back within the state's borders; the remainder of the 100,000 would include Arabs already in Israel as a result of infiltration or family unification. The proposal was put forward at the Lausanne talks in early August, but was rejected out of hand by representatives of the Arab states.[127] It is far from clear how Israel would have responded had the Arabs sent a more affirmative signal.[128] What is clearer is that, although conversations continued in Tel Aviv, Washington, and at the U.N. over the next couple of years, time was not on the side of the Palestinian refugees. As new Jewish immigrants streamed into the State of Israel and the international community's attention shifted away from the Middle East in the first years of the 1950s (in particular, toward the brewing Korean War), the question of Palestinian repatriation did not preoccupy Israeli diplomats or politicians as it had at Lausanne.[129]

Simon Rawidowicz, for his part, kept abreast of the various diplomatic machinations. Writing a few years after Lausanne (and the parallel armistice negotiations at Rhodes in 1949), he expressed considerable disappointment at Israel's tack in negotiations on the refugees, and particularly on the question of sequence. Adopting a first-person voice that collapsed the distance between Waltham and Jerusalem, he asserted: "The assumption in our strategies has been—first a peace agreement with the Arabs, and then a resolution to the refugee question, or a resolution as part of an agreement. From the outset, this position was never practical. And in retrospect, everyone knows that it has brought no benefit to the Jews in their relations with the world."[130]

In fact, Rawidowicz maintained, the pragmatic approach—and the only path to normalization with the Arab world—was through resolution of the refugee question. He felt similarly about the State of Israel's relationship with the international community beyond the Middle East. One ought not be deceived, he warned, by the fact that pressure from the West on Israel to resolve the refugee question was not yet insurmountable. In all likelihood, this "passive-neutral" stance drew from the reservoir of guilt built up in the immediate aftermath of the Holocaust (sec. VII). Eventually, it would dry up, leading to a new era of tension between Israel and the West—and diminished comfort and security for Diaspora Jewry. Were that not to happen, the West would simply continue to signal that it "understood" that Jacob had adopted Esau's ways. In either case, the "plight of the refugees" would be neither a "miracle" nor a "blessing," but a rather a "stain" and a "curse" on the name of Israel. [131]

### "Save the Honor of Israel: Open the Gate!"

In "Between Jew and Arab," Simon Rawidowicz gave voice to what few Jews of his day chose to or were capable of articulating—indeed, a position far more in line with frontline Arab states than with the State of Israel. He did so with a sense of genuine urgency, firmly believing that "every additional hour that this question remains alive in the world only adds a further blemish to the moral image of the Jewish people, and moreover, heightens the danger to its future existence" (sec. xv).

The onus to act, he announced, lay neither with the Arabs nor the international community, but with the Jews. Having gained control of a good chunk of western Palestine, the State of Israel could not comfort itself with claims that it did not initiate hostilities or that it did not hatch a premeditated plan to "transfer" Arabs out of the country. Even more remarkably, he believed that it could not claim that "five or six hundred thousand Arab refugees from the State of Israel outside of its borders are more dangerous to the State than five or six hundred thousand additional Arab citizens within its borders" (sec. xv).

As we have seen, Rawidowicz was quite certain that repatriation was the less injurious path for the State of Israel. His cost-benefit analysis of a prospective return of the refugees took note of potential advantages, but less so of possible liabilities. Thus, he never asked whether the return of large numbers of Palestinian refugees would, over the course of a generation or two, reshape the demographic landscape of the State of Israel to the point of erasing its Jewish character. Nor, to turn the question around, did he reveal whether he regarded the preservation of a Jewish state as a supreme value worth preserving—and if so, at what cost. These questions dwelt in a large gray area in "Between Jew and Arab," set between Rawidowicz's support for the creation of the state in 1948 and his disaffection for the behavior of the "servant who has come to reign."

These unresolved questions make clear that Rawidowicz's strength did not lie in forging a blueprint for a future State of Israel in which displaced Palestinians would find their home. Rather, it was in the assertion of an uncommon moral voice that, from an unapologetic position of *ahavat Yisra'el*, called for "repair [of] this injustice" in order that not "a single refugee from the State of Israel [remain] in the world." At stake was nothing less than "the very soul of the State, the very soul of Israel [that is, the Jewish people]" (sec. xv). Echoing a central point made at the beginning of the essay, Rawidowicz reiterated at its end that the "question of these refugees is not an Arab question; it is a *Jewish question*, a question that 1948 placed upon the Jewish people" (sec. xv).

What did Rawidowicz actually propose to do? Immediately upon concluding the last armistice agreement with Syria, the State of Israel should have declared that "every Arab man and woman who left the country at the outbreak of war is permitted to return to their property" (sec. xv). The underlying principle was framed in classic Rawidowiczian language, full of Hebrew wordplay and a clear nod to Maimonides: "the gates of return and repentance are not yet locked."[132]

But the hour had grown late, and the geopolitical fault lines in the Middle East had shifted since 1949. Writing some years later, Rawidowicz summoned up all his moral authority and announced:

> I dare to propose to the government of the State of Israel that it assume this moral—and terribly difficult—path. From an emotional, political, social, economic, and military standpoint, the severity of the situation does not escape me. It requires nothing less than this: opening the gates of the State to Arab refugees *after the Arab countries have arrived at a peace treaty with it*—excluding those Arabs who endanger the security of the State. (sec. xv; emphasis mine)

The proviso that repatriation should follow a peace treaty was new, hinting that in the years in which Rawidowicz wrote this chapter (primarily between 1951 and 1953) his views about the sequencing of repatriation—before or after a peace settlement—had changed. He was well aware of the pervasive fear in the State of Israel in this period that the Arab states were itching for a *sibuv sheni*—a second round of fighting in order to avenge their losses in the first.[133] He also knew well that the narrow window of time during which the state had considered repatriation on any scale had all but closed. After the Lausanne Conference, the leaders of the State of Israel tended to shift responsibility for the refugee problem either to the neighboring Arab states or to the international community; on the rare occasion when they did acknowledge a measure of responsibility, they focused not on repatriation, but on another angle of the refugee question mentioned in U.N. Resolution 194: financial compensation for the displaced.[134]

Feeling himself alone in the face of Jewish public opinion,[135] Rawidowicz was prepared—at least as late as 1956 (when he was still considering publishing his chapter)—to face the wrath of his compatriots by calling for repatriation: "It is better that I should be the target of the arrow of every archer in Israel than I should hold my tongue and say: Israel [that is, the Jewish people] has no sin. If Israel has sinned, then this sin is also part of me. If blood has been spilled in [the State of] Israel . . . if Israel has spilled blood outside of Israel, then no Jews can say: my hands did not spill it" (sec. XVII).

As committed as he was to upholding the preeminence of Jewish ethical propriety—which many in his day and afterward would regard as irresponsibly naïve—Rawidowicz was equally committed to the proposition that he was not a utopian dreamer. On the contrary, he believed that the utopian was the one who deceived himself through "total avoidance of the question of the refugees." What resulted was an "imagined *realism* that . . . brings us, in every generation, to human slaughter and pushes us into the abyss of loss—of life and land alike" (sec. XV). The true realist must confront the most vexing problems of the era with a depth of perspective that eschews the "Realpolitik of the hour, which destroys everything from one day to the next" (sec. XV).

Inverting the notions of utopian and realist was key to Rawidowicz's view of the Jewish Question in its post-1948 guise. Impelled by a strong sense of moral rectitude, he maintained that, as a true realist, his insistence on redress for the "plight of the refugees" was also a matter of Jewish self-interest. Conversely, the false realist was so dizzy with power as to ignore the peril to his own moral and political status.

To be sure, there was in Rawidowicz himself something of the false realist, detached from a clear sense of what was politically possible and unpersuasive in conceiving of the practical benefits and costs of repatriation. But there was also something of the far-reaching realist in him, an ability to intuit that the wound of Palestinian national suffering and indignity would continue to feed discontent and turmoil well into the future.

This, indeed, reflects the double-edged quality of Rawidowicz's advocacy: at once, high-minded and impractical as he sought to blend prophetic and realistic notes into a single key. True to form, Rawidowicz often embraced the role of the lonely critic over the course of his career. But he also sensed that, in a matter as controversial as Palestinian repatriation, he could not go it alone. Turning to fellow Jewish intellectuals, he beseeched them toward the end of "Between Jew and Arab" to demand resolution of the Arab Question: "And you, Jewish writers in the State of Israel, educators and thinkers—rise and awaken and help the government of the State of Israel to undertake this operation. Save the honor of Israel and of the State of Israel; preserve its peace and the peace of its sons and daughters for generations to come: Open the gate!" (sec. XVI).

At the end of the day, this stirring call, born of a sense of urgency and indignation, may have fallen victim to Rawidowicz's own self-censorship—a final act of realism intended to save the larger edifice of "Babylon and Jerusalem." Whether or not such was the case, Rawidowicz's distinctive vision of a dual-centered Jewish nation in fact did not reach a wide audience, owing both to linguistic constraints and an unreceptive Zeitgeist (in which the State of Israel had been established). Of course, even less known was "Between Jew and Arab," the unpublished chapter whose mix of prescience and utopianism, so characteristic of his thought in general, marked the dramatic passage from the Jewish Question to the Arab Question.

# "BETWEEN JEW AND ARAB"

From Simon Rawidowicz, *Bavel vi-Yerushalayim* (1957)
English translation by David N. Myers and Arnold J. Band

*The foreign policy of Zionism and the State of Israel; the "Arab question"
and the question of the homeland from 1948 on; Israel's transition from
powerlessness to power; improvement in the condition of the Arab in the
Hebrew state; a law for the Jew[1] and a law for the Arab; the Law of Return; the
law declaring the State of Israel;[2] the refugee problem in 1948; the moral and
practical facets of the refugee problem; the status of the State of Israel in the
world and the refugee problem; the claim that "it is not good for the State of
Israel to have a large national minority";[3] the refugee problem and the
beginning of the "ingathering of the Exiles," and Israel's role in building up the
state; between Jew and Arab and the education of the coming generation in
the State of Israel; what role Israel's morality? the ethics of Judaism and the
ethics of "Exile"; Zionism's guiding assumption in the matter of Jew and Arab
until 1948; religion of labor, people of humanity; "solutions" to the problem of
Jew and Arab: transfer, assimilation; the "Arab question" in the world and for
Jews; the danger in repatriating the refugees and the danger in not
repatriating them, aspirations from within and without; the participation of
the U.N. in finding a solution to the refugee problem; "utopia" and reality; the
shadow of 1948; responsibility for the existence of the State of Israel, and for
the well-being of the sons and daughters of Israel in the days to come.*

## I

From the day that I first broached the subject of Israel and Diaspora, I
made a vow[4] not to discuss publicly two issues: the foreign policy of

---

*Editorial note:* Rawidowicz's original footnotes have been retained; editorial comments
(in brackets) have been added where necessary. The endnotes are intended to provide
relevant bibliographic and historical context to the chapter.

the Zionist movement and [of the State of Israel],[5] and the "Arab question" in Erets Yisra'el. The central concern of my work has been the "House of Israel"[6]—the status of our "House" resting on its four pillars—with the goal of removing the stumbling blocks from the path of Israel in its home and its soul.

I still hold to my vow regarding foreign policy. Those who have discussed this matter, before and after 1948, speak in exaggerated terms of the sovereignty of foreign policy. For the most part, the State of Israel has not the slightest possibility of choosing its own course, as if it is able to make the sun rise and set in its relations with the outside world. Everything is predestined for her in the present, and the present is not brief. And she is not alone in this regard. Several states greater and more powerful than she have lost the ability in recent times to determine affairs outside of their borders, in their foreign policy.

But that is not the case regarding the Arab question, about which I shall now break my earlier vow. This is for the simple reason that with the creation of the state, the nature of the battle between Jew and Arab in the Land of Israel has been transformed. This is no longer about "two people holding on to a garment,"[7] both of whom claim to the master watching over them that the garment is all theirs. Rather, one has grabbed hold of it, dominates, and leads, while the other is led. The first rules as a decisive majority, as a nation-state. The other is dominated as a minority. And domination is in the hands of "Israel." Consequently, the "Arab Question," in its new guise, the guise of 1948, has become a question about the Jewish people and its national home: in its most profound sense, a question of "Israel" (that is, the Jewish Question) writ large, both for those who live outside of the country and especially those who live in the State of Israel.

Zionism (or at least its dominant parties) saw the "Jewish Question" as the product of impotence.[8] Accordingly, their argument was: Render power to a powerless people, make it a master of its fate like all strong nations in the world, autonomous like all peoples—and the problem will be solved. The very idea of power, with its roots in the nineteenth century (culturally and politically), fueled the struggle of modern Jewry for empowerment (the gift of power to a people without power)—actual social and political power, a matter that deserves its own study.[9]

The issue before us is: how did a people, after two thousand years, pass from impotence to power, from lack of sovereignty to sovereignty? What were its first steps, footsteps that were so instructive and decisive on its path to social and political empowerment, to the acquisition of power in the world? Did it display great maturity, age-old experience? Or was it afflicted with "childhood maladies" of a small and young country, which experts in such diseases have diagnosed in groups that have moved from illness to independence? Did it overcome temptation—or did the acquisition of power and dominance tip its judgment and make it like "the servant who now comes to reign,"[10] the weak one who now attacks and feels compelled to display excessive force (whose aggression fuels itself)? Specifically, has the State of Israel stood the test in the crucial realm of relations between Jew and Arab?

I am not interested in what transpired between Jew and Arab in the past—from the beginning in the Middle Ages on—but rather in the chapter that begins in 1948: the relationship between the State of Israel and the Arabs within its borders (that is, not the relationship between the State of Israel and the Arab countries, which concerns foreign affairs). This relationship is difficult, complex, and disturbing, and yet we are not at liberty to avoid it.

## II

I do not discount the seriousness of the political situation in which the State of Israel finds herself: there is no peace treaty between her and the Arab nations, and the latter long for a "second round."[11] And grave is the danger of infiltrators who attack from time to time.[12] As for the Arabs within the State of Israel, their economic situation has improved since 1948 in a number of regards. Like other citizens, they enjoy the services of the state: education, welfare, medical care, etc. Arab women have the right to vote. With the creation of the state, many Arab tillers of the soil were given the opportunity to throw off the yoke of the effendi.[13] From 1948 on, Arab farmers have suffered fewer food shortages than the majority of the Jewish population in the state's cities. And yet, in contrast to the many improvements in their lives, they are (or have been) subjected to a number of restrictive laws brought on by the state of emergency.[14] In general, they control their own fate in their domain of existence—in matters of religion, language, and social relations. But when we tally up the things that the State of Israel has done for the benefit of the Arabs within its borders, we should not join in with those who count "good deeds." The Arabs dwell in the State of Israel by right, not sufferance—just like any minority in the world, including the Jewish minority, which dwells where it dwells by right, not sufferance. The State of Israel must concern itself with the welfare of its citizens. They, in turn, must concern themselves with the welfare of the state—one concern in exchange for the other.

Of course, one cannot escape the fact that the Arab countries attacked the State of Israel in 1948, and that the decisive majority of Arabs in the state—one can even say all—prayed for the victory of the attackers. There is nothing surprising about this, just as it is "natural" that the suspicion between Jew and Arab in the State of Israel is mutual. In fact, it is not simply the Jews of the state, but the new Jewish immigrants, or refugees, from Arab countries who have so much bitterness toward the Arabs.[15] It is difficult for them, as members of the majority, to conquer this bitterness toward the Arab minority. This is understandable, and so the government, which is responsible for all its citizens, must distance itself from any discrimination directed against the minority—a minority that is the remnant of a one-time majority that became a minority in 1948.[16] We must educate the majority to overcome its natural inclinations, the inclinations of any majority to lash out at a minority that is subordinate to it.

The top decision-makers of the state from 1948 on are Zionists and socialists who always acknowledged the rights of Arabs to complete equality in this country; among them were those who spoke frequently of *brotherhood* between Jew and Arab. They do not need remonstrators to come and hold them to their obligation to the Arab remnant in a country that was established with newly found power for the remnant of the remnant of the Jews.

But in fact, are those who once preached equality so nicely able to practice it as nicely in the actual relationship between Jew and Arab from 1948 onward?

### III

Some of the laws legislated by the State of Israel between 1948 and 1953 are not equally applied to Arab and Jew. I shall not discuss them in all their details; it will suffice to offer a few examples here.

The Arabs—as far as I know—did not protest the Law of Return (20 Tammuz 5710),* which locks the gates of the country to their brethren, who are a minority in the State—while opening the gates widely only to members of the majority population in it. This is the harsh reality. On one hand, a "scattered and dispersed" people without a country wants to gather its far-flung and homeless children in the State of Israel.[17] On the other hand, the Arabs have numerous countries which are not sufficiently populated. They do not know the pain of migration, oppression, and persecution. We would be happy if the territory of the State were not so limited, and it were possible for Jews to establish a state open to all in this land. This would be in clear protest against the walling in of every living creature that was so pervasive in the world, a world of Jericho and Sodom[18] that makes one forget the law of free movement. But we have not yet achieved the possibility of free movement, and thus Jew and Arab alike must accept the harsh verdict. The State will arise in this small patch of land and will serve as a refuge for the children of Abraham, Isaac, and Jacob.

However, in contrast to the Law of Return, not only the Arabs but some Jews in the State of Israel, and not only members of "Ihud,"[19] have protested the discriminatory clauses against Arabs in the Nationality Law (Tammuz 5712)‡ according to which the children of Abraham, Isaac, and Jacob alone earn citizenship in the State of Israel through the Law of Return:

> Whereas "non-Jews must fulfill the following conditions in order to become citizens in (the State of) Israel by virtue of residence: (1) the first condition is status as a subject of [Mandatory] Palestine on the eve of the creation of the State; (2) candidates for citizenship must have been registered as inhabitants by 4 Adar 5712 (1 March 1952); (3) they must have been residents by the date on which the Law took effect . . . (4) the fact of their having been in (the State of) Israel from the day of the creation of the state until the day on which the Nationality Law took effect, or their having entered Israel legally (see above) during that period, must be clearly established. This applies even to those whose place of residence is on land that was annexed to the state after its creation (and not from the day of annexation) and who entered it during this

---

*Divre Ha-Keneset . . . [The reference is incomplete in Rawidowicz's text. For a full text of the Law of Return, see appendix B.]

‡See the deliberations of the Knesset in the matter of the Citizenship Law in Divre Ha-Keneset, vol. 11 (Jerusalem), appendix p. 1723, as well as the report on other sessions of the Knesset devoted to this subject that were published in Divre Ha-Keneset. [See appendix D.]

period legally. In addition to those who gained Israeli citizenship by virtue of their residence, their children—those born after the creation of the state and who were residents of the state on the day on which the Law took effect—become citizens as well. On the basis of this provision, therefore, only children who are not older than 4 years and 2 months can gain Israeli citizenship through their parents. With respect to children who are older than this, it is necessary to examine each case individually to determine if each of the conditions mentioned above is fulfilled.*

Morality itself protests against these discriminatory clauses. But there is also a practical consideration. It is well known that in contrast to the traces of discrimination practiced by the State of Israel against the Arab minority within its borders, the nations of the world would dole out to the Jews throughout the entire world a double dose of discrimination. One can see in these discriminatory clauses a violation of the U.N. Charter, and the Declaration of Human Rights embedded in it, which the State of Israel itself has endorsed.[20] From an internal political perspective, neither the ingathering of the exiles nor the security needs of the state require these discriminatory clauses. If they were required, they would not trump the obligation of the State of Israel toward the Arab minority in its midst. Discrimination is discrimination, even when it serves the security needs of a state.

Defenders who attempted to assert the legitimacy of the discriminatory clauses found after some effort that these clauses adversely affect "only" 15,000 Arabs out of a general population of approximately 180,000.[21] As opposed to them, one should respond that: (a) the number of those affected is not the point, but rather the very act of discrimination; (b) if the State of Israel is not required to issue protective regulations on behalf of the decisive majority of its Arab citizens, does it make sense, from a practical political standpoint, for it to discriminate against a small minority of the Arab minority within its borders?

Representatives of the State of Israel—ambassadors, attachés, and its angels of propaganda—used to declare in 1950 that the Nationality Law is the most "liberal" of Nationality Laws in the world, that there is nothing like the freedom in it, etc.[22] By contrast, one can find legal specialists of our own who discuss the laws of the State of Israel from a "professional

---

*Yehoshua Freudenheim, *Ha-shilton bi-medinat Yisrael* (1953), 190. [Cf. the English version, *Government in Israel* (Dobbs Ferry, N.Y.: Oceana Publicatgions, 1967), 257.]

legal" perspective, and who want to defend the government, but cannot hide their doubts about this matter. The words of Yehoshua Freudenheim in his above-mentioned book (n. 3) serve as a good example:

> From the outset it was clear that in this area, it was impossible to disregard the security needs of the state. However, the solution at which the legislator arrived aroused sharp criticism in Israel and abroad; many condemned the legislation as a clear case of racial discrimination. Although this accusation certainly has no legs to stand on, and there can be no doubt that the regulations against which the arrows of criticism were directed stem only from security considerations, it is difficult to claim that the legal arrangement is very successful or that solutions that better fit both the problem and the demand for justice, and are less likely to mar our reputation in the wide world, are beyond the realm of possibility. It appears that the discussion has not been concluded in this affair and that the injustice will be rectified in the not-distant future.*

May this be God's will. With respect to the Nationality Law, we read further:

> Since the burden of proof falls heavily upon the non-Jewish applicants for Israeli citizenship, it is clear that one cannot speak here—as is routinely done—of automatic granting of citizenship for non-Jews. It is better to designate this route of acquiring citizenship by naturalization according to the most demanding conditions, since it is almost impossible to bring evidence beyond all doubt to demonstrate fulfillment of each and every one of the conditions for citizenship prescribed by the law. As a result, the authorities have the power in every instance to deny claims to citizenship due to insufficient evidence.
>
> Therefore, those who claim that the law remands the minority to the mercy of the authorities and does not grant it any rights are correct. One can only hope that the practical implementation of the law will be better than the law itself.†

The Jewish press in the Diaspora has ignored these discriminatory clauses. According to one of the opponents of these clauses in the State of Israel, the Jewish press in America was "requested not to call attention to this matter."‡ Meanwhile, if our own writers had not heeded this request, and instead would have protested as they should have, they would have earned a reward for their protest, as would have the State of Israel itself.

---

*Freudenheim, 188.

†Ibid., 191.

‡Shershevsky, "Se'ife ha-haflayah be-hok ha-'ezrahut," *Be-terem*, 24, 24 Av 5712, 26.

But here the debt collectors have found a place to collect their debt: from the *Galut*.[23] A number of the opponents of this discrimination have linked it to the *Galut:* for example, the critic mentioned above who has said: "The depressing impression remains among the non-Jewish population in this country and abroad, and especially among our Jewish brethren here and abroad, that we could not liberate ourselves from our Exilic complexes."*

Is *Galut* the sources of sins, even those sins of which it knows nothing? No Jewish minority in the Diaspora would dream of discriminating in this fashion. And if it did dream of this, it would not have the chance to implement it. In *Galut,* the Jewish people was—and is—a discriminated minority, whether in actuality or in potential, on a small or large scale. In the State of Israel, the Jewish people became a majority with the potential to discriminate even when it did not actually do so. So what is the relevance of the *Galut* and its "complexes" here? In the *Galut,* whether old or new, the Jewish people has always been a victim of discrimination. At what point do we learn how to victimize? One veteran Zionist leader in the State of Israel, who fought in Poland against the discriminatory laws that the government imposed upon Jews within its borders, revealed in public his great disappointment that this country—of which he dreamt and for which he fought all his life—is proceeding along the very path that Poland and other countries followed.[24]

The protesters protest—even if they are not many in number, if their voices do not always carry like a trumpet, if they do not always persist in their protest. Meanwhile, the government proposes its laws, the Knesset approves them—with the required majority—and the state goes about its usual business. Custom becomes law, each law has its defenders, and the same discrimination continues to stand.

## IV

More severe than the above-mentioned clauses in the Nationality Law is the [ . . . ] Law, which was approved by the Knesset on 1 March 1953 by a vote of 22 in favor and five opposed (out of 120 votes in the Knesset).[25] Moshe Smilansky wrote an article in protest over this law: "How do you sit alone in Jerusalem, O Jewish conscience?"[26] In fact, both religious and

---

* Ibid.

socialist kibbutzim "acquired" land by virtue of this law from their Arab neighbors, who were evicted from this land and made homeless. The Knesset vote demonstrates that a majority of its members oppose this law or disagree with it. And yet, it is now law, for the "law of the kingdom is the law."[27] As if laws of this type are legislated by themselves! Can the legislature legislate against the will of its legislators?

Until 1948, Zionism was proud of the fact, and justifiably so, that it "redeemed Zion with justice";[28] it did not expel nor would it expel Arabs from their land. What was so felicitous and heartening to Israel and Zionism was that the Peel Commission and other commissions of inquiry that studied every nook and cranny of modern-day Palestine up to the Second World War, were never able to justify the claim of expulsion that haters of Zion used to raise.[29] Is our moral and practical political position in this matter—in the relationship of dominance that exists between one people and another—as attractive after 1948 as it was before? Some estimate that almost half of the Arabs who remained in the state (in fact, almost 90,000 souls), were evicted from their land, legally and illegally, and were exiled from their property by decree of the army and as a result of the security-related laws. And if it were only a matter of ten or twenty thousand out of 100,000, would it be possible to ignore them altogether?

You will say that Israel has entered an era of new fortune—not as a stateless community, but as a state, a government that breaches boundaries without anyone raising a voice. I would respond: (a) the Kingdom of Israel (that is, the State of Israel) must be careful not to breach boundaries. It is forbidden for Israel to adopt the laws of the Gentiles and expropriate the property of an enemy or combatant who was vanquished on the battlefield; (b) in fact, it is not advisable for a weak and poor people, weak and poor even with the crown of statehood on its head, to pillage and plunder. Plundering will not last long in its hands. In the end—and I should keep silent lest the devil hear—she will be pillaged and plundered twofold.

As alluded to above, voices have been heard in the State of Israel that are bitter over the discrimination against Arabs.[30] Blessed is the press in that country that does not lock its gates to these voices. Would that the Zionist press in the Diaspora, in all its manifold languages, follow suit! Particularly the Diaspora Hebrew press, to the extent that it exists, which brands as an outcast anyone who doesn't answer "amen" to the excess of propaganda that simply regurgitates old tales. Rest assured: the State of Israel, its government and the Jews within it, will ultimately rectify any wrong within its borders, either by choice or coercion. There will arise among the Jews those who will protest and struggle to eradicate the evil in their midst, on the one hand. On the other, the Arabs themselves will fight with their very lives to defend their rights in the State of Israel. Moreover, public opinion in the Arab countries—and the rest of the world—will also play a role. In light of this, it is far better for the State of Israel that this work not be done by others. One surely hopes that the relationship between Jew and Arab not become a subject for discussion in the U.N. or in the world press. The United Nations does not intervene in the domestic affairs of countries, and yet its platform is open to any and all denouncers. A number of those countries are burdened by their own minority problems. One country may say to another: "Remove the beam from between your eyes. And the other responds: Remove the splinter from between your teeth."[31] But many are the beams, and many are the splinters in this world. Indeed, sins abound on all sides, and thus there is no consolation.

It is not the discriminatory acts in the areas of citizenship and property—enacted in a particular time—that are the heart of the trouble between Jew and Arab. They are insignificant compared to one major act of discrimination: the denial of repatriation that was imposed upon the Arabs who left Palestine—or took flight from it—with the outbreak of war between the State of Israel and the Arab countries—or more accurately, with the attack of the Arab countries on the State of Israel.

V

The matter of the Arab refugees is extremely serious, now and in the future; anyone who ignores it does no favor to Israel. I don't know the number of refugees. The Arabs speak at times of a million souls or more. By contrast, there are those who set the figure at five, six, or seven hundred; that is, about the number of ʿolim (Jewish immigrants) to the State of Israel between 1948 and 1951.[32] The number is not significant here; nor is the reason for the Arabs' exit or flight. It matters little whether they left because their Arab brothers and British friends incited them to do so by promising them a quick return to a Palestine in which there would be no State of Israel, or whether they fled out of fear of the Jews (the Deir Yassin massacre,[33] for example, certainly could have frightened the Arabs of this country), or out of the chaos of war that uproots people from their place of residence and sweeps them beyond the borders, or out of political naïveté and "technical" ignorance (it is told that a night rain storm once drove the Arabs from their homes in Safed, and they believed that it was the "secret weapon" of the Jews that triggered the storm).

Nothing stands before me—before Israel and the entire world—except this simple fact: hundreds of thousands of Arabs, man, woman, and child, left this country, and the State of Israel will not permit them to return to their homes and settle on their land, the land of their fathers, and of their father's fathers. From 1948 on, I have spent much time thinking about this fact, from all angles, and to the best of my ability. But it is impossible for me to come to terms with it in any way, shape, or form.

If *all* of the hundreds of thousands of Arabs had fought as soldiers against the Israel Defense Forces, would they have lost the right to return to their property? Would they not be like prisoners of war, who are permitted to return to their territory at the end of the war or after the signing of a peace treaty?

Has even this custom been eliminated from our world? The Arabs in question do not have the status of prisoners of war. They are refugees. The State of Israel had the right—and obligation—to investigate each and every one of them upon his return home, and with the most thorough scrutiny; it could have shut its gates to spies and inciters. But it has instead shut its gates to *every* refugee, to men, women, and children who did not commit any wrong. When did this become a positive commandment in Israel?[34]

When I used to hear in 1948–49 and after Jewish leaders, ministers of the State of Israel, Zionist writers, and even non-Zionists offer fulsome praise for the miracle, indeed, to the greatest of all miracles to happen to Israel (in their words), the fact that six, seven, or eight hundred thousand residents of Palestine—even if it were four hundred thousand or less—became refugees, I would ask myself: is this really a miracle for "Israel"? On the contrary, it is a trap. A snare that history has set for us, and into which we have fallen. This is not the kind of miracle that "Israel" can or must bless. There is no place for it in the "About these Miracles" blessing recited by a people that has learned about miracles over the generations.[35] "Israel" should not rejoice at miracles of this sort.

If the flight of Arabs from the Land of Israel be a miracle in any way, it is only in that the State of Israel does not permit the exiled to return.[36] And the Arabs never imagined that they would be expelled from their lands for good because of the "sin" of their flight with the outbreak of the war. This really is our own handwork. And our hands, the hands of Jacob, were not created for this task.

## VI

There are several aspects of the refugee question before us. The first of these is the moral aspect, with which I have great difficulty. Indeed, it is very difficult to preach about morality in this world in the twentieth century. How much more difficult it is to preach morality to "Israel," the victim of the world's immorality for more than two thousand years! Is there any nation on the face of this earth that has the authority to admonish Israel? But "Israel" should admonish *itself.* The source of wisdom is morality: the first principle is that rule which governs the relationship between man and his neighbor. As a practical matter, if morality prevails in the world, Israel has a future—some hope—in it. If morality falters, having reached the lowest rung, Israel will go from bad to worse. The verdict that the State of Israel pronounced upon the Arab refugees is an act that should not have been undertaken as a matter of morality. We were once certain that such an act could never have been undertaken by Jews. Now that we have descended into the valley of "the shadow of death"[37]—that is, into the morality of the Gentile nations—we think and act like they do: an individual's morality is one thing, that of a country another; that which is considered an evil deed between individuals is deemed a moral obligation, a commandment, among nations, as if "Thou shall not murder" and "Thou shall not steal," and the rest of the Ten Commandments apply only to individuals in order to teach us that there is nothing in them that pertains to a large group of people, to a society at large or to its diverse parts. No defender of Israel can explain away this deed with his myriad justifications.

We need not continue elaborating on this point of morality. I shall limit myself to discussing in outline form the political and practical aspects of this decree[38] as it affects the Jewish people and the State of Israel as part of it:*

---

*See *Divre ha-Keneset.* [Rawidowicz includes this note in "Between Jew and Arab," although it does not correspond to any superscripted citation in the text.]

A. The economy of the state: According to experts in this matter, the prohibition against the return of refugees did not bring any economic blessing to the state. The rates of food and agricultural production would be much improved if the Arabs were able to return and perform their work. Their exit has hurt the food supply of the populace and made the state dependent on foreign currency for this purpose. Had the refugees been permitted to return to their property, this money could have been used for other purposes. I do not know if the damage to the economy was transitory, confined to the first years of the state—or if its impact will be felt in the coming years. In any event, the advantage that the state (and its Jewish citizens as individuals) seemingly gained from the new ownerless property[39]—that is, from the refugees' property—will not be an asset even from an economic perspective.*

B. From another economic perspective, which is also political at core, one must inquire about the "boycott" that Arab countries have imposed on the State of Israel, which gets worse and worse by the year. If the refugees were permitted to return home, it would surely weaken considerably, and eventually disappear altogether. Moreover, those hundreds of thousands of Arabs would surely serve as a bridge between the State of Israel and the Arab state[s]; they would assist not only in improving political relations between Jews and Arabs in the wider world, but also in strengthening the economic position of the State of Israel. That is to say, they would free it from its dependence on foreign assistance, or lessen it in a significant way.

---

*This point about the "uneconomical" aspect has been raised in the country's press. For example, the author of the article [Zvi Hefetz], "Observations on Hofein's Speech," writes in *Be-terem* 24 Av 5714: "Thus there fell into our hands houses, orchards, fields, vineyards, wells, and pipes, even whole factories with all their equipment and warehouses. I do not want to attempt to estimate the value of this property that fell into our houses, but it was not a little. The question is really whether they used all this property in efficient fashion (without speaking of theft, stealing, and so forth)." Our author is doubtful whether they "used it for their benefit or the benefit of the State"—that is, at the expense of the minority that was deprived of its property. Does that minority now require reparation? Our author does not ask this question at all. This is not the kind of question that even one in a hundred Jews in the State of Israel would ask.

C. Regarding political relations between Jews and Arabs: the presence of the refugees outside of the State of Israel is a major stumbling block to the normalization of relations between it and (1) the neighboring Arab countries, and (2) the broader Arab world. Were it not for the refugees, the Arab countries would not be able to hold fast to their refusal to come to terms with the existence of the State of Israel. And they would not find so much support for their refusal in the wider Arab world. This problem that we call the refugees is the source of all obstacles to the foreign policy of the State of Israel; its significance is not restricted to the Arab world alone. The assumption in our strategy has been: first a peace agreement with the Arabs, and then a resolution to the refugee question, or a resolution as part of an agreement. From the outset, this position was never practical. And in retrospect, everyone knows that it has brought no amelioration to the Jews in their relations with the world.

## VII

Beyond the Arab countries, is it beneficial for the State of Israel, in terms of its stature in the world, not to permit the return of the refugees to their homes? Many in the Jewish world say: The world understands that the State of Israel cannot cancel this decree.

First of all, does the entire world understand? Can the State of Israel regard the entire world, or a large part of it, as the West? Will the East (Asia and Africa) accept the oppression of a fellow Eastern people whose oppressor is returning to its origin? The latter's origin in the East is beginning to earn it a place there, even though it remains a Western people in the eyes of the East.* Can those in charge of the policy of the State of Israel

---

*I completed this chapter two years *before* the Bandung conference (Indonesia, April 1955), in which twenty-nine Asian and African states participated. This was the first meeting of its kind, inaugurating a new era in the political history of these countries and in the realm of relations between East and West in their fullest scope. The conference closed its gates to the State of Israel in the spirit of the Arab states that oppose it— as if it is not Eastern in the least. Moreover, the twenty-nine countries were divided on most of the questions with which they dealt—but they spoke in one voice (if not with one heart) when they arrived at the matter of Jews and Arabs. They expressed "their

express disdain for the rising star of the East? Perhaps the East is destined to determine the victor in the battle of the giants in our day, as a third plot among two other plots that cancel each other out.[40] What will come at the end of the State of Israel's plot if it be laden by the plight of the refugees, the refugees of the East?

Second, why does the State of Israel think that the Western world truly "understands" this plight and has readily come to terms with it? The Western world, which remembers what Hitler did to the Jewish people and whose nations have done some rather immoral things to one another—at least part of that world, adopts a "passive-neutral" stance on the refugee question. It is prepared to accept a resolution of this question outside of the State of Israel—for the sake of "peace" in Asia, etc. But there is a world within that world—even those who assisted in the creation of the State of Israel, especially the United States of America—that expresses the view from time to time that "the State of Israel [has] an obligation to contribute something" to the resolution of this problem: that is, to return some, or most, of the refugees to their land of origin.

State of Israel, do not mistake the silence of the enlightened liberal-democratic world—enlightened in fact or only in appearance—for tacit agreement. Do not raise up a storm over every politician in America, England, and elsewhere who occasionally breaks "the vow of silence and demands some form of assistance from the State of Israel" in this matter.

The world was silent in this matter after 1948. Should we not fear that its voice, which began to be heard several years later, will get continually louder and become a blaring trumpet? "Keep quiet," as noted above, because the destruction of the Jews of Europe led to some perplexity and aroused a certain amount of unpleasantness. But I doubt that the majority of the world is genuinely embarrassed by Hitler's deeds against "Israel."

---

full support for the rights of the Arabs in Palestine" and demanded "the implementation of U.N. resolutions on Palestine." The issue of the refugees was the most serious of those raised by the Arabs and their friends who oppose the State of Israel. And this is what decided the day against the State of Israel.

Many of our newspapers—in the State of Israel and the Diaspora—vehemently protested the decision of this Asian-African Conference, some deriding it and calling attention to its lack of substance. This criticism surely stands. One must look at the conference thoroughly if one feels a sense of responsibility for the State of Israel and its place in the world of the East. [See the firsthand account in Richard Wright's *The Color Curtain: A Report on the Bandung Conference* (Cleveland: World Publishing, 1956).]

Maybe they do not know anything about what that depraved devil did—just as some of our Jewish sons and daughters do not know. And those among the world's politicians who reflected on the Holocaust, whether extensively or not, hesitated to come in its wake and preach to us about morality. This too is Hitler's curse. That is, not only the destruction that was brought upon us, but also the new era of apology and silence that the destruction brought, among us Jews and among the Gentiles. Among Jews, there is one response to those who mumble incantations over the wounds inflicted by each defect or weakness that you find among the Jews following the "third catastrophe":[41] "'And Hitler was any better?' You want Hitler? As if there is no choice but this: either one of our mistakes—or Hitler. Among the Gentiles, there is, in their world of rationalizations following what Hitler did to the Jews, a sense that 'no one could come in judgment of them.'"

Third, even if the whole world understood the problem of the refugees and genuinely and sincerely accepted it, it is forbidden for us to understood and accept it willingly. Among our foundational principles is, Woe unto the Jew who has been rebuilt in the state of the Jews upon the ruin of the Arab!

## VIII

"The world understands"—this is what is terrifying. This world understood—it matters little whether a lot or a little, in theory or in practice—what Hitler did in Germany, Czechoslovakia, and later in Poland and in Europe. Many around the world "understood" his deeds against us. Understood and still understand every evil under the sun. If the same world that accepted Hitler and his ilk appeased him, made friendship and non-aggression treaties with him, now understands the State of Israel when it locks its gates to the refugees—this is a bad sign for it, indeed for us.

Jacob was "not understandable" to Esau his whole life. In this very "lack of understanding" lurks one of the sources of Esau's hatred for Jacob. When Esau does not comprehend the language of Jacob—"have no fear, O Jacob my servant."[42] But when Esau begins to comprehend the language of Jacob, woe unto Jacob. Everything of Jacob that can be understood by Esau will be altogether eliminated from the dwellings of Jacob, body and soul.

I fear that from 1948 onward, Esau has been defiling Jacob through this "understanding"; the two have become alike. The twins are no longer struggling with each other. They have begun to understand each other. Understand each other? Jacob is a brother to Esau, who always made of the credo "live by the sword" a positive commandment.

At present, it appears—so it seems—that Esau understands Jacob's deed. And "when it will no longer be worth his while" to understand it, he will not understand it. He will then surely say: I don't understand. He will demand a full accounting. Will the state of the Jews and the Jewish people be able to provide such an accounting, to be exonerated? Perhaps one day Esau and Ishmael will join forces in a single union to repay Jacob for the act that he committed in 1948.[43] And when the avengers are given the authority to avenge, will they know any limit?

Until 1948, there was not a single solid complaint in the arsenal of the haters of Israel. We knew, and many from the Gentile world also knew: the blood libel is a lie, the claim of poisoning wells is a falsehood. There is no blood in "the bread of affliction"[44] We did not destroy the economies of Europe and America nor did we undermine the existence of other countries. Rather, the Jews have been a tool of preserving peace in the world. How fine was our moral standing in the world! Our hands were as clean as clean could be. We did not spill blood, no blood at all, in any place or at any time—although we knew how to defend our lives in certain places and at certain times. We did not cause any man, woman, or child in this world to shed a tear. We had no part in the violence that the Gentiles committed under the sun. When the haters of Israel and the historians, for example, sought to prove that the hands of Israel were also full of blood, they were forced to reach as far back as the Hasmoneans. (Clarifying the perspective of these historians, though, is not my task.) From the days of the Hasmonean kingdom until the middle of the twentieth century, one could not find a trace of iniquity in Jacob: neither spilling of blood nor conquest of land, or anything else of that kind.[45]

And now in 1948, principally as a result of the refugee problem, there is ever-growing criticism of us not only from the haters of Israel in this world (who hardly need additional cause) nor from the politicians alone. Rather, it comes from intellectuals and historical scholars who distanced and still distance themselves from Jew-hatred. Even when they exaggerate greatly in insisting on links between the Jews' deed in 1948 in the State of Israel and the deeds of various dictators from ancient and modern times, are we able to deny the painful fact on which they seize: namely, that several hundred thousand men, women, and children were forced from their land because of our political revival? Can we dare face ourselves and say: We are righteous and did not sin. There is no thorn in the crown of our kingdom, the kingdom of 1948, no stain in the vestments of our glory; our garment is pure through and through.

When those of our enemies who are not Arab will say, look what you did the moment the door to statehood was opened to you, with that first small measure of strength and sovereignty that was given to you, what shall we say? Of what shall we speak? What is so painful—the pain is so deep that it is impossible to lift it from the heart to the mouth—are the German voices, the heirs of the Nazis who are full of wrath.[46] They have been heard to say at times: Go look at what the Jews have done to the Arabs, who lived in Palestine for more than one thousand years. Why should the Americans, the English, and the rest of the West complain about us and our parents?

Time blurs the basic distinctions between one evil and another, one instance of suffering and another. But the violence perpetrated by Hitler's regime has no precedent in modern times. And now his heirs, on one hand, and intellectuals, on the other, come and claim that while the present violence is not like Hitler's violence, it is violence nonetheless; whether large or small, every act of violence cries out to God.*

I fear that those who do not "understand" the plight of the refugees will only increase in number—and they will not be silent. And we shall anoint each of those who does not understand with the crown of Jew-hater. And therefore we make an enemy out of one who is not an enemy, as if he seeks

---

*Many in our midst complain, and justifiably so, about the English historian Arnold Toynbee, who compared the plight of the refugees to Hitler's deeds. One cannot avoid the fact that this historian was simply repeating a claim that is alive in the hearts of some Gentiles, including the righteous among them.

Clarifying the Toynbee matter is not my concern. If it were possible to remove from the world this claim through articles protesting Toynbee's words or through spirited declarations of the sort that have been published in the press in recent years, all would be well and good. In fact, this "literature" is growing in our midst by the day, but there is nothing in it to neutralize the cause of our vilifiers, nor, for that matter, to assuage those who are not Jews and whose vocation is not the hatred of Israel. [For a condensed version of Arnold Toynbee's highly critical view of Zionism, see the interview conducted by Louis Eaks, "Arnold Toynbee on the Arab-Israeli Conflict," *Journal of Palestine Studies* 2, no. 3 (Spring 1973): 3–13.]

to eliminate us from the world, as if he wants the life, limb, and property of Jews, though in fact he has no intention of doing so. They are all our enemies—and that's that? If you want to place some of those who are not haters of Jews among our enemies, does this help the State of Israel or the Jewish people in the world? Or should we not instead preserve something, like the opening toward shared understanding and feeling that has developed between "Israel" and the nations in the past two hundred years? Even if that opening is not very wide, are we at liberty to dismiss it? We want candor between "Israel" and the nations. Let the Gentiles think of us without prejudice, but also without "defending" or "tolerating" us. They should speak about and with us candidly, just as we approach them as free people, by right and not sufferance. In this matter [of the refugees], we force some of their best and brightest to vanquish their bitterness—they are afraid that they will be suspected of hating Jews, though this is far from their hearts—in order to sing the praise of the State of Israel. All the while they hide what is in their hearts. But they should speak to and of us from their heart of hearts. Otherwise, we will have reason to be sorry.

And if a miracle should happen and the plight of the refugees does not serve as "a fiery stream"[47] that ignites the flame of Jew-hatred in the world, it will certainly not increase love of the Jewish people and of the State of Israel. Thus, some say: it does not matter at all if the world will love us; it will respect and revere us because of our growing strength, and it will fear us, for it respects only the powerful.

Over the course of my life, I have never counted myself among those who chase after the world and its love for Israel; that grand illusion, embedded in the words of those who always praise the Jews, frightens me a great deal.

## IX

I am not able to examine here all the claims, one by one, made by those who defend the plight of the refugees. But I cannot avoid discussing the claim that has been repeated from 1948 on, in the State of Israel and outside of it—from the first president of the state, Chaim Weizmann, to the latest journalists and propagandists: *it is not good for the State of Israel if it has a large and alien national minority that is not Jewish.**

---

*See above.

When advancing the claim of a national homeland for the Jews, Pinsker supported as a key plank the idea of "welcoming guests." But when the State of Israel was created, it said then and still says: "We can't have guests, or citizens who are not of our own kind—that is, a national minority, even the Arab minority that was the majority in the land of Israel up to 1948." If only the State of Israel had sustained Pinsker's vision, and the scale of the state itself could sustain it, I would be silent.[48] But the fact that the world, according to our politicians, "agrees" that "it is not worthwhile to permit a large Arab minority in the State of Israel" is offensive to the Jewish people. The world does not at all trust that the Jewish people has the ability to proceed in proper fashion with "an alien national minority"; it is similarly skeptical of the ability of the State of Israel to support a minority of this kind, to pass the test.

If it is not good for the State of Israel to have "an alien national minority," then it is not good for any country in the world to have a national minority. That is, every national minority should be eliminated. And if one cannot eliminate it in an instant, then one should weaken and undermine it until it rots away and passes from the world by "natural means"—with the national majority assisting nature in its work of destruction. But don't those who make this claim realize that it actually undermines the existence of the Jewish Diaspora?

My query is not directed at those who negate the Diaspora. They say: "Yes, it is true that we want to remove the Diaspora from the world, to bring it to a point of crisis that will require that it dissolve itself either through aliyah or assimilation. Indeed, any thought or deed that hastens the process of dissolution is a blessing." The State of Israel, however, frequently speaks of a *partnership* between it and the Diaspora, which is to say, that it does not "officially" make use of the language of the negators![49] If the State of Israel is permitted to issue a decree of exile [*sic*] upon the "alien national minority"—upon its own residents, potential citizens by virtue of their residency within its borders—to cancel their right of property ownership and force them from their land, and no amount of material compensation can eliminate the spilling of blood associated with the forced removal, then how easy would it be for the enemies of the Jews to justify the right to persecute the Jewish minority in the Diaspora—in the very name of the State of Israel? For this is the way that you treated those residents of the land who preceded you, whose forefathers resided on this land for more than a thousand years.

Just as your brothers in Palestine treated the Arabs, so we shall treat you. There is no justice and there is no judge, either for them or you.

David Ben-Gurion used to go to great lengths to stress the responsibility of the State of Israel and its Jewish citizens to the rest of the Jewish world. For example, in his article "Like All the Gentiles?":*

> The Jewish citizen of the State of Israel bears responsibility not only for his state, but for his people wherever it is found. To the extent that the good and bad deeds of each Jewish citizen determine the fate of the state—and these deeds determine the fate of the state no less than the government—they also determine, directly or indirectly, the fate of every Jew in the world. . . . What happens in Laos, Ceylon, or Lebanon, concerns only the residents of the state. What happens in [the State of] Israel concerns all the press in every country in which Jews are found—for example, all the press in Europe, America, Australia, Africa, and large parts of Asia. The [renown of the] State of Israel spread to every country, even before it was established. And this is a binding fact for the state and its Jewish inhabitants. The citizen of Israel who does not recognize this fact and its consequences does not recognize the responsibility placed on the State of Israel and its inhabitants.

If the State of Israel is responsible for the "fate and status" of the Jewish people outside of it, and if every act that the state and its citizens undertake concerns the well-being of the Jewish people in the world, then doesn't this affect the "fate and status," as well as the future, of the Jewish people in the wide world out there? Does not the responsibility placed on the state, according to Ben-Gurion, compel it to regard the plight of the refugees also from the standpoint of the status of Jews in the Diaspora, of their struggle for rights in Gentile countries, whether the rights be those of a citizen or of a national minority? They should not be deprived of their right to property and land, and their possessions should not be plundered.

## X

Up to this point, we have discussed relations between "Israel" and the nations. From here on, we shall address the seriousness of the situation facing the Jewish people itself, from the standpoint of the Zionist vision (principally the matter of aliyah) and of life in the homeland of the Jews at present.

---

*Davar, 26 November 1954. [This paragraph is drawn from a series of quotes from Ben-Gurion's long article, "Ke-khol ha-goyim."]

It seems to me that when those who stand in judgment of the State of Israel deliver a final verdict, they will link, to a greater or lesser extent, the break[50] that began with the aliyah of 1948 to the locking of the [state's] gates to Arab refugees. The redemptive opening that was opened to the State of Israel, a redemption short and swift, a redemption worthy of the name and very long in coming—that sudden opening, a "miraculous" opening, that inadvertent discovery and then claiming of ownerless land, perhaps caused the failure, to some extent, of the initial process of the "ingathering of the exiles" (1948–1950) in two ways. First, one cannot ignore the fact that the "Arab miracle"[51] created an opening to the East (an ingathering of Eastern exiles), and to the extent that this opening to the East expanded, it placed upon the state an unbearable burden and forced its policy in a number of economic and political directions that were not beneficial. Second, from the point of view of Jewish immigration, this "opening" blocked, directly or indirectly, aliyah from Western countries. I do not distinguish between Jews, between Jews of the East and West.[52] But the opening to the West has greatly narrowed, indeed, has almost been entirely closed. Some might say that this is only a temporary closing. But this temporary closing of the gate during the first years of the existence of the State of Israel played a decisive role in shaping its image at home and its status abroad. As a result, the gain from the aliyah from the East was offset by a loss; that is, the absence of Western aliyah, which the State of Israel so desperately needed. It is not yet possible to calculate the value of these "openings" in minute detail. But it will be quite significant in our moral accounting. It should also serve to warn those who choose the short route about the obligation of taking the long route, which turns out to be shorter and more beneficial.

We turn now from aliyah and the "ingathering of exiles" to the assistance provided by Jews who are not likely to immigrate, and to the realization of the Zionist dream in its totality. The lack of a peace accord between the State of Israel and the Arab countries—which is connected to the plight of the refugees—certainly slows down a great deal the aliyah of Diaspora Jews, as well as their investments in the state, which sorely needs them.

Moreover, I fear that the plight of the refugees can damage—indeed, seriously damage—the charitable impulse[53] of Diaspora Jewry for the State of Israel. It is not in my nature to see the world in dark terms, but I am fearful. Perhaps the day will come when public opinion in America and other countries will scare off Jewish circles, among them wealthy Jews, and dissuade them from contributing charitable funds to the State of Israel. For the closing of the gates of the state to Arab refugees is an "undemocratic" act, and tramples on the principles of individual and collective freedom and rights. It introduces bitterness into the world, to the point that Jews in the Diaspora, or at least some of them, will be fearful of identifying with the State of Israel. At that point, a number of groups throughout the world, either out of love of Arabs or hatred of Jews, will begin to incite over the plight of the refugees—and the result will be confusion among Jews of the Diaspora.* Of course, the apologists will preach to the world about the plight of the refugees with all their might, but they will not achieve their objective. Fear in the world will be so great that Jews in the Diaspora, as well as in the State of Israel, will demand an accounting of the relationship between Jews and Arabs. Traces of this fear will be embedded into every philanthropic effort on behalf of the State of Israel.

## XI

We should not ignore the potential inhering in this matter to educate the future generation of Jews in the State of Israel. The normal course[54] of the

---

*And they have already begun. See, for example, the American press from 1954 to 1955. The improvements that the State of Israel made in the lives of Arabs within its borders receive no special mention. In contrast to these improvements, discrimination against Arabs—and particularly the plight of the refugees—is publicized in the world press with growing frequency from year to year.

In May 1955, a number of leading American newspapers published a picture of the "first" Arab refugee family that fled Jerusalem in 1948 and then came to New York according to a 1953 law that assists refugees. [Rawidowicz is referring here to the U.S. Congress's Refugee Relief Act, which permitted the immigration of some three thousand Palestinians to the United States between 1953 and 1963.] The family was allowed to settle in America through the help of a number of charitable organizations. Do those responsible for Zionist propaganda in America believe that this picture of the refugees wins friends for the State of Israel (and the various projects associated with it)? If the American papers continue to publicize pictures of this sort, will they not harm the *well-being* and *status* of American Jews too? And their ability to help the State of Israel? And if this assistance is not damaged by the plight of the refugees, then it is not really decisive in this matter before us. I only make this point, and others like it, in order to reach those responsible for Jewish philanthropy and propaganda who have before them such matters.

State of Israel in dealing with relations between Jew and Arab has the potential to distance its sons and daughters—the children of Abraham, Isaac, and Jacob—from the principle of "brotherly co-existence"[55] between nations (not just "tolerance," which is an insult both to the one who tolerates and the one who is tolerated), according to which diverse groups of people stand hand in hand with one another. This tension fuels and increases a sense of national "chauvinism" in Jewish youth that is pointless in itself and is likely to harm the underlying foundation of the State of Israel in the future. It undermines the *moral* basis of Zionism that developed from its inception to 1948, deepens the lack of faith of the young in the consistency of Zionism and the morality of the State of Israel, and induces in them grave disappointment in the leaders of the Zionists parties, educators, and writers who made grand promises about the relationship between Jews and Arabs. Our attention was directed to this issue by S. Yizhar, the one writer who salvaged the honor of our Hebrew literature in the State of Israel when he protested in his stories ("Sipur Hirbet Hiz'ah" and "Hashavui,") the injustice done to the Arabs.[56] From afar, I praise this noble development in literature and ethics that the new Land of Israel has nurtured; it is gaining a respectable place for itself among our writers. Here are S. Yizhar's words in response to questions from youth at a conference:*

> And so it was said in schools and in the Yishuv as a whole, as well as in the mouths of our leaders, regarding the Arabs before the establishment of the state. They planted deep in everyone's heart that there is place for two peoples in this country, that one does not need to push the other out.
>
> We used to speak with pride of the fact that the English commission that was appointed to investigate the expulsion of Arabs from their land found a very small number of actual cases.[57] We spoke of the intensification of the agricultural sector in this country, which opens up new possibilities without having to expel anyone. We spoke the language of "We and Our Neighbors,"[58] albeit in different tones and voices. But the content was more or less the same.
>
> Today, without even speaking of or analyzing the matter [we say that] there is no room for Arabs in this country. [We hear that] they are not trustworthy, that they can be a fifth column during wartime. This country is indeed only for Jews, because the Jew has no other place in the world other than this country. But Arabs can live in other countries without harming

---

*Divre siah*, 52–53. [The full citation is *Divre siah: hartsa'ot ve-diyune haverim* (Tel Aviv: Mifleget po'ale Erets Yisra'el, 1951), 2:52–53.]

their national sovereignty. The national existence [of the Arabs] does not depend on the Jews. And so they have no place in this country. All of this is now accepted in a simple and clear fashion without any serious debate.

What is the meaning of this? Where is the connection between these two sermons? When were we more just—before the creation of the state or after? When we were weak or strong? I see this as a psychic wound and a breach of faith by those same leaders who spoke in such a way and by those political parties that changed their flag. The key point is the manner of casting off, of forgetting, of adapting to the new way. I do not bring the question of the Arabs before you because it is particularly painful to me. My intention is only to show you of what I speak: phony education. I am not here to speak of cruelty to man or coldheartedness to Arabs or of ruthlessness with respect to the Arab question, but rather about the switching of the flag at the head of our camp—without so much as a peep. And thus, a certain miasma settles in the bottom of one's soul . . .

How could our educators and politicians divert their attention from this admonition, which issued from such a loyal soul?

## XII

It is distressing that a certain tendency is on the rise among our people and receives very clear expression in the case before us: one standard for the Jews, and another for non-Jews. When *they* commit an outrage, it cries out to heaven. But when we commit such an act with our own hand, it is an imperative that could not have been avoided. And if there is something about it that might assist our national revival, then that is well and good, and should be praised a hundred times every day.

Those who dreamt of our national revival—Pinsker, Ahad Ha-am and the ones who came after them—complained a great deal about our national-social, or national-political, weakness; at times, they cast doubt on the ability of the "flock" to become a "nation," according to the national-political education that it received in the nineteenth century. (Their words on this matter require closer examination). Just yesterday we earned the right to create a national movement capable of conquest—and today we speak of those weaker than us in the language of aggressive nations who designate the national movement of a minority that is not convenient to them as dark and "destructive," or as an "enemy of freedom and progress." Some of our writers and politicians speak of the Arabs—employing the language of the British, French, and Americans (and not the most clever or decent among them)—as purveyors of a nationalism typical of Oriental peoples. As if this nationalism is nothing but the product of inciters and seducers, demagogues thirsty for power—a foreign branch, "a passing contagion," as is said, along with other descriptions, in writing devoted to the national question in the "backwater" world that is now awakening from national slumber.

Sometimes it seems to me that just as the Arabs in the State of Israel and the broader Arab world misrepresent the Jewish national idea, so too do we fail to represent accurately the struggle of the Arabs to realize their nationalism. In their eyes, we are "agents" of the West. And Moscow spreads the flag of the West over the East too. Meanwhile, for us, they are backward "Asiatics," tools in the hands of exploitative effendis and of this or that state that uses them and their nationalism for their own purposes. When we fight for our revival, we are men of vision, heralding a national renaissance that has great value for the entire human race. And the Arabs who fight for their existence in their land of residence—what is the name, or names, by which we call them and their wars? As Moshe Smilansky has written: "Our brothers, the children of Israel, who return to their land after two thousand years of Exile, are daring ones;[59] they are national heroes worthy of the world's support—whereas the Arabs who return to their property after two or three years of exile are infiltrators, whose blood it is not forbidden [to spill]."

There is reason to fear that the plight of the refugees, and all that is bound up within it, will add to this notion of a "new national morality" that is steadily gaining strength in the State of Israel—and which is not new at all. In fact, it is like the man who conquers and subdues, and thus not like the Jewish morality of which the Jewish people has been proud from its inception—nor like the morality of the "new Jew" that some of our thinkers had envisaged in their haste in recent times.

As an example, take the manifesto of one of the founders of Nahalal, Shmuel Dayan,[60] who sought to defend the right of "Hebrew labor" in the State of Israel—that is, after the Arab refugees were not permitted to return to their homes within its borders and only 20 percent of the Arabs who had lived in the country up to 1948 remained there. It is important to ensure that the Jewish National Fund and the Jewish Agency and their settlements employ "only Jews and not Arabs"—according to Dayan's article, "Our Attitude to the Arabs," which was written in opposition to R. Binyomin and Hayim Greenberg,[61] who questioned this principle of "Hebrew labor."

This writer—like all Zionist writers and leaders of the state—insists on the uniqueness of the situation of the Jewish people in the State of Israel, as well as the state's tasks:

> The task of uniting the fragmentary tribes into a nation and reviving an ancient language that is incomprehensible to most of the people—no other nation has this kind of task. From this we understand that the standard assumptions about national minorities in all aspects of their life will not be part of this discussion, because what is understood and justified in normal countries and nations is not always justified and proper in our situation today in Israel.*

Even if we assume that there isn't a bit of exaggeration in emphasizing the lack of similarity, doesn't this lack of similarity serve to cover up an ethical, social, and political injustice done to another people, or to a national minority that was not molded by the same experiences as the Jews? Our writer denies everything; Jacob has no sin:

> Did we commit a wrong to the Arabs by taking their land, homes, and all their possessions? *Arabs as individuals surely suffered, but the Jewish people committed no wrong to the Arab people.* They waged a war against us, sought to throw us into the sea. We defended our lives, fought, and won. We acted like a man who is drowning and does everything in his power to save himself. *We pushed the Arabs from their homes to their neighbors and brothers by race,* and saved ourselves. Because we were slaughtered and destroyed in the land of the Gentiles, we acted to save ourselves. *And the Arabs, we shoved the Arabs to the homes of their brethren,* who have countries empty of people and amongst whom they can easily take root. Meanwhile, we can repair somewhat the injustice done to the individual. We fought and are fighting for our existence as individuals and as a nation. Those amongst us who do not agree with the ways of this war of survival are prepared to surrender, it seems, our existence as individuals and as a nation. Their Zionism is not comprehensible, because it is not consistent. Hayim Greenberg and R. Binyomin, who claim that there is racial discrimination, must admit that until the creation of the state they were parties to this discrimination. And now they argue against it.

If we did push the Arabs from their homes *as individuals and as a nation,* then the "Jewish people" committed an injustice to the "Arab

---

*Ha-po'el ha-tsa'ir, 45 (nos. 44–45).

people"—to Arabs as "individuals and as a people." A war on the battle-field is one thing, but the expulsion of men and women who were not combatants is another.

Our writer does not have the ability—which is typical of Zionist writers—to distinguish between morality and the political revival of a nation. Is anyone who assists in the political revival of the Jews in the Land of Israel, by definition, moral? And whoever obstructs is amoral?

> What after all is moral? To help the other, the person who suffers, who lacks a home or means of existence, who lacks hope, who lacks roots, who is oppressed, who comes from far-away countries without the language, who needs to break from his native traditions, to get used to the blazing sun and physical labor, and so forth. The people who suffer are the new ʿolim [Jewish immigrants]. Meanwhile, nothing of the sort happened to the Arabs residing in this land. Are not the contributions of Jews from abroad to the State of Israel intended to build up the tribes of Israel into a unified nation in its own home? The Zionist Organization collected contributions from the Jewish people and built Nahalal so that it would serve as a foundation and home for the ʿolim, who come to rebuild and root themselves in this country. And when Nahalal employs ʿolim, it is fulfilling its moral obligation to the nation. Tell us, please, what is in your heart and then we will know what your Zionism is and what your morals are. Is it for the Jews to be murdered and slaughtered in Exile, or is it to build up the Jewish people and the homeland? There is no halfway morality. The economic framework for our existence still needs to be built; it is not easy and demands sacrifices for an extended period of time. Political and economic morality will be measured by how much it serves Jews who have no bread to eat, who dwell in tattered tents, who fled various countries, including Arab countries, enduring physical and emotional torture and the expropriation of their property. *If this enterprise of ours—the "ingathering of the exiles" and the building up of a national economy—is not moral, then what is morality?*

An eye for an eye, an expropriation from an Arab for an expropriation from a Jew—this is morality? "To be murdered and slaughtered in Exile"—is there no choice but to expel Arabs from their land, to push and shove them out of their homes, as our writer would put it? Is it not possible "to build up the Jewish people and the homeland" *without* committing a grave injustice to the Arabs? And if there is no "halfway morality," can an injustice to one's fellow man be called morality?

If the idea of Hebrew labor was needed at the outset to lay down the roots of the Jewish people in the land of Israel, is it not possible to surrender this goal after 1948 when the Arabs have become a small minority, and after Jews have taken over their homes and property?* Or does morality dictate that even after 1948, one must discriminate between different kinds of citizens in the state in the realm of labor? Where are the Ten Commandments of this "national morality" in whose name our writer and his friends uphold the State of Israel?

Very troubling, indeed, is this "morality"—and frightening is the faith of our writer that:

> [t]he Americans will understand our situation, which is so clear and pronounced. And they will judge us positively, because if they regarded favorably those associated with "Brit Shalom," whom Magnes brought before them in his day, they would not have agreed to the creation of a Jewish state or to provide constant support for it to this day.[62]

The confidence in America shown by this exponent of "national morality" extends to this point: America will always understand discrimination against Arabs in Jewish settlements sponsored by the Jewish National Fund, etc.; it will always accept the reality of hundreds of thousands of Arabs living outside of the border of the State of Israel; it will answer "amen" in response to this "national morality" and "provide constant support" for it!†

---

*Michael Assaf—who does not believe in A. Sharon's plans for the "exodus of the Arabs," though in fact he accepts the idea of "transfer" in principle but has doubts about its practical implementation—comments in his article "The Bad Myth of the Military Government" (*Be-terem*, 15 May 1953) about the "problem of idolatry": "My heart goes out to my persecuted friend, Avraham Sharon! He lost all hope to earn the right to sit in a jail of the Jewish state, because of his romantic, fanatic defense of 'Hebrew labor.' Because the Employment Bureau controls all labor in the State of Israel and faithfully performs its task of protecting organized labor paid according to the Histadrut tariffs. At any point where there is an 'opportunity' to push out an Arab laborer, even a veteran worker with a large family, he is pushed out. There are so many diligent ones in this work that I am sure that if R. A. Sharon were called upon to assist them, he would rise up against them with all of his noble soul, which remains detached from reality." If I am not mistaken, the opening of the doors of the Histadrut (the General Federation of Labor in the Land of Israel) to Arabs a short while ago greatly improved their position in the country's workforce.

†Surely our writer could not write his words about this "constant support" in 1954–55, after a change took place in U.S. policy toward Israel and the Middle East. Even prior to this, only the truly naïve could claim that the support of America for the State of Israel in 1948 was "constant."

A last word about morality between Jew and Arab. The period between 1948 and now* places in question the very morality of Judaism itself. Is the morality of Judaism in which Jews have taken such pride, both religious and secular—that great joy in which "Israel" reveled as a result of its lack of appetite for iniquity, for doing wrong to its neighbor—is there nothing to this concern? Can our enemies and haters say of us that this is but the morality of *Galut,* the morality of a weak minority with its back to the wall, the morality of slaves, the morality of a group that does not have the ability to do what other normal groups do? So the Jew was given sovereignty in a small patch of land—and he acts like any Gentile under the sun. Your enemy lashed out, so kill him. He killed one or more from your camp, go seek him out and kill him—and his family and the family of his family. Because this is the "only language" understandable to your enemy.

---

*I wrote the bulk of this appendix two years before the Kibya episode. On the night of 14–15 October 1953, an "armed band" from the State of Israel undertook an attack on a village in Transjordan in which more than sixty people, including women and children, were killed—in retaliation for an attack by Arabs from Transjordan on 13 October on a single house in a Jewish village in which a woman and her two children were killed in their sleep (and others injured). The Kibya episode disturbed Diaspora Jewry greatly, but they did not hasten to criticize it in public in order not to cause harm to the State of Israel.

In the words of the author of the "Seventh Column," Nathan Alterman, it was important to give expression to the thought of those children of Abraham, Isaac, and Jacob who did not count themselves among the concealers of this episode: "Perhaps He knows / Who sits on high / Why it was with all its signs? / We labor to defend today / A dark act / Whose face is not His face / An act whose repudiation is not subject to debate among us, but we all secretly / Say it was necessary and imperative / And yet it *could have* been done differently / An act that those among us know / Can only with eyes forced shut / be pushed among the noble deeds / Among which we labor to place it squarely. / Only the celestial heavens know how and why / We cling to our righteousness rather than accept it as a wrong ... / What would the State and nation stand to lose / If we stood up and rejected it / In a loud voice in front of all / God only knows when we became reticent / To call it by a name that is known, and tremulous / And when we began to allow foreign preachers / To say what we should be saying in Hebrew. / And when we began to exercise ourselves so much / Not to open our mouths, Heaven forbid / Even though in this way (as was already proven) / We give it more salience rather than less. / For also from the legal standpoint / Not just from the instrumental or logical standpoint / We must object to the objectionable in order that / the just and wise be doubly affirmed." "Al devekut she-ena bimkoma," *Davar,* 23 October 1953.

In the same issue of *Davar,* M. A. opens his article "The Kibya Incident" with this paragraph: "The act of retaliation in the village of Kibya has stirred up debate anew about a whole range of ethics, policies, and instrumentalities, and so forth. In particular, debate has been revived around the question of restraint, and the question of a

We knew that we could not undertake an unjust act. And in our hearts we believed that we did not want to commit an injustice to another. We have no evil inclination to do wrong. And there were those who hung the essence of Judaism on the inability to do wrong.† And it has been revealed in retrospect that this is but a lie. I shall not exaggerate and say that "my sin is *worse* than all the other nations'." But I must say, to my regret, that "my sin is *like* all the other nations'." We have become like the Gentiles. Just

---

moral state within the global framework of nation-wolves, as well as the question of yearning for Arab-Israel peace and the impact of this incident on these yearnings." And further: "There is no reason in the world—moral, political, instrumental, and so forth— that Israel (the State of Israel) should not be enjoined to live in peace with its Arab neighbors. Each reason on its own—and all the reasons together—require of us peace. 'Thou shall not murder?' But how will the State of Israel live and survive if, from Cairo (haven of the Mufti and Nazi war criminals) to London and Washington, they are shocked and appalled by this one-sidedness?" And more: "Restraint and the destruction of the fabric of our life bit by bit, cell by cell over the years—how long can we preserve ourselves in this way?"

And yet with all of the difficulty in this complicated matter, the commandment not to murder, with all that is contained within it, still stands in place. In the language of our author: This is not a moral commandment alone, but a "political" and "instrumental" one as well.

†The words of David Frishman [Hebrew author and Zionist critic: 1859–1922] can serve as an example. Although we do not derive our deep thoughts or Jewish concerns from him, and because he spoke innocently and without any sense of the present stakes, there are in his words faithful testimony to the thinking of a simple Jew in his day, a Jew who sought to define Judaism as "a feeling of uprightness, or better yet, of the inability to do wrong to the other. This is it. If this uprightness came from music, I would say that the Jews have a better sense of hearing, while other peoples are not so musical. This Judaism came into the world and raised up a family from among the families of the world, and this family was filled up with a feeling of uprightness in every corner that it turned, night and day, and it could not, even if it wanted to, commit an evil deed." The Jewish nation "is distinguished by the fact that it has no ability to do wrong or evil to anyone, and we find that as a result, there developed within it a norm of absolute uprightness." And further, "it is possible that in the entire world, he [the Jew] is now the only representative of that idea. It is possible that this has become a stumbling block on the path of the rest of the nations." And further, "it is possible that this is the secret of the hatred that the nations instinctively feel for this nation, because it is the only one that still reminds them without saying a word of that old and worn version of silent morality and of justice and uprightness and of caution before doing wrong, wickedness, and evil" ("Al ha-Yahadut," *He-'atid* 4 [1914], 155). As for this hatred, will it pass from the world when the Jews will "earn" for themselves the ability to do evil, when they will be like all the evildoers in the world?

as they have done to us, we do to them. As has been said already, the world—the world of Esau and Ishmael—has no right to preach morality to the Jews. The world is no better than they—and too bad for that. Are Jews better and finer than the world, from every standpoint and at every moment on the stage of history? You may answer: The world, at the end of the day, is worse than the Jews. And my question is, Even if Israel is better in general, is that true in that which concerns us here?*

There are those who say that after 1948 an opening was created for Israel to become a Chosen People. Thus, David Ben-Gurion teaches us that "as long as we were merely a dispersed and scattered Diaspora people, removed from any territorial framework, subservient to foreign rule and dependent on the mercy of foreigners, there was no objective possibility for us to become the 'Chosen People.' Only 'Israel' sitting in its land and self-sufficient can ascend the rung to become a Chosen People."

My question is: Does not the plight of the refugees caused by 'Israel,' which now renews itself as a state, significantly delay the ascent of Israel to that noble and desired rank? Is it not the first negative commandment incumbent on any Chosen People: Do not uproot a man from his possessions, whether he be a member of your people or not? Everyone (Jew or not) is called "man." Do not build yourself up from the destruction of one who is weaker than you. Conquer your impulse to dominate, as well as all lesser impulses, and perhaps you can become a Chosen People.

This episode weighs very heavily upon us. The sun of Israel could have risen to the fullness of its light in 1948, without obstruction. There was no need, even in practical terms, to obstruct the light. In fact, from an ethical standpoint, an obstruction cannot be removed even when it serves a necessary function in the real world.

## XIII

Regardless of whether the Hibat Zion[63] and Zionist movements acknowledged the reality of an Arab majority in Palestine at their inception or not, or whether they delved deeply into the "Arab question" to fulfill their Zionism or not, it was impossible to ignore this reality in 1887, in 1917, and all the more so in 1948. The world knew of this reality, and so did we. We

*"Am segulah," *Davar*, 29 October 1954.

considered it and then accepted it. We said to the world and ourselves: We'll find a way out, a path of "common existence" for Jew and Arab in Palestine. Who among the leaders and writers of Zionism did not promise this path of *peace and honor,* whose guiding principle is total equality rooted in a single law for Jew and Arab in a future state of Palestine? Not only "democratic," "progressive," "radical," and socialist Zionists (including some religious Jews), but the leader of militant Zionism, the Zionism of both banks of the Jordan River, whose opponents have branded it as "imperialist" and "fascist": Zev Jabotinsky,[64] who was always among those who promised a path of peace with respect to the Arab question in the country. Even Avraham Sharon—the father of the negators of the Diaspora among Zionists who arouses passions with his call for the *exodus of Arabs* from the State of Israel for the sake of both Jew and Arab—wrote several years prior to the creation of the State of Israel:

> We Zionists must assume responsibility ourselves to solve the question of the Jews in its entirety. That is, over the course of a reasonable period of time, we will settle all of our people, or almost all of them, on the territory of Mandatory Palestine, west and east. *And this will be done on the condition, and with sufficient international guarantee, that its other residents will not be harmed.* If in the future twelve out of seventeen million of our own will support themselves in this land, *two million of the other people* will also be able to support themselves here.*

In the past two generations, almost every Jewish writer who was drawn to this question repeated this promise to the Arabs, and if only by allusion, it was taken for granted.†

If one had said to David Ben-Gurion, Chaim Weizmann, Yitzhak Ben-Zvi,[65] and their friends before 1948 that they were soon to stand as the leaders of a State of Israel that did not permit Arab refugees—men, women, and children—to return to their possessions, and thus *uprooted* and rendered them homeless, would they not have seen in this claim a contemptible libel

---

*Torat ha-Tsiyonut ha-akhzarit* (1944), 49.

†For example, Chaim Nachman Bialik in his lecture "Erets Yisra'el" (1929–30): "Right now, there is in Erets Yisra'el enough room for two peoples, as there will be in the future. We do not want to push the Arabs from the land. We do not say 'let's expel them to the desert, like Abraham the Patriarch did in his day to his son Ishmael.' In fact, they settled in this land and were laid bare in it." *Devarim she-be'al peh* [Tel Aviv: Dvir, 1935], 1:156.

of the haters of Israel and Zion who aimed to desecrate the name of Israel and besmirch Zionism in the world? Would they not have dismissed this prophecy with disgust? For the writings of the founding fathers of Zionism (of all stripes), as well as the Zionist press in Hebrew and all other languages that Jews used in the past two generations, are open to all who want to peruse them. Is it necessary to mention the abundance of information in them about solving the Arab Question without inflicting any damage whatsoever on their rights or property?

If Aharon David Gordon[66] were living in 1948, would he have permitted the children of Abraham, Isaac, and Jacob to dwell in expropriated and conquered Arab homes? Even if their expelled owners received compensation? What would this prophet of the religion of labor have done, for example, with the newspaper of his party, *Ha-poʿel ha-tsaʿir,* which declared (in an article by its editor) that the State of Israel "will not return refugees."* Would he have asked, as I do, how is it possible to say in the holy tongue

---

*"And our relations with the Arabs," A. D. G[ordon] writes in 'Letters to the Diaspora,' "to the extent that they depend on us, must be based on new grounds, on the same grounds that we designate in these letters as *exalted national and cosmic, universal humanitarian* interests" (*Kitve A. D. G.* [Jerusalem, 1952], 1:553). "And not only are relations between a man and his neighbor an important measure of truth, but also relations between one nation and another. 'Nation shall not lift sword against nation [Isaiah 2:4]— this was the verdict of truth that love did not fulfill. The truth will come and be fulfilled. Through the force of truth, we shall find a path toward a shared life with the Arabs and shared labor that is a blessing to the two sides.... We and they are natural allies. More than ethnic brotherhood from within unites us, hatred from the outside toward our two nations unites us" ("Ha-kongres," in ibid., 203).

A. D. G[ordon] is also sure that "apart from their right to live and work (in Palestine), the Arabs have only a historical right to this land, like us, except that our historical right is undeniably greater than theirs." With this degree of confidence, he demands that we be "very cautious in our relations with the Arabs, in purchasing land and the like, without trampling their human rights or forcing actual works from their land, etc. ... In general, it is incumbent upon us to maintain humane relations with the Arabs, and not relate to them in purely negative terms—just as the anti-Semites relate to us in purely negative terms" ("Avodatenu me-ʿata," in ibid., 244).

As for his demand to arrive at 'cosmic' humane relations with the Arabs in practice (for example, in his "Yesodot le-takanot le-moshav ʿovdim, in ibid., 460): "Regarding the choice of land, that which is allocated to the Arabs must be uppermost in the minds of the moshav (Nahalal), not just for its own benefit but for the benefit of the Arabs.... In general, all that the moshav can do to help Arab workers, we must do without taking into account whether their relations with the moshav are good or bad." At times, he appears to be opening a path to a solution to the Arab problem that is *far from the* "thou shall not restore the refugees?"† A state that seeks to elevate its people to the status of a *people of humanity*‡ locks its gate to men, women, and children who belong to a "foreign national minority?" Would he have kept silent or perhaps blurted out like his friends and disciples at Degania, Nahalal, and elsewhere that "we have no stain on our hands, we are righteous and have not sinned?" Doesn't the pride of Israel lie in the fact that the gates of "the religion of labor"[67] are open to each and every worker or to each and every future worker? In fact, the vision of a humane people applies, in Gordon's thought and in the thought of those that come after him, only to Israel. According to this vision, the Jewish people must purify its *Galut* "filth," its parasitism (to which they cling, in exaggerated fashion)—as if only Jews are human, only Jews will achieve the rank of a

---

*humane and cosmic ideals* [he values]. We cannot ignore this "opening" in Gordon's thought. For example, in "Pitaron lo-ratsyonali" (ibid., 96): "It is an undeniable fact that this land is ours as long as the Jewish people is alive and has not forgotten it. On the other hand, we cannot decide that the Arabs have no stake in it. The question is: in what sense and on what scale is this land ours, and in what ways is it theirs? And how to reconcile the claims of the two sides? The question is not so simple and requires a great deal of study. One thing that can be said with certainty is that the land will belong to the side that is more able to suffer on it and work it—or in fact suffers on it and works it more than the other. Logic dictates this, justice dictates this, and the nature of things dictates this as well."

Was the preacher of the religion of labor so certain that the "nature of things" between Jew and Arab would always be of a piece with "justice"; that is, not with the justice of a group or with that of a certain individual, but justice as it really is: "universal human" justice, justice between one people and another, justice between a majority and a minority, between the victor and the vanquished?

†"Ha-mefurash veha-satum," *Ha-po'el ha-tsa'ir,* 27 Sivan 5703.

‡Lovely were the words of A. D. G[ordon] in this matter which I heard from his mouth at the founding conference of the union of "Tse'ire tsiyon" and "Ha-po'el ha-tsa'ir" in Prague in 1920. [Rawidowicz here is referring to the union of two socialist-Zionist parties that would form the foundation of the Labor Zionist movement in Palestine.] Great was their encouragement for both Jews and Arab in the days ahead: "If there is no humane people, there will be no humane man, for there is no isolated individual. Who, if not us, the children of Israel, must reckon with this truth? We who learned first that man is created in God's image must move forward and say: the nation must be created in the image of God. And not because we are better than others, but rather because we bore and suffered all that was placed on our shoulders. For our tribulations, which have no parallel in the world, we earned the right to be the first to arrive at this teaching, and through the force of our tribulations we will find the force of this teaching." (*Kitve A. D. G.,* 260).

humane people. But when this people fails to reach this exalted level, does it do so by failing to recognize the "image of God"[68] in that group of people facing it? How have we forgotten—and so quickly—the lovely declarations we've been making for the last two generations about peaceful coexistence, some even said brotherly existence, between Jew and Arab in the Land of Israel? We feared that the opposing side would not want such peaceful coexistence, but is it not we who do not allow the Arabs to settle among us on their land in the Land of Israel? Who did not answer "amen" after every prayer for a single constitution for Jew and Arab? And if we forgot all this, didn't the world, including the Arabs, also forget it and continue to forget it?

Do not say: the Arab countries attacked the State of Israel in 1948—the seven countries that attacked, on the one hand, and the hundreds of thousands of Arab residents of Palestine, on the other. Do not say: there is no certainty in politics; it depends on the spur of the moment and circumstance. At first, we made declarations and promises, but afterward, we did not follow through. At first, we did not expel the Arabs, and in retrospect, since they left of their own accord, why should we bring them back? Zionism did not yearn for an expulsion of Arabs from Palestine. It was forbidden to do so. And it was not in its own interest to validate, with the royal stamp that it received in 1948, the retrospective expulsion of Arabs. There are principles among nations, between Jew and Arab, that are not time-bound, that must be preserved at all times and in all places. The demands of the hour are a challenge for those who meet the challenge, and a pit and snare to those who fail the test.

## XIV

Would that the true face of morality itself could have encouraged the government of the State of Israel to move quickly toward an examination of its policy toward the Arabs—and as I say this, I must add that I do not believe, God forbid, that my morality is better than that of the policymakers of the State of Israel, for whom 1948 and its exigencies compelled them to impose that fateful verdict on the Arabs within its borders. But now that morality alone cannot foment the desired revolution in the state's policy, it is necessary to make clear to the State of Israel the huge practical danger in a delayed resolution to the refugee question.

The state cannot delude itself with "dreams" of that which goes by the name of "transfer": the exchange of Jews of Arab countries for Arab refugees and their brethren who remained in the State of Israel.* Population transfers are undertaken either (1) forcibly by dictatorial regimes in which a population is moved from one country to another without being asked, "What do you want to do?" or (2) willingly by those being exchanged. Neither of these paths is the one before us in this case. Even if it were possible to undertake a "transfer," it would not bring much advantage to the State of Israel at present ( for the state will not be built by immigrants from Arab countries who have not answered the call for an ingathering of the exiles thus far and who would arrive to its shores as exiles without money or vocation in most cases). On the contrary, this proposal ( for transfer) has the potential to endanger the well-being of some of our Diaspora communities in the East and the West, now and in the foreseeable future, on the other. For all intents and purposes, the Jewish communities in Arab countries are at liberty to choose their own fate. The State of Israel cannot treat them as if they belong to it; that is, by forcing them to leave their country of residence, as part of a transfer. If it [the State of Israel] commenced such an "operation," there would be reason to fear that some countries, and not only in Asia and Africa, would help themselves to their own "transfer plans," or at least half a plan.[69] They would expel their Jews, whether the State of Israel was prepared to accept them or not. And they would ask:

---

*Avraham Sharon, the most "logical" and consistent of the negators of the Diaspora, is faithful to himself and his "cruel" logic when he links his demand for an exodus of Arabs—the Arab remnant—from the State of Israel to a "transfer" plan for the Arab refugees. "And thus I always insist that we do not have the correct answer to the demand to return the refugees that issues from the mouth of our enemy. We do not have the ability to return the Arabs who left. Rather, it is imperative that our answer take the form of a counterclaim: we must demand the departure of the Arabs who remained. To a certain extent, these arguments are interdependent. The only logical guard against their return is their departure. If for the past four years we had demanded—at least theoretically, in the gentlest and softest way—the departure of those who remained with us, we would not be compelled at all to return those outside; the demand for their departure would be based on security grounds. If we were to declare that on these same grounds, there is no possibility of returning refugees because they constitute an enemy, hostile, and antagonistic presence, then the question would arise: And those who remain in our state: in what way are they different from their brethren? Are not our people members of a different tribe altogether?" ("He'arot diplomatiyot shel lo-diplomat," *Be-terem* 4 [1953], 169).

Why are we undertaking this act of transfer? If the State of Israel does not send us anything in exchange for our citizens, or does not want an exchange, why should we lose?[70] In short, the "solution" [of transfer must be altogether removed from consideration, both in terms of Arab refugees outside of the country, and all the more so, regarding the remaining Arabs in the State of Israel. Here][71] the "solution" of assimilation (that is, assimilating the remaining Arabs in the state among the children of Abraham, Isaac, and Jacob) would be injurious. "That which is hateful to you, do not do to your neighbor."[72] From our beginnings, we fought every one who came to assimilate us. We saw assimilation as an oppressive act, as the murder of our soul, and self-assimilation as a moral sickness; we fought for our right to live as we were, preserving our distinctive visage, our national visage, our way of life, and thought, etc. Heaven forbid if we do the same grave evil to the Arab remnant in the State of Israel.*

## XV

Earlier, when the armistice between the Arab countries and the State of Israel was arranged,[73] the following should have been declared: every Arab man and woman who left the country with the outbreak of war is permitted to return to their possessions—or at the very least, they will be permitted to do so after the signing of a peace treaty between the state and the Arab countries, excluding those Arabs who have no desire or ability to be loyal citizens of the State of Israel, indeed, and who would endanger

---

*I am sorry that some of those drawn to the question of Jew and Arab at this time—especially in the State of Israel—find the solution in the assimilation of the Arab within the Jew. We must emphasize that there is no novelty in this "solution." Even a national Jew like Ahad Ha-'am, who rejected any form of assimilation by Jews (and permitted only a competitive kind of imitation of the Gentile), failed on this score and did not hesitate to permit the Arabs that which he forbade the children of Abraham, Isaac, and Jacob; that is, to hope that they would do this "disgraceful" deed: "The Arab question. After we become a cultural force in the land [Palestine] in the spirit of Judaism, it is possible that the Arabs will assimilate within us. Have they not inhabited this land for a long time? Perhaps some of them come from our people" ("Maskanot," *Kol kitve Ahad Ha-'am* [1947], 479).

But how will the evolution of a "cultural force in the land in the spirit of Judaism" lead to the assimilation of Arabs? What is the nature of the "spirit of Judaism" that will prompt the loss of a nation's essential character and hasten the assimilation of the Arab minority into the Jewish majority?

the security of the state. A declaration of this sort would surely have assisted in achieving a peace treaty. In retrospect, the gates of return and repentance were never locked.[74]

The State of Israel must fix this injustice. It affects the very soul of the state, the very soul of "Israel." The presence of the Arab refugees from the State of Israel is a blessing to those Arab countries that desire the destruction of the State of Israel—and a curse to the Jews. It would be comforting to the Arab countries to have the world (or the U.N.) settle these refugees in some region, a kind of "refugee-land" and haven for the Arab refugees that will serve as a monument of injustice against the State of Israel and the Jewish people wherever they may be. Or, it might disperse the refugees among the Arab countries, in which they will kindle (of their own will or not) the flame of hatred for the country that forced them from their land. The entire world will sit as judge over the resolution of this matter; perhaps the world itself could be judged tolerant and defer this matter year after year. Which the Jews can *not* do: they cannot afford to delay this resolution in any way. In fact, there can be no real resolution that does not entail the *complete elimination* of the refugee question. Every additional hour that this question remains alive in the world is a further blemish on the moral image of the Jewish people and heightens the danger to its future existence.

The question of these refugees is not an Arab question; it is a *Jewish question,* a question that 1948 placed upon the Jewish people. The Jewish people must deliver this problem from the world with all deliberate speed and thoroughness. Let not a single Arab refugee from the State of Israel remain in the world. This is an existential imperative for the State of Israel, from which it can not flinch.

Accordingly, I dare to propose to the government of the State of Israel that it assume the moral—and terribly difficult—path. From an emotional, political, social, economic, and military standpoint, the difficulty of the solution has not diminished at all. It requires nothing less than this: opening the gates of the state to Arab refugees after the Arab countries have arrived at a peace treaty with it (excluding those Arabs who endanger the security of the state). The State of Israel should appoint a committee of inquiry for refugees that includes members from outside the State of Israel (such as representatives of the U.N.), in order to show the world that the State of Israel is the state of "Israel," the Jewish people. Then the world would see how the Jewish people rectifies an injustice and solves the problem of the refugees.

I know well what has been oft-repeated: the State of Israel is still beset by deep economic troubles and requires a great deal of foreign assistance that has not yet been adequately provided. Moreover, more than forty million enemies surround her, whose animosity was deepened by the same "plight of the refugees." And the economic and security difficulties will multiply when the Arab refugees are permitted to return. Despite all this, it is hard for me to imagine that the return of several hundred thousand refugees will really endanger the existence of the state (which is prepared, it appears, to open its gates to one hundred thousand refugees, and maybe more, when the Arab countries reach a peace agreement with it).[75] The return of the refugees will burden the state, not destroy it. It is necessary for the state to take upon itself this large burden, and in particular *eliminate* by its own hand the very difficult problem of the refugees. The failure to return them will be far more burdensome.

Defenders of the plight of the refugees, including those among the Gentile nations, claim that if those hundreds of thousands of Arabs had not left Palestine in 1948, the State of Israel would not have arisen at all. And if they be permitted to return to settle in the State of Israel, it will be destroyed. Is this an argument of defense on behalf of the State of Israel? Reflect on it well and you will see that they are making a mockery of the dream of Zionism at its core. These defenders affirm that they never *believed in the dream of Zionism*. They always knew that it could not be undertaken without destroying the Arabs in the land of Israel. In their view, there was no Zionism to speak of between 1884 and 1948. Its goals were in fact nothing but an illusion.

State of Israel, beware of defenders of this sort and their arguments in your defense! Don't the leaders of the state and its representatives everywhere speak of a population of *four, five, or six million souls* in the state, sometimes adding "at least" to that number? If the State of Israel can only survive on the condition (that of the children of Gad and Reuben)[76] that those hundreds of thousands of refugees *not return* to their property, will the vision of Zionism, along with its scope and goals, inspire much faith in the future in the hearts of Jews and Gentiles alike?

I am ignorant in military and security matters, but I do know one thing: practically speaking, five or six hundred thousand Arab refugees from the State of Israel outside of its borders are much more dangerous to the state than five or six hundred thousand additional Arab citizens within its borders—even if most or all of them were a "fifth column," which they are not. Are they a danger to the state? Yes, they are a danger in the state, but they are also a danger outside of the State; and this latter danger is many times more serious than that within the state. Any aspiration that an Arab "fifth column" may have regarding the State of Israel is nothing compared to the aspiration of those hundreds of thousands of refugees who dream night and day, by virtue of their stateless existence, of the possibility of creating a state *right now,* of realizing this goal in the immediate future.

The State of Israel will not be redeemed by arguments of the following sort: "The Arabs have a number of unpopulated countries of their own, and we only have one little state." Arab states are not populated; this is one matter. The rights of the Arab refugees vis-à-vis the State of Israel is another matter. Or when it is said: "The houses of the refugees are now taken." What cries out to be heard is this: How were they occupied? The hand that takes is the hand that will return. Land cannot just be stolen, any land from any landowner. The ingathering of the exiles does not depend on the refugees; may it not come to pass that in our own quarters, we seek to bring the ingathering about completely and quickly in this age at the expense of several hundred thousand displaced and neglected refugees. It is better to repair an evil later, and with many sacrifices, than to let it fester all the way to the heart of heaven.

Sometimes, when there is trouble, a gain results at a future date. And sometimes when there is an apparent profit, there is subsequently trouble.

The State of Israel can ask the U.N., as well as America (and the Jews within it), to participate in solving the *economic problem* bound up with returning the refugees to its borders—and I am certain [that they would respond] with an open hand. Such would be a new direction in the State of Israel's policy regarding Jewish-Arab relations. The details of the arrangement are best left to experts in the many practical questions connected to this question, which is not my expertise. But certainly the arrangement would bring about a great triumph for the State of Israel. All the arguments of the Arab countries and their friends in the world would completely disappear. The Arab countries would be compelled to acknowledge the existence of the State of Israel and arrive at a peace treaty with it. The boycott against the State of Israel in Arab countries would lose its political and economic rationale. The moral standing of the State of Israel would rise dramatically. All the nations of the world would know that the vision that

Isaiah son of Amoz prophesied in the days of the kings of Judah—Uzziah, Jotham, Ahaz, and Hezekiah—is no mere rhetoric.[77] It is alive and well in the State of Israel that was established in 1948. "Zion shall be redeemed with justice; and they that return of her with righteousness."[78] "They that return" refers, on the one hand, to the children of Abraham, Isaac, and Jacob; and on the other, to the children of Ishmael: justice to all, without any discrimination whatsoever. The people of Zion, "Jerusalem," will not pollute their hands with the filth of the spoils of a minority that is not of the covenant. They will not resort to taking by force. Whoever takes by force, the measure of justice is not with him.

The practical-minded will say: the return of the refugees to their land in the State of Israel is a dream, a utopia. But in fact, what is "utopian" is the total avoidance of the question of the refugees, delaying its resolution from year to year. It is dangerous to leave the resolution to the U.N. or to the Arabs. There is no other path than the elimination [of this problem]—and by Jews themselves.

Our soul has tired of that imaginary *realism* that governs relations between the nations and brings us, in every generation, to human slaughter and pushes us into the abyss of loss—of life and land alike. There is a kind of Realpolitik of the hour, which turns out to be a total disaster the next day. If there is hope that "out of Zion will go forth Torah,"[79] this Torah will go forth without any trace of that kind of "realism." It will be a Torah of faith in humanity, a Torah of one law governing the state and "the stranger who sojourneth in it"[80] (though the Arab who lives in the state of the Jew is *not* a stranger), as well as the refugees who live outside of its borders. This Torah is time-honored to us, and its time is now.

Never in their history did Jews force refugees into the world. Let not the State of Israel begin its path by forcing refugees into the world.

## XVI

My words of plea to the State of Israel, its government, parliament, and political parties regarding the abolition of the decree of the refugees do not stem from Arab-Oriental *romanticism*.

Throughout my life, I have never been counted among those who bestow glory on the Arabs either in the past or the present. I am very dubious about descriptions of the beneficence that the Arabs bestowed upon the Jewish people in the Middle Ages that held sway in history books (theirs *and* ours). The Arabs did not do to us what the Christian Church did, but most of their countries were not a Garden of Eden for Jews either. They heaped much scorn on the "eternal wanderer,"[81] and vehemently opposed his national revival. I cannot close my eyes to the persecutions that they inflicted on Jews in their lands: before the establishment of the state, and even more so after;[82] nor from the disturbances that they organized in the Jewish *Yishuv* in Palestine in the days of the British Mandate.[83] I do not trust them, just as I do not trust the Christians and their ethic of "love." It is not for their honor that I am anxious; it is for *our* honor. I am concerned for *our* soul, for the purity of the garment of Israel.

The *shadow of redemption* (or the *athalta de-Geulah*)[84] is not signaled for me in the spiritual and social crisis present in the state today nor in the realm of ethical relations among Jews in the state. Such a crisis will not last forever. The temporary clouds will pass, the skies over the state of Israel will be clear blue. For the Jews in the state, the sun of 1948 is greater than its shadow. The ample light in it dispels any shadow that steals into its domain, despite the dirges that are chanted in the State of Israel and in the Diaspora over the decline of the state. The main part of the shadow of 1948 is the relationship between Jew and Arab. There will be a shadow without sunlight as long as the State of Israel leaves refugees out in the world. The State of Israel's refugees are not the only refugees in the world at this time. Millions of refugees—of war, famine, Communism, and so forth— wander from place to place in the countries of the Far East.[85] But that which is acceptable to the world is not acceptable to Israel. It is simply not possible this way. However many operations the State of Israel has undertaken since 1948, the time has come to undertake the most exalted and difficult of them: the operation to eliminate the problem of the refugees. The God of Isaac and Jacob promised the conquerors of Canaan, and Joshua bin Nun at their helm, "great and goodly cities, which thou didst not build and houses full of all good things which thou didst not fill, and cisterns hewn out, which thou didst not hew, vineyards and olive trees, which thou didst not plant."* To *them,* not to the returners to Zion from 1881 or to the creators of the State of Israel in 1948. Would that there be fixed in the Declaration of the State of Israel from 1948 the passage from the Scroll of

---

* Deuteronomy 6:10–11.

Esther about the Jews of Shushan; namely, "the other Jews that were in the king's provinces," who "assembled to defend their lives," did not lay their hands on the spoils.[86]

To summarize: there should not be a single refugee from the State of Israel in the world. The Arab refugees should return to their homes, and your state should be pure, O Israel.

And you, Jewish writers in the State of Israel, educators and thinkers—rise and awaken and help the government of the State of Israel to undertake this operation. Save the honor of Israel and of the State of Israel; preserve its peace and the peace of its sons and daughters for generations to come: Open the gate!

If that will happen, there will be peace unto its sons and daughters. The generation of the victors in the State of Israel, the 1948 generation, will be sure of justice in this affair. May the days to come not demand that we impose a debt on our children and their children's children, and not decree that they pay four, five, and seventy-seven times for this "benefit," this "miraculous benefit" that came to their forefathers in 1948, and that they hold on to with all their might for their sake and for the sake of those who come after them.

May there not have to be among Jews in coming generations those who will call to justice the generation of the gatekeepers of the state who locked the gate to former residents of the land—and who thereby opened, through this closing, the door to their defamers and persecutors in surrounding countries. It is in your hands, guides of the current generation in the state, to safeguard those who will come after you from the verdict of that future day of retribution. May it not come, but if it does come, what will be the price that the children of our sons and daughters will pay?

## XVII

In my notebook from 1948, I found the following entry: If this year angels came to sing a song before the Holy One, would He silence them? The results of His handiwork are drowning in a sea of refugees, a sea that came about, either directly or directly, through the work of the most exalted among his Chosen People, who lived the life of a refugee for thousands of years. Would they sing a song today?[87] The Arab refugees did not inflict even a fraction of the evil upon the Jews that the Egyptians inflicted upon their ancestors for more than four hundred years. And when the Egyptians drowned, no voice of song was heard from on high.

And if the God of Israel will not silence them, and the angels will sing a song, and the poets of Israel will lavish praise on the lamb that was privileged to become a lion, and they will continue to place the "miracle" of the Arab refugees above the other "miracles" that happened to our forefathers over the generations, what will a Jew utter at that moment? What will he do in the future?

I have spoken at length with Jewish men and women from 1948 on about this matter of Jews and Arabs, and I have not yet been privileged to hear them say: "This is no time for song, either from angels on high or from the Jews who dwell below, so long as hundreds of thousands of uprooted refugees are divested of their homes." I have learned this much. Those who are not Zionists, and even those who are opponents of Zion and national Judaism, the new antisemites and the neo-traditionalists, sometimes "understand" the plight of the refugees and justify it more forcefully than those children of Israel whose heart was always faithful to Zion and its revival. These people too, who wash their hands of the 1948 episode, are fearful of inquiring into the matter adequately. I fear that it is impossible to find one out of a hundred Jews from the State of Israel (and not only there) who doubts the justice of the verdict of the refugees.

I also know this. Many in our ranks have said that my words regarding the relationship between Jew and Arab suffice to disqualify the entire project of "Babylon and Jerusalem." The latter will surely find something in my words pertaining to other matters that will assist them in disqualifying it. And I would not be worthy of writing in the language of "the herdsman and dresser of sycamores," the man from Tekoa and those who come after him,[88] had I not vanquished that which was in my heart in this matter, whether spoken or unspoken. A Hebrew writing to Hebrews in our language, to his people, whose face is not facing outward, must think and write with heartfelt candor. It is forbidden to hide anything. Gath does not understand it. And Ashkelon does not need it. The fear of the daughters of the Philistines is not upon it: "Lest they rejoice, the daughters of the uncircumcised."[89]

It is better that I should be the target of the arrow of every crossbow in "Israel" than I should hold my tongue and say: "Israel" has no sin. If "Israel" has sinned, then this sin is part of me. If blood has been spilled in "Israel" (and there are several types of bloodletting), if "Israel" has spilled blood outside of "Israel," then no Jew is able to say: my hands did not spill it.

Do not say that as long as a Jew cannot finish the blessing for the "miracle of the refugees," he cannot rejoice in the political renewal of "Israel," and thus has no place or stake in "Israel." Do not say if he does not answer "amen" to this blessing, the blessing of making refugees, of uprooting men, women, and children from their property, he is our enemy. Woe unto the last of the last who wraps himself in the splendor of his ancestors! He should ask: those who rose up in antiquity against kings who breached the wall, usurped the vineyard, and transgressed the border, were called "troublers of Israel" in the language of the aggressors[90]—but were they and their descendants the ones who caused trouble to Israel?

I have always had faith in Israel. And I pray: may the remnant of Israel not commit acts of injustice. May the Guardian of Israel protect this remnant, which became the foundation of the State of Israel, from the injustice and destruction [keliyah] now associated with it.

# EPILOGUE

*"Historical enquiry brings to light deeds of violence which took place at the origin of all political formation . . ."*

—Ernest Renan, "What Is a Nation?" (1882)

The motif of awakening one's people from a deep and dangerous slumber is, as scholars remind us, a familiar theme in the history of modern nationalism.[1] In the case of the Jews, a number of nineteenth-century journals edited by incipient nationalists bore titles anticipating or imploring a revival, a new dawn, or a reawakening.[2] Curiously, one of the sharpest expressions of this motif came in a Hebrew poem imploring Jews in Russia to embrace the culture and language of their country, to join more fully not the Jewish, but the Russian nation. Judah Leib Gordon's "Awaken, My People!" calls out to Jews:

> Awake, my people! How long will you sleep?
> The night has passed, the sun shines through.
> Awake, cast your eyes hither and yon.
> Recognize your time and your place.[3]

Rawidowicz made neither explicit reference to this poem nor resonated with its integrationist ethos, though he surely knew of Gordon's earlier plea for Jews to awaken from their slumber. Like Gordon, he believed that the Jews should recognize their "time and place"; namely, that they were at the dawn of a new era in their history (in Rawidowicz's case, the era of 1948). And, again like Gordon, he believed that the task of awakening Jews to the new realities of the day fell to intellectuals: in this instance, to those who must implore Israel's political leaders to permit the return of Palestinian refugees. But unlike Gordon and (and many early Jewish nationalists), he did not believe that slumber was the centuries-old condition of the Jews; rather, their current torpor was a new development, induced by the hypnotic force of Zionism.

Rawidowicz's mission in overcoming this torpor took form during a period in which the boundary between the scholar and the active public intellectual was becoming more fixed. Rawidowicz traversed this border throughout his entire life, moving from his detailed studies of Maimonides, Nahman Krochmal, and Feuerbach to his more public mission of reviving a Hebrew cultural nation. Animating him was the conviction that ideas truly mattered, that they were indispensable stimuli to important deeds, not merely malleable constructs molded by and for professional academics. Even though his death in 1957 coincided with the period that Daniel Bell called "the end of ideology"—entailing, among other effects, the segregation of the functions of the scholar and the intellectual—Rawidowicz never forsook this conviction nor the weighty sense of responsibility that accompanied it.

Above all, he remained wedded to the principle of integrity until his last days. This meant that he was compelled at times to give voice to discomfiting opinions that, in his view, honesty or the Jewish commonweal demanded; most provocative among them was his call for Palestinian Arab repatriation to the State of Israel. But "integrity" also meant that he saw his lifelong corpus as an organic unit, not divisible into isolated fragments or genres. *Bavel vi-Yerushalayim,* the culmination of three decades of thought, combined a re-narration of Jewish history, especially a revaluation of the First and Second Temples, with an extended ideological meditation on Jewish life in his day. We may well fault the unwieldy book for its unsystematic quality. But one cannot dispute that it sought to meld the historical and the contemporary—for instance, by coupling the claim that the figurative "Babylon" has historically been one of the two centers of the Jewish nation with the persistent call to recognize present-day Jews as a nation both in their territorial homeland and beyond. Nor, for that matter, can one dispute that Rawidowicz saw a close link between the Jewish Question, to which he devoted much of his adult life, and the Arab Question, to which he was attentive in his last years.

Here too one could find fault in his presentation. While seeking to introduce practical political considerations into his discussion of the refugee problem, he evinced little understanding of the massive social and political upheaval that repatriation would cause in the State of Israel and even less of the delicate art of diplomacy that would be required for any agreement between Israel and the Arab side (particularly if it dealt with the refugee question). Moreover, his unbending allegiance to a Jewish moral exceptionalism sounded chauvinistic at times, naïve at others.

For these and other reasons, it would be easy to compile a long list of Simon Rawidowicz's defects and dismiss him as irrelevant. But to do so is to miss the honesty, depth of perspective, and again integrity that informed his worldview. Rawidowicz understood what was momentous in the restoration of sovereignty to the Jews, how it marked the fulfillment of millennial aspirations and a remedy to the ravages of the recent past. But he refused to surrender to the intoxicating feeling of historical virtue and sacred mission that often envelops nationalist movements—and that enveloped the Zionist movement and much of the Jewish world in 1946. He saw through the celebratory mist of the day to observe that the triumph of the Jewish people entailed the fall of another. He also observed that indifference and amnesia vis-à-vis the refugees were the norm among Jews in the State of Israel and the Diaspora. In response, he offered as fundamental a critique of this indifference and amnesia as any Jewish thinker of his—or, perhaps, any—day.

In this regard, Rawidowicz represents a stark contrast to those Jews (especially, but not exclusively, those from the Diaspora), who identify themselves as supporters—indeed, as self-described "advocates" on behalf—of the State of Israel. These advocates routinely turn a deaf ear to critics, branding opponents as misinformed and ill-intentioned while justifying or ignoring transgressions against Palestinians. They often convey the sense that the defense of Israel's position hinges on the diminution or denial of Palestinian suffering, when in fact acknowledgment of the pain of that suffering—and more broadly, of Palestinian national aspirations—can only lend credibility to their cause.[4]

Arrayed at the opposite end of the spectrum are those who are inclined to see in Zionism the source of the world's evils—and in the State of Israel the sole or primary state actor worthy of condemnation in the international order. Their keen apprehension of Zionism's flaws often prevents them from seeing that Jews in fact have a long-standing attachment, as well as an internationally recognized claim, to the Land of Israel. The inability of these critics to discern any legitimate grounds for Zionism, and their one-side application of empathy—little to Jewish aspirations and much to Palestinian aspirations—exposes an unfortunate historical and moral blindness.[5] This blindness encourages, in an unhealthy dynamic of interdependence, the ongoing myopia of some supporters of Israel who turn off their humanitarian sensors when it comes to the Palestinians.

Finding the middle point between these poles is not an easy task. A number of recent books, including the anthology *Prophets Outcast* and Jacqueline Rose's *The Question of Zion,* attempt to do so by excavating a lineage of critical Jewish thinkers who, while often drawn to Zionism in one form or another, were also acutely aware of the movement's pitfalls, especially regarding the Arab Question.[6] Rose, for her part, undertakes an extended and rather reductionist psychoanalytic reading of Zionism that is marred by inadequate historical nuance and knowledge. But her book does advance an argument that cannot be summarily swept away: namely, that there is a recurrent tendency within Zionism to suppress and overcompensate for painful wounds inflicted both upon Jews (in the Diaspora) and by Jews (in Palestine/Israel).

In the course of her discussion, Rose treats a number of those mentioned in this book—Ahad Ha-am, Hannah Arendt, Martin Buber, Judah Magnes—suggesting that they pursued an alternative Zionist course that confronted, rather than ignored, the more ignominious deeds of the past.[7] Of course, she does not include Simon Rawidowicz in her roster of Jewish critics; she could not have known of his impassioned brief nor of his belief that addressing the effects, if not the cause, of the "plight of the refugees" was an essential step for the State of Israel to take—indeed, a price worth paying sooner rather than later.

The fact that Rawidowicz is unknown to Rose, and most others, as one of the most sensitive *and* empathic critics of Zionism owes as much to him as to anyone else. As we know, he clung to a language, style, and genre that were not easy to understand. And in the matter that has concerned us here, he poured out his soul over, but ultimately published nary a word about, the Arab Question.

Rawidowicz still has a good deal to say to us today. In terms of his grand life project, the idea of a meaningful partnership between "Babylon and Jerusalem" remains quite germane, especially given the demographic parity between the Diaspora and Israeli populations. Moreover, his intuition that veneration for the State of Israel qua state mistook the means for the end of Jewish nationalism merits attention. His was not a call to oppose the existence of the state, but rather to question whether that state, as distinct from Jewish religion, culture, or the global nation, should be the foundation of Jewish group identity. This challenge to "statism" did not deny that the State of Israel could serve a variety of important aims, including the provision of physical defense, social services, and a framework for Hebrew culture for its Jewish citizens. But it stubbornly refused to regard Jewish sovereignty as a supreme value in itself, and surely not as commendable if it entailed the negation of the Diaspora or discrimination against Palestinian Arabs.

The lessons of Jewish history taught Rawidowicz that power, while necessary, was fraught with danger unless constantly checked by moral and political constraints. He could not accept the view of Zionists in his day—from David Ben-Gurion to Avraham Sharon—that the assumption of statehood was the fulfillment of Jewish history. He would perhaps have even more trouble understanding the claims of those today, such as Ruth Wisse in her recent *Jews and Power,* who move in an opposite direction and maintain that the State of Israel is not sufficiently unmoored from a self-destructive "Diaspora strategy of accommodation" (as, for example, when it engages in peace negotiations with the Palestinians).[8] Rawidowicz, for his part, thought that the state had abandoned that strategy at its inception and, in fact, would do well to recall the principle, born in conditions of exile, to respect the stranger—"for you were strangers in the land of Egypt" (Exodus 22:21).

This distinctive moral sensibility pulsates through Rawidowicz's chapter on the Arab Question. "Between Jew and Arab" brought to the fore his vocation as a moral critic more than as a pragmatic political actor engaged in the art of negotiation and compromise. Accordingly, his call to responsibility might be dismissed by some as irredeemably naïve. But its unrelenting introspection—a quality often lacking in the self-aggrandizing rhetoric of nationalist movements—bored through to a point that stands at the center of the conflict between Jews and Arabs over Palestine.

The "plight of the refugees"—ignored by some and inflamed by others—could not escape Simon Rawidowicz's attention. After more than fifty years, his exposé sees the light of day for the first time. It does so in an age in which reckoning with past misdeeds—exposing the wound in order to heal it—has occurred with increasing frequency among political states. On the one hand, this trend results from an unfortunate cause: the ever-expanding number and scale of state-sponsored acts of violence (from Cambodia and Rwanda to Serbia and Russia). On the other hand, it reflects a sense of growing responsibility that issues from international organizations (including the United Nations and various affiliated legal bodies), from the victims of the criminal acts themselves, and even from the citizenry and new leadership of perpetrator states, to overcome the criminal past by confronting it directly. Various types of redress—ranging from trials for war crimes to property restitution to truth and reconciliation commissions—have emerged since the end of the Second World War. With postwar Germany as a model, states have increasingly been compelled or encouraged to answer for their past actions, a process that, in the best of cases, enables their societies to restore a measure of normality. While there are notable cases in which countries manage to resist this process (Japan comes to mind), one need only scan the globe to see this process of confronting the past at different stages of development in Rwanda, South Africa, the Balkans, Liberia, East Timor, Australia, and Argentina.[9]

It is important to emphasize that the dispossession of Palestinian Arabs occurred in the midst of a war that the Jews did not initiate and during which they believed themselves to be fighting for survival. Consequently, some say that Israel should feel no obligation to examine its role in the dispossession. They point to the long history of population exchanges and expulsions in modern times—as well as to the unresolved matter of Jewish restitution efforts in Arab countries, an important cause in its own right— as reasons to ignore or explain away the Palestinian case. At the same time, there are critics of Israel who argue that the state was born in original sin and lacks all legitimate grounds to exist. While the fate of the Palestinians is uppermost in their minds, the fate of the Jews is of no moment.

As we have seen, Simon Rawidowicz assiduously avoided these two extremes. An unreconstructed partisan of his own people, he saw no option but for the State of Israel, and the entire Jewish world, to swallow a bitter pill and assume responsibility for the "plight of the refugees." "Anyone who ignores it," he warned," does no favor to 'Israel' [that is, the Jewish people]" ("Between Jew and Arab," sec. v). The cost of ignoring the predicament, he feared, could only breed more resentment and hatred among millions of Palestinians and require ever more costly mechanisms of repression from Israelis.

This is what Rawidowicz feared more than a half-century ago. To a great extent, his concerns have been borne out. This is not to say that the entire

Israeli-Palestinian conflict can be reduced to the refugee question. A host of other issues, from land to the status of Jerusalem to water rights, not to mention recognition of the State of Israel by its neighbors, remain unresolved. Nor is it to say that Israel bears exclusive responsibility for solving the Palestinian refugee problem. While U.N. Resolution 194 places the burden to repatriate or compensate the Palestinian refugees on "the Governments or authorities responsible" (that is, the State of Israel), international law in general situates the obligation to act on "the countries of asylum to which refugees flee" (which would include, in the case of the Palestinians, Jordan, Lebanon, and Syria, among others).[10] Bridging the gap between these two formulations is a complex matter that moves beyond the scope of this study. Even if one arrived at a position of theoretical clarity, it would have to be admitted that Rawidowicz's proposal for the repatriation of hundreds of thousands of refugees is not practicable in the present context. The State of Israel would never permit the return of millions of Palestinians to its territory, and a large majority of Palestinians, if we are to believe pollster Khalil Shikaki, are not interested in actual return to their pre-1948 homes.

This, however, does not mean that the question of the refugees has vanished or should be swept off the table. It was a factor—some would say a central one—in the ultimate failure of the Oslo peace process;[11] Palestinian leaders continue to insist to this day that "the plight of Palestinian refugees must be addressed holistically—that is, in its political, human, and individual dimensions in accordance with UNGA resolution 194."[12] By refusing to recognize this plight in any meaningful way, the State of Israel does little to advance its own interests or the cause of conflict resolution. As an alternative to denial, it might well behoove Israel to conclude, as Yoav Peled and Nadim Rouhana have argued, that "recognition of the narrative told by the victims of injustice is a necessary precondition for reconciliation."[13]

What precise consequences might follow from such recognition is unclear, with the gamut of options ranging from compensation and property restitution to partial or full return (to the State of Israel or, more likely, to a future state of Palestine).[14] The point of this book has *not* been to square the circle with a Solomonic policy recommendation. Rather, it is to recover an intriguing and forgotten text and to focus overdue attention on a thinker who presciently grasped the perils of ignoring the "plight of the refugees." Central to Rawidowicz's thinking was the proposition that the welfare of the Arabs of Palestine had become inextricably linked with the welfare of the Jewish state (and nation). This linkage remains as true today, if not more so. And thus, even though "Between Jew and Arab" was never published, lingering for more than half a century in silence, the ongoing relevance of its main theme prompts us to let Simon Rawidowicz's voice be heard.

# APPENDIX A

## HISTORICAL TIMELINE
*Relevant Dates in "Between Jew and Arab"*


1958
*Bavel vi-Yerushalayim* published (bearing 1957 imprint)

1957
Rawidowicz dies (20 July)

1956
Suez Canal War (October–November)

1955
Bandung Conference of nonaligned countries (18–24 April)

1953
Kibya attack: Israeli reprisal force kills sixty-nine civilians in Jordanian border village (14–15 October)

1953
Land Acquisition Law passed by Knesset (10 March)

1952
Nationality Law passed by Knesset (1 April)

1950
Law of Return passed by Knesset (5 July)

1949
U.N. General Assembly Resolution 273 (11 May): State of Israel admitted to the U.N.

1949
Lausanne Conference convened by U.N.. Israel provisionally offers to repatriate 100,000 Arab refugees. UNRWA created in wake of conference's failure (April–September)

1949
Publication of S. Yizhar's "Hirbet Hizah."

1948
U.N. Resolution 194 (11 December). Calls for Israel to repatriate Arab refugees who desire to live in peace "at the earliest practicable date" or pay compensation.

1948
New State of Israel is attacked by Arab states (15 May). Hostilities ensue.

1948
State of Israel is declared by Provisional Government (14 May).

1948
Deir Yassin attack by IZL and Stern Gang militia; more than one hundred Arab adults and children killed (9 April)

1947
Outbreak of hostilities between Arab and Jewish forces over the fate of Palestine. (Late November–December)

1947
U.N. Resolution 181 (29 November). Calls for partition of Palestine into Jewish and Arab states.

# APPENDIX B

## THE DECLARATION OF THE ESTABLISHMENT OF THE STATE OF ISRAEL (1948)

The Land of Israel was the birthplace of the Jewish people. Here their spiritual, religious and political identity was shaped. Here they first attained to statehood, created cultural values of national and universal significance and gave to the world the eternal Book of Books.

After being forcibly exiled from their land, the people kept faith with it throughout their Dispersion and never ceased to pray and hope for their return to it and for the restoration in it of their political freedom.

Impelled by this historic and traditional attachment, Jews strove in every successive generation to re-establish themselves in their ancient homeland. In recent decades they returned in their masses. Pioneers, defiant returnees, and defenders, they made deserts bloom, revived the Hebrew language, built villages and towns, and created a thriving community controlling its own economy and culture, loving peace but knowing how to defend itself, bringing the blessings of progress to all the country's inhabitants, and aspiring towards independent nationhood.

In the year 5657 (1897), at the summons of the spiritual father of the Jewish State, Theodore Herzl, the First Zionist Congress convened and proclaimed the right of the Jewish people to national rebirth in its own country.

This right was recognized in the Balfour Declaration of the 2nd November, 1917, and re-affirmed in the Mandate of the League of Nations which, in particular, gave international sanction to the historic connection between the Jewish people and Eretz-Israel and to the right of the Jewish people to rebuild its National Home.

The catastrophe which recently befell the Jewish people—the massacre of millions of Jews in Europe—was another clear demonstration of the urgency of solving the problem of its homelessness by re-establishing in Eretz-Israel the Jewish State, which would open the gates of the homeland wide to every Jew and confer upon the Jewish people the status of a fully privileged member of the community of nations.

Survivors of the Nazi holocaust in Europe, as well as Jews from other parts of the world, continued to migrate to Eretz-Israel, undaunted by difficulties, restrictions and dangers, and never ceased to assert their right to a life of dignity, freedom and honest toil in their national homeland.

SOURCE: Provisional Government of Israel, *Official Gazette*, no. 1 (Tel Aviv, 1948), 1

In the Second World War, the Jewish community of this country contributed its full share to the struggle of the freedom- and peace-loving nations against the forces of Nazi wickedness and, by the blood of its soldiers and its war effort, gained the right to be reckoned among the peoples who founded the United Nations.

On the 29th November, 1947, the United Nations General Assembly passed a resolution calling for the establishment of a Jewish State in Eretz-Israel; the General Assembly required the inhabitants of Eretz-Israel to take such steps as were necessary on their part for the implementation of that resolution. This recognition by the United Nations of the right of the Jewish people to establish their State is irrevocable.

This right is the natural right of the Jewish people to be masters of their own fate, like all other nations, in their own sovereign State.

Accordingly we, members of the People's Council, representatives of the Jewish Community of Eretz-Israel and of the Zionist Movement, are here assembled on the day of the termination of the British Mandate over Eretz-Israel and, by virtue of our natural and historic right and on the strength of the resolution of the United Nations General Assembly, hereby declare the establishment of a Jewish state in Eretz-Israel, to be known as the State of Israel.

We declare that, with effect from the moment of the termination of the Mandate being tonight, the eve of Sabbath, the 6th Iyar, 5708 (15th May, 1948), until the establishment of the elected, regular authorities of the State in accordance with the Constitution which shall be adopted by the Elected Constituent Assembly not later than the 1st October 1948, the People's Council shall act as a Provisional Council of State, and its executive organ, the People's Administration, shall be the Provisional Government of the Jewish State, to be called "Israel."

The State of Israel will be open for Jewish immigration and for the Ingathering of the Exiles; it will foster the development of the country for the benefit of all its inhabitants; it will be based on freedom, justice and peace as envisaged by the prophets of Israel; it will ensure complete equality of social and political rights to all its inhabitants irrespective of religion, race or sex; it will guarantee freedom of religion, conscience, language, education and culture; it will safeguard the Holy Places of all religions; and it will be faithful to the principles of the Charter of the United Nations.

The State of Israel is prepared to cooperate with the agencies and representatives of the United Nations in implementing the resolution of the General Assembly of the 29th November, 1947, and will take steps to bring about the economic union of the whole of Eretz-Israel.

We appeal to the United Nations to assist the Jewish people in the building-up of its State and to receive the State of Israel into the community of nations.

We appeal—in the very midst of the onslaught launched against us now for months— to the Arab inhabitants of the State of Israel to preserve peace and participate in the up-building of the State on the basis of full and equal citizenship and due representation in all its provisional and permanent institutions.

We extend our hand to all neighbouring states and their peoples in an offer of peace and good neighbourliness, and appeal to them to establish bonds of cooperation and mutual help with the sovereign Jewish people settled in its own land. The State of Israel is prepared to do its share in a common effort for the advancement of the entire Middle East.

We appeal to the Jewish people throughout the Diaspora to rally round the Jews of Eretz-Israel in the tasks of immigration and upbuilding and to stand by them in the great struggle for the realization of the age-old dream—the redemption of Israel.

Placing our trust in the Almighty, we affix our signatures to this proclamation at this session of the provisional Council of State, on the soil of the Homeland, in the city of Tel-Aviv, on this Sabbath eve, the 5th day of Iyar, 5708 (14th May, 1948).


*David Ben-Gurion*

*Daniel Auster; Mordekhai Bentov; Yitzchak Ben Zvi; Eliyahu Berligne; Fritz Bernstein; Rabbi Wolf Gold; Meir Grabovsky; Yitzchak Gruenbaum; Dr. Abraham Granovsky; Eliyahu Dobkin; Meir Wilner-Kovner; Zerach Wahrhaftig; Herzl Vardi; Rachel Cohen; Rabbi Kalman Kahana; Saadia Kobashi; Rabbi Yitzchak Meir Levin; Meir David Loewenstein; Zvi Luria; Golda Myerson; Nachum Nir; Zvi Segal; Rabbi Yehuda Leib Hacohen Fishman; David Zvi Pinkas; Aharon Zisling; Moshe Kolodny; Eliezer Kaplan; Abraham Katznelson; Felix Rosenblueth; David Remez; Berl Repetur; Mordekhai Shattner; Ben Zion Sternberg; Bekhor Shitreet; Moshe Shapira; Moshe Shertok*

# APPENDIX C

# THE "LAW OF RETURN" (5710/1950)

Right of *'aliyah*\* (1).

1.  Every Jew has the right to come to this country as an *'oleh.*\*

*'Oleh's* visa.

2.  (a) *'Aliyah* shall be by *'oleh's* visa.

    (b) An *'oleh's* visa shall be granted to every Jew who has expressed his desire to settle in Israel, unless the Minister of Immigration is satisfied that the applicant

    (1) is engaged in an activity directed against the Jewish people; or

    (2) is likely to endanger public health or the security of the State.

*'Oleh's* certificate.

3.  (a) A Jew who has come to Israel and subsequent to his arrival has expressed his desire to settle in Israel may, while still in Israel, receive an *'oleh's* certificate.

    (b) The restrictions specified in section 2(b) shall apply also to the grant of an *'oleh's* certificate, but a person shall not be regarded as endangering public health on account of an illness contracted after his arrival in Israel.

Residents and persons born in this country.

4.  Every Jew who has immigrated into this country before the coming into force of this Law, and every Jew who was born in this country, whether

---

Passed by the Knesset on the 20th Tammuz, 5710 (5th July, 1950) and published in *Sefer Ha-Chukkim*, No. 51 of the 21st Tammuz, 5710 (5th July, 1950), p. 159; the Bill and an Explanatory Note were published in *Hatza'ot Chok*, No. 48 of the 12th Tammuz, 5710 (27th June, 1950), p. 189.

\* Translator's Note: *'aliyah* means immigration of Jews, and *'oleh* (plural, *'olim*) means a Jew immigrating, into Israel.

SOURCE: *The Law of Return, 5710–1950*. Official Records of the Laws of the State of Israel. Authorized translation from the Hebrew (Jerusalem: Government Printer, 1950), 4:114.

before or after the coming into force of this Law, shall be deemed to be a person, who has come to this country as an 'oleh under this Law.

Implementation and regulations.

5. The Minister of Immigration is charged with the implementation of this Law and may make regulations as to any matter relating to such implementation and also as to the grant of 'oleh's visas and 'oleh's certificates to minors up to the age of 18 years.

DAVID BEN-GURION
*Prime Minister*

MOSHE SHAPIRA
*Minister of Immigration*

YOSEF SPRINZAK
*Acting President of the State*
*Chairman of the Knesset*

## APPENDIX D

## THE "NATIONALITY LAW" (5712/1952)

### Part One: Acquisition of Nationality

Preliminary.

1.  Israel nationality is acquired—
    - by return (section 2),
    - by residence in Israel (section 3),
    - by birth (section 4) or
    - by naturalisation (section 5 to 9).
    - There shall be no Israel nationality save under this Law.

Nationality by Return.

2.  (a) Every *'oleh** under the Law of Return, 5710/1950,[1] shall become an Israel national.

    (b) Israel nationality by return is acquired—

    (1) by a person who came as an *'oleh* into, or was born in, the country before the establishment of the State—with effect from the day of the establishment of the State;

    (2) by a person having come to Israel as an *'oleh* after the establishment of the State—with effect from the day of his *'aliyah*;

    (3) by a person born in Israel after the establishment of the State— with effect from the day of his birth;

    (4) by a person who has received an *'oleh's* certificate under section 3 of the Law of Return, 5710/1950—with effect from the day of the issue of the certificate.

---

Passed by the Knesset on the 6th Nisan, 5712 (1st April, 1952). and published in *Sefer Ha-Chukkim*, No. 95 of the 13th Nisan, 5712 (8th April, 1952), p. 146; the Bill was published in *Hatza'ot Chok*, No. 93 of the 22nd Cheshvan, 5712 (21st November, 1951), p. 22.

\* Translator's Note: *'oleh* and *'aliyah* mean, respectively, a Jew immigrating, and the immigration of a Jew, into the Land of Israel.

SOURCE: *Nationality Law, 5512/1952*. Official Records of the Laws of the State of Israel. Authorized translation from the Hebrew (Jerusalem: Government Printer, 1952), 6:50–53.

(c) This section does not apply

(1) to a person having ceased to be an inhabitant of Israel before the coming into force of this Law;

(2) to a person of full age who, immediately before the day of his ʿaliyah or the day of his ʿoleh's certificate is a foreign national and who, on or before such day, declares that he does not desire to become an Israel national;

(3) to a minor whose parents have made a declaration under paragraph (2) and included him therein.

Nationality by Residence in Israel.

3. (a) A person who, immediately before the establishment of the State, was a Palestinian citizen and who does not become a Israel national under section 2, shall become an Israel national with effect from the day of the establishment of the State if—

(1) he was registered on the 4th Adar, 5712 (1st March 1952) as an inhabitant under the Registration of Inhabitants Ordinance, 5709/1949;[2] and

(2) he is an inhabitant of Israel on the day of the coming into force of this Law; and

(3) he was in Israel, or in an area which became Israeli territory after the establishment of the State, from the day of the establishment of the State to the day of the coming into force of this Law, or entered Israel legally during that period.

(b) A person born after the establishment of the State who is an inhabitant of Israel on the day of the coming into force of this Law, and whose father or mother becomes an Israel national under subsection (a), shall become an Israel national with effect from the day of his birth.

Nationality by Birth.

4. A person born while his father or mother is an Israel national shall be an Israel national from birth; where a person is born after his father's death, it shall be sufficient that his father was an Israel national at the time of his death.

Naturalisation.

5. (a) A person of full age, not being an Israel national, may obtain Israel nationality by naturalisation if—

(1) he is in Israel; and

(2) he has been in Israel for three years out of five years proceeding the day of the submission of his application; and

(3) he is entitled to reside in Israel permanently; and

(4) he has settled, or intends to settle, in Israel, and

(5) he has some knowledge of the Hebrew language, and

(6) he has renounced his prior nationality or has proved that he will cease to be a foreign national upon becoming an Israel national.

(b) Where a person has applied for naturalisation, and he meets the requirements of subsection (a), the Minister of the Interior, if he thinks fit to do so, shall grant him Israel nationality by the issue of a certificate of naturalisation.

(c) Prior to the grant of nationality, the applicant shall make the following declaration:

*"I declare that I will be a loyal national of the State of Israel."*

(d) Nationality is acquired on the day of the declaration.

Exemption from conditions of naturalisation.

6.   (a) (1) A person who has served in the regular service of the Defence Army of Israel or who, after the 16th Kislev, 5708 (29th November 1947) has served in some other service which the Minister of Defence, by declaration published in *Reshumot,* has declared to be military service for the purpose of this section, and who has been duly discharged from such service; and

(2) a person who has lost a son or daughter in such service, is exempt from the requirements of section 5 (a), except the requirement of section 5 (a) (4).

(b) A person applying for naturalisation after having made a declaration under section 2 (c) (2) is exempt from the requirement of section 5 (a) (2).

(c) A person who immediately before the establishment of the State was a Palestinian citizen is exempt from the requirement of section 5 (a) (5).

(d) The Minister of the Interior may exempt an applicant from all or any of the requirements of section 5 (a) (1), (2), (5) and (6) if there exists in his opinion a special reason justifying such exemption.

Naturalisation of husband and wife.

7.   The spouse of a person who is an Israel national or who has applied for Israel nationality and meets or is exempt from the requirements of section 5 (a) may obtain Israel nationality by naturalisation even if she or he is a minor or does not meet the requirements of section (5) (a).

Naturalisation of Minors.

8.   Naturalisation confers Israel nationality also upon the minor children of the naturalised person.

Grant of Nationality to Minors.

9.  (a) Where a minor, not being an Israel national, is an inhabitant of Israel, and his parents are not in Israel or have died or are unknown, the Minister of the Interior, on such conditions and with effect from such day as he may think fit, may grant him Israel nationality by the issue of a certificate of naturalisation.

(b) Nationality may be granted as aforesaid upon the application of the father or mother of the minor or, if they have died or are unable to apply, upon the application of the guardian or person in charge of the minor.

## Part Two: Loss of Nationality

Renunciation of Nationality.

10. (a) An Israel national of full age, not being an inhabitant of Israel, may declare that he desires to renounce his Israel nationality; such renunciation is subject to the consent of the Minister of the Interior; the declarant's Israel nationality terminates on the day fixed by the Minister.

(b) The Israel nationality of a minor, not being an inhabitant of Israel, terminates upon his parents' renouncing their Israel nationality; it does not terminate so long as one of his parents remains an Israel national.

Revocation of Naturalisation.

11. (a) Where a person, having acquired Israeli nationality by naturalisation—

(1) has done so on the basis of false particulars; or

(2) has been abroad for seven consecutive years and has no effective connection with Israel, and has failed to prove that his effective connection with Israel was severed otherwise than by his own volition; or

(3) has committed an act of disloyalty towards the State of Israel, a District Court may, upon the application of the Minister of the Interior, revoke such person's naturalisation.

(b) The Court may, upon such application, rule that the revocation shall apply also to such children of the naturalised person as acquired Israel nationality by virtue of his naturalisation and are inhabitants of a foreign country.

(c) Israel nationality terminates on the day on which the judgment revoking naturalisation ceases to be appealable or on such later day as the Court may fix.

Saving of Liability.

12. Loss of Israel nationality does not relieve from a liability arising out of such nationality and created before its loss.

**Part Three: Further Provisions**

Interpretation.

13.  In this Law—

"of full age" means of the age of eighteen years or over;

"minor" means a person under eighteen years of age;

"child" includes an adopted child, and "parents" includes adoptive parents;

"foreign nationality" includes foreign citizenship, and "foreign national" includes a foreign citizen, but does not include a Palestinian citizen.

Dual nationality and dual residence.

14.  (a) Save for the purposes of naturalisation, acquisition of Israel nationality is not conditional upon renunciation of a prior nationality.

(b) An Israel national who is also a foreign national shall, for the purposes of Israel law, be considered an Israel national.

(c) An inhabitant of Israel residing abroad shall, for the purposes of this Law, be considered an inhabitant of Israel so long as he has not settled abroad.

Evidence of Nationality.

15.  An Israel national may obtain from the Minister of the Interior a certificate attesting to his Israel nationality.

Offence.

16.  A person who knowingly gives false particulars as to a matter affecting his own or another person's acquisition or loss of Israel nationality is liable to imprisonment for a term not exceeding six months or to fine not exceeding five hundred pounds, or to both such penalties.

Implementation and regulations.

17.  (a) The Minister of the Interior is charged with the implementation of this Law and may make regulations as to any matter relating to its implementation, including the payment of fees and exemption from the payment thereof.

(b) The Minister of Justice may make regulations as to proceedings in District Courts under this Law, including appeals from decisions of such Courts.

Repeal, adaptation of laws and validation.

18.  (a) The Palestinian Citizenship Orders, 1925–1942,[3] are repealed with effect from the day of the establishment of the State.

(b) Any reference in any provision of law to Palestinian citizenship or Palestinian citizens shall henceforth be read as a reference to Israel nationality or Israel nationals.

(c) Any act done in the period between the establishment of the State and the day of the coming into force of this Law shall be deemed to be valid if it were valid had this Law been in force at the time it was done.

Commencement.

19.  (a)  This Law shall come into force on the 21st Tammuz, 5712 (14th July, 1952).

(b)  Even before that day, the Minister of the Interior may make regulations as to declarations under section 2(c)(2).

MOSHE SHARETT
*Minister of Foreign Affairs*

MOSHE SHAPIRA
*Minister of the Interior*

YOSEF SPRINZAK
*Chairman of the Knesset*
*Acting President of the State*

# APPENDIX E

## "THE LAND ACQUISITION (VALIDATION OF ACTS AND COMPENSATION) LAW" (5713/1953)

Interpretation,

1. (a) In this Law—

"the Minister" means the member of the Government whom the Government shall authorise for the purposes of this Law by notice published in *Reshumot;*

"Development Authority" means the Development Authority established under the Development Authority (Transfer of Property) Law, 5710–1950;[1]

"property" means land;

"acquired property'" means property vested in the Development Authority in pursuance of section 2;

"date of acquisition" means the date on which property vests in the Development Authority in pursuance of section 2;

"owners," in relation to acquired property, means the persons who immediately before the date of acquisition were the owners of, or had a right or interest in such property, and includes their successors;

"the Court" means the District Court in the area of whose jurisdiction acquired property is situated.

(b) In the case of a person who has a right or interest in property, any reference in this Law to property shall be deemed to be a reference to such right or interest.

Passed by the Knesset on the 23rd Adar, 5713 (10th March, 1953) and published in *Sefer Ha-Chukkim,* No. 122 of the 4th Nisan, 5713 (20th March, 1953), p. 58; the Bill and an Explanatory Note were published in *Hatza'ot Chok,* No. 118 of the 2nd Sivan, 5712 (26th May, 1952), p. 232.

SOURCE: *Land Acquisition (Validation of Acts and Compensation)* Law, 5713/1953. Official Records of the Law of the State of Israel. Authorized translation from the Hebrew (Jerusalem: Government Printer, 1953), 1:43–45.

Acquisition of land for purposes of development, settlement, or security.

2.  (a) Property in respect of which the Minister certifies by certificate under his
    hand—

    (1) that on the 6th Nisan, 5712 (1st April, 1952) it was not in the
    possession of its owners; and

    (2) that within the period between the 5th Iyar, 5708 (14th May, 1948) and
    the 6th Nisan, 5712 (Ist April 1952) it was used or assigned for purposes
    of essential development, settlement or security; and

    (3) that it is still required for any of these purposes—

    shall vest in the Development Authority and be regarded as free from any
    charge, and the Development Authority may forthwith take possession
    thereof.

    (b) The property shall vest in the Development Authority as from the date
    specified in the said certificate; the certificate may only be issued within one
    year from the day of the coming into force of this Law, and shall be published
    in *Reshumot* as early as possible after the day of its issue.

    (c) Property vested in the Development Authority as aforesaid shall be
    registered in the Land Register in its name, but non-registration shall not
    affect the validity of the vesting of the property in the Development
    Authority.

    (d) A certificate under this section shall not constitute an admission that
    acquired property is not or was not State property or that the State has not or
    had not a right or interest therein.

Right to Compensation.

3.  (a) The owners of acquired property are entitled to compensation therefore
    from the Development Authority. The compensation shall be given in money,
    unless otherwise agreed between the owners and the Development
    Authority. The amount of compensation shall be fixed by agreement between
    the Development Authority and the owners or, in the absence of agreement,
    by the Court, as hereinafter provided.

    (b) Where the acquired property was used for agriculture and was the main
    source of livelihood of its owner, and he has no other land sufficient for his
    livelihood, the Development Authority shall, on his demand, offer him other
    property, either for ownership or for lease, as full or partial compensation. A
    competent authority, to be appointed for this purpose by the Minister, shall,
    in accordance with rules to be prescribed by regulations, determine the

category, location, area, and, in the case of lease, period of lease (not less than 49 years) and the value of the offered property, both for the purpose of calculating the compensation and for determination of the sufficiency of such property for a livelihood.

(c) The provisions of subsection (b) shall add to, and not derogate from, the provisions of subsection (a).

Determination of compensation by the court.

4. In the following cases, the right to and amount of compensation shall, on the application of the Development Authority or the owner of the acquired property, be determined by the Court:

(1) in the absence of agreement between the Development Authority and the owner of the acquired property as to the grant or amount of compensation;

(2) where the owner of the acquired property did not file a claim for compensation with the Development Authority within one year from the day of publication of a certificate under section 2;

(3) where a claim as aforesaid was filed but was not supported by sufficient evidence;

(4) where different or conflicting claims were filed in relation to the acquired property.

Rules for determining compensation.

5. (a) In fixing the amount of compensation, the Court shall follow *mutatis mutandis* the rules laid down in section 12 of the Land (Acquisition for Public Purposes) Ordinance, 1943;[2] provided that the 12th Tevet, 5710 (Ist January, 1950) shall be regarded as the day on which notice of the intended acquisition was published for the purposes of the said section.

(b) Any amount fixed by the Court as aforesaid shall be increased by an addition of three per centum per annum as from the 12th Tevet 5710 (1st January, 1950).

Decision of the Court in the case of deposit of compensation.

6. (a) The decision of the Court or, in the case of appeal, of the Court of Civil Appeal shall be final with regard to all parties to whom notices of an application under section 4 have been sent or who have attended and claimed compensation either personally or by attorney.

(b) A person to whom notice as aforesaid has not been sent or who has not attended and claimed as aforesaid may file a claim within one year from the date of the final decision.

(c) Where the Court has awarded compensation, but has not issued directions as to the mode of payment thereof, the compensation shall be deposited with the Court, and the Court shall pay it only upon the expiration of one year, or such shorter period as it may decide, from the date of the final decision, and after application has been made to it by a person claiming the compensation; and the compensation shall be paid as the Court may direct.

(d) Deposit of the compensation with the Court has the effect of full discharge, and relieves the Development Authority from liability as to any claim in relation to the property, unless the Court otherwise orders in connection with a claim under subsection (b).

(e) A person who alleges that he has a right to compensation deposited with the Court and the whole or any part of which has not been paid, may, within three years from the date of the final decision, apply to the Court for payment of the whole or any part thereof; and any person who alleges that he has a better right to the whole or any part of the compensation, may file a claim against the person to whom compensation has been paid.

Relief from liability for use of compensation.

7. The giving of compensation, whether in money or in land, and whether by agreement or under a decision of the Court, or the deposit of compensation under section 6, relieves the Development Authority from any liability for the manner in which such compensation is used or for the misuse thereof.

Inapplicability.

8. Section 3(4)(a) of the Development Authority (Transfer of Property) Law, 5710/1950, shall not apply to property of the Development Authority offered or given to the owner of acquired property as full or partial compensation for the acquired property.

Immunity.

9. Where the Minister certifies by certificate under his hand that an act done on behalf of the State or the Development Authority in respect of any property was done after such property had first been used or assigned for purposes of essential development, settlement or security, and before it became acquired property, such act shall not serve as cause for an action on the part of the owner of the property or of his predecessor in title, or as basis for a charge.

Regulations.

    10. The Minister may make regulations as to any matter relating to the implementation of this Law.

DAVID BEN-GURION
*Prime Minister*

YITZCHAK BEN-ZVI
*President of the State*

## APPENDIX F

## UNITED NATIONS UNIVERSAL DECLARATION OF HUMAN RIGHTS
*General Assembly Resolution 217 A (III)*


On December 10, 1948 the General Assembly of the United Nations adopted and proclaimed the Universal Declaration of Human Rights (resolution 217A [III]), the full text of which appears in the following pages. Following this historic act the Assembly called upon all Member countries to publicize the text of the Declaration and "to cause it to be disseminated, displayed, read and expounded principally in schools and other educational institutions, without distinction based on the political status of countries or territories."


*PREAMBLE*

Whereas recognition of the inherent dignity and of the equal and inalienable rights of all members of the human family is the foundation of freedom, justice and peace in the world,

Whereas disregard and contempt for human rights have resulted in barbarous acts which have outraged the conscience of mankind, and the advent of a world in which human beings shall enjoy freedom of speech and belief and freedom from fear and want has been proclaimed as the highest aspiration of the common people,

Whereas it is essential, if man is not to be compelled to have recourse, as a last resort, to rebellion against tyranny and oppression, that human rights should be protected by the rule of law,

Whereas it is essential to promote the development of friendly relations between nations,

Whereas the peoples of the United Nations have in the Charter reaffirmed their faith in fundamental human rights, in the dignity and worth of the human person and in the equal rights of men and women and have determined to promote social progress and better standards of life in larger freedom,

---

SOURCE: U.N. General Assembly, Third Session, Official Records, *International Bill of Human Rights.* Prepared in pursuance of U.N. General Assembly Resolution 217A, A/PV 183, 1948.

Whereas Member States have pledged themselves to achieve, in co-operation with the United Nations, the promotion of universal respect for and observance of human rights and fundamental freedoms,

Whereas a common understanding of these rights and freedoms is of the greatest importance for the full realization of this pledge,

Now, Therefore THE GENERAL ASSEMBLY proclaims THIS UNIVERSAL DEC-LARATION OF HUMAN RIGHTS as a common standard of achievement for all peoples and all nations, to the end that every individual and every organ of society, keeping this Declaration constantly in mind, shall strive by teaching and education to promote respect for these rights and freedoms and by progressive measures, national and international, to secure their universal and effective recognition and observance, both among the peoples of Member States themselves and among the peoples of territories under their jurisdiction.

## *Article 1.*

All human beings are born free and equal in dignity and rights. They are endowed with reason and conscience and should act towards one another in a spirit of brotherhood.

## *Article 2.*

Everyone is entitled to all the rights and freedoms set forth in this Declaration, without distinction of any kind, such as race, colour, sex, language, religion, political or other opinion, national or social origin, property, birth or other status. Furthermore, no distinction shall be made on the basis of the political, jurisdictional or international status of the country or territory to which a person belongs, whether it be independent, trust, non-self-governing or under any other limitation of sovereignty.

## *Article 3.*

Everyone has the right to life, liberty and security of person.

## *Article 4.*

No one shall be held in slavery or servitude; slavery and the slave trade shall be prohibited in all their forms.

## *Article 5.*

No one shall be subjected to torture or to cruel, inhuman or degrading treatment or punishment.

*Article 6.*

Everyone has the right to recognition everywhere as a person before the law.

*Article 7.*

All are equal before the law and are entitled without any discrimination to equal protection of the law. All are entitled to equal protection against any discrimination in violation of this Declaration and against any incitement to such discrimination.

*Article 8.*

Everyone has the right to an effective remedy by the competent national tribunals for acts violating the fundamental rights granted him by the constitution or by law.

*Article 9.*

No one shall be subjected to arbitrary arrest, detention or exile.

*Article 10.*

Everyone is entitled in full equality to a fair and public hearing by an independent and impartial tribunal, in the determination of his rights and obligations and of any criminal charge against him.

*Article 11.*

(1) Everyone charged with a penal offence has the right to be presumed innocent until proved guilty according to law in a public trial at which he has had all the guarantees necessary for his defence.

(2) No one shall be held guilty of any penal offence on account of any act or omission which did not constitute a penal offence, under national or international law, at the time when it was committed. Nor shall a heavier penalty be imposed than the one that was applicable at the time the penal offence was committed.

*Article 12.*

No one shall be subjected to arbitrary interference with his privacy, family, home or correspondence, nor to attacks upon his honour and reputation. Everyone has the right to the protection of the law against such interference or attacks.

*Article 13.*

(1) Everyone has the right to freedom of movement and residence within the borders of each state.

(2) Everyone has the right to leave any country, including his own, and to return to his country.

*Article 14.*

(1) Everyone has the right to seek and to enjoy in other countries asylum from persecution.

(2) This right may not be invoked in the case of prosecutions genuinely arising from non-political crimes or from acts contrary to the purposes and principles of the United Nations.

*Article 15.*

(1) Everyone has the right to a nationality.

(2) No one shall be arbitrarily deprived of his nationality nor denied the right to change his nationality.

*Article 16.*

(1) Men and women of full age, without any limitation due to race, nationality or religion, have the right to marry and to found a family. They are entitled to equal rights as to marriage, during marriage and at its dissolution.

(2) Marriage shall be entered into only with the free and full consent of the intending spouses.

(3) The family is the natural and fundamental group unit of society and is entitled to protection by society and the State.

*Article 17.*

(1) Everyone has the right to own property alone as well as in association with others.

(2) No one shall be arbitrarily deprived of his property.

*Article 18.*

Everyone has the right to freedom of thought, conscience and religion; this right includes freedom to change his religion or belief, and freedom, either alone or in community with others and in public or private, to manifest his religion or belief in teaching, practice, worship and observance.

*Article 19.*

Everyone has the right to freedom of opinion and expression; this right includes freedom to hold opinions without interference and to seek, receive and impart information and ideas through any media and regardless of frontiers.

*Article 20.*

(1) Everyone has the right to freedom of peaceful assembly and association.

(2) No one may be compelled to belong to an association.

*Article 21.*

(1) Everyone has the right to take part in the government of his country, directly or through freely chosen representatives.

(2) Everyone has the right of equal access to public service in his country.

(3) The will of the people shall be the basis of the authority of government; this will shall be expressed in periodic and genuine elections which shall be by universal and equal suffrage and shall be held by secret vote or by equivalent free voting procedures.

*Article 22.*

Everyone, as a member of society, has the right to social security and is entitled to realization, through national effort and international co-operation and in accordance with the organization and resources of each State, of the economic, social and cultural rights indispensable for his dignity and the free development of his personality.

*Article 23.*

(1) Everyone has the right to work, to free choice of employment, to just and favourable conditions of work and to protection against unemployment.

(2) Everyone, without any discrimination, has the right to equal pay for equal work.

(3) Everyone who works has the right to just and favourable remuneration ensuring for himself and his family an existence worthy of human dignity, and supplemented, if necessary, by other means of social protection.

(4) Everyone has the right to form and to join trade unions for the protection of his interests.

*Article 24.*

Everyone has the right to rest and leisure, including reasonable limitation of working hours and periodic holidays with pay.

*Article 25.*

(1) Everyone has the right to a standard of living adequate for the health and wellbeing of himself and of his family, including food, clothing, housing and medical

care and necessary social services, and the right to security in the event of unemployment, sickness, disability, widowhood, old age or other lack of livelihood in circumstances beyond his control.

(2) Motherhood and childhood are entitled to special care and assistance. All children, whether born in or out of wedlock, shall enjoy the same social protection.

## Article 26.

(1) Everyone has the right to education. Education shall be free, at least in the elementary and fundamental stages. Elementary education shall be compulsory. Technical and professional education shall be made generally available and higher education shall be equally accessible to all on the basis of merit.

(2) Education shall be directed to the full development of the human personality and to the strengthening of respect for human rights and fundamental freedoms. It shall promote understanding, tolerance and friendship among all nations, racial or religious groups, and shall further the activities of the United Nations for the maintenance of peace.

(3) Parents have a prior right to choose the kind of education that shall be given to their children.

## Article 27.

(1) Everyone has the right freely to participate in the cultural life of the community, to enjoy the arts and to share in scientific advancement and its benefits.

(2) Everyone has the right to the protection of the moral and material interests resulting from any scientific, literary or artistic production of which he is the author.

## Article 28.

Everyone is entitled to a social and international order in which the rights and freedoms set forth in this Declaration can be fully realized.

## Article 29.

(1) Everyone has duties to the community in which alone the free and full development of his personality is possible.

(2) In the exercise of his rights and freedoms, everyone shall be subject only to such limitations as are determined by law solely for the purpose of securing due recognition and respect for the rights and freedoms of others and of meeting the just requirements of morality, public order and the general welfare in a democratic society.

(3) These rights and freedoms may in no case be exercised contrary to the purposes and principles of the United Nations.

*Article 30.*

Nothing in this Declaration may be interpreted as implying for any State, group or person any right to engage in any activity or to perform any act aimed at the destruction of any of the rights and freedoms set forth herein.

## APPENDIX G

## UNITED NATIONS GENERAL ASSEMBLY RESOLUTION 181, NOVEMBER 29, 1947

The General Assembly,

Having met in special session at the request of the mandatory Power to constitute and instruct a Special Committee to prepare for the consideration of the question of the future Government of Palestine at the second regular session;

Having constituted a Special Committee and instructed it to investigate all questions and issues relevant to the problem of Palestine, and to prepare proposals for the solution of the problem, and

Having received and examined the report of the Special Committee (document A/364)[1] including a number of unanimous recommendations and a plan of partition with economic union approved by the majority of the Special Committee,

Considers that the present situation in Palestine is one which is likely to impair the general welfare and friendly relations among nations;

Takes note of the declaration by the mandatory Power that it plans to complete its evacuation of Palestine by 1 August 1948;

Recommends to the United Kingdom, as the mandatory Power for Palestine, and to all other Members of the United Nations the adoption and implementation, with regard to the future Government of Palestine, of the Plan of Partition with Economic Union set out below;

Requests that

The Security Council take the necessary measures as provided for in the plan for its implementation;

The Security Council consider, if circumstances during the transitional period require such consideration, whether the situation in Palestine constitutes a

SOURCE: U.N. General Assembly, Second Session, Official Records, *Future Government of Palestine.* Prepared in pursuance of U.N. General Assembly Resolution 181, A/PV 128, 1947.

threat to the peace. If it decides that such a threat exists, and in order to maintain international peace and security, the Security Council should supplement the authorization of the General Assembly by taking measures, under Articles 39 and 41 of the Charter, to empower the United Nations Commission, as provided in this resolution, to exercise in Palestine the functions which are assigned to it by this resolution;

The Security Council determine as a threat to the peace, breach of the peace or act of aggression, in accordance with Article 39 of the Charter, any attempt to alter by force the settlement envisaged by this resolution;

The Trusteeship Council be informed of the responsibilities envisaged for it in this plan;

Calls upon the inhabitants of Palestine to take such steps as may be necessary on their part to put this plan into effect;

Appeals to all Governments and all peoples to refrain from taking any action which might hamper or delay the carrying out of these recommendations, and

Authorizes the Secretary-General to reimburse travel and subsistence expenses of the members of the Commission referred to in Part 1, Section B, Paragraph I below, on such basis and in such form as he may determine most appropriate in the circumstances, and to provide the Commission with the necessary staff to assist in carrying out the functions assigned to the Commission by the General Assembly.*

The General Assembly,

Authorizes the Secretary-General to draw from the Working Capital Fund a sum not to exceed 2,000,000 dollars for the purposes set forth in the last paragraph of the resolution on the future government of Palestine.

## PLAN OF PARTITION WITH ECONOMIC UNION

### Part I. Future Constitution and Government of Palestine

*A. Termination of Mandate, Partition and Independence*

The Mandate for Palestine shall terminate as soon as possible but in any case not later than 1 August 1948.

The armed forces of the mandatory Power shall be progressively withdrawn from Palestine, the withdrawal to be completed as soon as possible but in any case

---

*At its hundred and twenty-eighth plenary meeting on 29 November 1947 the General Assembly, in accordance with the terms of the above resolution, elected the following members of the United Nations Commission on Palestine: Bolivia, Czechoslovakia, Denmark, Panama, and Philippines.

not later than 1 August 1948. The mandatory Power shall advise the Commission, as far in advance as possible, of its intention to terminate the mandate and to evacuate each area. The mandatory Power shall use its best endeavours to ensure that an area situated in the territory of the Jewish State, including a seaport and hinterland adequate to provide facilities for a substantial immigration, shall be evacuated at the earliest possible date and in any event not later than 1 February 1948.

Independent Arab and Jewish States and the Special International Regime for the City of Jerusalem, set forth in Part III of this Plan, shall come into existence in Palestine two months after the evacuation of the armed forces of the mandatory Power has been completed but in any case not later than 1 October 1948. The boundaries of the Arab State, the Jewish State, and the City of Jerusalem shall be as described in Parts II and III below.

The period between the adoption by the General Assembly of its recommendation on the question of Palestine and the establishment of the independence of the Arab and Jewish States shall be a transitional period.

## B. Steps Preparatory to Independence[2]

A Commission shall be set up consisting of one representative of each of five Member States. The Members represented on the Commission shall be elected by the General Assembly on as broad a basis, geographically and otherwise, as possible.

The administration of Palestine shall, as the mandatory Power withdraws its armed forces, be progressively turned over to the Commission, which shall act in conformity with the recommendations of the General Assembly, under the guidance of the Security Council. The mandatory Power shall to the fullest possible extent coordinate its plans for withdrawal with the plans of the Commission to take over and administer areas which have been evacuated.

In the discharge of this administrative responsibility the Commission shall have authority to issue necessary regulations and take other measures as required. The mandatory Power shall not take any action to prevent, obstruct or delay the implementation by the Commission of the measures recommended by the General Assembly.

On its arrival in Palestine the Commission shall proceed to carry out measures for the establishment of the frontiers of the Arab and Jewish States and the City of Jerusalem in accordance with the general lines of the recommendations of the General Assembly on the partition of Palestine. Nevertheless, the boundaries as described in Part II of this Plan are to be modified in such a way that village areas as a rule will not be divided by state boundaries unless pressing reasons make that necessary.

The Commission, after consultation with the democratic parties and other public organizations of the Arab and Jewish States, shall select and establish in each State as rapidly as possible a Provisional Council of Government. The activities of both the Arab and Jewish Provisional Councils of Government shall be carried out under the general direction of the Commission.

If by 1 April 1948 a Provisional Council of Government cannot be selected for either of the States, or, if selected, cannot carry out its functions, the Commission shall communicate that fact to the Security Council for such action with respect to that State as the Security Council may deem proper, and to the Secretary-General for communication to the Members of the United Nations.

Subject to the provisions of these recommendations, during the transitional period the Provisional Councils of Government, acting under the Commission, shall have full authority in the areas under their control including authority over matters of immigration and land regulation.

The Provisional Council of Government of each State, acting under the Commission, shall progressively receive from the Commission full responsibility for the administration of that State in the period between the termination of the Mandate and the establishment of the State's independence.

The Commission shall instruct the Provisional Councils of Government of both the Arab and Jewish States, after their formation, to proceed to the establishment of administrative organs of government, central and local.

The Provisional Council of Government of each State shall, within the shortest time possible, recruit an armed militia from the residents of that State, sufficient in number to maintain internal order and to prevent frontier clashes.

This armed militia in each State shall, for operational purposes, be under the command of Jewish or Arab officers resident in that State, but general political and military control, including the choice of the militia's High Command, shall be exercised by the Commission.

The Provisional Council of Government of each State shall, not later than two months after the withdrawal of the armed forces of the mandatory Power, hold elections to the Constituent Assembly which shall be conducted on democratic lines.

The election regulations in each State shall be drawn up by the Provisional Council of Government and approved by the Commission. Qualified voters for each State for this election shall be persons over eighteen years of age who are (a) Palestinian citizens residing in that State; and (b) Arabs and Jews residing in the State, although not Palestinian citizens, who, before voting, have signed a notice of intention to become citizens of such State.

Arabs and Jews residing in the City of Jerusalem who have signed a notice of intention to become citizens, the Arabs of the Arab State and the Jews of the Jewish State, shall be entitled to vote in the Arab and Jewish States respectively.

Women may vote and be elected to the Constituent Assemblies.

During the transitional period no Jew shall be permitted to establish residence in the area of the proposed Arab State, and no Arab shall be permitted to establish residence in the area of the proposed Jewish State, except by special leave of the Commission.

The Constituent Assembly of each State shall draft a democratic constitution for its State and choose a provisional government to succeed the Provisional

Council of Government appointed by the Commission. The Constitutions of the States shall embody Chapters 1 and 2 of the Declaration provided for in section C below and include, inter alia, provisions for:

Establishing in each State a legislative body elected by universal suffrage and by secret ballot on the basis of proportional representation, and an executive body responsible to the legislature;

Settling all international disputes in which the State may be involved by peaceful means in such a manner that international peace and security, and justice, are not endangered;

Accepting the obligation of the State to refrain in its international relations from the threat or use of force against the territorial integrity or political independence of any State, or in any other manner inconsistent with the purpose of the United Nations;

Guaranteeing to all persons equal and non-discriminatory rights in civil, political, economic and religious matters and the enjoyment of human rights and fundamental freedoms, including freedom of religion, language, speech and publication, education, assembly and association;

Preserving freedom of transit and visit for all residents and citizens of the other State in Palestine and the City of Jerusalem, subject to considerations of national security, provided that each State shall control residence within its borders.

The Commission shall appoint a preparatory economic commission of three members to make whatever arrangements are possible for economic cooperation, with a view to establishing, as soon as practicable, the Economic Union and the Joint Economic Board, as provided in section D below.

During the period between the adoption of the recommendations on the question of Palestine by the General Assembly and the termination of the Mandate, the mandatory Power in Palestine shall maintain full responsibility for administration in areas from which it has not withdrawn its armed forces. The Commission shall assist the mandatory Power in the carrying out of these functions. Similarly the mandatory Power shall co-operate with the Commission in the execution of its functions.

With a view to ensuring that there shall be continuity in the functioning of administrative services and that, on the withdrawal of the armed forces of the mandatory Power, the whole administration shall be in the charge of the Provisional Councils and the Joint Economic Board, respectively, acting under the Commission, there shall be a progressive transfer, from the mandatory Power to the Commission, of responsibility for all the functions of government, including that of maintaining law and order in the areas from which the forces of the mandatory Power have been withdrawn.

The Commission shall be guided in its activities by the recommendations of the General Assembly and by such instructions as the Security Council may consider necessary to issue.

The measures taken by the Commission, within the recommendations of the General Assembly, shall become immediately effective unless the Commission has previously received contrary instructions from the Security Council.

The Commission shall render periodic monthly progress reports, or more frequently if desirable, to the Security Council.

The Commission shall make its final report to the next regular session of the General Assembly and to the Security Council simultaneously.

## C. Declaration

A declaration shall be made to the United Nations by the Provisional Government of each proposed State before independence. It shall contain, inter alia, the following clauses:

### GENERAL PROVISION

The stipulations contained in the Declaration are recognized as fundamental laws of the State and no law, regulation or official action shall conflict or interfere with these stipulations, nor shall any law, regulation or official action prevail over them.

### CHAPTER I: HOLY PLACES, RELIGIOUS BUILDINGS AND SITES

Existing rights in respect of Holy Places and religious buildings or sites shall not be denied or impaired.

In so far as Holy Places are concerned, the liberty of access, visit, and transit shall be guaranteed, in conformity with existing rights, to all residents and citizens of the other State and of the City of Jerusalem, as well as to aliens, without distinction as to nationality, subject to requirements of national security, public order and decorum. Similarly, freedom of worship shall be guaranteed in conformity with existing rights, subject to the maintenance of public order and decorum.

Holy Places and religious buildings or sites shall be preserved. No act shall be permitted which may in any way impair their sacred character. If at any time it appears to the Government that any particular Holy Place, religious, building or site is in need of urgent repair, the Government may call upon the community or communities concerned to carry out such repair. The Government may carry it out itself at the expense of the community or community concerned if no action is taken within a reasonable time.

No taxation shall be levied in respect of any Holy Place, religious building or site which was exempt from taxation on the date of the creation of the State. No change in the incidence of such taxation shall be made which would either discriminate between the owners or occupiers of Holy Places, religious buildings or sites, or would place such owners or occupiers in a position less favourable in relation to the general incidence of taxation than existed at the time of the adoption of the Assembly's recommendations.

The Governor of the City of Jerusalem shall have the right to determine whether the provisions of the Constitution of the State in relation to Holy Places, religious buildings and sites within the borders of the State and the religious rights appertaining thereto, are being properly applied and respected, and to make decisions on the basis of existing rights in cases of disputes which may arise between the different religious communities or the rites of a religious community with respect to such places, buildings and sites. He shall receive full co-operation and such privileges and immunities as are necessary for the exercise of his functions in the State.

CHAPTER 2: RELIGIOUS AND MINORITY RIGHTS

Freedom of conscience and the free exercise of all forms of worship, subject only to the maintenance of public order and morals, shall be ensured to all.

No discrimination of any kind shall be made between the inhabitants on the ground of race, religion, language or sex.

All persons within the jurisdiction of the State shall be entitled to equal protection of the laws.

The family law and personal status of the various minorities and their religious interests, including endowments, shall be respected.

Except as may be required for the maintenance of public order and good government, no measure shall be taken to obstruct or interfere with the enterprise of religious or charitable bodies of all faiths or to discriminate against any representative or member of these bodies on the ground of his religion or nationality.

The State shall ensure adequate primary and secondary education for the Arab and Jewish minority, respectively, in its own language and its cultural traditions. The right of each community to maintain its own schools for the education of its own members in its own language, while conforming to such educational requirements of a general nature as the State may impose, shall not be denied or impaired. Foreign educational establishments shall continue their activity on the basis of their existing rights.

No restriction shall be imposed on the free use by any citizen of the State of any language in private intercourse, in commerce, in religion, in the Press or in publications of any kind, or at public meetings.[3]

No expropriation of land owned by an Arab in the Jewish State (or by a Jew in the Arab State)[4] shall be allowed except for public purposes. In all cases of expropriation full compensation as fixed by the Supreme Court shall be said previous to dispossession.

CHAPTER 3: CITIZENSHIP, INTERNATIONAL CONVENTIONS AND FINANCIAL OBLIGATIONS

1. Citizenship Palestinian citizens residing in Palestine outside the City of Jerusalem,

as well as Arabs and Jews who, not holding Palestinian citizenship, reside in Palestine outside the City of Jerusalem shall, upon the recognition of independence, become citizens of the State in which they are resident and enjoy full civil and political rights. Persons over the age of eighteen years may opt, within one year from the date of recognition of independence of the State in which they reside, for citizenship of the other State, providing that no Arab residing in the area of the proposed Arab State shall have the right to opt for citizenship in the proposed Jewish State and no Jew residing in the proposed Jewish State shall have the right to opt for citizenship in the proposed Arab State. The exercise of this right of option will be taken to include the wives and children under eighteen years of age of persons so opting.

Arabs residing in the area of the proposed Jewish State and Jews residing in the area of the proposed Arab State who have signed a notice of intention to opt for citizenship of the other State shall be eligible to vote in the elections to the Constituent Assembly of that State, but not in the elections to the Constituent Assembly of the State in which they reside.

**2. International conventions** The State shall be bound by all the international agreements and conventions, both general and special, to which Palestine has become a party. Subject to any right of denunciation provided for therein, such agreements and conventions shall be respected by the State throughout the period for which they were concluded.

Any dispute about the applicability and continued validity of international conventions or treaties signed or adhered to by the mandatory Power on behalf of Palestine shall be referred to the International Court of Justice in accordance with the provisions of the Statute of the Court.

**3. Financial obligations** The State shall respect and fulfil all financial obligations of whatever nature assumed on behalf of Palestine by the mandatory Power during the exercise of the Mandate and recognized by the State. This provision includes the right of public servants to pensions, compensation or gratuities.

These obligations shall be fulfilled through participation in the Joint Economic Board in respect of those obligations applicable to Palestine as a whole, and individually in respect of those applicable to, and fairly apportionable between, the States.

A Court of Claims, affiliated with the Joint Economic Board, and composed of one member appointed by the United Nations, one representative of the United Kingdom and one representative of the State concerned, should be established. Any dispute between the United Kingdom and the State respecting claims not recognized by the latter should be referred to that Court.

Commercial concessions granted in respect of any part of Palestine prior to the adoption of the resolution by the General Assembly shall continue to be valid according to their terms, unless modified by agreement between the concession-holders and the State.

CHAPTER 4: MISCELLANEOUS PROVISIONS

The provisions of chapters 1 and 2 of the declaration shall be under the guarantee of the United Nations, and no modifications shall be made in them without the assent of the General Assembly of the United Nations. Any Member of the United Nations shall have the right to bring to the attention of the General Assembly any infraction or danger of infraction of any of these stipulations, and the General Assembly may thereupon make such recommendations as it may deem proper in the circumstances.

Any dispute relating to the application or interpretation of this declaration shall be referred, at the request of either party, to the International Court of Justice, unless the parties agree to another mode of settlement.

## D. Economic Union and Transit

The Provisional Council of Government of each State shall enter into an undertaking with respect to Economic Union and Transit. This undertaking shall be drafted by the Commission provided for in section B, paragraph 1, utilizing to the greatest possible extent the advice and cooperation of representative organizations and bodies from each of the proposed States. It shall contain provisions to establish the Economic Union of Palestine and provide for other matters of common interest. If by 1 April 1948 the Provisional Councils of Government have not entered into the undertaking, the undertaking shall be put into force by the Commission.

THE ECONOMIC UNION OF PALESTINE

The objectives of the Economic Union of Palestine shall be:

A customs union;

A joint currency system providing for a single foreign exchange rate;

Operation in the common interest on a non-discriminatory basis of railways inter-State highways; postal, telephone and telegraphic services and ports and airports involved in international trade and commerce;

Joint economic development, especially in respect of irrigation, land reclamation and soil conservation;

Access for both States and for the City of Jerusalem on a non-discriminatory basis to water and power facilities.

There shall be established a Joint Economic Board, which shall consist of three representatives of each of the two States and three foreign members appointed by the Economic and Social Council of the United Nations. The foreign members shall be appointed in the first instance for a term of three years; they shall serve as individuals and not as representatives of States.

The functions of the Joint Economic Board shall be to implement either directly or by delegation the measures necessary to realize the objectives of the Economic Union. It shall have all powers of organization and administration necessary to fulfil its functions.

The States shall bind themselves to put into effect the decisions of the Joint Economic Board. The Board's decisions shall be taken by a majority vote.

In the event of failure of a State to take the necessary action the Board may, by a vote of six members, decide to withhold an appropriate portion of the part of the customs revenue to which the State in question is entitled under the Economic Union. Should the State persist in its failure to cooperate, the Board may decide by a simple majority vote upon such further sanctions, including disposition of funds which it has withheld, as it may deem appropriate.

In relation to economic development, the functions of the Board shall be planning, investigation and encouragement of joint development projects, but it shall not undertake such projects except with the assent of both States and the City of Jerusalem, in the event that Jerusalem is directly involved in the development project.

In regard to the joint currency system, the currencies circulating in the two States and the City of Jerusalem shall be issued under the authority of the Joint Economic Board, which shall be the sole issuing authority and which shall determine the reserves to be held against such currencies.

So far as is consistent with paragraph 2(b) above, each State may operate its own central bank, control its own fiscal and credit policy, its foreign exchange receipts and expenditures, the grant of import licences, and may conduct international financial operations on its own faith and credit. During the first two years after the termination of the Mandate, the Joint Economic Board shall have the authority to take such measures as may be necessary to ensure that—to the extent that the total foreign exchange revenues of the two States from the export of goods and services permit, and provided that each State takes appropriate measures to conserve its own foreign exchange resources—each State shall have available, in any twelve months' period, foreign exchange sufficient to assure the supply of quantities of imported goods and services for consumption in its territory equivalent to the quantities of such goods and services consumed in that territory in the twelve months' period ending 31 December 1947.

All economic authority not specifically vested in the Joint Economic Board is reserved to each State.

There shall be a common customs tariff with complete freedom of trade between the States, and between the States and the City of Jerusalem.

The following items shall be a first charge on the customs and other common revenue of the Joint Economic Board:

The expenses of the customs service and of the operation of the joint services;

The administrative expenses of the Joint Economic Board;

The financial obligations of the Administration of Palestine, consisting of:

The service of the outstanding public debt;

The cost of superannuation benefits, now being paid or falling due in the future, in accordance with the rules and to the extent established by paragraph 3 of chapter 3 above.

After these obligations have been met in full, the surplus revenue from the customs and other common services shall be divided in the following manner: not less than 5 per cent and not more than 10 per cent to the City of Jerusalem; the residue shall be allocated to each State by the Joint Economic Board equitably, with the objective of maintaining a sufficient and suitable level of government and social services in each State, except that the share of either State shall not exceed the amount of that State's contribution to the revenues of the Economic Union by more than approximately four million pounds in any year. The amount granted may be adjusted by the Board according to the price level in relation to the prices prevailing at the time of the establishment of the Union. After five years, the principles of the distribution of the joint revenue may be revised by the Joint Economic Board on a basis of equity.

All international conventions and treaties affecting customs tariff rates, and those communications services under the jurisdiction of the Joint Economic Board, shall be entered into by both States. In these matters, the two States shall be bound to act in accordance with the majority of the Joint Economic Board.

The Joint Economic Board shall endeavour to secure for Palestine's exports fair and equal access to world markets.

All enterprises operated by the Joint Economic Board shall pay fair wages on a uniform basis.

## FREEDOM OF TRANSIT AND VISIT

The undertaking shall contain provisions preserving freedom of transit and visit for all residents or citizens of both States and of the City of Jerusalem, subject to security considerations; provided that each State and the City shall control residence within its borders.

## TERMINATION, MODIFICATION AND INTERPRETATION OF THE UNDERTAKING

The undertaking and any treaty issuing therefrom shall remain in force for a period of ten years. It shall continue in force until notice of termination, to take effect two years thereafter, is given by either of the parties.

During the initial ten-year period, the undertaking and any treaty issuing therefrom may not be modified except by consent of both parties and with the approval of the General Assembly.

Any dispute relating to the application or the interpretation of the undertaking and any treaty issuing therefrom shall be referred, at the request of either party, to the International Court Of Justice, unless the parties agree to another mode of settlement.

### E. Assets

The movable assets of the Administration of Palestine shall be allocated to the Arab and Jewish States and the City of Jerusalem on an equitable basis. Allocations should be made by the United Nations Commission referred to in section B, paragraph 1, above. Immovable assets shall become the property of the government of the territory in which they are situated.

During the period between the appointment of the United Nations Commission and the termination of the Mandate, the mandatory Power shall, except in respect of ordinary operations, consult with the Commission on any measure which it may contemplate involving the liquidation, disposal or encumbering of the assets of the Palestine Government, such as the accumulated treasury surplus, the proceeds of Government bond issues, State lands or any other asset.

### F. Admission to Membership in the United Nations

When the independence of either the Arab or the Jewish State as envisaged in this plan has become effective and the declaration and undertaking, as envisaged in this plan, have been signed by either of them, sympathetic consideration should be given to its application for admission to membership in the United Nations in accordance with article 4 of the Charter of the United Nations.

## PART II. BOUNDARIES

### A. The Arab State

The area of the Arab State in Western Galilee is bounded on the west by the Mediterranean and on the north by the frontier of the Lebanon from Ras en Naqura to a point north of Saliha. From there the boundary proceeds southwards, leaving the built-up area of Saliha in the Arab State, to join the southernmost point of this village. There it follows the western boundary line of the villages of Alma, Rihaniya and Teitaba, thence following the northern boundary line of Meirun village to join the Acre-Safad Sub-District boundary line. It follows this line to a point west of Es Sammu'i village and joins it again at the northernmost point of Farradiya. Thence it follows the sub-district boundary line to the Acre-Safad main road. From here it follows the western boundary of Kafr-I'nan village until it reaches the Tiberias-Acre Sub-District boundary line, passing to the west of the junction of the Acre-Safad and Lubiya-Kafr-I'nan roads. From the south-west corner of Kafr-I'nan village the boundary line follows the western boundary of the Tiberias Sub-District to a point close to the boundary line between the villages of Maghar and 'Eilabun, thence bulging out to the west to include as much of the eastern part of the plain of Battuf as is necessary for the reservoir proposed by the Jewish Agency for the irrigation of lands to the south and east.

The boundary rejoins the Tiberias Sub-District boundary at a point on the Nazareth-Tiberias road south-east of the built-up area of Turʿan; thence it runs southwards, at first following the sub-district boundary and then passing between the Kadoorie Agricultural School and Mount Tabor, to a point due south at the base of Mount Tabor. From here it runs due west, parallel to the horizontal grid line 230, to the north-east corner of the village lands of Tel Adashim. It then runs to the northwest corner of these lands, whence it turns south and west so as to include in the Arab State the sources of the Nazareth water supply in Yafa village. On reaching Ginneiger it follows the eastern, northern and western boundaries of the lands of this village to their south-west comer, whence it proceeds in a straight line to a point on the Haifa-Afula railway on the boundary between the villages of Sarid and El-Mujeidil. This is the point of intersection. The south-western boundary of the area of the Arab State in Galilee takes a line from this point, passing northwards along the eastern boundaries of Sarid and Gevat to the north-eastern corner of Nahalal, proceeding thence across the land of Kefar ha Horesh to a central point on the southern boundary of the village of ʿIlut, thence westwards along that village boundary to the eastern boundary of Beit Lahm, thence northwards and north-eastwards along its western boundary to the north-eastern corner of Waldheim and thence north-westwards across the village lands of Shafa ʿAmr to the southeastern corner of Ramat Yohanan. From here it runs due north-north-east to a point on the Shafa ʿAmr-Haifa road, west of its junction with the road of Iʿbillin. From there it proceeds north-east to a point on the southern boundary of Iʿbillin situated to the west of the Iʿbillin-Birwa road. Thence along that boundary to its westernmost point, whence it turns to the north, follows across the village land of Tamra to the north-westernmost corner and along the western boundary of Julis until it reaches the Acre-Safad road. It then runs westwards along the southern side of the Safad-Acre road to the Galilee-Haifa District boundary, from which point it follows that boundary to the sea.

The boundary of the hill country of Samaria and Judea starts on the Jordan River at the Wadi Malih south-east of Beisan and runs due west to meet the Beisan-Jericho road and then follows the western side of that road in a north-westerly direction to the junction of the boundaries of the Sub-Districts of Beisan, Nablus, and Jenin. From that point it follows the Nablus-Jenin sub-District boundary westwards for a distance of about three kilometres and then turns north-westwards, passing to the east of the built-up areas of the villages of Jalbun and Faqquʿa, to the boundary of the Sub-Districts of Jenin and Beisan at a point north-east of Nuris. Thence it proceeds first northwestwards to a point due north of the built-up area of Zieʿin and then westwards to the Afula-Jenin railway, thence north-westwards along the District boundary line to the point of intersection on the Hejaz railway. From here the boundary runs southwestwards, including the built-up area and some of the land of the village of Kh. Lid in the Arab State to cross the Haifa-Jenin road at a point on the district boundary between Haifa and Samaria west of El-Mansi. It follows this boundary to the southernmost point of the village of El-Buteimat. From here it follows the northern and eastern boundaries of the village of Ar'ara rejoining the Haifa-Samaria district boundary at Wadi 'Ara, and thence proceeding south-south-westwards in an approximately straight line joining up with the western boundary of Qaqun to a point east of the railway line on the eastern boundary of Qaqun village. From here it runs along the railway line some distance to the east of it to a point just east of the Tulkarm railway station. Thence the boundary follows a line half-way between the railway and the Tulkarm-Qalqiliya-Jaljuliya and Ras El-Ein road to a point just east of Ras El-Ein station, whence it proceeds along the railway some distance to the east of it to the point on the railway line south of the junction of the Haifa-Lydda and Beit Nabala lines, whence it proceeds along the southern border of Lydda airport to its south-west corner, thence in a south-westerly direction to a point just west of the built-up area of Sarafand El 'Amar, whence it turns south, passing just to the west of the built-up area of Abu El-Fadil to the north-east corner of the lands of Beer Ya'aqov. (The boundary line should be so demarcated as to allow direct access from the Arab State to the airport.) Thence the boundary line follows the western and southern boundaries of Ramle village, to the north-east corner of El Na'ana village, thence in a straight line to the southernmost point of El Barriya, along the eastern boundary of that village and the southern boundary of 'Innaba village. Thence it turns north to follow the southern side of the Jaffa-Jerusalem road until El-Qubab, whence it follows the road to the boundary of Abu-Shusha. It runs along the eastern boundaries of Abu Shusha, Seidun, Hulda to the southernmost point of Hulda, thence westwards in a straight line to the north-eastern corner of Umm Kalkha, thence following the northern boundaries of Umm Kalkha, Qazaza and the northern and western boundaries of Mukhezin to the Gaza District boundary and thence runs across the village lands of El-Mismiya El-Kabira, and Yasur to the southern point of intersection, which is midway between the built-up areas of Yasur and Batani Sharqi.

From the southern point of intersection the boundary lines run north-westwards between the villages of Gan Yavne and Barqa to the sea at a point half way between Nabi Yunis and Minat El-Qila, and south-eastwards to a point west of Qastina, whence it turns in a south-westerly direction, passing to the east of the built-up areas of Es Sawafir Esh Sharqiya and 'Ibdis. From the south-east corner of 'Ibdis village it runs to a point southwest of the built-up area of Beit 'Affa, crossing the Hebron-El-Majdal road just to the west of the built-up area of Iraq Suweidan. Thence it proceeds southward along the western village boundary of El-Faluja to the Beersheba Sub-District boundary. It then runs across the tribal lands of Arab El-Jubarat to a point on the boundary between the Sub-Districts of Beersheba and Hebron north of Kh. Khuweilifa, whence it proceeds in a south-westerly direction to a point on the Beersheba-Gaza main road two kilometres to the north-west of the town. It then turns south-eastwards to reach Wadi Sab' at a point situated one kilometer to the west of it. From here it turns north-eastwards and proceeds along Wadi Sab' and along the Beersheba-Hebron road for a distance of one kilometer, whence it turns eastwards and runs in a straight line to Kh. Kuseifa to join the Beersheba-Hebron Sub-District boundary. It then follows the Beersheba-Hebron boundary eastwards to a point north of Ras Ez-Zuweira, only departing from it so as to cut across the base of the indentation between vertical grid lines 150 and 160.

About five kilometres north-east of Ras Ez-Zuweira it turns north, excluding from the Arab State a strip along the coast of the Dead Sea not more than seven kilometres in depth, as far as 'Ein Geddi, whence it turns due east to join the Transjordan frontier in the Dead Sea.

The northern boundary of the Arab section of the coastal plain runs from a point between Minat El-Qila and Nabi Yunis, passing between the built-up areas of Gan Yavne and Barqa to the point of intersection. From here it turns south-westwards, running across the lands of Batani Sharqi, along the eastern boundary of the lands of Beit Daras and across the lands of Julis, leaving the built-up areas of Batani Sharqi and Julis to the westwards, as far as the north-west corner of the lands of Beit-Tima. Thence it runs east of El-Jiya across the village lands of El-Barbara along the eastern boundaries of the villages of Beit Jirja, Deir Suneid and Dimra. From the south-east corner of Dimra the boundary passes across the lands of Beit Hanun, leaving the Jewish lands of Nir-Am to the eastwards. From the south-east corner of Beit Hanun the line runs south-west to a point south of the parallel grid line 100, then turns north-west for two kilometres, turning again in a southwesterly direction and continuing in an almost straight line to the north-west corner of the village lands of Kirbet Ikhza'a. From there it follows the boundary line of this village to its southernmost point. It then runs in a southerly direction along the vertical grid line 90 to its junction with the horizontal grid line 70. It then turns south-eastwards to Kh. El-Ruheiba and then proceeds in a southerly direction to a point known as El-Baha, beyond which it crosses the Beersheba-El 'Auja main road to the west of Kh. El-Mushrifa. From there it joins Wadi El-Zaiyatin just to the west of El-Subeita. From there it turns to the north-east and then to the south-east following this Wadi and passes to the east of 'Abda to join Wadi Nafkh. It then bulges to the south-west along Wadi Nafkh, Wadi Ajrim and Wadi Lassan to the point where Wadi Lassan crosses the Egyptian frontier.

The area of the Arab enclave of Jaffa consists of that part of the town-planning area of Jaffa which lies to the west of the Jewish quarters lying south of Tel-Aviv, to the west of the continuation of Herzl street up to its junction with the Jaffa-Jerusalem road, to the south-west of the section of the Jaffa-Jerusalem road lying south-east of that junction, to the west of Miqve Yisrael lands, to the northwest of Holon local council area, to the north of the line linking up the north-west corner of Holon with the northeast corner of Bat Yam local council area and to the north of Bat Yam local council area. The question of Karton quarter will be decided by the Boundary Commission, bearing in mind among other considerations the desirability of including the smallest possible number of its Arab inhabitants and the largest possible number of its Jewish inhabitants in the Jewish State.

## B. The Jewish State

The north-eastern sector of the Jewish State (Eastern Galilee) is bounded on the north and west by the Lebanese frontier and on the east by the frontiers of Syria and Transjordan. It includes the whole of the Huleh Basin, Lake Tiberias, the whole of the Beisan Sub-District, the boundary line being extended to the crest of the Gilboa mountains and the Wadi Malih. From there the Jewish State extends north-west, following the boundary described in respect of the Arab State. The Jewish section of the coastal plain extends from a point between Minat El-Qila and Nabi Yunis in the Gaza Sub-District and includes the towns of Haifa and Tel-Aviv, leaving Jaffa as an enclave of the Arab State. The eastern frontier of the Jewish State follows the boundary described in respect of the Arab State.

The Beersheba area comprises the whole of the Beersheba Sub-District, including the Negeb and the eastern part of the Gaza Sub-District, but excluding the town of Beersheba and those areas described in respect of the Arab State. It includes also a strip of land along the Dead Sea stretching from the Beersheba-Hebron Sub-District boundary line to 'Ein Geddi, as described in respect of the Arab State.

## C. The City of Jerusalem

The boundaries of the City of Jerusalem are as defined in the recommendations on the City of Jerusalem. (See Part III, section B, below).

## PART III. CITY OF JERUSALEM[5]

### A. Special Regime

The City of Jerusalem shall be established as a *corpus separatum* under a special international regime and shall be administered by the United Nations. The Trusteeship Council shall be designated to discharge the responsibilities of the Administering Authority on behalf of the United Nations.

### B. Boundaries of the City

The City of Jerusalem shall include the present municipality of Jerusalem plus the surrounding villages and towns, the most eastern of which shall be Abu Dis; the most southern, Bethlehem; the most western, 'Ein Karim (including also the built-up area of Motsa); and the most northern Shu'fat, as indicated on the attached sketch-map (annex B).

*C. Statute of the City*

The Trusteeship Council shall, within five months of the approval of the present plan, elaborate and approve a detailed statute of the City which shall contain, inter alia, the substance of the following provisions:

1. *Government machinery; special objectives.* The Administering Authority in discharging its administrative obligations shall pursue the following special objectives:

   (a) To protect and to preserve the unique spiritual and religious interests located in the city of the three great monotheistic faiths throughout the world, Christian, Jewish and Moslem; to this end to ensure that order and peace, and especially religious peace, reign in Jerusalem;

   (b)To foster cooperation among all the inhabitants of the city in their own interests as well as in order to encourage and support the peaceful development of the mutual relations between the two Palestinian peoples throughout the Holy Land; to promote the security, well-being and any constructive measures of development of the residents having regard to the special circumstances and customs of the various peoples and communities.

2. *Governor and Administrative staff.* A Governor of the City of Jerusalem shall be appointed by the Trusteeship Council and shall be responsible to it. He shall be selected on the basis of special qualifications and without regard to nationality. He shall not, however, be a citizen of either State in Palestine. The Governor shall represent the United Nations in the City and shall exercise on their behalf all powers of administration, including the conduct of external affairs. He shall be assisted by an administrative staff classed as international officers in the meaning of Article 100 of the Charter and chosen whenever practicable from the residents of the city and of the rest of Palestine on a non-discriminatory basis. A detailed plan for the organization of the administration of the city shall be submitted by the Governor to the Trusteeship Council and duly approved by it.

3. *Local autonomy*

   (a) The existing local autonomous units in the territory of the city (villages, townships and municipalities) shall enjoy wide powers of local government and administration.

   (b) The Governor shall study and submit for the consideration and decision of the Trusteeship Council a plan for the establishment of special town units consisting, respectively, of the Jewish and Arab sections of new Jerusalem. The new town units shall continue to form part the present municipality of Jerusalem.

4. *Security measures*

   (a) The City of Jerusalem shall be demilitarized; neutrality shall be declared and preserved, and no para-military formations, exercises or activities shall be permitted within its borders.

   (b) Should the administration of the City of Jerusalem be seriously obstructed or prevented by the non-cooperation or interference of one or more sections of the population the Governor shall have authority to take such measures as may be necessary to restore the effective functioning of administration.

   (c) To assist in the maintenance of internal law and order, especially for the protection of the Holy Places and religious buildings and sites in the city, the Governor shall organize a special police force of adequate strength, the members of which shall be recruited outside of Palestine. The Governor shall be empowered to direct such budgetary provision as may be necessary for the maintenance of this force.

5. *Legislative Organization.* A Legislative Council, elected by adult residents of the city irrespective of nationality on the basis of universal and secret suffrage and proportional representation, shall have powers of legislation and taxation. No legislative measures shall, however, conflict or interfere with the provisions which will be set forth in the Statute of the City, nor shall any law, regulation, or official action prevail over them. The Statute shall grant to the Governor a right of vetoing bills inconsistent with the provisions referred to in the preceding sentence. It shall also empower him to promulgate temporary ordinances in case the Council fails to adopt in time a bill deemed essential to the normal functioning of the administration.

6. *Administration of Justice.* The Statute shall provide for the establishment of an independent judiciary system, including a court of appeal. All the inhabitants of the city shall be subject to it.

7. *Economic Union and Economic Regime.* The City of Jerusalem shall be included in the Economic Union of Palestine and be bound by all stipulations of the undertaking and of any treaties issued therefrom, as well as by the decisions of the Joint Economic Board. The headquarters of the Economic Board shall be established in the territory City. The Statute shall provide for the regulation of economic matters not falling within the regime of the Economic Union, on the basis of equal treatment and non-discrimination for all members of the United Nations and their nationals.

8. *Freedom of Transit and Visit: Control of residents.* Subject to considerations of security, and of economic welfare as determined by the Governor under the

directions of the Trusteeship Council, freedom of entry into, and residence within the borders of the City shall be guaranteed for the residents or citizens of the Arab and Jewish States. Immigration into, and residence within, the borders of the city for nationals of other States shall be controlled by the Governor under the directions of the Trusteeship Council.

9. *Relations with Arab and Jewish States.* Representatives of the Arab and Jewish States shall be accredited to the Governor of the City and charged with the protection of the interests of their States and nationals in connection with the international administration of the City.

10. *Official languages.* Arabic and Hebrew shall be the official languages of the city. This will not preclude the adoption of one or more additional working languages, as may be required.

11. *Citizenship.* All the residents shall become ipso facto citizens of the City of Jerusalem unless they opt for citizenship of the State of which they have been citizens or, if Arabs or Jews, have filed notice of intention to become citizens of the Arab or Jewish State respectively, according to Part 1, section B, paragraph 9, of this Plan. The Trusteeship Council shall make arrangements for consular protection of the citizens of the City outside its territory.

12. *Freedoms of citizens.*

    (a) Subject only to the requirements of public order and morals, the inhabitants of the City shall be ensured the enjoyment of human rights and fundamental freedoms, including freedom of conscience, religion and worship, language, education, speech and press, assembly and association, and petition.

    (b) No discrimination of any kind shall be made between the inhabitants on the grounds of race, religion, language or sex.

    (c) All persons within the City shall be entitled to equal protection of the laws.

    (d) The family law and personal status of the various persons and communities and their religious interests, including endowments, shall be respected.

    (e) Except as may be required for the maintenance of public order and good government, no measure shall be taken to obstruct or interfere with the enterprise of religious or charitable bodies of all faiths or to discriminate against any representative or member of these bodies on the ground of his religion or nationality.

    (f) The City shall ensure adequate primary and secondary education for the Arab and Jewish communities respectively, in their own languages and in accordance with their cultural traditions.

The right of each community to maintain its own schools for the education of its own members in its own language, while conforming to such educational requirements of a general nature as the City may impose, shall not be denied or impaired. Foreign educational establishments shall continue their activity on the basis of their existing rights.

(g) No restriction shall be imposed on the free use by any inhabitant of the City of any language in private intercourse, in commerce, in religion, in the Press or in publications of any kind, or at public meetings.

13. *Holy Places.*

(a) Existing rights in respect of Holy Places and religious buildings or sites shall not be denied or impaired.

(b) Free access to the Holy Places and religious buildings or sites and the free exercise of worship shall be secured in conformity with existing rights and subject to the requirements of public order and decorum.

(c) Holy Places and religious buildings or sites shall be preserved. No act shall be permitted which may in any way impair their sacred character. If at any time it appears to the Governor that any particular Holy Place, religious building or site is in need of urgent repair, the Governor may call upon the community or communities concerned to carry out such repair. The Governor may carry it out himself at the expense of the community or communities concerned if no action is taken within a reasonable time.

(d) No taxation shall be levied in respect of any Holy Place, religious building or site which was exempt from taxation on the date of the creation of the City. No change in the incidence of such taxation shall be made which would either discriminate between the owners or occupiers of Holy Places, religious buildings or sites or would place such owners or occupiers in a position less favourable in relation to the general incidence of taxation than existed at the time of the adoption of the Assembly's recommendations.

14. *Special powers of the Governor in respect of the Holy Places, religious buildings and sites in the City and in any part of Palestine.*

(a) The protection of the Holy Places, religious buildings and sites located in the City of Jerusalem shall be a special concern of the Governor.

(b) With relation to such places, buildings and sites in Palestine outside

234 | APPENDIX G

the city, the Governor shall determine, on the ground of powers granted to him by the Constitution of both States, whether the provisions of the Constitution of the Arab and Jewish States in Palestine dealing therewith and the religious rights appertaining thereto are being properly applied and respected.

(c) The Governor shall also be empowered to make decisions on the basis of existing rights in cases of disputes which may arise between the different religious communities or the rites of a religious community in respect of the Holy Places, religious buildings and sites in any part of Palestine. In this task he may be assisted by a consultative council of representatives of different denominations acting in an advisory capacity.

### D. Duration of the Special Regime

The Statute elaborated by the Trusteeship Council on the aforementioned principles shall come into force not later than 1 October 1948. It shall remain in force in the first instance for a period of ten years, unless the Trusteeship Council finds it necessary to undertake a re-examination of these provisions at an earlier date. After the expiration of this period the whole scheme shall be subject to examination by the Trusteeship Council in the light of experience acquired with its functioning. The residents the City shall be then free to express by means of a referendum their wishes as to possible modifications of regime of the City.

## PART IV. CAPITULATIONS

States whose nationals have in the past enjoyed in Palestine the privileges and immunities of foreigners, including the benefits of consular jurisdiction and protection, as formerly enjoyed by capitulation or usage in the Ottoman Empire, are invited to renounce any right pertaining to them to the re-establishment of such privileges and immunities in the proposed Arab and Jewish States and the City of Jerusalem.

ADOPTED AT THE 128TH PLENARY MEETING

*In favour: 33*

Australia, Belgium, Bolivia, Brazil, Byelorussian S.S.R., Canada, Costa Rica, Czechoslovakia, Denmark, Dominican Republic, Ecuador, France, Guatemala, Haiti, Iceland, Liberia, Luxemburg, Netherlands, New Zealand, Nicaragua, Norway, Panama, Paraguay, Peru, Philippines, Poland, Sweden, Ukrainian S.S.R., Union of South Africa, U.S.A., U.S.S.R., Uruguay, Venezuela.

*Against: 13*

Afghanistan, Cuba, Egypt, Greece, India, Iran, Iraq, Lebanon, Pakistan, Saudi Arabia, Syria, Turkey, Yemen.

*Abstained: 10*

Argentina, Chile, China, Colombia, El Salvador, Ethiopia, Honduras, Mexico, United Kingdom, Yugoslavia.

## APPENDIX H

## UNITED NATIONS GENERAL ASSEMBLY
## RESOLUTION 194 (III)
*Palestine—Progress Report of the United Nations Mediator*


*The General Assembly,*

*Having considered further* the situation in Palestine,

1. *Expresses* its deep appreciation of the progress achieved through the good offices of the late United Nations Mediator in promoting a peaceful adjustment of the future situation of Palestine, for which cause he sacrificed his life; and

   *Extends* its thanks to the Acting Mediator and his staff for their continued efforts and devotion to duty in Palestine;

2. *Establishes* a Conciliation Commission consisting of three States members of the United Nations which shall have the following functions:

   (a) To assume, in so far as it considers necessary in existing circumstances, the functions given to the United Nations Mediator on Palestine by resolution 186 (S-2) of the General Assembly of 14 May 1948;

   (b) To carry out the specific functions and directives given to it by the present resolution and such additional functions and directives as may be given to it by the General Assembly or by the Security Council;

   (c) To undertake, upon the request of the Security Council, any of the functions now assigned to the United Nations Mediator on Palestine or to the United Nations Truce Commission by resolutions of the Security Council; upon such request to the Conciliation Commission by the Security Council with respect to all the remaining functions of the United Nations Mediator on Palestine under Security Council resolutions, the office of the Mediator shall be terminated;

3. *Decides* that a Committee of the Assembly, consisting of China, France, the Union of Soviet Socialist Republics, the United Kingdom and the United States

SOURCE: U.N. General Assembly, Third Session, Official Records, *Admission of Israel to the United Nations.* Prepared in pursuance of U.N. General Assembly Resolution 173, A/PV 207, 1949.

of America, shall present, before the end of the first part of the present session of the General Assembly, for the approval of the Assembly, a proposal concerning the names of the three States which will constitute the Conciliation Commission;

4. *Requests* the Commission to begin its functions at once, with a view to the establishment of contact between the parties themselves and the Commission at the earliest possible date;

5. *Calls upon* the Governments and authorities concerned to extend the scope of the negotiations provided for in the Security Council's resolution of 16 November 1948 and to seek agreement by negotiations conducted either with the Conciliation Commission or directly, with a view to the final settlement of all questions outstanding between them;

6. *Instructs* the Conciliation Commission to take steps to assist the Governments and authorities concerned to achieve a final settlement of all questions outstanding between them;

7. *Resolves* that the Holy Places—including Nazareth—religious buildings and sites in Palestine should be protected and free access to them assured, in accordance with existing rights and historical practice; that arrangements to this end should be under effective United Nations supervision; that the United Nations Conciliation Commission, in presenting to the fourth regular session of the General Assembly its detailed proposals for a permanent international regime for the territory of Jerusalem, should include recommendations concerning the Holy Places in that territory; that with regard to the Holy Places in the rest of Palestine the Commission should call upon the political authorities of the areas concerned to give appropriate formal guarantees as to the protection of the Holy Places and access to them; and that these undertakings should be presented to the General Assembly for approval;

8. *Resolves* that, in view of its association with three world religions, the Jerusalem area, including the present municipality of Jerusalem plus the surrounding villages and towns, the most eastern of which shall be Abu Dis; the most southern, Bethlehem; the most western, Ein Karim (including also the built-up area of Motsa); and the most northern, Shu'fat, should be accorded special and separate treatment from the rest of Palestine and should be placed under effective United Nations control;

*Requests* the Security Council to take further steps to ensure the demilitarization of Jerusalem at the earliest possible date;

*Instructs* the Conciliation Commission to present to the fourth regular session of the General Assembly detailed proposals for a permanent international regime for the Jerusalem area which will provide for the maximum local autonomy for distinctive groups consistent with the special international status of the Jerusalem area;

The Conciliation Commission is authorized to appoint a United Nations representative, who shall co-operate with the local authorities with respect to the interim administration of the Jerusalem area;

9. *Resolves* that, pending agreement on more detailed arrangements among the Governments and authorities concerned, the freest possible access to Jerusalem by road, rail or air should be accorded to all inhabitants of Palestine;

*Instructs* the Conciliation Commission to report immediately to the Security Council, for appropriate action by that organ, any attempt by any party to impede such access;

10. *Instructs* the Conciliation Commission to seek arrangements among the Governments and authorities concerned which will facilitate the economic development of the area, including arrangements for access to ports and airfields and the use of transportation and communication facilities;

11. *Resolves* that the refugees wishing to return to their homes and live at peace with their neighbours should be permitted to do so at the earliest practicable date, and that compensation should be paid for the property of those choosing not to return and for loss of or damage to property which, under principles of international law or in equity, should be made good by the Governments or authorities responsible;

*Instructs* the Conciliation Commission to facilitate the repatriation, resettlement and economic and social rehabilitation of the refugees and the payment of compensation, and to maintain close relations with the Director of the United Nations Relief for Palestine Refugees and, through him, with the appropriate organs and agencies of the United Nations;

12. *Authorizes* the Conciliation Commission to appoint such subsidiary bodies and to employ such technical experts, acting under its authority, as it may find necessary for the effective discharge of its functions and responsibilities under the present resolution;

The Conciliation Commission will have its official headquarters at Jerusalem. The authorities responsible for maintaining order in Jerusalem will be responsible for taking all measures necessary to ensure the security of the Commission. The Secretary-General will provide a limited number of guards to the protection of the staff and premises of the Commission;

13. *Instructs* the Conciliation Commission to render progress reports periodically to the Secretary-General for transmission to the Security Council and to the Members of the United Nations;

14. *Calls upon* all Governments and authorities concerned to co-operate with the Conciliation Commission and to take all possible steps to assist in the implementation of the present resolution;

15. *Requests* the Secretary-General to provide the necessary staff and facilities and to make appropriate arrangements to provide the necessary funds required in carrying out the terms of the present resolution.

*At the 186th plenary meeting on 11 December 1948, a committee of the Assembly consisting of the five States designated in paragraph 3 of the above resolution proposed that the following three States should constitute the Conciliation Commission:*

FRANCE, TURKEY, UNITED STATES OF AMERICA.

*The proposal of the Committee having been adopted by the General Assembly at the same meeting, the Conciliation Commission is therefore composed of the above-mentioned three States.*

# APPENDIX I

## UNITED NATIONS GENERAL ASSEMBLY
## RESOLUTION 273 (III)
### Admission of Israel to Membership in the United Nations
## MAY 11, 1949

*Having received* the report of the Security Council on the application of Israel for membership in the United Nations,[1]

*Noting* that, in the judgment of the Security Council, Israel is a peace-loving State and is able and willing to carry out the obligations contained in the Charter,

*Noting* that the Security Council has recommended to the General Assembly that it admit Israel to membership in the United Nations,

*Noting* furthermore the declaration by the State of Israel that it "unreservedly accepts the obligations of the United Nations Charter and undertakes to honour them from the day when it becomes a Member of the United Nations,"[2]

*Recalling* its resolutions of 29 November 1947[3] and 11 December 1948[4] and taking note of the declarations and explanations made by the representative of the Government of Israel[5] before the *ad hoc* Political Committee in respect of the implementation of the said resolutions,

*The General Assembly,*

*Acting* in discharge of its functions under Article 4 of the Charter and rule 125 of its rules of procedure,

1. *Decides* that Israel is a peace-loving State which accepts the obligations contained in the Charter and is able and willing to carry out those obligations;

2. *Decides* to admit Israel to membership in the United Nations.

---

SOURCE: U.N. General Assembly, Third Session, Official Records, *Admission of Israel to Membership in the United Nations.* Prepared in pursuance of U.N. General Assembly Resolution 273, A/PV 207, 1949.

# NOTES

Introduction *(pages 1–19)*

1. This was British High Commissioner Herbert Samuel's warning to Chaim Weizmann from 1921. I thank Liora Russman Halperin for this citation. See her superb bachelor's thesis, "The Arabic Question: Zionism and the Politics of Language in Palestine, 1918–1948" (Harvard University, 2005), 74.

2. This desire is deeply embedded in the founding document of the State of Israel, the Declaration of the Establishment of the State from 14 December 1948, which declares: "After being forcibly exiled from their land, the people kept faith with it throughout their Dispersion and never ceased to pray and hope for their return to it and for the restoration in it of their political freedom. . . . Impelled by this historic and traditional attachment, Jews strove in every successive generation to re-establish themselves in their ancient homeland."

3. The Arabic term *Nakba* was coined in 1948 by the historian Constantine Zureik. The literature on the *Nakba* and the Palestinian right of return is large and growing. In terms of literary representation, Elias Khoury's *Gate of the Sun* is peerless in evoking the sense of longing, neglect, and misfortune that the *Nakba* caused Palestinian refugees. It bred, on one hand, a kind of psychic malady among displaced Palestinians that Khoury's narrator calls "Return fever." It also generated a well-developed sense of self-deprecation, no more poignantly expressed in the novel than by a Palestinian woman to an Israeli officer: "We're the Jews' Jews." See Khoury, *Gate of the Sun* (Bab al-Shams), trans. Humphrey Davies (Brooklyn, N.Y.: Archipelago, 2006), 62, 381.

4. Khalil Shikaki, "The Right of Return," *Wall Street Journal,* 30 July 2003. This point was affirmed by a recent *New York Times* article that concluded that "(a)lmost no Palestinian questions the demand for Israel's recognition of the right to return; many, however, now say returning is becoming less and less feasible." See Hassan M. Fattah, "For Many Palestinians, 'Return Is Not a Goal,'" *New York Times,* 26 March 2007.

5. For critical voices on his conclusions, see, for example, Salman Abu Sitta, "Inalienable and Sacred," http://weekly.ahram.org.eg/2003/651/op11/htm, 13–20 August 2003 and Ghada Karmi, "The Right of Return: The Heart of the Israeli-Palestinian Conflict," http://www.opendemocracy.net/conflict-debate_97/article_1456.jsp, 27 August 2003. For another critical voice from a different angle, see Max Abrams, "The 'Right of Return' Debate Revisited," *Middle East Intelligence Bulletin* 5 (August–September 2003), accessed at http://www.meib.org/articles/0308_pal1.htm.

6. Said offered his assessment while polemicizing against Palestinian political leaders who were prepared to compromise on the question of return. See his "Introduction: The

Right of Return at Last" in Naseer Aruri, *Palestinian Refugees: The Right of Return* (London: Pluto, 2001), 4. Meanwhile, the interview with Olmert in the *Jerusalem Post* from 29 March 2007 can be found at http://www.jpost.com/servlet/Satellite?apage=4&cid =1173879210818&pagename=JPost%2FJPArticle%2FShowFull.

7. See Rawidowicz's lecture at a symposium on the new State of Israel held in 1949, "Two That are One," in Rawidowicz, *State of Israel, Diaspora, and Jewish Continuity: Essays on the "Ever-Dying People"* (1986; reprint, Hanover, N.H.: University Press of New England, 1998), 155.

8. There were some exceptions, as we shall explore in part II, especially in the midst of and after Israel's wars in 1956 and 1967.

9. In addition to those discussed here, groups ranging from the Reform-oriented American Council for Judaism to the ultra-Orthodox Neturei Karta attacked the Zionist goal of statehood on religious grounds. In its opening "Digest of Principles" from August 1943, the American Council for Judaism (ACJ) declared its opposition to "the efforts to establish a Jewish National State in Palestine or elsewhere," as well as to "all philosophies that stress the racialism, the nationalism and the homelessness of the Jews." Later, after the state was created, the ACJ accepted the principle of the partition of Palestine, but strenuously affirmed the loyalty of American Jews to the United States. The first article of a new statement of principles from 19 January 1948 proclaimed: "Nationality and religion are separate and distinct. Our nationality is American. Our religion is Judaism. Our homeland is the United States of America. We reject any concept that Jews are at home only in Palestine." See the discussion in Thomas A. Kolsky, *Jews against Zionism: The American Council for Judaism, 1942–1948* (Philadelphia: Temple University Press, 1990), 71, 177. Perhaps the most renowned and vociferous among religious critics was Rabbi Yoel Teitelbaum, the Satmar Rebbe and author of the theological polemic against Zionism, *Va-yo'el Mosheh* (1958), who famously called Zionism "the greatest form of spiritual impurity in the entire world." See http://www.jewsagainstzionism .com/quotes/teitelbaum.htm#SomeWords.

10. See, for example, Yoram Hazony, *The Jewish State: The Struggle for Israel's Soul* (New York: Basic Books, 2000), Michael B. Oren, "Jews and the Challenge of Sovereignty," *Azure* 23 (Winter 5766/2006), 27–38, and Ruth Wisse, *Jews and Power* (New York: Schocken, 2007).

11. See Avraham Sharon, *Torat ha-Tsiyonut ha-akhzarit* (Tel Aviv: Sifriyat De'ot, 1943–44). This viewpoint bears a strong resemblance to—and became more famous among—the Canaanites, the literary and political movement that arose in the *Yishuv* in the 1940s. Inspired by the Hebrew poet Yonatan Ratosh, the Canaanites constructed a rather fantastical image of a radical Hebrew culture at home in the native soil of ancient Canaan— and genetically unrelated to Jewish religion, Diaspora Jewish life, or even Zionism (with its European origins). Rawidowicz, for his part, regarded the Canaanites as the flip side of the coin of the anti-Zionist American Council for Judaism. Both groups denied an organic relationship between Babylon and Jerusalem: the American Council, because it rejected the notion of a national bond of any sort among Jews; and the Canaanites, because they "absorbed (the idea of) the negation of the Diaspora with their mothers' milk." See *Bavel vi-Yerushalayim* (Waltham, Mass.: Ararat, 1957), 1:188–89.

12. In a related vein, Anita Shapira has traced a shift in the dominant Socialist Zionist movement from a defensive to an offensive posture vis-à-vis the native Palestinian Arab population, marked by the outbreak of the general Arab strike and rebellion of 1936. See her *Land and Power: The Zionist Resort to Force, 1881–1948*, trans. William Templer (New York: Oxford University Press, 1992).

13. Yizhar's short piece, "'Al dodim ve-'Arvim" is included in a section on "The Arab Question as a Jewish Problem," in *Mordekhai Martin Buber be-mivhan ha-zeman,* ed. Kalman Yaron and Paul Mendes-Flohr (Jerusalem: Magnes Press, 1993), 14–15. See also the English translation by Steven Bowman, "About Uncles and Arabs," *Hebrew Studies* 47 (2006), 325–26. I thank Yael Feldman for calling this source to my attention.

14. Yizhar, "'Al dodim ve-'Arvim," 14.

15. See Joseph B. Schechtman, *Postwar Population Transfers in Europe, 1945–55* (Philadelphia: University of Pennsylvania Press, 1962), ix, and Schechtman, *The Arab Refugee Problem* (New York: Philosophical Library, 1952). 31.

16. This, for example, is the argument of the Israeli writer Hillel Halkin, who describes the Palestinian claim to repatriation as "absurd," given that "no such right was ever demanded on behalf of far larger refugee populations in the 20th century." Halkin does not mention in his article United Nations General Assembly Resolution 194 of 1948, which specifically addresses the plight of Palestinian refugees by calling for either repatriation or compensation; see Hillel Halkin, "The Peace Planners Strike Again," *Commentary* (January 2008), 16. For a more nuanced legal discussion that dismisses the right of return for Palestinians (but not the idea of compensation), see Ruth Lapidot, *Israel and the Palestinians: Some Legal Issues* (Jerusalem: Jerusalem Institute for Israel Studies, 2003), 43–54.

17. See, for example, Salman Abu-Sitta, "The Right of Return: Sacred, Legal and Possible," in Aruri, *Palestinian Refugees: The Right of Return*, 195–207. On the inalienability of the right of return, see the introduction by Said and Joseph Massad's chapter, "Return or Permanent Exile?" in Aruri, *Palestinian Refugees*. Elsewhere, Ali Abunimah and Hussein Ibish argue that with respect to the Palestinians' right of return, "[n]o state or authority has the right to bargain it away, any more than it could bargain away its people's other human rights." See Abunimah and Ibish, *The Palestinian Right of Return* (Washington, D.C.: American-Arab Anti-Discrimination Committee, 2001), 7. Ibish has recently offered, in a private exchange, a refinement of this position that draws upon his reading of current political realities and his own commitment to a two-state solution. He writes: "Israel must recognize and accept the right of return as an inviolable principle of international law, and Palestinians must recognize and accept that in practice Israeli sovereignty will dictate the modalities for the implementation of any such return of refugees" (e-mail correspondence, 10 July 2007). A competing view that suggests that the right of return is not rooted in international law is offered by Israeli legal scholar Eyal Benvenisti who argues: "[I]nstead of an individual right of each Palestinian refugee, or any refugee, to return, international law recognizes the full authority of the relevant governments (including those representing the refugees) to reach any compromise they deem to be just and appropriate." See Benvenisti, "The Right of Return in International Law: An Israeli Perspective," http://www.idrc.ca/uploads/user-S/10576079920 Session_2_Eyal_Benvenisti_paper.doc, 1.

18. An exception to this pattern is provided by Sari Nusseibeh, who argues of the Palestinian cause: "We have two rights. We have the right of return, in my opinion. But we also have the right to live in freedom and independence. And very often in life one has to forgo the implementation of one right in order to implement other rights." See Nusseibeh (with Anthony David), *Once Upon a Country: A Palestinian Life* (New York: Farrar, Straus, and Giroux, 2007), 446. See also the observation of Hannah Arendt in 1948; she notes in Jews and Arabs in Palestine "the complete incompatibility of claims which until now has frustrated every attempt to compromise and every effort to find a common denominator between two peoples whose common interests are patent to all except themselves." Arendt, "Peace or Armistice in the Near East?" in her *The Jewish Writings*, ed. Jerome Kohn and Ron H. Feldman (New York: Schocken, 2007), 430.

19. The question, following the groundbreaking work of Israeli scholars, particularly Benny Morris, is no longer whether expulsions took place in 1948. As Derek Penslar has commented in a recent book: "[I]t is now conventional wisdom that, as Benny Morris argued back in 1988, substantial numbers of Palestinians were expelled from their homes in 1948." See Derek J. Penslar, *Israel in History: The Jewish State in Comparative Perspective* (New York: Routledge, 2007), 44–45. However, two key questions remain: the extent of the expulsions (i.e., how many Palestinians were forcibly removed) and whether the expulsions were deliberately organized according to a master plan or not. On the latter question, Ilan Pappé has recently advanced a sweeping thesis, arguing that a small group of Zionist officials led by David Ben-Gurion—and which he refers to as "The Consultancy"—came together "solely for the purpose of plotting and designing the dispossession of the Palestinians." Ilan Pappé, *The Ethnic Cleansing of Palestine* (Oxford: Oneworld, 2006), 5. Pappé presents a seamless plot line based on a wide range of sources (including Arab accounts and oral histories), though the documentary evidence he uses is at times fragmentary and ignores countervailing statements that point toward a more complicated set of Zionist/Israeli intentions vis-à-vis the Arab population of Palestine up to and including 1948 (i.e., professions from Zionist officials speaking of the desire for peace, friendship, or fraternity with them). The position at which Pappé is taking aim, most famously associated with Morris, asserts that the expulsion of Palestinian Arabs was far more episodic and partial than premeditated, dependent, as it was, on local conditions and the discretion accorded individual commanders by the Haganah's "Plan D." That said, Morris in the revised edition of his 1988 book arrived at a new conclusion: "pre-1948 'Transfer' thinking had a greater effect on what happened in 1948 than I had allowed for." Morris, in this sense, tries to avoid the pole of Pappé's sweeping determinism and his erstwhile assertion of a lack of premeditation. In this view, pre-1948 Zionist discussions of "transfer" (the forced removal of Palestinian Arabs) did not necessarily provide the blueprint for expulsions in 1948, but rather offered a policy option that was acted upon in moments of crisis or stress. See Morris, *The Birth of the Palestinian Refugee Problem Revisited* (Cambridge: Cambridge University Press, 2004), 5–6.

20. We shall see that Simon Rawidowicz was well aware of and deeply disturbed by the fact that various Israeli government officials, including the first president of the State of Israel, Chaim Weizmann, referred to the Arab flight from Palestine as "a miracle." Meanwhile, David Ben-Gurion, the towering founding father of the State of Israel and its first prime minister tended to see the creation of the state in messianic terms,

indeed, as "a messianic event"—notwithstanding his confirmed secularism. His writings are replete with this kind of messianic resonance from 1948 to his last years. See David Ohana's study and source collection dealing with Ben-Gurion's messianism, *Meshihiyut u-mamlakhtiyut: Ben-Guryon veha-intelektu'alim ben hazon medini le-te'ologyah politit* (Beer Sheva: Makhon Ben-Guryon, 2003), 57ff.

21. In addition, it is important to note that at various times, and with increasing frequency today, Jewish advocates have countered the claims of Palestinian dispossession with claims of Jewish dispossession from Arab countries in 1948. Indeed, some 850,000 Jews left Arab countries in 1948 and thereafter, many under the dark cloud of threat to their physical well-being. Recently, the group Justice for Jews from Arab Countries has claimed to unearth evidence that the Arab League drafted a law that called on its seven member countries to discriminate against Jews in response to Zionism. See "Group Spotlights Jews who Left Arab Lands," *New York Times*, November 5, 2007. As we shall see in part II, it has been proposed on different occasions that the flight of Arabs from Palestine/Israel and of Jews from Arab countries be deemed a population exchange. Such a proposal has the effect of ignoring both the sense of historical injustice and the legitimate demands for compensation of both Arabs and Jews.

22. In this regard, Don Peretz's early and excellent treatment of Israel's stance on the refugee question (1958) concludes on an overly optimistic note: "Time as a healing element is the most important factor in coping with the psychological disturbances created by the Palestine conflict." See Peretz's important study, based on his 1954 Columbia dissertation, *Israel and the Palestine Arabs* (Washington, D.C.: Middle East Institute, 1958), 247.

23. The intent of this discussion of parallel but opposing vectors of change is *not* to equate the Nakba with the Holocaust; the latter remains a unique example of premeditated state-sponsored mass murder.

24. One such figure is Palestinian philosopher, Sari Nusseibeh. Nusseibeh is hardly the only Israeli Jew or Palestinian Arab to be able to grasp with empathy the perspective of the other. He is, however, an especially noteworthy one, given his commitment to serve his people (as president of Al-Quds University) and to advance with an Israeli counterpart what they see as the most equitable and practical solution: a two-state arrangement between the Jordan River and the Mediterranean Sea. And yet, as a telling symbol of the suspension of reality in which Nusseibeh must engage, he commences his recent memoir by describing how he felt compelled to pen a fairy tale in order to lure his British wife to leave the comforts of Oxford for the travails of Jerusalem. How else, he pondered, "do you break the news that your fate will be tied to one of the most volatile corners on the planet, with two major wars in its recent history and the Arab leaders worldwide calling for another?" The fairy-tale quality is preserved in the title of the book. See Nusseibeh, *Once Upon a Country: A Palestinian Life*, 4.

25. Arendt's response to Scholem from 24 July 1963 is found in *The Jewish Writings*, 466–67.

26. The journalist J. J. Goldberg captures this dynamic in reporting an exchange in 1992 between Yossi Beilin, then Israel's deputy foreign minister, and American Jewish leader Ruth Popkin. Beilin insisted to an audience of Jewish community leaders: "We want you to disagree with us." Popkin responded: "We can't do that. Our job here is to defend

you." See Goldberg, *Jewish Power: Inside the American Jewish Establishment* (Cambridge, Mass.: Perseus, 1996), 347.

27. The example of Cubans, Hindus, Irish, and Armenians in the United States, to mention but a few, illustrates the point about diaspora or exile communities adopting a political stance that is more conservative than in the homeland. For a discussion of this tendency, see María de los Angeles Torres, *In the Land of Mirrors: Cuban Exile Politics in the United States* (Ann Arbor, Mich.: University of Michigan Press, 1999), Prema Kurien, "Multiculturalism, Immigrant Religion, and Diasporic Nationalism: The Development of an American Hinduism," *Social Problems* 51, no. 3 (2004), 362–85; and Yossi Shain, "The Role of Diasporas in Conflict Perpetuation or Resolution," *SAIS Review* 22, no. 2 (Summer–Fall 2002), 115–44. As against the declared intention of the organized Jewish community in America to provide unstinting support to the government of the State of Israel, the Oslo peace process prompted some Jewish groups to break ranks. Shain notes the efforts of some of these groups to resist conciliatory steps by Israel or the United States toward the Palestinians despite the strong support of both the Israeli and American governments. Shain, "The Role of Diasporas," 124.

28. Benny Morris seemed to justify the practice of ethnic cleansing in a well-publicized interview with Ari Shavit from 2004: "A Jewish state would not have come into being without the uprooting of 700,000 Palestinians. Therefore it was necessary to uproot them. There was no choice but to expel that population. It was necessary to cleanse the hinterland and cleanse the border areas and cleanse the main roads." See Morris's interview of 9 January 2004, "Survival of the Fittest," in *Ha-arets,* accessed on 22 June 2007 at http://www.haaretz.com/hasen/objectspages/PrintArticleEn.jhtml?itemNo=380986.

29. Shlomo Ben-Ami, *Scars of War, Wounds of Peace: The Israeli-Arab Tragedy* (Oxford: Oxford University Press, 2006), 42.

30. See Oz, "No right of return, but Israel must offer a solution," from 12 May 2007 at http://globeandmail.workopolis.com/servlet/Content/fasttrack/20070512/COOZ12?gateway=cc.

31. Ben-Ami, *Scars of War*, 50.

32. For example, the Parameters presented at Camp David by President Clinton, which were accepted by the Israelis, offered five possible venues for refugee resettlement, including a new state of Palestine ( first) and, in limited fashion, the State of Israel (last). Moreover, the Clinton Parameters suggested one of two alternative formulations regarding recognition of the Palestinian right of return: (1) "Both sides recognize the right of Palestinian refugees to return to historic Palestine"; and (2) "Both sides recognize the right of Palestinian homeland." Dennis Ross includes the Parameters in his careful account of the Camp David peace talks, *The Missing Peace: The Inside Story of the Fight for Middle East Peace* (New York: Farrar, Straus, and Giroux, 2005), 804–805.

33. It is especially interesting to note the efforts of a number of Israeli legal theorists to mediate between the Palestinian right of return and the right of Jews to a state of their own, including Eyal Benvenisti, Chaim Gans, and Andrei Marmur. Gans, for example, makes an admirable though at times convoluted attempt to balance the competing interests at hand before arriving at the following two conclusions. First, Israel should

accept responsibility for those who were expelled (as against all Palestinian refugees). Second, Israel should allow (a) the return of refugees to their original homes if the land on which they stand is unpopulated, and (b) the return of more refugees—ranging between the poles of "negligible" and "mass" in number—as part of a broader peace agreement. See Gans's paper, "The Palestinian Right of Return and the Justice of Zionism," *Theoretical Inquiries in Law* 5 (2004), 269–304; a Hebrew version of this essay, along with a number of others dealing with the right of return can be found in his *Me-Rikhard Vagner ʿad zekhut ha-shivah: nituah filosofi shel beʿayot tsibur Yisreʾeliyot* (Tel Aviv: Am Oved, 2006), especially 200–285. The above-noted issue of *Theoretical Inquiries in Law* is devoted to the question of return and includes contributions by Lukas Meyer, Jeremy Waldron, Alon Harel, and David Enoch. Meanwhile, Andrei Marmur offers a somewhat sharper and more straightforward account than Gans in which he also concludes that Israel must accept partial responsibility for the refugee problem, as well as a limited number of returnees. See Marmor, "Entitlement to Land and the Right of Return: An Embarrassing Challenge for Liberal Zionism," in *Justice in Time: Responding to Historical Injustice*, ed. Lukas H. Meyer (Baden-Baden: Nomos, 2004), 319–33. The Meyer volume includes a range of views on the right of return, including Gans's critique of Marmor, 335–38.

34. The Beilin–Abu Mazen text calls, on one hand, for the Palestinians to acknowledge that full implementation of the right of return is "impracticable," and on the other, for the Israelis to acknowledge "the moral and material suffering caused to the Palestinian people as a result of the war of 1947–1949." See the text at http://www.bitterlemons .org/docs/beilinmazen.html (accessed on 29 June 2007). For the Geneva Accord, see http://www.geneva-accord.org/Accord.aspx?FolderID=33&lang=en (accessed on 29 June 2007).

35. Nusseibeh makes this remark, a version of which he once delivered to an Israeli audience, just after describing the Arab tradition of the *sulha* (the act of making amends for a wrong through a ritualized expression of contrition) in his memoir: "It doesn't matter whether you set out premeditatedly to cause the Palestinian refugee tragedy.... the tragedy did occur, even as an indirect consequence of your actions. In our tradition, you have to own up to this. You have to come and offer an apology. Only this way will Palestinians feel that their dignity has been recognized, and be able to forgive" (*Once Upon a Country*, 169).

36. See Ravid's Hebrew biography of his father, "Le-hayav veli-khetavav shel Shimon Rawidowicz," *ʿIyunim be-mahshevet Yisrael* (Jerusalem: Rubin Mass, 1969), 1:xvii–lxxii. The English version, "The Life and Writings of Simon Rawidowicz," is found in Rawidowicz, *State of Israel, Diaspora, and Jewish Continuity*, 13–50 (citation at 43–44). Michael A. Meyer's brief foreword to this volume makes a number of incisive and important points about Rawidowicz, but does not mention the chapter. See also Ravid's introduction, similar to the other English version, to Simon Rawidowicz, *Studies in Jewish Thought*, ed. Nahum N. Glatzer (Philadelphia: Jewish Publication Society, 1974), 3–42. Among other studies that address Rawidowicz's significance to the field of Jewish thought, see the tribute of his Brandeis colleague, Nahum N. Glatzer, "Simon Rawidowicz on his 10th Yahrzeit," *Judaism* 16 (Summer 1967); Jay Harris's discussion of his contribution to the study of Nachman Krochmal in his *Nachman Krochmal: Guiding*

*the Perplexed of the Modern Age* (New York: New York University Press, 1991), passim; and my "A Third Guide for the Perplexed? Simon Rawidowicz 'On Interpretation,'" in *History and Literature: New Readings of Jewish Texts in Honor of Arnold J. Band*, ed. William Cutter and David C. Jacobson. (Providence, R.I.: Brown Judaic Studies, 2002), 75–87.

37. See, for example, Yosef Gorny, *The State of Israel in Jewish Public Thought: The Quest for Collective Identity* (New York: New York University Press, 1994), passim; Ehud Luz, *Wrestling with an Angel: Power, Morality, and Jewish Identity* (New Haven, Conn.: Yale University Press, 1998), 82–83. Gordon Tucker's review of Rawidowicz's *State of Israel* collection and James Diamond's *Homeland or Holy Land? The Canaanite Critique of Israel* is found in *Judaism* 37 (Summer 1988), 364–75. One of the most perceptive analyses of Rawidowicz's attitude toward Zionism was offered by Arnold Band in an unpublished lecture, "Simon Rawidowicz: An Early Critic of the Zionist Narrative," delivered as the 35th Simon Rawidowicz Memorial Lecture at Brandeis University in Waltham, Massachusetts, in 1998. See also David N. Myers, "Simon Rawidowicz, 'Hashpaitis,' and the Perils of Influence," *Transversal* 7 (2006), 13–26.

38. See Noam F. Pianko, "Diaspora Jewish Nationalism and Identity in America, 1914–1967" (Ph.D. diss., Yale University, 2004), 195–96. It is noteworthy that Rawidowicz has attracted recent attention from two aspiring scholars in their respective B.A. theses. See Ronch Willner, "Mobilising Diaspora: Identity beyond Sovereignty" (Monash University, 2007), especially 46–70, and Jason Lustig, "Between Berlin and Tel Aviv: Simon Rawidowicz and the Politics of Culture (Brandeis University, 2008).

39. See Arendt's short opinion piece from 14 August 1942, "Confusion," originally published in the German-American newspaper, *Aufbau*, and newly reprinted in *The Jewish Writings*, 170.

40. A more updated existentialist expression of this predicament is offered by Jeffrey Goldberg in describing his own tortuous path from a Jewish boy in Long Island to military sentry in an Israeli prison: "My love for Israel was so bottomless that my disappointment with it was bottomless, too." See Goldberg, *Prisoners: A Muslim and a Jew across the Middle East Divide* (New York: Knopf, 2006), 175.

41. For recent attempts to treat the Jews and Arabs in Palestine as part of a single historical sphere, see the collection, *Reapproaching Borders: New Perspectives on the Study of Israel-Palestine*, ed. Sandy Sufian and Mark Levine (Lanham, Md.: Rowman and Littlefield, 2007), and Adam LeBor, *City of Oranges: An Intimate History of Arabs and Jews in Haifa* (New York: Norton, 2007).

PART I | The Jewish Question *(pages 21–87)*

1. Fifty years after its publication, this book remains largely unknown to the world of Jewish letters. While portions of the book have been translated in *State of Israel, Diaspora, and Jewish Continuity* and *Studies in Jewish Thought*, a complete translation and critical analysis of *Bavel vi-Yerushalayim* remain an overdue desideratum.

2. Rawidowicz recalls at the end of the introduction to *Bavel vi-Yerushalayim* that he wrote the text between 1951 and 1955, though he made some modifications in 1956 upon

reading the completed draft. See Rawidowicz's recollections in *Bavel vi-Yerushalayim* (Waltham, Mass: Ararat, 1957), 49.

3. See the account of Avraham Greenbaum in *A History of the Ararat Publishing Society* (Jerusalem: Rubin Mass, 1998), 22.

4. The question of the number of refugees remains an open one. A report by the United Nations Conciliation Commission for Palestine (PCC) from 28 March 1949 estimated that "the number of refugees to be repatriated or resettled (in Palestine or elsewhere), amounts to approximately 650,000," while also noting a figure of 910,000 by another U.N. official, Stanton Griffis, director of the U.N. Relief for Palestine Refugees. By contrast, officials of the State of Israel argued that there were 530,000 refugees. See the PCC's "Observations on Some of the Problems Relating to Palestine Refugees," 5256cf40073bfe6/1c4639213dbdfad985256cafoo726eec!OpenDocument. A commonly quoted figure today, drawn from British Foreign Office analysis, is 711,000 refugees. See Morris's summary, "The Number of Palestinian Refugees" in *The Birth of the Palestinian Refugees Problem Revisited*, 602–604.

5. In the early 1930s, Rawidowicz had to combat claims that his distinctive position violated the spirit and essence of Zionism. See his response to Zionist critics who deemed him an apostate in *Im lo kan—hekhan?* (Lvov: Brit 'Ivrit 'Olamit, 1933), viii. More than a decade later, at a London reception to celebrate the appearance of the first volume of *Metsudah,* the journal he edited, Simon Rawidowicz came under attack from his fellow Hebraist and occasional collaborator, Sir Leon Simon. Simon complained that Rawidowicz's opening article contained "unfair and bitter attacks on the Zionist movement" that "went beyond the bounds of fair criticism." See "Publication of 'Metsudah': Sir L. Simon's Attack," *The Jewish Chronicle*, 18 February 1944, as well as the discussion by Ravid in a lengthy note in Rawidowicz, *State of Israel, Diaspora, and Jewish Continuity,* 252. Some years later, the German-born British rabbi and scholar Alexander Carlebach reported that Rawidowicz had been branded, unfairly to his mind, with the epithet "anti-Zionist" by a recent commentator. See his review of Rawidowicz's journal *Metsudah,* "Solving the Jewish Problem?" *Hayenu* 12, nos. 9–10 (October 1948), 13. By contrast, a year later, the State of Israel's first Ambassador to the United States, Eliahu Eilat, participated in a forum (in Yiddish) with Rawidowicz in New York in which he casually referred to Rawidowicz, along with Ahad Ha-am, Jacob Klatzkin, and Yehezkel Kaufmann, as "Zionist thinkers who have grappled with the problem of the relationship between Jews in the Land of Israel and those outside of it." See Eilat's remarks at the forum of 20 February 1949, "Yisroel un di tsukunft fun dem yidishn folk," *Di tsukunft* 54 (May–June 1949), 279. See also the postmortem appreciations of Rawidowicz by Israeli intellectuals and writers who challenge the perception of his hostility to Zionism; for example, G. Kressel's analysis in *Davar* from 12 December 1958 or Robert Weltsch's review of *Bavel vi-Yerushalayim* from 3 April 1959 in *Ha-arets*.

6. As we shall see later, Rawidowicz was borrowing the title from an article written by a young Bernard Lewis in Hebrew, "'Ever ve-'arav," in a Hebrew journal that Rawidowicz edited in London. Lewis's essay was an early and compressed version of his more renowned later work on the peaks and valleys in Jewish-Muslim relations. See Bernard Dov Lewis, "'Ever ve-'arav," *Metsudah* 1 (1943), 104–112. The term was also the title of a book by the scholar, A. S. Yahuda, in 1946, and has recently been evoked by Gil Anidjar

in his chapter "'*Eber ve-'Arab* (The Arab Literature of the Jews),'" in his *Semites: Race, Religion, Literature* (Stanford, Calif.: Stanford University Press, 2008), 84ff.

7. Perhaps the most obvious borrowing by Rawidowicz from this classicizing Hebrew style was the term "'ever" itself. In the eighteenth century, the Hebrew language was often referred to as "sefat 'ever." See for example the volume by N. H. Wessely, *Gan na'ul, le-va'er u-lelaben yesode sefat 'ever veha-shorashi mi-ha-nirdafim* (Amsterdam: Y. Y. and A. Props, 1765–66). This usage abounds in the later Haskalah journal *Ha-shahar*, edited by Peretz Smolenskin.

8. See "Between Jew and Arab," sec. xii.

9. Ibid., sec. vii.

10. The earliest that Rawidowicz could have received proofs that included a mention of the Bandung conference, it would seem, was late summer/early fall 1955.

11. "Between Jew and Arab," sec. vii.

12. See Marion Aptroot's introduction to Moshe Sanders and Marion Aptroot, *Jewish Books in Whitechapel: A Bibliography of Narodiczky's Press* (London: Duckworth, 1991), ix.

13. See Greenbaum, *A History of the Ararat Publishing Society*, 17 and 26 n.46. On Fink, see the *Leksikon ha-sifrut ha-'ivrit be-dorot ha-aharonim*, 1st ed., s.v., "Ya'akov Yisra'el Fink."

14. Rawidowicz, *Bavel vi-Yerushalayim*, 50.

15. See Rawidowicz's brief approbation, "Ahare ma'atayim shanah: divre berakha le-Shevivim," *Shevivim* 1 (1955), 3–6.

16. See Benjamin Ravid's comment in Rawidowicz, *State of Israel, Diaspora, and Jewish Continuity*, 44.

17. A collection of a dozen letters from Fink to Rawidowicz dealing with a variety of publishing matters from 1949 to 1955 can be found in the Simon Rawidowicz archive in Newton, Massachusetts.

18. Greenbaum, "Rawidowicz at Brandeis University (A Memoir)," in *A History of the Ararat Publishing Society*, 50. Greenbaum has confirmed (in an interview on April 10, 2005) that this information emerged out of a conversation he had with Rawidowicz in 1957.

19. Jacob Neusner notes that the traditional use of the term was layered with powerful theological resonances: "The word 'Israel' today generally refers to the overseas political nation, the State of Israel. . . . But the word 'Israel' in Scripture and in the canonical writings of the religion, Judaism, speaks of the holy community that God has called forth through Abraham and Sarah, to which God has given the Torah ('teaching') at Mt. Sinai. The Psalmists and the Prophets, the Sages of Judaism in all ages, the prayers that Judaism teaches, all use the word 'Israel' to mean 'the holy community.'" Neusner, "Jew and Judaism, Ethnic and Religious: How They Mix in America," *Issues* [American Council for Judaism] (Spring 2002), 3–4, quoted in Yakov M. Rabkin, *A Threat from Within: A Century of Jewish Opposition to Zionism* (London: Zed Publishing, 2006), 6. Meanwhile, Rabkin also recalls, following Aviezer Ravitzky, early twentieth-century rabbinic disdain for the very idea of a "state of Israel." The ultra-Orthodox rabbi,

Elyakum Shlomo Shapira of Grodno, asked in 1900: "How can I bear that something be called the 'State of Israel' without the Torah and the commandments (heaven forbid)?" See Aviezer Ravitzky, *Messianism, Zionism, and Jewish Religious Radicalism*, trans. Michael Swirsky and Jonathan Chipman (Chicago: University of Chicago Press, 1996), 4, and Rabkin, *A Threat from Within*, 59.

20. The text was sent on to Waltham either by Jacob Fink, or perhaps after Fink's death, by the person in Paris responsible for the actual printing of Rawidowicz's and Fink's Hebrew books, Yehudah Shapnik.

21. Rawidowicz's letter of 12 June 1948 to Avraham Ravid is excerpted in Benjamin Ravid's detailed biographical introduction to S. Rawidowicz, *'Iyunim be-mahshevet Yisra'el* (Jerusalem: Rubin Mass, 1969), 1:lviii. In a later lecture, Rawidowicz raised this personal reflection to the level of a broad principle: "If people in general could always remain as 'guests' to each other, and never become too 'residential' or 'familiar'—we might live in somewhat more cheerful circumstances." See Rawidowicz, *On Jewish Learning: Address delivered at the opening convocation of the College of Jewish Studies, September 1948* (Chicago: College of Jewish Studies, 1950), 5. Cf. the statement of Dubnow in 1934, when asked by a colleague to move to Palestine: "I move easily in time, but not in space. In my researches I can move swiftly from period to period, from the twelfth to the sixteenth century, for example; but to move several thousand kilometers from Riga to Jerusalem is not within my powers." This letter to Abraham Levinson is quoted in Koppel S. Pinson's introduction to Dubnow, *Nationalism and History: Essays on Old and New Judaism* (New York: Atheneum, 1970), 33.

22. Greenbaum, *A History of the Ararat Publishing Society*, 12.

23. Fifty years after "Between Jew and Arab," Rawidowicz's concerns seem more apposite than ever. Debates over the status of Palestinian Israelis arise periodically, often in response to a cyclical pattern of Arab protest and government response. Perhaps the most notable instance of this cycle occurred on 30 March 1976, when six Arab Israelis were killed in the Galilee by Israeli police at a protest over confiscated land. This event has come to be known and commemorated by Palestinians as *Yom al-ard* (Land Day). Meanwhile, in October 2000, an outbreak of heated Palestinian Israeli demonstrations in support of the second Intifada prompted a fierce Israeli response in which thirteen Arab citizens were killed. In the wake of this episode, a state-sponsored commission headed by Supreme Court Justice Theodor Or was appointed to investigate the events and the larger issue of Israel's treatment of its Arab citizens. The Or Commission produced a lengthy and, in many respects, remarkable report in the summer of 2003 that called into question the behavior of the Israeli police, noted with concern the radicalization of Israel's Arab population, and issued a series of recommendations to ameliorate tensions between Palestinian citizens and the State of Israel. In the first chapter, the Or Commission report offered a powerful evocation of Simon Rawidowicz's concerns a half century ago (without, of course, being aware of his plea). It stated with striking candor that "the embitterment and disquiet among citizens from the Arab sector, to a great (though not exclusive) extent, stem from the attitude of the State toward them in various realms." The report went on to assert that "Arab citizens of the State live a reality in which they are discriminated against as Arabs," and then proceeded to detail the nature of that discrimination, ranging from land expropriations in

the early years to unequal distribution of government resources in education and social services today. See *Din ve-heshbon: va'adat ha-hakirah ha-mamlakhtit le-verur ha-hitnagshuyot ben kohot ha-bitahon le-ven ezrahim yisre'elim be-Oktober 2000* (Jerusalem: Ha-madpis ha-memshalti, 2003), 1:33ff. I thank Professor Shimon Shamir, a member of the Or Commission, for providing me with a copy of this report. See also the detailed explanation of the commission's exhaustive work by its chair, Justice Theodor Or (ret.) in "The Report by the State Commission of Inquiry into the Events of October 2000," *Israel Studies* 11, no. 2 (2006), 25–53.

24. See http://daccessdds.un.org/doc/RESOLUTION/GEN/NR0/043/65/IMG/NR004365 .pdf?OpenElement. This resolution is mentioned in a subsequent General Assembly Resolution of 11 May 1949 (273) that admitted the State of Israel to the United Nations.

25. Glatzer arrived at Brandeis in 1950, while Altmann came in 1959, two years after Rawidowicz's death.

26. Daniel Bell, *The End of Ideology: On the Exhaustion of Political Ideas in the Fifties* (Glencoe, Ill.: Free Press, 1960), 374.

27. Alongside them are admirers of Rawidowicz's Berlin dissertation on Ludwig Feuerbach (later expanded in a book in 1931 and reprinted in 1964).

28. See Abram L. Sachar, *Brandeis University: A Host at Last* (Hanover, N.H.: University Press of New England, 1995), 204.

29. *Sihotai 'im Bialik* (Jerusalem: Devir, 1983), 15.

30. See Ben-Gurion's letter of 5 November 1958 to Zev Margalit (William Margolies) acknowledging receipt of the two volumes of *Bavel vi-Yerushalayi*—( fig. 6). Rawidowicz Archive.

31. Nahum G. Glatzer, "Simon Rawidowicz on his 10th Yahrzeit," 343.

32. *Kitve Rabbi Nahman Krochmal* (Berlin, 1924; 2nd ed., Waltham, Mass.: Ararat, 1961).

33. The published results of the research on Maimonides include a number of Hebrew articles from 1935 on the *Guide*, "She'elat mivnehu shel 'Moreh Nevukhim'" and "Hovatenu ha-mada'it le-'Moreh Nevukhim,'" as well as studies on *Sefer ha-mada'* extending back to 1922. For a discussion, see Benjamin C. I. Ravid's introduction to Simon Rawidowicz, *State of Israel, Diaspora, and Jewish Continuity*, 29–30.

34. See the following important discussions by Ravid: "Le-hayav veli-khetavav shel Shimon Rawidowicz," in Rawidowicz, *'Iyunim be-mahshevet Yisra'el*, I: xvii–lxxxii; "Ha-reka 'ha-histori," in Rawidowicz, *Sihotai 'im Bialik*, 7–17; and a shortened English version of the first piece above, "The Life and Writings of Simon Rawidowicz," in *State of Israel, Diaspora, and Jewish Continuity*, 15–52.

35. See the comments in Zvi Woyslawski's recollections about the Jewish community of Grayewo in "Grayewo" in *Grayeve yizker-bukh* (New York: United Grayever Relief Committee, 1950), 159. On the origins of the town in general, see S. Y. Fishbein's article in the same volume, "Grayeve fun amol," 11–12.

36. *Encyclopaedia Judaica*, 1972 ed., s.v. "Grajewo."

37. Fishbein, "Grayeve fun amol," 15. See also the discussion of the railway's impact on commercial travel on the waterways in Eugene van Cleef, "Eastern Baltic Waterways and Boundaries with Special Reference to Königsberg," *Geographic Review* 35, no. 2 (April 1945), 266.

38. See Ravid, "Le-hayav veli-khetavav shel Shimon Rawidowicz," xviii–xix.

39. Rawidowicz draws here on Deuteronomy 11:19. See Ibid., xxi–xxii. See also his contribution (in Yiddish) to the Grayewo memorial book, "Grayeve: di strebendike troymendike," *Grayeve yizker-bukh*, 39.

40. See Ravid, "Le-hayav veli-khetavav shel Shimon Rawidowicz," xx.

41. Rawidowicz, "Grayeve," 38.

42. Ravid, introduction to *State of Israel, Diaspora, and Jewish Continuity*, 14.

43. Rawidowicz, "Grayeve," 42.

44. For a recent discussion, see Yael Chaver, *What Must be Forgotten: The Survival of Yiddish in Zionist Palestine* (Syracuse, N.Y.: Syracuse University Press, 2004).

45. According to Ravid, Yiddishist opponents of Rawidowicz insisted that these speeches were pearls of Yiddish oratory, and hence the best advertisement for Yiddish itself. See "Le-hayav veli-khetavav shel Shimon Rawidowicz," xxiii.

46. This retrospective claim came in a brief autobiography that Rawidowicz penned in 1937 at the request of the editor of the Yiddish journal, *Di tsukunft*. It was published as the introduction to a collection of Rawidowicz's Yiddish writings published after his death, *Shriftn* (Buenos Aires: Argentiner opteyl fun Alyeltlekhn Yidish kultur-kongres, 1962), 11.

47. An important step in this direction, though limited in temporal scope, is the excellent dissertation of Kenneth Moss, "'A Time to Tear Down and a Time to Build Up': Recasting Jewish Culture in 1917–1921" (Ph.D. diss., Stanford University, 2003).

48. "Le-hayav veli-khetavav shel Shimon Rawidowicz," xxii.

49. Ibid., xxiii.

50. The schools, however, did not last long after Rawidowicz's migration to Berlin in 1919. See his account in "Le-yisud keren ha-tarbut ha-'Ivrit," *Ha-'olam* 12 May 1932.

51. For a brief but helpful discussion of Rawidowicz's relationship to and critique of Ahad Ha-am, see Barbara Schäfer, "Jewish Renaissance and *Tehiyya:* Two that are One?" *Jewish Studies Quarterly* 10 (2003), esp. 322–23.

52. See Michael Brenner, The Renaissance of Jewish Culture in Weimar Germany (New Haven, Conn.: Yale University Press, 1996), 198, as well as David N. Myers, "'Distant Relatives Happening onto the Same Inn': The Meeting of East and West as Literary Theme and Cultural Ideal," *Jewish Social Studies* 1, no. 2 (1994–95), 75–100.

53. See Benjamin Ravid's introduction to Rawidowicz, *Sihotai 'im Bialik*, 9.

54. Edward Kaplan and Samuel Dresner observe in their biography of Heschel that "(a)lthough his basic beliefs had taken shape—a certainty of God's attachment to humankind—he hoped to reconcile them with Western categories of thought" while in Berlin. See Kaplan and Dresner, *Abraham Joshua Heschel: Prophetic Witness* (New Haven, Conn.: Yale University Press, 1998), 108.

55. Kaplan and Dresner, *A Prophetic Witness*, 108–109. For Soloveitchik's involvement with Dessoir and Maier, see the autobiographical curriculum vitae of Soloveitchik quoted by Manfred Lehmann at http://www.manfredlehmann.com/sieg439.html. See also Reuven Kimelman, "Rabbis Joseph B. Soloveitchik and Abraham Joshua Heschel on Jewish-Christian Relations," *Modern Judaism* 24, no. 3 (2004), 251.

56. Details of Rawidowicz's studies can be gleaned from the autobiographical "Lebenslauf" included in his file at the University of Berlin. Humboldt Universität zu Berlin Archiv, Phil. Fak., 656, Bl. 26.

57. Rawidowicz devoted a long chapter of his 1924 Krochmal introduction to "Hegalianism." See Rawidowicz, ed., *Kitve R. Nahman Krochmal*, 160–201. See also his well-known article, "War Nachman Krochmal Hegelianer?" *Hebrew Union College Annual* 5 (1928), 535–82, published in English as "Was Nachman Krochmal a Hegelian?" in Rawidowicz, *Studies in Jewish Thought* (Philadelphia: Jewish Publication Society), 1974, 350–86.

58. See Rawidowicz's sixty-four-page dissertation, which was included in a much larger (500-page) study that he wrote on Feuerbach's thought and reception, *Ludwig Feuerbachs Philosophie: Ursprung und Schicksal* (Berlin: Reuther und Reichard, 1931). The volume was later burned by the Nazis, but then republished in Germany in 1964.

59. Ibid.

60. *Sihotai 'im Bialik,* 28. See also Brenner, *The Renaissance of Jewish Culture,* 198–99.

61. Rawidowicz discusses Bialik's hesitations about Ayanot in a letter to him from 15 March 1922 which is published in *Sihotai 'im Bialik,* 99–100; see also Ravid's comments in *Sihotai 'im Bialik,* 11.

62. Brenner, *The Renaissance of Jewish Culture,* 200–201.

63. Rawidowicz's letter to Avraham Ravid of 26 May 1925 is excerpted in *Sihotai 'im Bialik,* 12. According to Genesis 4:12, "ground, it shall not henceforth yield unto thee her strength; a fugitive and a wanderer shalt thou be in the earth."

64. The first M.A. degrees were awarded at the Hebrew University in 1931, and the first Ph.D in 1936. *The Hebrew University of Jerusalem (1957)* (Jerusalem: Jerusalem Post Press, 1957), 33.

65. Over the course of his fourteen years in Berlin, Rawidowicz was employed variously as an editor for Hebrew and Yiddish publications, researcher and coeditor for the Moses Mendelssohn jubilee volume for the Akademie für die Wissenschaft des Judentums, and librarian and lecturer for the Jewish community of Berlin. It is essential to add that his wife, Esther, maintained a full-time job as a researcher at the Charité Hospital in Berlin (until her dismissal in 1933).

66. Rawidowicz's letter to Joseph Klausner from 20 June 1928 is found in the Jewish National and University Archives, Joseph Klausner Papers, $4^0$ 1086/469.

67. Letter to Joseph Klausner from 4 February 1931 in the Jewish National and University Archives, Joseph Klausner Papers, $4^0$ 1086/469.

68. Letter to Joseph Klausner from 17 December 1930 in the Jewish National and University Archives, Joseph Klausner Papers, $4^0$ 1086/469.

69. Letters of 16 September 1931 and 4 January 1932 in the Jewish National and University Archives, Joseph Klausner Papers, $4^0$ 1086/469.

70. See Myers, *Re-Inventing the Jewish Past: European Jewish Intellectuals and the Zionist Return to History* (New York: Oxford University Press, 1995).

71. Rawidowicz suggests this in letters to Klausner from 16 September 1931 and 4 January 1932. However, the minutes of the Institute faculty reveal that Scholem raised Rawidowicz's name as a prospect, along with Wiener and Strauss, in 1931 when it seemed unlikely that Julius Guttmann would accept the offer to come to Jerusalem. Protocols of the Institute for Jewish Studies, 14 Iyar (1 May 1931). Central Archive for the Hebrew University (CAHU).

72. For example, the protocol of the meeting of the Institute for Jewish Studies held on 10 Tevet (30 December 1930) states: "Prof. Klausner reads the names of the candidate for this field (Jewish philosophy); proposes Prof. Guttmann, and also reads out the names of Rawidowicz and Tsifroni as possible experiments for a year." Protocols of the Institute for Jewish Studies, 10 Tevet (30 December 1930), CAHU. In a later meeting of the institute held on the Fast of Esther (2 March 1931), Klausner indicated that Guttmann was the candidate of choice with whom negotiations were being conducted. He did not mention Rawidowicz on this occasion, but did express his opposition to the appointment of Max Wiener. Protocols of the Institute for Jewish Studies (2 March 1930).

73. Protocols of the Institute for Jewish Studies, 10 Tevet (30 December 1930), CAHU. Rawidowicz did have an advocate in the scholar of Hebrew language and literature, David Yellin, who wrote Judah Magnes from Berlin that "renowned scholars here [deem] him to be worthy and appropriate to receive a position" at the Hebrew University. Yellin's letter of 8 Elul (1 September 1930) is found in the CAHU, 5-R. By contrast, Rawidowicz received strong support for his candidacy at the Hebrew University from two leading scholars of Jewish philosophy in the Diaspora. Harry Austryn Wolfson of Harvard wrote to Judah Magnes on 30 August 1933 "recommending him most highly for a position in the field of Jewish philosophy." Meanwhile, Isaac Husik of the University of Pennsylvania wrote Magnes on the same day with a request to "give him a post in your university at least for a year." The letters are contained in the Central Archive of the Hebrew University, file 165 (1933).

74. In a series of letters between 1926 and 1928, Rawidowicz kept Morgenstern apprised of his scholarly progress; Morgenstern, for his part, expressed interest in Rawidowicz's research, but never offered or promised a job to him at HUC. Morgenstern's letters are included in Benjamin Ravid, "The Human Dimension of *Wissenschaft des Judentums*: Letters from the Rawidowicz Archive," in *Studies in Arabic and Hebrew Letters in Honor*

*of Raymond P. Scheindlin,* ed. Jonathan P. Decter and Michael Rand (Piscataway, NJ: Gorgias Press, 2007), 92–97.

75. Rawidowicz's letter of 16 May 1928 is in the Klausner Papers. In fact, Schorr did write Rawidowicz on 10 May 1928 to "inquire whether you are ready to accept the position of a permanent teacher of the history of Jewish philosophy and also medieval poetic literature at our Institute." Although Rawidowicz asserted that he did not take the job because he did not like the intellectual climate of Warsaw, in fact, neither the precise contours of the job nor exact financial arrangements for it were ever detailed. See the letters regarding this matter printed in Ravid, "The Human Dimension of *Wissenschaft des Judentums,*" 97–102.

76. Rawidowicz's letter to Judah L. Magnes of 17 July 1930 is found in the CAHU 5-R.

77. Rawidowicz's letter of 7 June 1931 is in the Klausner Papers. Rawidowicz alludes to Maier's antisemitism in a letter to his father from 6 July 1931 in Ravid, "Le-hayav," xl–xli.

78. See Brenner, *The Renaissance of Jewish Culture,* 209–210.

79. Rawidowicz to Klausner, 7 June 1931, in the Klausner Papers.

80. Rawidowicz's letter of 12 November 1933 is in the Klausner Papers.

81. Rawidowicz's letter to Avraham Ravid from 6 December 1948 is quoted in Ravid, "Le-hayav," lxvii.

82. As he wrote in a letter to Asher Barash on 27 July 1939: "You wrote: 'In my view, you should come here (to Palestine).' Between us, the situation of [Hebrew] literature and writers, scholarship and scholars in the country is not a happy one. The country cannot support those from our family who are already there, and you want to add more?" This letter is found in the Schwadron Autograph Collection of the Jewish National and University Library.

83. See Rawidowicz's comments in "Mi-bene ha-arets," *Ha-ʿavodah* 1 (1919–20), 18, quoted in Ravid, "Le-yahav," xxv.

84. See Delphine Bechtel, "Les revues modernistes Yiddish à Berlin et à Varsovie de 1922 à 1924: La quête d'une nouvelle Jéruslaem," *Etudes germaniques* (April–June 1991), 164, and Myers, "'Distant Relatives Happening on the Same Inn,'" 87.

85. Rawidowicz recalls his relationship with Dubnow—and includes ninety-seven letters from him—in the memorial volume that he edited, *Sefer Shimon Dubnow* (Waltham, Mass.: Ararat, 1954), 402ff.

86. This description from a 1919 pamphlet is quoted in Brenner, *The Renaissance of Jewish Culture,* 52. However, in a recent article, Simon Rabinovitch notes that Dubnow was not especially attracted to the German Volkspartei as "it only vaguely resembled its Russian forebear, the *Folkspartey.*" See Rabinovitch, "Simon Dubnov and the Dawn of a New Diaspora," *Leo Baeck Institute Year Book* 50 (2005), 280.

87. In the introduction to his ten-volume history of the Jews, Dubnow did actually make a Rawidowiczian move. Writing in 1924, he asserted that "the dualism of the European-

American West and of the Palestinian East now becomes possible." See Dubnow, *History of the Jews*, trans. Moshe Spiegel (South Brunswick, N.J.: T. Yosseloff, 1967), 1:36.

88. See "Le-irgun ha-golah ha-'Ivrit," *Moznayim* 3, no. 9 (1931), 2. A fuller version of the speech was published by the Lvov branch of the Brit 'Ivrit 'Olamit as *Im lo kan—hekhan?*, 10. See also Ravid's extensive discussion of Rawidowicz and the Brit, "Shimon Rawidowicz u-Vrit 'Ivrit 'Olamit: perek be-yahasim ben tarbut 'Ivrit be-tefutsah le-ide'ologyah ha-Tsiyonit," in *Studies and Essays in Hebrew Language and Literature: Berlin Congress: Proceedings of the 16th Hebrew Scientific European Congress* (Brit Ivrit Olamit: Jerusalem, 2005), 119–54.

89. "Le-irgun ha-golah ha-'Ivrit," 3.

90. See Ahad Ha-am's discussion of imitation in his well-known essay, "Hikui ve-hitbolelut" (1893), reprinted in his collection of essays, *'Al parashat derakhim*, new ed. (Berlin: Jüdischer Verlag, 1930), 169–177. See also Barbara Schäfer's discussion, "Jewish Renaissance and *Tehiyya*," 322–23.

91. "Le-irgun ha-golah ha-'Ivrit," 3. Rawidowicz's view is a telling contrast to the more historically nuanced perspective of Gerson Cohen in his essay, *The Blessing of Assimilation in Jewish History* (Brookline, Mass.: Hebrew Teachers College, 1966).

92. Mishnah Baba Metzia 1:1. See Rawidowicz, "Le-irgun ha-golah ha-'Ivrit," 4.

93. Quoted in Ravid, "Le-hayav veli-khetavav shel Shimon Rawidowicz," xxxix–xl.

94. "Le-irgun ha-golah ha-'Ivrit," *Moznayim* 3, no. 10 (1931), 3. See also Rawidowicz's essay from 1934, "Kiyum ha-tefutsah," which enshrined the principle of affirming the Diaspora and thus stood in pointed contrast to the Zionist goal of "negating the Diaspora" (*shelilat ha-golah*).

95. "Le-irgun ha-golah ha-'Ivrit," *Moznayim* 3, no. 9 (1931), 5.

96. Ibid., 4. The motif of "two that are one" was recurrent in Rawidowicz's thinking. See, for example, his essay, "Shete she'elot she-hen ahat," *Moznayim* 44 (1931), 7–9, and 45 (1931), 8–9. See also his essay, "Two that are One," in *State of Israel, Diaspora, and Jewish Continuity*, 147–61, based on a Yiddish lecture from 1949.

97. Bialik, *Devir* 1 (1923), xii, cited in "'Distant Relatives Happening onto the Same Inn,'" 89.

98. F. Lachover, "Ha-kenesiyah ha-'Ivrit le-ma'aseh ule-halakhah," *Moznayim* 3, no. 10 (1931), 1.

99. Ibid., 2.

100. Rawidowicz's letter to his brother Avraham from 16 November 1932 is quoted in Ravid, *Sihotai 'im Bialik*, 14. Among those given credit for the Brit at Rawidowicz's expense was his conversation partner from Berlin in the early 1920s, Bialik. See Benjamin Ravid's discussion of this "revisionist" account of the Brit in "Shimon Rawidowicz u-Vrit 'Ivrit 'Olamit," 146–48.

101. See Renner's 1899 book, *Staat und Nation*, translated as "State and Nation" in *National Cultural Autonomy and its Contemporary Critics*, ed. Ephraim Nimni (London:

Routledge, 2005), 33, and quoted in Roni Gechtman's excellent article, "Conceptualizing National-Cultural Autonomy—From the Austro-Marxists to the Jewish Labor Bund," *Simon Dubnow Yearbook* 4 (2005), 30.

102. See Gechtman, "Conceptualizing National-Cultural Autonomy," 43–49.

103. There were, it must be said, disagreements between the Eastern Europeans, on the one hand, and the Western Europeans and Americans, on the other, over the extent to which Jewish national rights should be explicitly recognized (and what form of political organization these rights should assume). For an elaboration of these differences, see the exchange between Bernard G. Richards and Solomon Zeitlin in the *Jewish Quarterly Review* 36, no. 1 (July 1945), 89–103.

104. This language comes from Wilson's proposed Paragraph VI to the Covenant. See Jacob Robinson et al., *Were the Minorities Treaties a Failure?* (New York: Antin Press, 1943), 8.

105. Ibid., 45. See also the comprehensive account of Carole Fink, *Defending the Rights of Others: The Great Powers, the Jews, and International Minority Protection, 1878–1938* (Cambridge: Cambridge University Press, 2004), especially 133–70.

106. Ezra Mendelsohn, *The Jews of East Central Europe between the World Wars* (Bloomington, Ind.: Indiana University Press, 1983), 81.

107. See Fink, *Defending the Rights of Others,* 344–45. Dimitry Shumsky has recently argued, in a lecture that is the kernel for a larger book project, that Zionist leaders, including Ben-Gurion and Jabotinsky, had a more favorable attitude toward national minority rights for Jews in the Diaspora than is commonly thought. Shumsky, "Me-'ever le-ribonut: Tsiyonut otonomistit ben mizrah u-mercaz Eropa le-Erets Yisra'el ha-mandatorit," unpublished lecture, p. 5.

108. See Rawidowicz's letter to Chaim Yitzhak Ravid from 2 July 1933 excerpted in Ravid, "Le-hayav veli-khetavav shel Shimon Rawidowicz," xl.

109. Rawidowicz letter to Joseph Klausner from 12 November 1933 in the Klausner Papers.

110. The discussions over Rawidowicz's status at Jews' College are contained in the minutes of the Staff and Education Committee beginning on 3 October 1933. London Municipal Archive 4180/JC/B/03/012.

111. A perusal of the list of annual public lectures and publications of the School of Oriental Studies' affiliated faculty from 1935 to 1947 reveals that Rawidowicz was among the most active lecturers and most prolific researchers. See the *Report of the Governing Body and Statement of Accounts* of the School of Oriental Studies, London Institution (Hertford: Stephen Austin, 1935–47).

112. In this labor, he was joined by the Anglo-Jewish civil servant, Leon Simon (later Sir Leon), who served as president of the Tarbut Association while Rawidowicz served as chairman. As we have noted (n. 5 of this part), Simon would become a vocal critic of Rawidowicz's, accusing him of leveling unfair attacks on the Zionist movement.

113. *Vé'idat ha-histadrut "Tarbut" be-London: din ve-heshbon* (London: Tarbuth Association, 1938), 6. It is interesting to compare this optimistic account with the more tempered opinion that Rawidowicz voiced in a letter from 1936 to the Hebrew activist in Palestine,

Avraham Schwadron (Sharon). While Rawidowicz would later criticize Schwadron-Sharon for his doctrine of "cruel Zionism," he confided in 1936 that "I pray like you for the 'uprooting of the exile.' But a prayer is one thing, and reality is another." Rawidowicz's letter to Schwadron-Sharon from 15 November 1936 is found in the Jewish National and University Library Archive, Schwadron Autograph Collection, Rawidowicz letters.

114. "Kiyum ha-tefutsah" (Affirmation of the Diaspora). See Ravid, "Le-hayav veli-khetavav shel Shimon Rawidowicz," xlvi.

115. Rawidowicz, "'Al ha-shelihut," *Ha-'olam* 28 May 1936, 383.

116. "'Al ha-shelihut," 668.

117. See Rawidowicz, "Ha-Yalkut: Petikha," *Yalkut: Musaf-hodesh le-hashkafah ha-Tsiyonit* 1 (December 1940), 1. Rawidowicz repeated this warning in the first number of the second year, albeit with increasing urgency. See his opening essay, "'Et litko'a yated," *Yalkut* 2 (1941), 1.

118. *Yalkut* 1:3 (1940), 1.

119. "Et likto'a yated," 7.

120. See Ish Boded, "Shivre devarim," *Yalkut* 2, nos. 2–3 (1942), 95.

121. Rawidowicz was informed of his appointment in a letter of 28 July 1941 by the Registrar of the University of Leeds. Archives of the Central Records Office of the University of Leeds.

122. Letter of H. A. R. Gibb to Rawidowicz from 14 August 1941 in the Rawidowicz Archive, Newton, Massachusetts.

123. This description comes in a departmental memorandum from 10 October 1944. A copy of the contract between the University of Leeds and Rawidowicz (dated 14 October), as well as correspondence relating to the appointment from July 1941, are preserved in the Archives of the Central Records Office of the University of Leeds. I thank Mr. David Wardle, assistant secretary of the university, for sending me copies of the documents relating to Rawidowicz's tenure there.

124. Telephone interview with Professor Bernard Lewis, 24 November 2004.

125. "Editor's Preface," *Melilah* 1 (1944), vii.

126. Avraham Greenbaum observes that the name "Ararat" also offered up a glimmer of hope, as a place from which "to foresee the renewal of life on earth." *A History of the Ararat Publishing Society*, 10.

127. Letter of 27 April 1941 to Avraham Ravid in "Le-hayav veli-khetavav shel Shimon Rawidowicz," lxii. Although there was underground Hebrew publishing in Eastern Europe during this period, England was one of the last sites in Europe where it was possible to publish freely in Hebrew until the demise of the Third Reich. We should recall that the journal *Melilah* was produced in Manchester, not London.

128. Rawidowicz, *Metsudah* 1 (1943), 20. In a letter from November 1942, Rawidowicz also evoked this theme in a letter to his brother, Avraham: "I cannot, under any circumstance, accept the idea that at this hour in Europe when the Hebrew language is banned, we

do nothing here in London, the last fortress of freedom at home and abroad." Quoted in Ravid, "Le-hayav veli-khetavav shel Shimon Rawidowicz," lxii.

129. Rawidowicz, "Bi-metsudah zo," *Metsudah* 1 (1943), 16, 18.

130. "Ish Boded," "Shivre devarim," *Metsudah* 1 (1943), 165.

131. "Ish Boded," "'Am ve-lashon lo," *Metsudah* 1 (1943), 168.

132. Ibid., 170.

133. See Arendt's articles from the *Aufbau* from 14 November 1941 and 26 December 1941, in Arendt, *The Jewish Writings*, 137, 143.

134. Arendt's meditation on "The Minority Question" from the summer of 1940 was copied from a letter to Erich Cohn-Bendit and is found in *The Jewish Writings*, 131–32. As Arendt grew increasingly troubled by the course of Zionism in the 1940s, she came to favor a variation of the commonwealth idea—namely, a federation or confederation of nations—in Palestine and/or the Middle East more broadly.

135. This image was reprinted at the opening of the memorial volume for Simon Dubnow, who was murdered by a Nazi soldier in Riga in 1941.

136. Dedication page, *Metsudah* 2 (1943). The last two lines are modifications of Job 16:18 and the famous Psalm 137:5.

137. The familiar language of right and sufferance harks back to a British government document, the Churchill White Paper of June 1922, which declared to the Jewish people: "it is essential that it should know that it is in Palestine as of right and not on the sufferance." See the 1922 White Paper at http://www.yale.edu/lawweb/avalon/mideast/brwh1922.htm. Hannah Arendt relies on the formulation in support of a Jewish army in this period, noting that "if the Jews are to live in Palestine by right and not by sufferance, it will only be by the right they have earned and continue to earn every day with their labor." See her *Aufbau* essay from 26 December 1941 in *The Jewish Writings*, 144.

138. "Yisra'el ba-'olam," *Metsudah* 2 (1943), especially sec. 1 (pp. 7–20).

139. "Kiyum lelo tenai (Unconditional Survival)," *Metsudah* 3–4 (1945), 5.

140. Ibid., 8. This right calls to mind Mordecai Kaplan's earlier insistence that "the task now before the Jew is to save the otherness of Jewish life" by preserving its "differentia" (for example, language, arts, religion, and law). See the classic account in Mordecai M. Kaplan, *Judaism as A Civilization: Toward a Reconstruction of American-Jewish Life* (New York: Macmillan, 1934; reprint, Philadelphia: Jewish Publication Society, 1981), 173, 178, 180.

141. "Kiyum lelo tenai," 13. Rawidowicz then enumerated the ways in which "Israel" is different, especially its language.

142. "Kiyum lelo tenai," 18.

143. "Li-keliyah oli-tekumah," *Metsudah* 5–6 (1948), 30 n.7.

144. Yaakov Fleischer, "She'elat Yisra'el bi-ve'idat ha-shalom bi-shenat 1946," *Metsudah* 5–6 (1948), 162–194. The rights accorded to national minorities in the paradigmatic Polish Minorities Treaty that emerged out of the Paris Peace Conference included a declaration of

basic human rights, full citizenship rights, as well as the right to preserve the group's language and to education in the group's language (with state subvention). In addition, specific clauses were included with respect to Jews; for example, that affirming their right to observe the Sabbath without discrimination. These rights were to be enforced by the League of Nations. See Janowsky, *Nationalities and National Minorities (With Special Reference to East-Central Europe)* (New York: Macmillan, 1945), 112–15. See also Janowsky's more detailed study *The Jews and Minority Rights* (New York: Macmillan, 1933), as well as the discussion of the Jewish delegation to Paris in Shlomo Netzer, *Ma'avak Yehude Polin 'al zekhuyotehem ha-ezrahiyot ha-le'umiyut* (Tel Aviv: Tel Aviv University, 1980), especially chap. 4.

145. Fleischer borrowed Rawidowicz's language in concluding that the evidence at hand in the wake of the Second World War "proved that the era of *libertas differendi* still remains a future vision." Fleischer, "She'elat Yisra'el bi-ve'idat ha-shalom bi-shenat 1946," 168, 170.

146. Ibid., 160.

147. See Ravid, "Le-hayav," lviii.

148. Ish Boded, "Shivre devarim," *Metsudah* 7 (1954), 661.

149. This view can be seen in a letter Rawidowicz wrote to the Leeds registrar, Mr. Loach, on 30 May 1948, as well as in his official letter of resignation to the Leeds vice-chancellor of 12 June 1948. Both are in the Leeds University Central Records Archive.

150. Rawidowicz's letter to Avraham Ravid is quoted in Ravid, "Le-hayav," lviii.

151. Ish Boded, "Shivre devarim," *Metsudah* 5–6 (1948), 544–45.

152. Ibid., 560.

153. Consistent with his interest in local Jewish culture, he initiated and edited a bilingual volume devoted to the history of the Jewish community in Chicago. This volume, which was published by the college in 1952 as *Pinkas Chicago,* evoked the legacy of the record books of the great semi-autonomous communities of premodern Jewish history. Rawidowicz did note that *Pinkasim* usually came from older communities which had passed through many travails, while the Chicago *Pinkas* dealt with a young community that bore few scars of persecution. See his introduction to *Pinkas Chicago* (Chicago: College of Jewish Studies, 1952), viii–ix.

154. Rawidowicz here refers to Judah Ha-Levi's famous poetic lament that "my heart is in the east, while I am in the west." See "Divre hatimah," *Metsudah* 7 (1954), 673.

155. Rawidowicz, "Yisra'el," *Metsudah* 7 (1954), 36. Rawidowicz was not alone in this belief. The Orthodox rabbi and philosopher, Joseph B. Soloveitchik, who was friendly with Rawidowicz from their days in Berlin, shared his reservation. Soloveitchik confessed in 1960 that "I have never called the state in the Holy Land by the name 'Israel.' . . . In the letters that I send to the land of our Patriarchs, I write instead of 'Israel' State of Israel, Erets Yisra'el." See Soloveitchik's "Response to a Questioner" in *Divre hashkafah* (Jerusalem: Sifriyat Eliner, 1992), 242.

156. These opponents included Michael Assaf, Bechor Shetreet, and David Remez. See Nissan's brief article, "Ha-lebatim seviv ha-shem Yisra'el: zikaron mi-yeme hakhrazat Medinat Yisra'el," *Ha-umah* 91 (1988), 410–11.

157. The exchange is published with a postscript by Rawidowicz under the heading "Ben Yerushalayim u-Bavel-Yerushalayim" in *Bavel vi-Yerushalayim*, 2:872–909. Substantial excerpts appear in English in his *State of Israel, Diaspora, and Jewish Continuity*, 194–204.

158. Rawidowicz, "Yisra'el," 36.

159. Ben-Gurion's letter of 24 November 1954 to Rawidowicz is quoted in Rawidowicz, *State of Israel, Diaspora, and Jewish Continuity*, 197.

160. Rawidowicz quoted Ben-Gurion to the effect that "the creation of the state of Israel has not concluded . . . not from the perspective of the land in its possession nor from that of the surrounding environment." Ben-Gurion's comments were published in *Ha-Dor* 15 Elul 5712 (1951–52), and quoted in "Yisra'el," *Metsudah* 7 (1954), 14 n.5.

161. In inverting the famous phrase from Zechariah 4:6, Rawidowicz called this new sensibility "the *pathos* of 'by might and by power.'" Ish Boded, "Shivre devarim," *Metsudah* 7 (1954), 647.

162. Ibid., 648.

163. Rawidowicz liked to recall his reaction when asked "Have you ever been to Israel?" He would respond in a confounding way that reflected his distinctive commitment to a global "Israel": "I have been all my life in Israel. As a matter of fact I was born in Israel, got my name in Israel." See Rawidowicz, "Yisra'el," 25.

164. Aryeh Tartakower, "Mishtar-demokratyah bi-medinat Yisra'el," *Metsudah* 7 (1954), 77. Tartakower may have had in mind the 1922–23 population exchange between Turkey and Greece following the Greco-Turkish War as a possible model. A more recent example, far larger and more disruptive, was the population exchange of some 14.5 million people following the 1947 partition that led to the rise of the independent states of India and Pakistan.

165. Ibid., 77.

166. Cf. Joseph Schechtman, who notes in his detailed study of post–WWII population transfers and exchanges: "After this war, just as after World War I, the peacemakers did not—and apparently could not—succeed in creating such a territorial settlement in Europe that would eliminate, or at least reduce, the scope and the intensity of the minorities problem." See Schechtman, *Postwar Population Transfers in Europe*, 4. We should note that Rawidowicz declared in no uncertain terms in 1945 that "the political solution of moving national minorities from one country to another (transfer), of which many speak favorably, is not at all an exalted or desirable ideal." See "Kiyum lelo tenai," 18.

167. Tartakower, "Mishtar," 78. Tartakower had no illusions about the difficulty inhering in relations between the State of Israel and the Arab minority in its midst: "History has placed before us one of the most difficult and yet responsible tasks in the annals of the minority problem in the world: to realize the principle of full equality of rights and, at the same time, to safeguard the well-being of a most neglected and distinct minority which sees us as its enemy and does not know to recognize the hand extended to it in assistance and friendship."

PART II. The Arab Question *(pages 89–134)*

1. See Arendt's brief essay, "Confusion," from 14 August 1942 in *The Jewish Writings*, 171.

2. Rawidowicz reports in a long note at the end of the introduction to *Bavel vi-Yerusha-layim* that he wrote the book in the years 5711 (1950–51) to 5714 (1953–54). He adds: "In 5716 (1955–56), most of it was already in press, except for a few additions that I made in 5717 (1956–57) upon reading the galley pages." He goes on to state that the main sections of the book—parts I and II—were drafted on multiple occasions, but that they were composed "in a single breath." See *Bavel vi-Yerushalayim*, I:49.

3. Rawidowicz, *Bavel vi-Yerushalayim*, I:17–18.

4. Ibid., I:27.

5. Kaplan stressed that neither the State of Israel nor any state, for that matter, could serve as "the nerve center of world Jewry." Rather, what was needed was "a formal and publicly recognized renewal of covenantship among all the Jews of the world" as the embodiment of *Klal Yisrael* (the entirety of Israel). Mordecai M. Kaplan, "The State of Israel and the Status of the Jew," *The Reconstructionist* 15, no. 10 (24 June 1949), 10, 14.

6. Rawidowicz, *Bavel vi-Yerushalayim*, I:35.

7. The First Temple period ran from the mid-10th century BCE to 586 BCE; the Second Temple period ran from 520 BCE to 70 CE.

8. Rawidowicz noted that the two were not strictly markers of time, and the boundaries between them far from fixed. Indeed, one is inclined to argue that they represented two distinct systems as much as phases. See *Bavel vi-Yerushalayim*, I:104.

9. Rawidowicz elaborated on the distinction between interpretive modes in one of his last published essays, "On Interpretation," *Proceedings of the American Academy for Jewish Research* 26 (1957), 83–126. See also David N. Myers, "A Third Guide for the Perplexed? Simon Rawidowicz 'On Interpretation,'" in *History and Literature: New Readings of Jewish Texts in Honor of Arnold J. Band,* ed. William Cutter and David C. Jacobson (Providence, R.I.: Brown Judaic Studies, 2002), 75–90.

10. See *Bavel vi-Yerushalayim*, I: 84–85.

11. See Rawidowicz's comments about messianic and antimessianic impulses in Zionism in *Bavel vi-Yerushalayim*, I:131.

12. Rawidowicz argued that the very nature of Jewish peoplehood—that is, the presence of centers in both "Babylon" and "Jerusalem"—distinguished Jews from other nations and made their path toward normalization a unique one. Ibid., I:190, 217.

13. "Sha'ar TaShaH" can be translated as "The Chapter of 1948."

14. There were, in fact, two impulses present in Rawidowicz's ideological worldview. The first was to assert a strong and resilient Diaspora culture in the face of Zionism's insistence on a single Palestine-based center; the second, and somewhat countervailing impulse, was to defend the proposition of a single Jewish nation that could not be

divided With respect to the latter, Rawidowicz often asserted that "there is no ʿeruv in Israel"—referring to the line of demarcation within which it is permitted for Jews to carry certain objects and perform certain tasks otherwise proscribed on the Sabbath. *Bavel vi-Yerushalayim,* I:205.

15. Ibid., I:243.

16. Ibid., I:506.

17. See the discussion of Jewish anti-Zionism in Rabkin, *A Threat from Within,* and Ravitzky, *Messianism, Zionism, and Jewish Religious Radicalism,* especially chapters 2 and 4.

18. For a still valuable summary of the history of the binational idea and the organizational forms it assumed, see Susan Hattis, *The Bi-National Idea in Palestine During Mandatory Times* (Haifa: Shikmona Publishing, 1970).

19. S. H. Bergmann, letter to the editor, *Ner* 1, no. 4 (31 March 1950), 3.

20. See Buber's speech from spring 1949, "Should the Ichud Accept the Decree of History?" in Buber, *A Land of Two Peoples,* ed. Paul Mendes-Flohr (Oxford: Oxford University Press, 1983), 251–52.

21. Buber, "Bene Amos," *Ner* 1, no. 1 (February 1950), 4. See also the translation, "The Children of Amos," in Buber, *A Land of Two Peoples,* 257.

22. They included *Be-terem, Davar, Ha-arets,* and *Ha-poʿel ha-tsaʿir.*

23. Rawidowicz, "Tsvay vos zaynen eyns," *Di Tsukunft* 54 (May–June 1949), 288; "Two that are One," 158.

24. As noted in the introduction, the attachment of young Jews in America to Israel is declining, according to a study undertaken by sociologists Steven Cohen and Ari Kelman. Indeed, the rate of strong attachment of Jews under thirty-five is less than 20 percent. See "Attachment to Israel Declining among American Jews," *The Forward,* 5 September 2007.

25. For recent discussions of this relationship, see Yossi Shain, *Kinship and Diasporas in International Affairs* (Ann Arbor, Mich.: University of Michigan, 2007), and Gabriel Sheffer, *Diaspora Politics: At Home Abroad* (Cambridge: Cambridge University Press, 2003).

26. The number fourteen, represented by the Hebrew letters "yod" and "dalet" that spell the word "hand," refers in traditional Jewish literature to God (the strong hand). It was also the number of chapters in Maimonides' *Mishneh Torah* (known as the "yad hahazakah" or strong hand)—a fact of which Rawidowicz was well aware.

27. Fink to Rawidowicz, 5 September 1955, Rawidowicz Archive. Jacob Fink died in Paris on October 26, 1955. We have in our possession a copyedited typed version of the manuscript, with marginal notes in both French and Yiddish (suggesting Fink's hand), as well as a more polished set of galleys. I thank Benjamin Ravid for sharing both texts with me from the Rawidowicz Archive.

28. Simon Rawidowicz to Avraham Ravid, 10 May 1956, Rawidowicz Archive.

29. I owe this speculation to Professor Jonathan Sarna, who proposed a version of it in response to my lecture, "'Between Jew and Arab': Simon Rawidowicz and the Jewish

Politics of the Arab Question," delivered as the 41st Simon Rawidowicz Memorial Lecture at Brandeis University on 28 March 2004. A small piece of evidence in support of this claim is the clipping preserved among Rawidowicz's papers of an article by the New York Yiddish writer, B. Z. Goldberg. Goldberg wrote a pair of articles on the Arab question on 7 and 14 February 1956 in the *Tog-morgn zhurnal*. In the first of the articles, Goldberg writes, perhaps with Rawidowicz in mind, that he is in touch with "Jews who are concerned about the Arabs in Israel and more so about the Arab refugees from Palestine." While allowing for the possibility of improved treatment for Arabs in Israel and even the prospect of some limited return at a later juncture, Goldberg declares that "now is not the time to speak . . . The danger of an assault is great. . . . And if ever there were a danger of an Arab fifth column in Israel, such a danger is present today." See Goldberg, "In gang fun tog," from 7 February 1956 in the *Tog-morgn zhurnal*.

30. *Bavel vi-Yerushalayim*, II:819.

31. Proverbs 30:21–22: "For three things the earth doth quake, and for it cannot endure: *For a servant when he reigneth*; and a churl when he is filled with food; For an odious woman when she is married; and a handmaid that is heir to her mistress" (emphasis mine).

32. Emphasis mine. Ahad Ha-'am's essay, "Emet me-Erets Yisra'el," originally appeared in the Russian Hebrew newspaper *Ha-melits* and was republished in *Kol kitve Ahad Ha-'am* (Tel Aviv: Devir, 1947), 23–30 (citation at 29). I have relied upon and at times modified the English translation by Alan Dowty, "Much Ado about Little: Ahad Ha'am's 'Truth from Eretz Yisrael,' Zionism, and the Arabs," *Israel Studies* 5, no. 2 (2000), 174. Dowty also offers a helpful introduction to the piece, though consciously understates the significance of the paragraphs dealing with the Arab population of Palestine.

33. "Emet me-Erets Yisra'el," 24.

34. Yitzhak Epstein, "She'elah ne'elamah," *Ha-shiloah* (1907), 203–204.

35. On the origins of Brit Shalom and a detailed analysis of the binational idea, see Hattis, *The Bi-National Idea in Palestine during Mandatory Times*, 39ff. On the Central European circle that became the core of Brit Shalom, see Shalom Ratzabi, *Between Zionism and Judaism: The Radical Circle in Brith Shalom, 1925–1933* (Leiden: Brill, 2002).

36. See Yosef Gorny, *Zionism and the Arabs, 1992–1948: A Study of Ideology* (Oxford: Oxford University Press, 1987), 134. See also Shabtai Teveth, *Ben-Gurion and the Palestinian Arabs: From Peace to War* (Oxford: Oxford University Press, 1995), 70–71.

37. Zeev Sternhell has argued strenuously for the ascendance of nationalist over socialist values in the Labor Zionist movement of which Ben-Gurion was the dominant figure. See Sternhell, *The Founding Myths of Israel*, trans. David Meisel (Princeton, N.J.: Princeton University Press, 1997).

38. See Ben-Gurion's response to Brit Shalom's stance from 1930, "Mi-tokh ha-vikuah: siha 'im havre Brit Shalom," in his essays *Anahnu u-shekhenenu* (Tel Aviv: Davar, 1931), 184.

39. Shabtai Teveth asserts that in Ben-Gurion's view, "the Arab right to Palestine was inferior to that of the Jewish people." Teveth, *Ben-Gurion and the Palestinian Arabs*, 94.

40. Ibid., 129–48.

41. Benny Morris discusses a shift in rhetoric and tactic by the 1930s in *The Birth of the Palestinian Refugee Problem Revisited*, 44–45. Dimitry Shumsky points out that Ben-Gurion held on to the view of a federated arrangement with autonomous Jewish and Arab cantons as late as 1931. Shumsky, "Me'ever le-ribonut," 2.

42. Benny Morris notes the sentiment of some Mapam members (from the more left-leaning kibbutz faction) in favor of a return of refugees in late 1948/early 1949. See Morris, "Mapai, Mapam, and the Arab Problem in 1948," in *1948 and After: Israel and the Palestinians* (Oxford: Clarendon, 1990), 63–64. As an example, see the critique of the Mapai leader, Moshe Shertok (Sharett) by Moshe Sneh in the Mapam newspaper, *Al ha-mishmar* (5 December 1948), 2.

43. Morris, "Mapai, Mapam, and the Arab Problem," 39, 43. I have modified Morris's own translation of Yavne'eli's remark from "slaves who have become kings" to the more common "servants who have come to reign."

44. Indeed, there was a concerted effort by Israeli politicians, government officials, and researchers to count and categorize the refugees and then to rebut their claims to return to their homes. See the study of this effort during the years 1948–52 by Haya Bombaji-Sasportas, "Kolo shel mi nishma/kolo shel mi mushtak: havnayat ha-siah 'al 'be'ayat ha-pelitim ha-falastinim' ba-mimsad ha-Yisre'eli" (master's thesis, Ben-Gurion University, 2000). Meanwhile, Gil Eyal studies the impact of the "Orientalist" profession in the Yishuv and the first decades of the State of Israel in *The Disenchantment of the Orient: Expertise in Arab Affairs and the Israeli State* (Stanford, Calif.: Stanford University Press, 2006).

45. See the published version of his speech in "Ki tetsu le-milhamah," *'Al ha-mishmar*, 30 July 1948. Meanwhile, the first number of *Ner* 1, no. 1 (February 1950) reported on a meeting involving Rabbi Binyomin, S. H. Bergmann, and a Maronite priest to discuss the expulsion of the village of Kafr Bir'im (near Safed) in November 1948. The next two numbers (1, no. 2, and 1, no. 3) discuss the case of the coastal village of al-'Abbasiyya in which, it is argued, villages were unjustly expelled given their peaceable relations with neighboring Jews. (On the fate of these two villages during the 1948 war, see Walid Khalidi, ed., *All That Remains: The Palestinian Villages Occupied and Depopulated by Israel in 1948* [Washington, D.C.: Institute for Palestine Studies, 1992], 232–33, 460–61.) Subsequent issues of the journal are filled with reports on legal and social discrimination against Arabs, discussions of cases of expulsions (and responses to *Ner*'s own coverage in other journals or papers), and meditations on the question of the return of refugees. On the last point, see R. Binyomin's article in *Ner* 2, nos. 1–2 (27 October 1950), in which he argues that Israel was responsible for the war and should thus agree to the return of the refugees. To neglect the refugee problem is, he argued, to perpetuate the spirit of fascism that led to the war in the first place. In the next number (2, nos. 3–4 [1 December 1950]), R. Binyomin continues this theme, challenging the claim of a writer in *'Al ha-mishmar* that the refugees should only be permitted to return following a peace agreement with the Arab nations. R. Binyomin says that no such linkage should be drawn, though he

published an article by Shlomo Shershevsky (3, nos. 1–4, October–November 1951) that made a similar point. Curiously, R. Binyomin's own views seemed to change a bit by 1951. In an article on the refugee problem from 13 July 1951 (*Ner* 2, nos. 18–21), he asserted that responsibility for the refugee problem should be divided among three parties, the Jews, the Arabs, and the international community—each of whom should take responsibility for one-third of the refugees; that is to say, 250,000 people.

46. Alexander Prag, "Medinat Yisra'el veha-kefar ha-'Arvi," '*Al ha-mishmar*, 1 August 1948. And yet, this view was not uniformly maintained throughout '*Al ha-mishmar*. For example, Avraham Benshalom argued some months earlier (7 May) that the responsibility for Arab flight lay not with Jewish forces, but with Arab political leaders. Moshe Shertok (Sharett) affirmed this view in an article from 20 June, and went on to maintain that the flight could actually help in demarcating borders with Israel's Arab neighbors. He also cited the population exchange of Greeks and Turks in 1923 as an example of the irreversibility of the movement of people. Moshe Sneh rejects the logic of Shertok's claims (5 December), arguing that those refugees who accept the State of Israel should be permitted to return with the war's end. I discuss these views in my essay, "Simon Rawidowicz on the Arab Question: A Prescient Gaze into the 'New History,'" in *Mediating Modernity: Challenges and Trends in the Jewish Encounter with the Modern World: Essays in Honor of Michael A. Meyer*, ed. Lauren B. Strauss and Michael Brenner (Detroit, Mich.: Wayne State University Press, 2008).

47. R. Binyomin (né Yehoshua Radler-Feldmann [1880–1957] was a prolific Hebrew author and editor, as well as the possessor of a unique Zionist perspective. That is, he held that the fulfillment of Zionism would come with the integration of Jews and Arabs in a single "pan-Semitic" project of renewal. See the brief memorial volume published on the thirtieth day after his death, *R. Binyomin: Zikhrono li-verakha*, ed. Yehudah ibn Shmuel, Naftali Ben-Menahem, and Shraga Kadri (Jerusalem: R. H. Ha-Cohen, 1958), 11. R. Binyomin edited a number of Hebrew journals other than *Ner* including the earlier Brit Shalom organ, *She'ifotenu*.

48. The reference to the "servant who has come to rule" is actually an excerpted section of Ahad Ha-'am's 1891 essay, "Emet me-Erets Yisra'el" in *Ner* 1, nos. 10–11 (29 June 1950), 11. Meanwhile, Natan Hofshi invokes Hillel's dictum in the opening issue of *Ner* 1, no. 1 (February 1950), 5.

49. See R. Binyomin, "Be-shule ha-sefer veha-zeman," *Moznayim* 4 (1935), 76. In that response, R. Binyomin reveals himself to be a most curious Zionist, at once committed to territorial maximimalism and yet also to a political state for Jews and Arabs alike (hence, his early involvement in Brit Shalom). Ibid., 73–74. See Rawidowicz's discussion of R. Binyomin's criticism of him in a 1957 symposium, translated as "Jewish Existence: The End and the Endless," in *State of Israel, Diaspora, and Jewish Continuity*, 81. There Rawidowicz notes, with a trace of self-vindication, that R. Binyomin began to change his views by the 1940s.

50. Rawidowicz, "Levatser velo le'ar'er," *Moznayim* 5 (1935–36), 290–94, quoted in Ravid, "Le-hayav," xlviii.

51. Benny Morris notes that the tide began to turn decisively in favor of the Jewish side toward the end of the first stage of the war (what he calls the "civil war" stage)—that is, in April/May 1948. See Morris's new account in *1948: A History of the First Arab-Israeli*

*War* (New Haven: Yale University Press, 2008), 77–78. For a demographic perspective on the pace of flight, see Charles S. Kamen, "After the Catastrophe I: The Arabs in Israel, 1948–1951," *Middle Eastern Studies* 23 (October 1987), 453.

52. See the discussion of Sasson's memo of 13 August 1948 and the meeting of 18 August 1948 in Morris, *The Birth of the Palestinian Refugee Problem Revisited*, 327–28.

53. See Bernadotte's "Progress Report of the United Nations Mediator to Palestine," 16 September 1948 at http://domino.un.urg/unispal.nsf/9a798adbf322aff38525617b006d88d7/ab14d4aafc4e1bb985256204004f55fa!OpenDocument&Highlight=0,Bernadotte,progress. See also Morris, *The Birth of the Palestinian Refugee Problem Revisited*, 331.

54. Morris, *The Birth of the Palestinian Refugee Problem Revisited*, 330.

55. Anita Shapira, "Hirbet Hiz'ah: Between Remembrance and Forgetting," *Jewish Social Studies* 7, no. 1 (2000), 25.

56. See Don Peretz, *Israel and the Palestine Arabs* (Washington, D.C.: Middle East Institute, 1958), passim.

57. Rony Gabbay, *A Political Study of the Arab-Jewish Conflict: The Arab Refugee Problem* (Paris: E. Droz, 1959), 109–110.

58. Ibid., 110, no. 158.

59. Exceptions to the rule are Benny Morris and Avi Shlaim, who both lauded Gabbay's book, with the former calling it "a remarkable achievement." See Morris, "The New Historiography: Israel and its Past," in *1948 and After: Israel and the Palestinians*, 16–17, as well as Avi Shlaim, "The Debate about 1948," *International Journal of Middle Eastern Studies* 27 (1993), 289.

60. In the famous words of veteran Labor Zionist novelist Aharon Megged, the "New Historians" were motivated by a "suicide drive." See his "The Israeli Suicide Drive," *Haarets* (supp.), 10 June 1994, quoted in Neil Caplan, "The 'New Historians,'" *Journal of Palestine Studies* 24 (Summer 1995), 103. Subsequently, Israeli parliamentarian and later minister of education, Limor Livnat, argued that the "New Historians" posed the gravest of dangers to Israeli society. In a speech in New York on 17 August 2000, she declared: "These academics would have us believe that the Holocaust was not unique and that, therefore, Israel's creation and continued existence lacks any particular moral justification. To them, we have no legitimate past. Post-Zionists go on to say we do not have a legitimate future." Livnat's speech, "Post-Zionism and Israeli Politics," can be found at htt://www.meforum.org/article/185 (accessed on 27 December 2006).

61. In the case of 1956, the Israeli government considered a variety of options ( for example, resettlement outside of the country and preserving the status quo) regarding the 300,000 residents (more than 200,000 of whom were refugees) in the Gaza Strip, which Israel captured in November. Before making any definitive decision, it exited the Strip in March 1957. See the discussion by Nur Masalha, "The 1956–57 Occupation of the Gaza Strip: Israeli Proposals to Resettle the Palestinian Refugees," *British Journal of Middle Eastern Studies* 23, no. 1 (May 1996), 55–68. Meanwhile, Tom Segev chronicles the extensive deliberations within the Israeli cabinet and beyond over what to do with the new refugee problem created by the Six-Day War in 1967. Segev shows that Israel's conquest of the

West Bank, and the subsequent entry of Israelis into that territory, occasioned a renewed awareness of the presence of refugees from 1948. Moreover, the 1967 war created its own refugee problem, with Palestinians from the West Bank fleeing beyond Israeli control into Jordan; reports indicated that some 80,000 took shelter in tents in Jordan. The presence of the new refugees, whose plight was publicized through the medium of television, prompted new international pressure on Israel, including from the United States. As a result, Israeli politicians (Levi Eshkhol, Menachem Begin, and Pinhas Sapir among others), as well as academics (such as Michael Bruno and Roberto Bacchi), came up with a variety of plans to address the new and old refugee problems, but none gained traction. Tom Segev, *1967 veha-arets shinta et paneha* (Jerusalem: Keter, 2005), 548–68.

62. See Shapira's exhaustive analysis of public debate, especially after a film version of the story in 1978, in "Hirbet Hiz'ah: Between Remembrance and Forgetting," 30–50.

63. See Tom Segev, *The Seventh Million: The Israelis and the Holocaust*, trans. Haim Watzman (New York: Hill and Wang, 1973), 421–45. See also Idit Zertal, *Israel's Holocaust and the Politics of Nationhood*, trans. Chaya Galai (Cambridge: Cambridge University Press, 2005), 84–88.

64. Ben-Gurion's interview in the *New York Times Magazine*, 18 December 1960, is excerpted in Zertal, *Israel's Holocaust and the Politics of Nationhood*, 98. See also the famous discussion in Hannah Arendt, *Eichmann in Jerusalem: A Report on the Banality of Evil*, rev. and enlarged ed. (New York: Penguin, 1977), 10.

65. Zertal, *Israel's Holocaust and the Politics of Nationhood*, 98–99.

66. The first official census by the State of Israel in November 1948 listed 69,000 Arabs. Meanwhile, it is estimated that 156,000 Arabs lived in the State of Israel by the time of the armistice agreements in 1949, and more than 170,000 in 1953. See the detailed demographic analysis in Kamen, "After the Catastrophe I", 454, 458.

67. See the text of the White Paper at http://www.yale.edu/lawweb/avalon/mideast/brwh1922.htm (consulted on 24 August 2006). Two new books discuss Churchill's relationship to Zionism, pointing out his supportive stance. That said, his task in 1922 was to restrain more optimistic Zionist readings of the Balfour Declaration focused on Jewish self-administration in a "wholly Jewish Palestine" by instead referring to the creation of a Jewish center "in which the Jewish people as a whole may take, on grounds of religion and race, an interest and pride." Such a center, the paper instructed, would not alter the fact that "the status of all citizens of Palestine in the eyes of the law shall be Palestinian." See Michael Makovsky, *Churchill's Promised Land: Zionism and Statecraft* (New Haven, Conn.: Yale University Press, 2007), 130; for a more sanguine reading of the White Paper's affirmation of Zionism, see Martin Gilbert, *Churchill and the Jews: A Lifelong Friendship* (New York: Henry Holt, 2007), 85. Meanwhile, Rawidowicz quotes (and critiques) Churchill's "rights, not sufferance" formulation in a discussion of the relationship between Diaspora Jews and Jews in Palestine. See his "Yisra'el ba-'olam," *Metsudah* 2 (December 1943), 8.

68. The literature is extensive, but among the leading scholarly contributors to the discussion are As'ad Ghanem, Sabri Jiryis, Ian Lustick, Sara Ozacky-Lazar, Ilan Pappé, Shira Robinson, Nadim Rouhana, Sammy Smooha, and Oren Yiftachel.

69. Meron Benvenisti, *Sacred Landscape: The Buried History of the Holy Land since 1948*, trans. Maxine Kaufman-Lacusta (Berkeley and Los Angeles: University of California Press, 2000).

70. David Grossman, *Sleeping on a Wire: Conversations with Palestinians in Israel*, trans. Haim Watzman (New York: Farrar, Straus, and Giroux, 1992), 82–84.

71. http://www.knesset.gov.il/docs/eng/megilat_eng.htm (accessed on 25 August 2006).

72. Shira Nomi Robinson, "Occupied Citizens in a Liberal State: Palestinians under Military Rule and the Colonial Formation of Israeli Society, 1948–1956" (Ph.D. diss., Stanford University, 2005), 55.

73. See Schmitt's 1922 book, *Politische Theologie*, translated as *Political Theology: Four Chapters on the Concept of Sovereignty*, trans. George Schwab (Cambridge, Mass.: MIT Press, 1985).

74. On the operation of the military government, see Ian Lustick, *Arabs in the Jewish State: Israel's Control of a National Minority* (Austin, Tex.: University of Texas Press, 1980), 123–29.

75. See Don Handelman, "Contradictions between Citizenship and Nationality: Their Consequences for Ethnicity and Inequality in Israel," *International Journal of Politics, Culture and Society* 7, no. 3 (1994), 441–59; qtd. in Robinson, "Occupied Citizens in a Liberal State," 63.

76. For a discussion of the uphill battle faced by an Israel government figure such as Shetreet who saw his role as safeguarding the interests of Arabs, see Tom Segev, *1949: The First Israelis* (New York: Free Press, 1986), 43–91. See also Ilan Pappé, "An Uneasy Coexistence: Arabs and Jews in the First Decade of Statehood," in *Israel: The First Decade of Independence,* ed. S. Ilan Troen and Noah Lucas (Albany: State University of New York Press, 1995), 642–49.

77. See appendix C, "Law of Return," *Laws of the State of Israel: Authorized Translation from the Hebrew* (Jerusalem, 1948–87), 4:114. Israeli legal scholar David Kretzmer observes in his thorough book: "The right given in the Law of Return to Jews to immigrate to Israel is one of the only cases in Israeli legislation in which an overt distinction is made between the rights of Jews and non-Jews." David Kretzmer, *The Legal Status of the Arabs in Israel* (Boulder, Colo.: Westview Press, 1990), 35.

78. See the report of the Knesset debate, "Vikuah so'er 'al hok ha-'ezrahut," *Ha-arets*, 27 March 1952. Meanwhile, the Communist Hebrew daily, *Kol ha-'am*, ran a story several days after the law's implementation (on 12 July 1952) under the headline "Protest Strike in Arab Locales against the Racist Law." See "Shevitat meha'ah ba-yishuvim ha-'Arviyim neged ha-hok ha-giz'ani," *Kol ha-'am*, 14 July 1952.

79. See appendix D.

80. See Benny Morris's discussion of "infiltration" in his article on the government response to and public debate over the Kibya episode of 1953 in "Ha-'itonut ha-yisre'elit be-farashat Kibya," in his *Tikun ta'ut: Yehudim ve-'Arvim be-Erets-Yisra'el, 1936–1956* (Tel Aviv: Am Oved, 2000), 175–97.

81. The Universal Declarations contains a number of articles (2, 7, 12, 13, 15, and 21) that relate to the right of members of a national minority to express themselves as such, to move freely, and to participate fully in the government of their host country.

82. "Between Jew and Arab," (sec. III). See Yehoshua Freudenheim, *Ha-shilton bi-medinat Yisrael* (Jerusalem: Rubin Mass, 1950), 190.

83. See, for example, the opinions expressed in the recent collection assembled in Tony Kushner and Alisa Solomon, eds., *Wrestling with Zion: Progressive Jewish-American Responses to the Israeli-Palestinian Conflict* (New York: Grove Press, 2003).

84. The press release announcing the agreement from 10 September 1950 can be found at http://www.ajcarchives.org/AJC_DATA/Files/508.PDF. See also the discussion in Jonathan Sarna, *American Judaism: A History* (New Haven, Conn.: Yale University Press, 2004), 334–35. For Rawidowicz's analysis and critique of the agreement between Ben-Gurion and Blaustein, see *Bavel vi-Yerushalayim*, I:225–45.

85. For a detailed discussion of the term, see Nir Kedar, "Ben-Gurion's *Mamlakhtiyut*: Etymological and Theoretical Roots," *Israel Studies* 7, no. 3 (2002), 117–33.

86. Israel Land Acquisition (Validation of Acts and Compensation) Law, 2.a.3. See appendix E.

87. Benvenisti estimates that the number of "present absentees" has grown from 30,000–35,000 in 1951 to 150,000 in 1998. See *Sacred Landscape*, 209.

88. Kretzmer, *The Legal Status of the Arabs in Israel*, 49–76, esp. 50. Kretzmer also notes, without accepting, Sabri Jiryis' figure of one million dunams of expropriated Arab land. Ibid., 50, and Jiryis, *The Arabs in Israel* (Beirut: Institute for Palestine Studies, 1969), 138. For his part, Meron Benvenisti estimates that 4.5 million dunams of land were either confiscated or abandoned by Arabs in Israel. See *Sacred Landscapes*, 315. Meanwhile, Michael R. Fischbach maintains that in terms of "the Palestinian refugees' land, the exact scope and value . . . has been and continues to be debated by scholars and governments alike." See his thorough study, *Records of Dispossession: Palestinian Refugee Property and the Arab-Israeli Conflict* (New York: Columbia University Press, 2003), xxii.

89. Together, kibbutzim and moshavim, Israel's two main forms of collective settlements, "held 45 percent of the land abandoned by Arabs or confiscated from Arab citizens." Benvenisti, *Sacred Landscape*, 182.

90. The multivalent Hebrew term *gezerah* can be rendered in English as "verdict" or "plight." It also connotes a violent pogrom, as in *gezerat Ta'H ve-Ta'T* (the Chmielnicki massacres of 1648–49).

91. On the question of numbers, Rawidowicz observed: "The Arabs speak at times of a million souls or more. By contrast, there are those who set the figure of five, six, or seven hundred thousand—that is, about the number of *'olim* to the State of Israel between 1948–1951." "Between Jew and Arab," sec. V.

92. See the account of a conversation with the first American ambassador to Israel, James McDonald, in his book *My Mission in Israel, 1948–1951* (London: Victor Gollancz, 1951), 176.

93. See most prominently Nur Masalha, *Expulsion of the Palestinians: The Concept of "Transfer" in Zionist Political Thought, 1882–1948* (Washington, D.C.: Institute for Palestine Studies, 1992).

94. Shapira, "Hirbet Hiz'ah: Between Remembrance and Forgetting," 1–62. In her analysis of the story, Nurith Gertz observes that the "Israeli protagonists disengage from the historical past, from the shared communal future, from the natural environment surrounding them, from human values in which they once believed, and from a connection to the metaphysical world that had accompanied them from biblical times." See Gertz, *Hirbet Hiz'ah veha-boker shele-mohorat* (Tel Aviv: Ha-kibuts ha-me'uhad, 1983), 77.

95. S. Yizhar, "Hirbet Hiz'ah," in *Shiv'ah Sipurim* (Tel Aviv: ha-Kibuts ha-Me'uhad, 1971), 82, 86.

96. Ibid., 86, 87.

97. Shapira, "Hirbet Hiz'ah," 6–7.

98. See Shmuel Dayan, "'Al yahasenu la-'Arvim," *Ha-po'el ha-tsa'ir* 45, nos. 44–45 (1952), 16.

99. Ibid., qtd. in "Between Jew and Arab," sec. XII.

100. "Between Jew and Arab," sec. XIII.

101. "It is a rare occurrence indeed," Sharon wrote, "when a bad episode, which everyone regrets, largely turns out well in the vicissitudes of time and circumstance." Avraham Sharon (Schwadron), *He'arot shovinistiyot le-'inyan ha-'Arvim* (Tel Aviv, n.p., 1949), 7.

102. Sharon, *He'arot shovinistiyot le-'inyan ha-'Arvim*, 8. Sharon had been, by his own account, an advocate of population exchange for decades, first proposing the idea in a Swiss newspaper in 1916. Ibid., 14. Notwithstanding this commitment (and his many post-1948 remarks), Rawidowicz notes that Sharon seemed at one point to adopt the rhetoric of accommodation between Jews and Arabs: "Zionists must assume for themselves the responsibility to solve the question of the Jews in its entirety. That is, over the course of a reasonable period of time, we will settle all of our people, or almost all of them, on the territory of Mandatory Palestine, west and east. *And this will be done on the condition, and with sufficient international guarantee, that its other residents will not be harmed.* If in the future 12 out of 17 million of our own will earn their keep in this land, *two million of the other people* will also be able to earn their keep here." Sharon, *Torat ha-Tsiyonut ha-akhzarit* (Tel Aviv: Sifriyat De'ot, 1944), 49.

103. "Between Jew and Arab," sec. XI. The text of Yizhar's remarks can be found in *Divre siah: hartsa'ot ve-diyune haverim* (Tel Aviv, 1951), 2:52–53. Yizhar made reference in his remarks to an earlier era in which Zionists used the language of "we and our neighbors"; this was a clear reference to a volume of that name containing David Ben-Gurion's essays on the Arab question: *Anahnu u-shekhenenu*.

104. Reflecting his deep-rooted sense of Jewish ethical virtue prior to 1948, Rawidowicz asserted that from the time of the time of the Hasmonean kingdom (2nd century BCE) until the present, "there was not a single solid complaint in the arsenal of the haters of Israel." "Between Jew and Arab," sec. VIII.

105. Ibid. For a helpful discussion of the association of Esau with Christianity, see Gerson D. Cohen, "Esau as Symbol in Early Medieval Thought," in his collected essays, *Studies in the Variety of Rabbinic Cultures* (Philadelphia: Jewish Publication Society, 1991), esp. 245–50.

106. See Leibowitz essay, "After Kibya," originally published in the Israeli journal *Beterem* in 1953 and reprinted in his *Judaism, Human Values, and the Jewish State* (Cambridge, Mass.: Harvard University Press, 1992), 189–90. According to Leibowitz, "morality does not admit a modifying attribute and cannot be 'Jewish' or 'not Jewish.'" See the discussion of Leibowitz and, more broadly, debates over the balance of power and ethics by Ehud Luz, "'Jewish Ethics' as an Argument in the Public Debate over the Israeli Reaction to Palestinian Terror," *Israel Studies* 7 (2002), 134–56.

107. It is noteworthy that Leibowitz, despite his disavowal of a specific Jewish morality, *did* conclude his essay on Kibya by suggesting that "the curse of our father Jacob" (pronounced upon the tribes Simon and Levi after they killed the men of Shekhem in retaliation for the defiling of their sister Dinah) could fall on Israel for the dangerous arrogation of holiness to the state and its activity. Leibowitz, "After Kibiyeh," 190.

108. For a more recent version of this argument, see Daniel and Jonathan Boyarin, "Diaspora: Generation and the Ground of Jewish Identity," *Critical Inquiry* 19, no. 4 (Summer 1993), 693–725.

109. See Dvora Hacohen, trans. Gila Brand, *Immigrants in Turmoil: Mass Immigration to Israel and its Repercussions in the 1950s and After* (Syracuse, N.Y.: Syracuse University Press, 2003), 103. See also Nachum T. Gross's discussion of the system of rationing and economic controls in the name of "austerity" (*tsena*) in "The Economic Regime during Israel's First Decade," in *Israel: The First Decade of Independence*, ed. Troen and Lucas, 232.

110. By contrast, a group of nineteen American theologians, academics, and university administrators submitted a proposal to the United Nations in 1951 to resettle Palestinian refugees in Arab countries. Among their arguments was that "(f)or Israel to absorb the Arab refugees would be to dislocate the economy of a state which in the space of three years has been compelled to fight a war of defense, establish itself under democratic constitutional forms, and open its doors to almost 700,000 Jewish refugees." See H. Dewey Anderson, *The Arab Refugee Problem: How It Can be Solved (Proposals Submitted to the General Assembly of the United Nations)* (New York: Nation Associates, 1951), 12.

111. A leading force in this effort is the World Organization of Jews from Arab Countries (WOJAC), founded in France in 1976 whose mandate is "is to document the assets Jewish refugees lost as they fled Arab countries following the establishment of the state of Israel." See the group's website at http://wojac.com. For a critique of WOJAC's linkage between this demand and the Palestinian refugee problem, see Yehouda Shenhav, "Hitching a Ride on the Magic Carpet," *Ha-arets*, 15 August 2003.

112. See the discussion by Yehouda Shenhav, "Arab-Jews, Population Exchange, and the Palestinian Right of Return," in *Exile and Return: Predicaments of Palestinians and Jews*, ed. Ann M. Lesch and Ian S. Lustick (Philadelphia: University of Pennsylvania Press, 2005), 228–32.

113. On rates of immigration and economic development in Israel, see Linda Sharaby, "Israel's Economic Growth: Success without Security," *MERIA: Middle East Review of International Affairs* 6, no. 3 (September 2002); http://meria.idc.ac.il/journal/2002/issue3/jvbn3a3.html#Linda%20Sharaby.

114. Ironically, the immigrants who did come in large numbers from the West to the State of Israel were Holocaust survivors, who bore the same stigma of being unproductive that was placed on Jews from the Middle East. See Hacohen, *Immigrants in Turmoil*, 109.

115. In terms of the largest concentration of Jews in the world, one scholar has noted: "Despite Ben-Gurion's exhortations, American Jews simply ignored the Jewish state's call for their immigration." Steven T. Rosenthal, *Irreconcilable Differences: The Waning of the American Jewish Love Affair with Israel* (Waltham,Mass.: Brandeis University Press, 2001), 27. That said, between 1948 and 1951, slightly more than half of the Jewish immigrants to the State of Israel (50.1 percent) were from the West (99 percent of whom came from Europe)—as opposed to 49.9 percent from the Middle East. Between 1952 and 1954, the tide had turned decisively toward the east, with 76.4 percent of Jewish immigrants coming from the Middle East and the remainder from the west. See the figures from the Israeli Central Bureau of Statistics *Statistical Abstract of Israel (2006)* at http://www.jewishvirtual library.org/jsource/Immigration/Immigration_by_region.html. For the broader period from 1946 to 1953, estimates are that 48.6 percent of all Jewish immigrants to the State of Israel were Holocaust survivors. See Dalia Ofer, "Holocaust Survivors as Immigrants: The Case of Israel and the Cyprus Detainees," *Modern Judaism* 16 (1996), 2.

116. According to the United Jewish Communities, nearly $12 billion was raised by the United Jewish Appeal, the United Israel Appeal, and the Jewish Federations in the United States for Israel between 1948 and 2004. See the table "American Jewish Contributions to Israel" at http://wwwjewishvirtuallibrary.org/jsource/US-Israel/ujatab.html.

117. Benny Morris, "The Crystallization of Israeli Policy Against a Return of the Arab Refugees: April–December 1948," *Studies in Zionism* 6, no. 1 (1985), 87, 90. The sequence of events described in this paragraph and the next owes much to Morris's article.

118. Morris describes the wave of Palestinian flight from Palestine beginning in April 1948 as the "mass exodus." See *The Birth of the Palestinian Refugee Problem Revisited*, 163ff.

119. In a discussion with members of the UN's Palestine Conciliation Commission in 1949, David Ben-Gurion asserted that the question of repatriation depended on "the establishment of peace, because so long as the Arab States refused to make peace . . . Israel could not fully rely upon the declarations that Arab refugees might make concerning their intention to live in peace with their neighbors." He went on to express his preference for the resettlement of refugees in Arab countries, not Israel. Quoted in Edward H. Buehrig, *The UN and the Palestinian Refugees: A Study in Nonterritorial Administration* (Bloomington, Ind.: Indiana University Press, 1971), 15.

120. For example, all of the Arab states voting in December 1948 (Egypt, Iraq, Lebanon, Saudi Arabia, Syria, and Yemen) opposed U.N. Resolution 194 with its call for repatriation of or compensation for Palestinian refugees. Later, the Arab states shifted to the view that it was better to insist on the return of refugees to Israel than to absorb them

in their own countries. See Morris, *The Birth of the Palestinian Refugee Problem Revisited*, 550. Meanwhile, Rashid Khalidi observes that Jordan and Egypt kept tight lids on Palestinian political activism in the wake of 1948 and that, in general, "constraints (were) placed on Palestinian activism by the Arabs regimes." Khalidi, *The Iron Cage: The Story of the Palestinian Struggle for Statehood* (Boston: Beacon Press, 2006), 136, 138. See also the earlier observation of Ben Halpern that the "tactics adopted by the Arabs were designed to derive the greatest possible political advantage from the humanitarian and quasi-legal claims of the refugees." Halpern, *The Idea of the Jewish State*, 2nd ed. (Cambridge, Mass.: Harvard University Press, 1969).

121. Quoted in Neil Caplan, "A Tale of Two Cities: The Rhodes and Lausanne Conference, 1949," *Journal of Palestine Studies* 21, no. 3 (Spring 1992), 15.

122. Shenhav, "Arab Jews, Population Exchange, and the Palestinian Right of Return," 226.

123. Truman's frustration was evident in a number of communications from the spring of 1949. On April 29, he wrote Mark Ethridge, the American representative of the Palestine Conciliation Commission: "I am rather disgusted with the manner in which the Jews are approaching the refugee problem." A month later, on 29 May 1949, he sent a very stern classified note to Ben-Gurion via Ambassador James McDonald that began: "The Govt of the US is seriously disturbed by the attitude of Israel with respect to a territorial settlement in Palestine and to the question of Palestinian refugees." The lengthy note concluded: "if the Govt of Israel continues to reject the basic principles set forth by the res of the GA of Dec. 11, 1948 [that is, U.N. Resolution 194] and the friendly advice offered by the US Govt for the sole purpose of facilitating a genuine peace in Palestine, the US Govt will regretfully be forced to the conclusion that a revision of its attitude toward Israel has become unavoidable." *Foreign Relations of the United States, 1949: The Near East, South Asia, and Africa* (Washington, D.C.: GPO, 1977), 957, 1072, 1074 n. For further discussion, see Simha Flapan, The Birth of Israel: Myths and Realities (New York: Pantheon, 1987), 214–22, as well as Joseph Schechtman, *The Arab Refugee Problem*, 26.

124. The resolution can be seen at http://daccessdds.un.org/doc/RESOLUTION/GEN/NR0/043/65/IMG/NR004365.pdf?OpenElement (accessed on 22 December 2006.) It is important to add that this clause was part of a larger document that called for the creation of the Palestine Conciliation Commission (PCC) and urged the conflicting parties to engage in negotiations "with a view to the final settlement of all questions outstanding between them."

125. In his massive biography of Israeli Foreign Minister Moshe Sharett, Gabriel Sheffer notes: "Sharett tried to cut the new Gordian knot and separate the question of Israel's membership in the UN and its participation in the Lausanne Conference, but to no avail." See Sheffer, *Moshe Sharett: Biography of a Political Moderate* (Oxford: Clarendon, 1996), 458. Indeed, the decision to admit the State of Israel to the U.N. on 11 May 1949 hardly seems unconnected to its agreement to sign the "Lausanne Protocol" on 12 May. The protocol detailed the shared principles of the parties to that conference (Israel, Egypt, Jordan, Lebanon, Syria, and the members of the PCC—France, Turkey, and the United States), including agreement to realize "as quickly as possible the objectives of the General Assembly resolution of December 11, 1948, regarding the refugees, respect for their rights, and the preservation of their property, as well as territorial and other

questions." http://domino.un.ort/UNISPAL.NSF/90634F6F0DC1B85256d0a00549202/ 4a5ef29a5e977e2e852561010079e43c!OpenDocument. See also Flapan, *The Birth of Israel*, 214.

126. See the discussion in Morris, *The Birth of the Palestinian Refugee Problem Revisited*, 561–66 (and here at 565). Cf. Joseph Schechtman, who places the initiative for the proposal in the hands of Mark Ethridge, the United States representative to the Palestine Conciliation Commission. See Schechtman, *The Arab Refugee Problem*, 36–37.

127. See Morris's discussion of the "100,000 Offer" in *The Birth of the Palestinian Refugee Problem Revisited*, 570–80. Cf. Schechtman, *The Arab Refugee Problem*, 39–40. For an early discussion of the proposal to repatriate 100,000, see Jon Kimche, "Mahen ef-sharuyot le-yishuv be'ayat ha-pelitim ha-'Arvim," '*Al ha-mishmar*, 10 August 1948.

128. One Israeli researcher argues that Israel's "100,000 Offer" was made without "any intention of implementation." See Varda Schiffer, "The 1949 Israeli Offer to Repatriate 100,000 Palestinian Refugees," *Middle East Focus* 9 (Fall 1986), 18, quoted in Caplan, "A Tale of Two Cities," 31. See Caplan's broader study as well, *The Lausanne Conference, 1949: A Case Study in Middle East Peacemaking* (Tel Aviv: Moshe Dayan Center for Middle Eastern and African Studies, 1993). Morris asserts that "Israel hesitantly brandished the refugees as a carrot in the multilateral negotiations." Morris, *The Birth of the Palestinian Refugee Problem Revisited*, 551. In fact, there was a not insignificant current in Israeli policymaking that held to the view of the notorious "Transfer Committee" chaired by Yosef Weitz: namely, that far from being the heart of the problem, the "uprooting of the Arabs should be seen *as a solution* to the Arab question in the State of Israel'" qtd. in Morris, "Israel Policy and the Arab Refugees," 92.

129. Joshua Landis has argued that the United States continued to concern itself with the refugee question after Lausanne, turning its attention from repatriation in Israel to resettlement in Syria (via negotiations with Husni Za'im). See Landis, "Early U.S. Policy toward Palestinian Refugees: the Syria Option," in *The Palestinian Refugees: Old Problems—New Solutions*, ed. Joseph Ginat and Edward J. Perkins (Norman, Okla.: University of Oklahoma Press, 2001), 77–87. See also Avi Shlaim's discrete study of the Za'im proposal noted in note 130.

130. "Between Jew and Arab," sec. VI. Rawidowicz was joined in this view by one of the Israeli government's chief intermediaries with Arab regimes, Eliahu Sasson. Sasson opined in June 1949 that the "Jews think they can achieve peace without paying any price, maximal or minimal." That is, they expect the Arabs to cede all territory held by Israel, absorb all the refugees, and agree to all border modifications, among other concessions. Sasson's communication is quoted in Avi Shlaim, "Husni Za'im and the Plan to Resettle Palestinian Refugees in Syria," *Journal of Palestine Studies* 15, no. 4 (Summer 1986), 76.

131. The language of "blessings" and "curses" in response to the behavior of "Israel" is a recurrent theme in the Bible, especially in Deuteronomy 26.

132. נעלו לא עדין ותשובה שיבה שערי The Hebrew cognates "שיבה"and "תשובה"in this sentence convey the interrelated notions of return—in the physical sense for the Arab refugees—and repentance, in the moral sense for those Jews putatively responsible for their fate. The phrase immediately evokes Maimonides' well-known claim in *The*

*Guide for the Perplexed* (II:25) that the "gates of figurative interpretation are (not) shut in our faces."

133. "Between Jew and Arab," sec. II. See, for example, the reference to a "second round" in "Mi-yom le-yom," *Ha-arets*, 9 June 1950. See also the discussion in Zaki Shalom, *David Ben-Guryon: Medinat Yisra'el veha-'olam ha-'Arvi* (Sde Boker: Ha-merkaz le-moreshet Ben-Guryon, 1995), 5–7. For a skeptical assessment of this fear, see Flapan, *The Birth of Israel*, 212.

134. In response to a question posed by the Ihud journal *Ner* to a number of experts or public officials in 1952 regarding the rights of refugees to their property or compensation, Moshe Sharett offered the following formula: the United Nations is responsible for solving the refugee problem in political-diplomatic terms; the Arab States for the actual absorption of the refugees, and Israel for paying a fair share of reparations per Resolution 194. See the issue devoted in large part to the refugee question, *Ner* 3, nos. 7–8 (February–March 1952), 9.

135. In fact, Rawidowicz was not alone. To recall one obvious example with similarities to Rawidowicz in style and substance, Rabbi Binyomin continued to call for at least partial repatriation of refugees in the pages of *Ner* in a variety of forms and under a variety of noms de plume throughout the early 1950s. Similarly, one can find pro-repatriation advocates in M. R. Cohen (from a lecture at the Israel Oriental Society printed in *Ner* 3, no. 9–10 [April 1956], 2–3); Akiva Ernst Simon, *Ner* 5, nos. 6–7 (March–April 1954), 19–23; and Heinrich Strauss, *Ner* 6, nos. 3–4 (December 1954–January 1955), 43–48.

## "Between Jew and Arab" *(pages 135–80)*

1. We have chosen to translate the word "'ever," whose literal meaning is "Hebrew," as Jew. This usage was commonly found in the Jewish Enlightenment movement, the *Haskalah,* and reflects Rawidowicz's own fealty to an archaic Hebrew style. In the context of this chapter, "Jew" is a more suitable translation.

2. The typescript version of the manuscript includes here a reference not to Israel's Declaration of Independence, but rather to the state's Nationality Law (1952). The latter more accurately reflects the content of Rawidowicz's chapter.

3. This formulation hints of Rawidowicz's debt to the sociologist Aryeh Tartakower, who (as noted in part I) authored an article on democratic principles in the State of Israel that dealt with the status of the Arab minority. In the midst of that discussion, Tartakower articulated the general principle that "it is not good to be a minority in a state." Rawidowicz inverted the principle, but used quotations, I surmise, to acknowledge Tartakower's formulation. See Tartakower, "Mishtar-ha-demokratyah bi-Medinat Yisra'el," *Metsudah* 7 (1954), 77.

4. Rawidowicz here uses a verb of early rabbinic vintage (קִנֵּם) to indicate a pledge of abstinence. The more familiar form of this root קוֹנָם (*konam*), connoted a vow of abstinence in lieu of a sacrificial offering (*korban*).

5. Rawidowicz was adamant that the word "Israel" should be understood in its traditional meaning, to refer to the Jewish people at large, not to the State of Israel. For that

reason, we have often retained his use of the word "Israel" to refer to the Jewish people, retaining quotation marks around it to indicate his distinctive meaning. As noted
earlier, Rawidowicz insisted that the State of Israel (*Medinat Yisra'el*) be known only
as that. Rawidowicz engaged in an interesting exchange of letters on this theme in
1954–55 with Israeli Prime Minister David Ben-Gurion. See his essay "Israel: The People, the State, followed by the exchange with Ben-Gurion in Rawidowicz, *State of Israel, Diaspora, and Jewish Continuity,* 182–204.

6. Here Rawidowicz relies on one of the most familiar and versatile words in his linguistic arsenal, the Hebrew word בית (bayit). In much of his writing, including *Bavel vi-
Yerushalayim,* he makes frequent reference to the *bayit rishon* and *bayit sheni,* usually
translated as the First and Second Temples. Rawidowicz, however, understands these
terms less as markers of a physical space than of differing cultural dispositions of the
Jews. These two dispositions continually competed with each other for primacy in the
Jewish people throughout its long history—a battle that Rawidowicz described as
"bayit ve-bayit" in *Bavel vi-Yerushalayim,* I:105ff. He also believed that the events that
culminated in the creation of the State of Israel in 1948 marked the inauguration of *ha-
bayit ha-shlishi* (the third house) in the history of the Jewish people. Ibid., 148ff. In the
present chapter, Rawidowicz uses the term *bayit* to refer both to the Jewish homeland
in the Land of Israel and to the people of Israel in a larger, extraterritorial sense.

7. This phrase figures in the opening of Baba Metzia in the Mishnah tractate Nezikin:
"If two people are holding on to a garment and each one says it belongs to him, the law
is to divide it and each must swear that he for sure did not have less than half." Baba
Metzia 1:1.

8. Rawidowicz has in mind here political Zionists à la Herzl for whom the key problem
facing the Jewish people was not a desiccated culture or language but the absence of
a physical home.

9. Rawidowicz's term for empowerment—אִיּוּל—is an uncommon variation of the Hebrew word, אִיל, which connotes power. Rawidowicz's use of an obscure form of this
word reflects a number of important qualities in his prose: his search for antiquated
and rare usage from ancient and Hebrew texts; and his willingness to modify that usage
to create neologisms for a still developing modern Hebrew idiom.

10. This expression, "'eved ki yimlokh," comes from Proverbs 30:22.

11. Rawidowicz is here making reference to the recurrent fear in Israel that the Arab
countries might attempt a "second round" of fighting (known in Hebrew as a "sibuv
sheni"). See, for example, the reference to a "second round" in "Mi-yom le-yom," *Ha-
arets,* 9 June 1950.

12. "Infiltrators," known in Hebrew as *mistanenim,* were those Palestinians who attempted to reenter Israel's boundaries from Jordan, Egypt, and Lebanon. While it is
reasonable to assume that a large majority of "infiltrators" were seeking to reclaim their
property or rejoin their families, a smaller number harbored the desire to inflict harm
on the Israeli population.

13. This term, from the Turkish word "effendi" (lord or master), refers to wealthy and dis-
liked absentee landlords.

14. The new State of Israel declared in May 1948 a state of emergency (sec. 9a of the Law and Administration Ordinance). This declaration carried over previous British Mandatory regulations (including the Defense [Emergency] Regulations of 1945). See the discussion in Menachem Hofnung, *Democracy, Law and National Security in Israel* (Aldershott, Eng.: Dartmouth Publishing, 1996), 47ff.

15. Rawidowicz is referring to the nearly 600,000 Jews who had fled Arab countries and moved to Israel by 1951.

16. In a provocative move, Rawidowicz employs here the Hebrew term for remnant, "she-'erit," that was most commonly used to refer to Holocaust survivors (she'erit ha-peletah).

17. The phrase "scattered and dispersed," in reference to the Jewish people, can be found in Megilat Esther 3:8: "King Ahasuerus: 'There is a certain people scattered abroad and dispersed among the peoples in all the provinces of thy kingdom; and their laws are diverse from those of every people; neither keep they the king's laws; therefore it profit not the king to suffer them.'"

18. The reference is to two well-known walled cities in antiquity.

19. The Ihud Association was founded in September 1942 to advocate for "Jewish-Arab co-operation in a bi-national state, on the basis of parity of numbers and parity of political rights." Its initial membership included Judah Magnes, Martin Buber, and Moshe Smilansky, all of whom spoke on the behalf of the group at a meeting of the Anglo-American Inquiry Commission of 1946. See *Arab-Jewish Unity: Testimony before the Anglo-American Commission for the Ihud (Union) Association by Judah Magnes and Martin Buber* (London: Victor Gollancz, 1947), 9 The group also included among its prominent members Rabbi Binyomin, who edited the Ihud's journal, *Ner.*

20. Rawidowicz here refers to the U.N. Charter (1945) and the Universal Declaration of Human Rights (1948). He most likely had in mind the 13th clause of the latter document, which declares that "everyone has the right to leave any country, including his own, and to return to his country." The Universal Declaration is included in appendix D.

21. This figure presumably refers to the number of IDPs (internally displaced persons) whose land was annexed and were prevented from returning to it. According to Charles Kamen, there were 23,000 IDPs by the time of the conclusion of the 1948 war. Kamen, "After the Catastrophe I: The Arabs in Israel, 1948–1951," *Middle Eastern Studies* 23, no. 4 (October 1987), 466–69, quoted in Meron Benvenisti, *Sacred Landscape: The Buried History of the Holy Land since 1948* (Berkeley and Los Angeles: University of California Press, 2002), 201. Benvenisti estimates that there were 30,000–35,000 IDPs in 1951, double the number that Rawidowicz mentions.

22. It should be noted that a Nationality Law was first presented to the Knesset for discussion in June 1950, but was not approved until 1 April 1952.

23. Rawidowicz uses here the derogatory term (especially in the Zionist lexicon) "Galut" (exile) to signify the Diaspora.

24. Rawidowicz most likely had in mind Yitzhak Gruenbaum (1879–1970), the Polish-born Zionist activist who wrote about and defended (as a member of the Sejm) the

rights of Jews and other minorities in Poland. Gruenbaum was the first interior minister in the State of Israel and later a member of a kibbutz associated with the leftist Mapam party.

25. The text does not include the name of the law, though Rawidowicz was referring to the Land Acquisition (Validation of Acts and Compensation) Law of March 1953, which facilitated the transfer of annexed Arab land to the Israel Development Authority. The Development Authority then redistributed the land to kibbutzim, moshavim, and other bodies for their use. While Rawidowicz claims that the majority of Knesset members opposed or disagreed with the law, Menachem Hofnung notes that "the Law was passed with the support of all the Zionist parties." See Hofnung, *Democracy, Law, and National Security in Israel,* 115. What is true is that the law was passed with a fraction of the Knesset in audience, by a vote of 22–5. Finally, Rawidowicz provides the wrong date for the passage of the law; it was on 10 March 1953, not 1 March. See *Divre ha-Keneset: moshav sheni shel ha-Keneset ha-sheniyah* (Jerusalem: The Knesset, 1953), 13:923.

26. Smilansky's article is a play on the opening line of Lamentations: "How doth the city sit solitary, that was full of people!" Smilansky (1874–1953) was born in Kiev and emigrated to Palestine in 1890 as part of the First Aliyah. He settled in Rehovot, where he owned groves and vineyards. Smilansky opposed the efforts of the subsequent wave of Zionist immigrants to introduce a regime in the Yishuv of "Hebrew labor." He devoted a good deal of his energies and literary efforts to Arab-Jewish harmony, albeit with a rather pronounced paternalism. Nonetheless, Smilansky wrote a number of works of fiction, including one collection, *Bene 'Arav,* that depicted rural Arab life in Palestine. Smilansky was also, as noted earlier, the uncle of S. Yizhar, the renowned Hebrew author.

27. Rawidowicz is referring here to the maxim articulated by the third-century Babylonian sage, Samuel: "Dina de-malkhuta dina." This principle held that it was incumbent upon Jews to observe the law of the land.

28. Isaiah 1:27.

29. The Peel Commission was a British commission of inquiry that came to Palestine to investigate the circumstances surrounding the Arab revolt in 1936. After hearing testimony from various parties, the commission issued a recommendation in 1937, calling for the abolition of the British Mandate and partition of Palestine into Arab and Jewish states. Rawidowicz may also have been making reference to the Anglo-American Inquiry Commission, which was established in 1945 to explore Jewish immigration to Palestine in the wake of the Holocaust.

30. See the discussion in part II of those Israelis critical of the treatment of Palestinian Arabs, both inside Israel and beyond.

31. Rawidowicz here refers to a Talmudic passage (Arakhin 16b) that deals with the competing claims of disputants: "For if one says to [his fellow]: Remove the splinter from between your eyes [that is, refrain from a minor infraction], his fellow can retort, 'Remove the beam from between your eyes [refrain from a major transgression].'"

32. Slightly fewer than 700,000 'olim, or Jewish immigrants, came to Israel in the period between 1948 and 1951.

33. Deir Yassin was a village on the outskirts of Jerusalem which Jewish fighters from the Irgun Zvai Leumi and Lehi groups entered on 9 April 1948. As part of their efforts to ward off an Arab assault on Jerusalem, the Jewish soldiers laid siege to the village, killing between 110 and 120 residents (according to most current accounts). The event sent shock waves through both Jewish and Arab communities in Palestine, inducing fear, panic, and flight among members of the latter. Since that time, it has stood as a symbol of the excesses of Jewish military activity during the hostilities of 1948.

34. Rawidowicz here uses the rabbinic term "mitsvat 'aseh," referring to an affirmative commandment; that is, a commandment of commission.

35. The reference is to the "'al ha-nisim" blessing said at the Hanukah and Purim festivals.

36. Rawidowicz here uses a term for "exiled" (נסים from לנוס the verb for "to flee") whose unvocalized Hebrew form also means miracles.

37. Psalms 23:4.

38. Rawidowicz uses a Hebrew term "gezerah," abundantly present in medieval and early modern Jewish literature, which can be translated variously as "plight," "decree" (especially an *evil* decree), or "catastrophe" (as in "gezerot ta"h ve-ta"t," referring to the Chmielnicki massacres of 1648–49). Rawidowicz's usage contains elements of all three of these English words.

39. Rawidowicz uses the Jewish legal term "hefker" to refer to the lands abandoned by the Arab refugees.

40. This is an obvious reference to the Cold War tensions between the United States and the Soviet Union.

41. Rawidowicz's term "hurban shelishi" refers to the Holocaust as the "third catastrophe" after the destruction of the First and Second Temples.

42. Jeremiah 46:27. Rawidowicz here uses the biblical siblings Jacob and Esau to represent, as was common in late antique and medieval Jewish literature, Judaism and Christianity respectively. See part II.

43. Rawidowicz is suggesting that perhaps one day Christians (Esau) and Muslims (Ishmael) will unite to punish the Jews (Jacob) for their hand in the Palestinian refugee crisis.

44. Rawidowicz here refers to the series of recurrent accusations labeled against Jews, initially in medieval Europe, but spreading throughout the world, including in the present. The most common accusation involving the blood libel was that Jews murdered Christian children, whose blood was used either to poison wells or to make *matsah,* the ritual unleavened bread eaten during Passover. The "bread of affliction" (*ha-lakhma anya*) is another name for *matsah* used in the Passover Haggadah.

45. The Hasmoneans refer to the familial Maccabean band which initially rose up in rebellion against the Greek ruler, Antiochus IV Epiphanes in 165 BCE, and then went on to establish a ruling dynasty in Palestine from 140–37 BCE.

46. Here Rawidowicz performs a clever linguistic trick by describing "the heirs of the Nazis"— נאצים—as full of wrath (מנואצים), two words composed of similar Hebrew letters.

47. Daniel 7:10.

48. Leo Pinsker (1821–91) was a Russian-Jewish physician and early exponent of Jewish nationalism, especially in his 1882 treatise *Auto-emancipation*. Pinsker maintained that Jews were everywhere guests and nowhere at home, constantly subjected to the malady of "Judeophobia." The remedy was to find a place where the erstwhile guests were at home.

49. The idea of a vibrant partnership, or *shutafut,* between the State of Israel and the Diaspora was a key pillar of Rawidowicz's worldview.

50. Rawidowicz would seem to be making the counterintuitive claim that in an era in which hundreds of thousands of Jewish immigrants were arriving in the State of Israel, there was nonetheless a "break" or "interlude" of sorts (implied by the word *hafsakah*) in the current of immigration to the country after 1948. He somewhat clarifies this seeming incongruity further in the text, arguing that the Zionist ideal of "kibuts galuyot" (an ingathering of the dispersed exiles from around the Jewish world) had failed.

51. That is to say, the "miracle of Arab flight." As we have seen in part II (and will have occasion to see later in the text), Rawidowicz understood this notion that the flight of refugees was a "miracle" in the most ironic of terms.

52. This statement defies credulity, given Rawidowicz's manifestly Eurocentric orientation, according to which the Western Jews are culturally superior and, hence, more valuable than Jewish immigrants from the Middle East.

53. Rawidowicz makes a clever play on words with "masekhet terumah," referring to the Mishnaic tractate of that name. As noted, this prediction of Rawidowicz's was not borne out by subsequent charitable giving—or by the Jewish communal ethos of supporting the State of Israel as a cardinal article of faith.

54. There is a printer's error in the galleys version of the manuscript. The earlier typewritten version of the text clarifies, however, that the word in question is נוהג, meaning habit, custom, or in this case, norm.

55. The Hebrew term Rawidowicz uses, "shevet ahim," comes from the well-known Psalm 133:1: "How good it is, and how pleasant when we dwell together in unity."

56. S. Yizhar (né Yizhar Smilansky [1916–2006]) was a leading Hebrew writer, intellectual, and political figure. His two powerful stories, "Hirbet Hiz'ah" and "Ha-shavui" were published together in 1949. See the discussion of Yizhar and "Hirbet Hiz'ah" in part II.

57. Yizhar actually has in mind the Anglo-American Committee of Inquiry, which declared in 1946: "In Palestine there has been no expulsion of the indigenous population, and exploitation of cheap Arab labor has been vigorously opposed as inconsistent with Zionism." The report can be found at http://www.yale.edu/lawweb/avalon/anglo/angcov.htm.

58. This refers to a collection of essays by David Ben-Gurion on relations between Jews and Arabs; among them are some with a rather conciliatory message, especially those prior to 1929. See Ben-Gurion, *Anahnu u-shekhenenu* (Tel Aviv: Davar, 1931).

59. Smilansky uses the term "ma'apilim" here, which was commonly used to refer to Jewish immigrants who entered Palestine in defiance of stringent British restrictions during the Second World War.

60. Nahalal was the first collective *moshav* established in Palestine in 1921. Shmuel Dayan (1891–1961) was one of the founders of Nahalal, a veteran farmer and Labor Zionist political figure, as well as the father of Moshe Dayan.

61. Rabbi Binyomin, as noted in part II, was a passionate cultural Zionist, long-standing advocate of Jewish-Arab reconciliation, and editor of the Ihud's journal *Ner.* Hayim Greenberg (1889–1953) was a writer, editor, and socialist Zionist leader affiliated with Po'ale Zion in the United States.

62. Dayan refers here to "Brit Shalom," the organization of progressive Zionists (largely from Central Europe) who advocated dialogue, reconciliation, and power sharing with Arabs in Palestine. A key guide to this circle was the American-born rabbi, Judah L. Magnes (1878–1947), who immigrated to Palestine in 1922 and became the founding chancellor of the Hebrew University in Jerusalem. Neither Brit Shalom nor Magnes believed in the necessity of a Jewish state, preferring instead a binational polity in which governance was shared by Jews and Arabs. While Brit Shalom lost momentum by 1933, Magnes continued to adhere to the principle of a binational state until his death. In fact, he spoke in favor of the idea in his testimony before the Anglo-American Committee of Inquiry in 1946.

63. Hibat Zion was a proto-Zionist movement that arose in the 1880s in order to stimulate Jewish immigration to and agricultural settlement in Palestine.

64. Vladimir Zev Jabotinsky (1880–1940) was a Russian Jewish writer and charismatic orator who became the leader of the Revisionist Zionist movement, which broke away from the mainstream World Zionist Organization in 1935 and advocated a maximalist territorial agenda for Zionism (a Jewish state on both sides of the Jordan River). Jabotinsky was the mentor of Israeli Prime Minister Menachem Begin, and the inspirational force behind the contemporary Likud party in Israel.

65. Weizmann (1874–1952) and Ben-Zvi (1884–1963) were veteran Zionist leaders who became the first and second presidents of the State of Israel.

66. A. D. Gordon (1856–1922) was a Russian Jew who left behind his life as an estate manager at the age of 47 to move to Palestine and assist in the work of redeeming the land through physical labor. Gordon exhibited a quasi-religious devotion to physical labor (the Hebrew word for which, עבודה, also connotes worship). As a result of his own example, Gordon became a beloved and inspiring figure to the Labor Zionist movement.

67. The term "religion of labor" (*dat ha-'avodah*) points to the sacred quality that Zionist immigrants, especially from the various socialist Zionist movements, attributed to

the task of physical labor, which was seen by many of them as the antithesis to the stereotypical figure of the cerebral and unproductive Diaspora Jew.

68. The expression "image of God" (*tselem Elohim*) draws from Genesis 1:26: "Then God said, 'Let us make man in our image, in our likeness, and let them rule over the fish of the sea and the birds of the air, over the livestock, over all the earth, and over all the creatures that move along the ground.'"

69. The Hebrew "זופא" should be read as "זו,א." This typographical error is contained in both the typescript and galleys version of the text, but not in the original handwritten version (p. 79).

70. The content of this sentence is somewhat unclear. Rawidowicz is conjuring up a hypothetical situation in which countries would exchange their Jewish population in return for the refugees. In fact, the topic of a population exchange was discussed variously by British, Israeli, and Arab leaders. According to the various suggestions, the displaced Palestinian refugees would be resettled in an Arab country (e.g., Iraq) in exchange for the settlement of Jews from Arab lands in Israel. See, for example, Yehouda Shenhav, "What do Palestinians and Arab-Jews Have in Common: Nationalism and Ethnicity Examined through the Compensation Question," http://www.arts.mcgill/ca/MEPP/PRRN/PAPERS/shenhav1.htm. See also his article "Arab Jews, Population Exchange, and the Palestinian Right of Return," in Ann M. Lesch and Ian S. Lustick, eds., *Exile and Return: Predicaments of Palestinians and Jews,* 225–45.

71. The section in brackets was excluded by the printer in the galleys version, but appears in the typescript version.

72. This line is a famous principle attributed to the first-century sage Hillel, the entirety of which reads: "That which is hateful to you, do not do to your neighbor. That is the whole Torah; the rest is commentary; go and study it." BT Shabbat 31a. A similar point is expressed by Natan Hofshi in the first volume of *Ner* 1 (February 1950), 5–8.

73. Hostilities between Israel and four Arab states came to an end through a series of armistice agreements signed in the first half of 1949: on 6 January with Egypt; on 23 March with Lebanon; on 3 April with Jordan; and on 20 July with Syria.

74. Here Rawidowicz modifies a famous phrase of Maimonides to the effect that "the gates of interpretation are open to us" (*Guide to the Perplexed,* II:25). His own formulation entails a word play between the cognates שיבה and תשובה. See 276, n. 132.

75. As noted in part II, the State of Israel, through Foreign Minister Moshe Sharett, offered to the Arab states at Lausanne the 100,000 plan. According to this plan, Israel would repatriate 100,000 Palestinian refugees (25,000 of whom had already made their way back to the state and 10,000 who would qualify under a family reunification program).

76. The tribes of Gad and Reuben were prepared, on the eve of the Israelite entry into Canaan, to remain where they were in Transjordan. Numbers 32:5.

77. Isaiah 1:1.

78. Isaiah 1:27.

79. Isaiah 2:3.

80. Rawidowicz is here referring to the well-known injunction from Leviticus 19:34: "The stranger that sojourneth with you shall be unto you as the home-born among you, and thou shalt love him as thyself; for ye were strangers in the land of Egypt: I am the Lord your God."

81. This refers to the well-known image of the rootless "wandering Jew."

82. With the intensification of the conflict between Jews and Arabs in Palestine in the 1940s, threats to and violence against Jews increased in various countries in the Arab world. More violence broke out against Jews in Egypt and Iraq, among others, following the declaration of the State of Israel in 1948.

83. Rawidowicz probably has in mind the disturbances that broke out in Palestine in 1920–21, 1929, 1936–39, and throughout the 1940s.

84. This is an Aramaic term indicating the beginning of the messianic redemptive process, which is usually imagined to be a time of difficulty, duress, and crisis.

85. Rawidowicz may have in mind here the massive displacement of people caused by two Asian conflicts: the French Indochina War (1946–1954) and the Korean War (1950–1953).

86. Rawidowicz here plays on the double use of the term "megilah," as in the Declaration of the State and the Scroll of Esther. It is curious that in quoting from the Scroll of Esther (9:16), Rawidowicz neglects an essential passage (in italics) that would seem to undermine his more felicitous reading of Jewish behavior in ancient Persia: "And the other Jews that were in the king's provinces gathered themselves together, and stood for their lives, and had rest from their enemies, *and slew of them that hated them seventy and five thousand*—but on the spoil they laid not their hand."

87. The previous sentences echo the Song of the Sea (Exodus 15:1–21), in which the Israelites sing their gratitude to God for their exodus from Egypt and the drowning of Pharaoh's army in the sea.

88. Rawidowicz is referring here to Amos, the humble prophet of justice who stated: "I was no prophet, neither was I a prophet's son; but I was a herdsman, and a dresser of sycamore-trees." Amos 7:14.

89. Rawidowicz is here drawing on King David's admonition not to publicize the death of Saul and Jonathan: "Tell it not in Gath, publish it not in the streets of Ashkelon; lest the daughters of the Philistines rejoice, lest the daughters of the uncircumcised triumph." 2 Samuel 1:20.

90. It was this term—"troubler of Israel"—that King Ahab used to describe the prophet Elijah when the latter came to chastise the king for his worship of idols. 1 Kings 18:16.

## Epilogue *(pages 181–88)*

1. For example, Ernest Gellner calls attention to the frequently uttered nineteenth-century belief that "the 'nations' are there, in the very nature of things, only waiting to

be 'awakened' (a favorite nationalist expression and image) from their regrettable slumber, by the nationalist 'awakener.'" He judges this slumber image to be the "nationalist ideologue's most misguided claim." See Ernest Gellner, *Nations and Nationalism* (Oxford: Basil Blackford, 1983), 47–48.

2. See, for example, *Ha-shahar* (The dawn [1868]), *Ha-me'orer* (The awakener [1906]), and *Rasszvets* (Dawn [1860]).

3. Gordon's "Ha-kitsa 'ami" is translated and discussed in Michael Stanislawski's *For Whom do I Toil? Judah Leib Gordon and the Crisis of Russian Jewry* (New York: Oxford University Press, 1988), 49–50.

4. Among the leading sources of inspiration and information for this group of supporters of Israel are Alan Dershowitz, *The Case for Israel* (Hoboken, N.J.: John Wiley, 2002), and Mitchell Bard, *Myths and Facts Online: A Guide to the Arab-Israeli Conflict* at http://www.jewishvirtuallibrary.org/jsource/myths/mftoc.html. Both texts deal with the refugee question in partial fashion, minimizing or ignoring altogether any Jewish/Israeli responsibility, past or present, for the plight.

5. See, most recently, Joel Kovel, *Overcoming Zionism: Creating a Single, Democratic State in Israel/Palestine* (London: Pluto, 2007).

6. See Tony Kushner and Alisa Solomon, eds., *Wrestling with Zion: Progressive Jewish-American Responses to the Israeli-Palestinian Conflict* (New York: Grove Press, 2003), and Adam Shatz, ed., *A Century of Dissident Jewish Writing about Zionism and Israel* (New York: Nation Books, 2004).

7. *Question of Zion*, 86. Rose concludes her analysis by recalling the insight offered by a non-Zionist, the late nineteenth-century French Jewish thinker, Bernard Lazare, who feared that Theodor Herzl's plan to restore Jewish pride through the creation of a state would inevitably ignore the depths of misery of Eastern European Jews. Lazare retorted with an observation that resonates powerfully in our own day: "We die from hiding our shames, from burying them in deep caves, instead of bringing them out into the pure light of day where the sun can cauterise and purify them." Lazare's retort is found in Nelly Wilson, *Bernard Lazare: Antisemitism and the Problem of Jewish Identity in Late Nineteenth-Century France* (Cambridge: Cambridge University Press, 1978), quoted in Rose, *Question of Zion*, 144–45.

8. Wisse, *Jews and Power*, 169.

9. Much of the momentum to "come to terms with the past" owes to the regime of accountability set in place by the Nuremberg trials from 1945 to 1949. Since that time, a number of European countries and business concerns have examined the history of their complicity with Nazism, expressed contrition, provided financial compensation to victims and, in so doing, lifted the stigma of criminality that had enveloped them. For a recent discussion of the postwar regime of accountability in Europe, see the essays in Dan Diner and Gotthard Wunberg, eds., *Restitution and Memory: Material Restoration in Europe* (New York: Berghahn Books, 2007). In addition, there is a large and ever-expanding body of literature dealing with "truth and reconciliation" as part of the process of transitional justice (most notable in the South African case, but evident as well in countries from Liberia to Chile). For a discussion of this important development,

see the volume edited by Tristan Anne Borer, *Telling the Truths: Truth Telling and Peace Building in Post-Conflict Societies* (Notre Dame, Ind.: University of Notre Dame Press, 2006). For the less well known South Korean case, see "After Long Wait in Korea, Unearthing War's Horrors," *New York Times*, 3 December 2007.

10. See Mark Cutts, ed., *The State of the World's Refugees, 2000: Fifty Years of Humanitarian Action* (Oxford: Oxford University Press, 2000), 2. A central tenet of the United Nations Convention Relating to the Status of Refugees (1951) is that host countries should not "expel or return [*refouler*] a refugee in any manner." At the same time, the convention explicitly excluded from its mandate "persons who are at present receiving from organs or agencies of the United Nations other than the United Nations High Commissioner for Refugees protection or assistance." See http://www.unchr.ch/html/menu3/b/0_c_ref.htm. Given that Palestinians received assistance from the United Nations Agency for Palestine Refugees (UNRWA) as of December 1949, they were not subject to the 1951 convention.

11. See, for example Ann M. Lesch and Ian S. Lustick, "The Failure of Oslo and the Abiding Question of the Refugees," in their edited volume, *Exile and Return: Predicaments of Palestinians and Jews*, 3–16, See also the various opinions on this question in Shimon Shamir and Bruce Maddy-Weitzman, eds. *The Camp David Summit—What Went Wrong? Americans, Israelis, and Palestinians Analyze the Failure of the Boldest Attempt Ever to Resolve the Palestinian-Israeli Conflict* (Brighton, Eng.: Sussex Academic Press, 2005).

12. See the remarks of Palestinian President Mahmoud Abbas at the Annapolis conference on 27 November 2007 at http://domino.un.org/UNISPAL.NSF/c25aba03fle079db 85256cf40073bfe6/36a4fb9b0a4de40d852573a1006be3f6!OpenDocument.

13. Yoav Peled and Nadim Rouhana, "Transitional Justice and the Right of Return of the Palestinian Refugees," *Theoretical Inquiries in Law* 5, no. 2 (2004), accessed online at file:///C:/DOCUME~1/DAVIDM~1LOCALS~1/Temp/Download%20Document.html. Rouhana has written extensively on the importance of a truth and reconciliation process in the case of Israel and the Palestinian refugees. See, for example, his essay, "Truth and Reconciliation: The Right of Return in the Context of Past Injustice," in *Exile and Return: Predicaments of Palestinians and Jews*, ed. Lesch and Lustick, 261–78.

14. The Palestinians have been accumulating data on property claims, relying on old maps and other sources, as well as studying the restitution claims process elsewhere (for example, Bosnia-Herzegovina), for use in negotiations with the Israelis. See the discussion in Fischbach, *Records of Dispossession*, 336–58. For a recent Israeli perspective laying out the contours of a peace settlement, including the refugees question, see Menachem Klein, *A Possible Peace between Israel and Palestine: An Insider's Account of the Geneva Initiative*, trans. Haim Watzman (New York: Columbia University Press, 2007).

APPENDIX D: "The Nationality Law" *(pages 196–201)*

1. *Sefer Ha-Chukkim*, No. 51 of the 21st Tammuz, 5710 (6th July, 1950), p. 159.

2. *I.R.*, No. 48 of the 5th Shevat, 5709 (4th February, 1949), Supp. I, p. 164.

3. *Palestine Gazette,* English edition, No. 1210 of the 16th July, 1942, Supp. 11, p. 1193.


## APPENDIX E: The "Land Acquisition (Validation of Acts and Compensation Law" *(pages 202–6)*

1. *Sefer Ha-Chukkim,* No. 57 of the 26th Av; 5710 (9th August, 1950), p. 278.

2. *P.G.* (English edition), No. 1305 of the 10th December, 1943, Supp. 1, p. 44.


## APPENDIX G: United Nations General Assembly Resolution 181 *(pages 214–35)*

1. See Official Records of the General Assembly, Second Session, Supplement No. 11, Volumes 1–4.

2. This resolution was adopted without reference to a Committee.

3. The following stipulation shall be added to the declaration concerning the Jewish State: "In the Jewish State adequate facilities shall be given to Arabic-speaking citizens for the use of their language, either orally or in writing, in the legislature, before the Courts and in the administration."

4. In the declaration concerning the Arab State, the words "by an Arab in the Jewish State" should be replaced by the words "by a Jew in the Arab State."

5. The boundary lines described in Part II are indicated in the Annex. The base map used in marking and describing this boundary is "Palestine 1:250000" published by the Survey of Palestine, 1946.


## APPENDIX I: United Nations General Assembly Resolution 273 (III) *(page 240)*

1. See document A/818.

2. See document S/1093.

3. See *Resolutions adopted by the General Assembly* during its second session, pages 131–32.

4. See *Resolutions adopted by the General Assembly* during Part I of its third session, pages 21–25.

5. See documents A/AC.24/SR.45–48, 50 and 51.

# BIBLIOGRAPHY

## Archives Consulted

Brandeis University Archive: Rawidowicz's faculty assignments and contracts.

Central Zionist Archives: files A 71/64 and A 115/26; letters, articles about Rawidowicz, and obituaries.

Central Archive of the Hebrew University: files 165 (correspondence); 2010 (Protocols of the Institute of Jewish Studies); and 2254 (correspondence).

Chicago Jewish Archives, Spertus Institute of Jewish Studies: related materials from the institution's newsletter, "Alon."

Humboldt-Universität zu Berlin, Universitätsarchiv: Rektorat files 112 and 116, Phil. Fak. file 656, records relating to Rawidowicz's enrollment, coursework, dissertation, and promotion.

Jacob Rader Marcus Center, American Jewish Archives, Cincinnati, Ohio: correspondence with Adolph Oko.

Jewish National and University Library Archives: Schwadron Autograph Collection, Rawidowicz letters (Ben-Zion Dinur, Judah Magnes, Joseph Klausner, David Yellin)

Leeds University Central Records Office: records relating to Rawidowicz's tenure as lecturer and Montague Burton Lecturer.

London Metropolitan Archives: files 4180/JC/B/02/009 and 4180/JC/B/03/012: records relating to Rawidowicz and Jews' College.

Rawidowicz Archive, Newton, Massachusetts: correspondence, manuscripts, institutional records, and photographs.

## Interviews

Chimen Abramsky, 24 July 2005 (London).

Ben-Zion Gold, 5 August 2005 (Cambridge, Massachusetts).

Bernard Lewis, October–November 2004.

William Margolies, 1 August 2005 (Jerusalem).

Alice Shalvi, 1 August 2005 (Jerusalem).

## Main Periodical Sources Consulted

*'Al ha-mishmar*

*Be-terem*

*Davar*

*Divre ha-keneset*

*Ha-arets*
*Ha-ʿolam*
*Kol ha-ʿam*
*Metsudah*
*Moznayim*
*Ner*
*Shevivim*
*Yalkut*


## Main Works by Simon Rawidowicz

*Bavel vi-Yerushalayim.* 2 vols. Waltham, Massachusetts: Ararat, 1957.

"Between Jew and Arab" (unpublished manuscript, 1951–55).

*Im lo kan—hekhan?* Lvov: Brit ʿIvrit ʿOlamit, 1933.

*ʿIyunim be-mahshevet Yisraʿel.* 2 vols. Jerusalem: Rubin Mass, 1969.

*Kitve Rabbi Nachman Krochmal* [editor]. 2nd ed. Waltham, Massachusetts: Ararat, 1961.

*Ludwig Feuerbachs Philosophie: Ursprung und Schicksal.* Berlin: de Gruyter, 1964.

*Pinkas Chicago.* Chicago: College of Jewish Studies, 1952.

*Sefer Shimon Dubnow* [editor]. London and Waltham, Massachusetts: Ararat, 1954.

*Sihotai ʿim Bialik.* Jerusalem: Devir, 1983.

*State of Israel, Diaspora, and Jewish Continuity: Essays on the "Ever-Dying People."* 1986. Reprint. Hanover, N.H.: University Press of New England, 1998.

*Studies in Jewish Thought.* Philadelphia: Jewish Publication Society, 1974.


## Other Works

Abbas, Mahmoud. Speech given at the Annapolis conference, 27 November 2007. http://domino.un.org/UNISPAL.NSF/c25aba03f1e079db85256cf40073bfe6/36a4f b9b0a4de40d852573a1006be3f6!OpenDocument.

Abrams, Max. "The 'Right of Return' Debate Revisited." *Middle East Intelligence Bulletin* 5, August–September 2003. http://www.meib.org/articles/0308_pal1.htm.

Abunimah, Ali, and Hussein Ibish. *The Palestinian Right of Return.* Washington, D.C.: American-Arab Anti-Discrimination Committee, 2001.

Abu Sitta, Salam. "Inalienable and Sacred." 13–20 August 2003. http://weekly.ahram .org.eg/2003/651/op11.htm.

Ahad Haʿam (Asher Ginzberg). *ʿAl parashat derakhim.* Berlin: Jüdischer Verlag, 1930.

———. *Kol kitve Ahad Ha-ʿam.* Tel Aviv: Devir, 1947.

American Jewish Committee. "Israeli Premier's First Official Declaration Clarifying Relationships Between Israel and Jews in United States and Other Free Democracies Hailed by Blaustein as 'Document of Historic Significance.'" 10 September 1950. New York. http://www.ajcarchives.org/AJC_DATA/Files/508.PDF.

Anderson, H. Dewey. *The Arab Refugee Problem: How It Can be Solved (Proposals Submitted to the General Assembly of the United Nations).* New York: Nation Associates, 1951.

Anidjar, Gil. *Semites: Race, Religion, Literature.* Stanford: Stanford University Press, 2008.

Arendt, Hannah. *Eichmann in Jerusalem: A Report on the Banality of Evil.* 1963. Revised and enlarged edition, New York: Penguin, 1977.

———. *The Jewish Writings.* Edited by Jerome Kohn and Ron H. Feldman. New York: Schocken, 2007.

Aruri, Naseer. *Palestinian Refugees: The Right of Return.* London: Pluto, 2001.

Band, Arnold. "Simon Rawidowicz: An Early Critic of the Zionist Narrative." Unpublished lecture delivered as the 35th Simon Rawidowicz Memorial Lecture, Brandeis University, Waltham, Massachusetts, 1998.

Bard, Mitchell. *Myths and Facts Online: A Guide to the Arab-Israeli Conflict.* http://www.jewishvirtuallibrary.org/jsource/myths/mftoc.html.

Beilin, Yossi, and Abu Mazen (Mahmoud Abbas). "Beilin-Abu Mazen Agreement." 31 October 1995. http://www.bitterlemons.org/docs/beilinmazen.html (29 June 2007).

Bell, Daniel. *The End of Ideology: On the Exhaustion of Political Ideas in the Fifties.* Glencoe, Ill.: Free Press, 1960.

Ben-Ami, Shlomo. *Scars of War, Wounds of Peace: The Israeli-Arab Tragedy.* Oxford: Oxford University Press, 2006.

Ben-Gurion, David. *Anahnu u-shekhenenu.* Tel Aviv: Davar, 1931.

Benvenisti, Eyal. "The Right of Return in International Law: An Israeli Perspective." Paper presented at the Stocktaking Conference on Palestinian Refugee Research, Ottawa, Canada, 17–20 June 2003. http://www.idrc.ca/uploads/user-S /10576079920Session_2_Eyal_Benvinisti_paper.doc.

Benvenisti, Meron. *Sacred Landscape: The Buried History of the Holy Land since 1948.* Berkeley and Los Angeles: University of California Press, 2000.

Bergmann, S. H. "Letter to the Editor." *Ner* 1, no. 4 (31 March 1950): 3.

Bernadotte, Count Folke. "Progress Report of the United Nations Mediator to Palestine," 16 September 1948. http://domino.un.org/unispal.nsf/9a798adbf322aff3852 5617b006d88d7/ab14d4aafc4e1bb985256204004f55fa!OpenDocument&Highlight =0,Bernadotte,progress

Bombaji-Sasportas, Haya. "Kolo shel mi nishma/kolo shel mi mushtak: havnayat ha-siah 'al 'be'ayat ha-pelitim ha-falastinim' ba-mimsad ha-Yisre'eli" (Master's thesis, Ben-Gurion University, 2000.

Borer, Tristan Anne, ed. *Telling the Truths: Truth Telling and Peace Building in Post-Conflict Societies.* Notre Dame, Ind.: University of Notre Dame Press, 2006.

Bowman, Steven. "About Uncles and Arabs." *Hebrew Studies* 47 (2006): 325–26.

Boyarin, Daniel, and Jonathan Boyarin. "Diaspora: Generation and the Ground of Jewish Identity." *Critical Inquiry* 19, no. 4 (Summer 1993): 693–725.

Brenner, Michael. *The Renaissance of Jewish Culture in Weimar Germany.* New Haven, Conn.: Yale University Press, 1996.

Buber, Martin. "Bene Amos." *Ner* 1, no. 1 (February 1950): 4.

———. *A Land of Two Peoples.* Edited by Paul R. Mendes-Flohr. Oxford: Oxford University Press, 1983.

Buehrig, Edward H. *The UN and the Palestinian Refugees: A Study in Nonterritorial Administration.* Bloomington, Ind.: Indiana University Press, 1971.

Caplan, Neil. *The Lausanne Conference, 1949: A Case Study in Middle East Peacemaking.* Tel Aviv: Moshe Dayan Center for Middle Eastern and African Studies, 1993.

———. "A Tale of Two Cities: The Rhodes and Lausanne Conference, 1949." *Journal of Palestine Studies* 21, no. 3 (Spring 1992): 15, 31.

———. "The New Historians." *Journal of Palestine Studies* 24, no.. 4 (Summer 1995): 103.

Carlebach, Alexander. "Solving the Jewish Problem?" *Hayenu* 12, nos. 9–10 (October 1948): 13.

Chaver, Yael. *What Must be Forgotten: The Survival of Yiddish in Zionist Palestine.* Syracuse, N.Y.: Syracuse University Press, 2004.

Cohen, Gerson D. *The Blessing of Assimilation in Jewish History.* Brookline, Mass.: Hebrew Teachers College, 1966.

———. *Studies in the Variety of Rabbinic Cultures.* Philadelphia: Jewish Publication Society, 1991.

Cohen, Steven, and Ari Kelman. "Attachment of U.S. Jews to Israel Falls in Past 2 Years." *The Forward*, 4 March 2005.

Cutter, William, and David C. Jacobson, eds. *History and Literature: New Readings of Jewish Texts in Honor of Arnold J. Band.* Providence, R.I.: Brown Judaic Studies, 2002.

Cutts, Mark. *The State of the World's Refugees, 2000: Fifty Years of Humanitarian Action.* Oxford: Oxford University Press, 2000.

Dayan, Shmuel. "'Al yahasenu la-'Arvim." *Ha-po'el ha-tsa'ir* 45, nos. 44–45 (1952): 16.

Decter, Jonathan P., and Michael Rand, eds. *Studies in Arabic and Hebrew Letters in Honor of Raymond P. Scheindlin.* Piscataway, N.J.: Gorgias Press, 2007.

Dershowitz, Alan. *The Case for Israel.* Hoboken, N.J.: John Wiley, 2002.

Diner, Dan, and Gotthard Wunberg, eds. *Restitution and Memory: Material Restoration in Europe.* New York: Berghahn Books, 2007.

*Divre siah: hartsa'ot ve-diyune haverim.* Volume 2. Tel Aviv: Mifleget po'ale Erets Yisra-'el, 1951.

Dowty, Alan. "Much Ado about Little: Ahad Ha'am's 'Truth from Eretz Yisrael,' Zionism, and the Arabs." *Israel Studies* 5, no. 2 (2000): 174.

Eaks, Louis. "Arnold Toynbee on the Arab-Israeli Conflict." *Journal of Palestine Studies* 2, no. 3 (Spring 1973): 3–13.

Elath, Eliahu. "Yisroel un di tsukunft fun dem yidishn folk." *Di tsukunft* 54 (May–June 1949): 279.

Epstein, Yitzhak. "She'elah ne'elamah." *Ha-Shiloah* (1907): 203–4.

Eyal, Gil. *The Disenchantment of the Orient: Expertise in Arab Affairs and the Israeli State.* Stanford, Calif.: Stanford University Press, 2006.

Fattah, Hassan M. "For Many Palestinians, 'Return' is Not a Goal," *New York Times*, 26 March 2007.

Fink, Carole. *Defending the Rights of Others: The Great Powers, the Jews, and International Minority Protection, 1878–1938.* Cambridge: Cambridge University Press, 2004.

Fischbach, Michael R. *Records of Dispossession: Palestinian Refugee Property and the Arab-Israeli Conflict.* New York: Columbia University Press, 2003.

Flapan, Simha. *The Birth of Israel: Myths and Realities.* New York: Pantheon, 1987.

Fleischer, Yaakov. "She'elat Yisrael bi-ve'idat ha-shalom bi-shenat 1946." *Metsudah* 5–6 (1948): 162–94.

*Foreign Relations of the United States, 1949: The Near East, South Asia, and Africa.* U.S. Department of State. Washington, D.C.: GPO, 1977.

Freudenheim, Yehoshua. *Ha-shilton bi-medinat Yisrael.* Jerusalem: Rubin Mass, 1950.

Gabbay, Rony. *A Political Study of the Arab-Jewish Conflict: The Arab Refugee Problem.* Geneva: E. Droz, 1959.

Gans, Chaim. *Me-Rikhard Vagner 'ad zekhut ha-shivah: nituah filosofi shel be'ayot tsibur Yisre'eliyot.* Tel Aviv: Am Oved, 2006.

———. "The Palestinian Right of Return and the Justice of Zionism." *Theoretical Inquiries in Law* 5 (2004): 269–304.

Gechtman, Roni. "Conceptualizing National-Cultural Autonomy—From the Austro-Marxists to the Jewish Labor Bund." *Simon Dubnow Yearbook* 4 (2005): 30, 43–49.

Gellner, Ernest. *Nations and Nationalism.* Oxford: Basil Blackford, 1983.

Geneva Accord, 1 December 2003. http://www.geneva-accord.org/Accord.aspx?Folder ID=33&lang=en, 29 June 2007.

Gertz, Nurith. *Hirbet Hiz'ah veha-boker shele-mohorat.* Tel Aviv: Ha-kibuts ha-me'uhad, 1983.

Gilbert, Martin. *Churchill and the Jews: A Lifelong Friendship.* New York: Henry Holt, 2007.

Ginat, Joseph, and Edward J. Perkins, eds. *The Palestinian Refugees: Old Problems – New Solutions.* Norman, Okla.: University of Oklahoma Press, 2001.

Glatzer, Nahum N. "Simon Rawidowicz on his 10th Yahrzeit." *Judaism* 16 (Summer 1967): 343.

Goldberg, Jeffrey. *Prisoners: A Muslim and a Jew across the Middle East Divide.* New York: Knopf, 2006.

Goldberg, J. J. *Jewish Power: Inside the American Jewish Establishment.* Cambridge, Mass.: Perseus, 1996.

Gorny, Yosef. *The State of Israel in Jewish Public Thought: The Quest for Collective Identity.* New York: New York University Press, 1994.

———. *Zionism and the Arabs, 1992–1948: A Study of Ideology.* Oxford: Oxford University Press, 1987.

Gorin, G., ed. *Grayeve yizker-bukh.* New York: United Grayever Relief Committee, 1950.

Greenbaum, Avraham. *A History of the Ararat Publishing Society.* Jerusalem: Rubin Mass., 1998.

Grossman, David. *Sleeping on a Wire: Conversations with Palestinians in Israel.* Translated by Haim Watzman. New York: Farrar, Straus, and Giroux, 1992.

Hacohen, Dvora. *Immigrants in Turmoil: Mass Immigration to Israel and Its Repercussions in the 1950s and After.* Translated by Gila Brand. Syracuse, N.Y.: Syracuse University Press, 2003.

Halkin, Hillel. "The Peace Planners Strike Again." *Commentary* (January 2008): 3–18.

Halpern, Ben. *The Idea of the Jewish State.* 2nd ed. Cambridge, Mass.: Harvard University Press, 1969.

Harris, Jay. *Nachman Krochmal: Guiding the Perplexed of the Modern Age.* New York: New York University Press, 1991.

Hattis, Susan. *The Bi-National Idea in Palestine during Mandatory Times.* Haifa: Shikmona Publishing, 1970.

Hazony, Yoram. *The Jewish State: The Struggle for Israel's Soul.* New York: Basic Books, 2000.

*Hebrew University of Jerusalem.* Jerusalem: Jerusalem Post Press, 1957.

Hofnung, Menahem. *Democracy, Law, and National Security in Israel.* Aldershot, Eng.: Dartmouth Publishing, 1996.

Ibn Shmuel, Yehuda, Naftali Ben-Menahem, and Shraga Kadri, eds. *R. Binyomin: Zikhrono li-verakha.* Jerusalem: R. H. Ha-Cohen, 1958.

Israeli Central Bureau of Statistics. *Statistical Abstract of Israel*, 2006. http://www.jewish virtuallibrary.org/jsource/Immigration/Immigration_by_region.html.

Janowsky, Oscar. *The Jews and Minority Rights*. New York: Macmillan, 1933.

——. *Nationalities and National Minorities (With Special Reference to East-Central Europe)*. New York: Macmillan, 1945.

Jiryis, Sabri. *The Arabs in Israel*. Beirut: Institute for Palestine Studies, 1969.

Kamen, Charles S. "After the Catastrophe I: The Arabs in Israel, 1948–1951." *Middle Eastern Studies* 23 (October 1987): 453–54.

Kaplan, Edward, and Samuel Dresner. *Abraham Joshua Heschel: Prophetic Witness*. New Haven, Conn.: Yale University Press, 1998.

Kaplan, Mordecai M. *Judaism as a Civilization: Toward a Reconstruction of American Jewish Life*. 1934. Reprint, Philadelphia: Jewish Publication Society, 1981.

——. "The State of Israel and the Status of the Jew." *The Reconstructionist* 15, no. 10 (24 June 1949): 10, 14.

Karmi, Ghada. "The Right of Return: The Heart of the Israeli-Palestinian Conflict." 27 August 2003. http://www.opendemocracy.net/conflict-debate_97/article_1456.jsp.

Kedar, Nir. "Ben-Gurion's *Mamlakhtiyut*: Etymological and Theoretical Roots." *Israel Studies* 7, no. 3 (2002): 117–33.

Khalidi, Rashid. *The Iron Cage: The Story of the Palestinian Struggle for Statehood*. Boston: Beacon, 2006.

Khalidi, Walid, ed. *All That Remains: The Palestinian Villages Occupied and Depopulated by Israel in 1948*. Washington, D. C.: Institute for Palestine Studies, 1992.

Khoury, Elias. *Gate of the Sun*. Translated by Humphrey Davies. Brooklyn, N.Y.: Archipelago, 2006.

Kimche, Jon. "Mahen efsharuyot le-yishuv be'ayat ha-pelitim ha-'Arvim." *'Al ha-mishmar*, 10 August 1948.

Kimelman, Reuven. "Rabbis Joseph B. Soloveitchik and Abraham Joshua Heschel on Jewish-Christian Relations." *Modern Judaism* 24, no. 3 (2004): 251.

Klein, Menachem. *A Possible Peace between Israel and Palestine: An Insider's Account of the Geneva Initiative*. Translated by Haim Watzman. New York: Columbia University Press, 2007.

Kolsky, Thomas A. *Jews against Zionism: The American Council for Judaism, 1942–1948*. Philadelphia: Temple University Press, 1990.

Kovel, Joel. *Overcoming Zionism: Creating a Single, Democratic State in Israel/Palestine*. London: Pluto, 2007.

Kretzmer, David. *The Legal Status of the Arabs in Israel*. Boulder, Colo.: Westview Press, 1990.

Kurien, Prema. "Multiculturalism, Immigrant Religion, and Diasporic Nationalism: The Development of an American Hinduism." *Social Problems* 51, no. 3 (2004): 431–450.

Kushner, Tony, and Alisa Solomon, eds. *Wrestling with Zion: Progressive Jewish-American Reponses to the Israeli-Palestinian Conflict*. New York: Grove, 2003.

Lachover, F. "Ha-kinesiyah ha-'ivrit le-ma'aseh ule-halakhah." *Moznayim* 3, no. 10 (1931): 1.

Lapidot, Ruth. *Israel and the Palestinians: Some Legal Issues*. Jerusalem: Jerusalem Institute for Israel Studies, 2003.

LeBor, Adam. *City of Oranges: An Intimate History of Arabs and Jews in Haifa*. New York: Norton, 2007.

Leibowitz, Yeshayahu. *Judaism, Human Values, and the Jewish State.* Cambridge, Mass.: Harvard University Press, 1992.

Lesch, Ann M., and Ian S. Lustick, eds. *Exile and Return: Predicaments of Palestinians and Jews.* Philadelphia: University of Pennsylvania Press, 2005.

Lewis, Bernard Dov. "'Ever ve-'arav." *Metsudah* 1 (1943): 104–12.

Livnat, Limor. "Post-Zionism and Israeli Politics." 17 August 2000. http://www.meforum .org/article/185, 27 December 2006.

Lustick, Ian. *Arabs in the Jewish State: Israel's Control of a National Minority.* Austin, Tex.: University of Texas Press, 1980.

Luz, Ehud. "'Jewish Ethics' as an Argument in the Public Debate over the Israeli Reaction to Palestinian Terror." *Israel Studies* 7 (2002): 134–56.

———. *Wrestling with an Angel: Power, Morality, and Jewish Identity.* New Haven, Conn.: Yale University Press, 1998.

Magnes, Judah L., and Martin Buber. *Arab-Jewish Unity: Testimony before the Anglo-American Commission for the Ihud (Union) Association by Judah Magnes and Martin Buber.* London: Victor Gollancz, 1947.

Makovsky, Michael. *Churchill's Promised Land: Zionism and Statecraft.* New Haven, Conn.: Yale University Press, 2007.

Masalha, Nur. *Expulsion of the Palestinians: The Concept of "Transfer" in Zionist Political Thought, 1882–1948.* Washington, D.C.: Institute for Palestine Studies, 1992.

———. "The 1956–57 Occupation of the Gaza Strip: Israeli Proposals to Resettle the Palestinian Refugees." *British Journal of Middle Eastern Studies* 23, no. 1 (May 1996): 55–68.

McDonald, James. *My Mission in Israel, 1948-1951.* London: Victor Gollancz, 1951.

Mendelsohn, Ezra. *The Jews of East Central Europe between the World Wars.* Bloomington, Ind.: Indiana University Press, 1983.

Meyer, Lukas H., ed. *Justice in Time: Responding to Historical Injustice.* Baden-Baden: Nomos Verlagsgesellschaft, 2004.

Morris, Benny. *The Birth of the Palestinian Refugee Problem Revisited.* Cambridge: Cambridge University Press, 2004.

———. "The Crystallization of Israeli Policy Against a Return of the Arab Refugees: April–December 1948," *Studies in Zionism* 6, no. 1 (1985): 87, 90.

———. *1948 and After: Israel and the Palestinians.* Oxford: Clarendon, 1990.

———. "Survival of the Fittest." Interview with Morris, 9 January 2004. *Ha-arets,* http://www.haaretz.com/hasen/objects/pages/PrintArticleEn.jhtml?itemNo=380986, 22 June 2007.

———. *Tikun ta'ut: Yehudi ve-'Arvi be-Erets-Yisra'el, 1936–1956.* Tel Aviv: Am Oved, 2000.

Moss, Kenneth. "'A Time to Tear Down and a Time to Build Up': Recasting Jewish Culture in 1917–1921." Ph.D. diss., Stanford University, 2003.

Myers, David N. "'Distant Relatives Happening onto the Same Inn': The Meeting of East and West as Literary Theme and Cultural Ideal." *Jewish Social Studies* 1 no. 2 (1994–95): 75–100.

———. *Re-Inventing the Jewish Past: European Jewish Intellectuals and the Zionist Return to History.* New York: Oxford University Press, 1995.

———. "Simon Rawidowicz, 'Hashpaitis,' and the Perils of Influence." *Transversal* 7 (2006): 13–26.

———. "Simon Rawidowicz on the Arab Question: A Prescient Gaze into the 'New History.'" In *Mediating Modernity: Challenges and Trends in the Jewish Encounter with the*

*Modern World: Essays in Honor of Michael A. Meyer*, edited by Lauren B. Strauss and Michael Brenner, 143–67. Detroit, Mich.: Wayne State University Press.

———. "A Third Guide for the Perplexed? Simon Rawidowicz 'On Interpretation.'" In *History and Literature: New Readings of Jewish Texts in Honor of Arnold J. Band*, edited by William Cutter and David C. Jacobson, 75–87. Providence, R.I.: Brown Judaic Studies, 2002.

Netzer, Shlomo. *Ma'avak Yehude Polin 'al zekhuyotehem ha-ezrahiyot ha-le'umiyot.* Tel Aviv: Tel Aviv University, 1980.

Nimni, Ephraim, ed. *National Cultural Autonomy and its Contemporary Critics.* London: Routledge, 2005.

Nissan, Mordechai. "Ha-lebatim seviv ha-shem Yisra'el: zikaron mi-yeme hakhrazat Medinat Yisra'el." *Ha-umah* 91 (1988): 410–11.

Nusseibeh, Sari, and Anthony David. *Once upon a Country: A Palestinian Life.* New York: Farrar, Straus, and Giroux, 2007.

Ofer, Dalia. "Holocaust Survivors as Immigrants: The Case of Israel and the Cyprus Detainees." *Modern Judaism* 16 (1996): 2.

Office for the High Commissioner for Human Rights. "Convention relating to the Status of Refugees. Adopted on 28 July 1951 by the United Nations Conference of Plenipotentiaries on the Status of Refugees and Stateless Persons convened under General Assembly resolution 429 (V) of 14 December 1950. http://www.unhchr.ch/html/menu3/b/o_c_ref.htm.

Ohana, David. *Meshihiyut u-mamlakhtiyut: Ben-Guryon veha-intelektu'alim ben hazon medini le-te'ologyah politit.* Beer Sheva: Makhon Ben-Guryon, 2003.

Or Commission. *Din ve-heshbon: va'adat ha-hakirah ha-mamlakhtit le-verur ha-hitnagshuyot ben kohot ha-bitahon le-ven ezrahim yisre'elim be-Oktober 2000.* Jerusalem: Ha-madpis ha-memshalti, 2003.

Or, Theodor. "The Report by the State Commission of Inquiry into the Events of October 2000." *Israel Studies* 11, no. 2 (2006): 25–53.

Oren, Michael B. "Jews and the Challenge of Sovereignty." *Azure* (Winter 5766 [2006]): 27–38.

Oz, Amos. "No right of return, but Israel must offer a solution." 12 May 2007. http://globeandmail.workopolis.com/servlet/Content/fasttrack/20070512/COOZ12?gateway=cc.

Pappé, Ilan. *The Ethnic Cleansing of Palestine.* Oxford: Oneworld, 2006.

———. *A History of Modern Palestine: One Land, Two Peoples.* Cambridge: Cambridge University Press, 2003.

Peled, Yoav, and Nadim Rouhana. "Transitional Justice and the Right of Return of the Palestinian Refugees." *Theoretical Inquiries in Law* 5, no. 2 (2004); http://www.springerlink.com/content/j033273564q206u3/fulltext.pdf.

Penslar, Derek J. *Israel in History: The Jewish State in Comparative Perspective.* New York: Routledge, 2007.

Peretz, Don. *Israel and the Palestine Arabs.* Washington, D.C.: Middle East Institute, 1956.

Pianko, Noam F. "Diaspora Jewish Nationalism and Identity in America, 1914–1967." Ph.D. diss., Yale University, 2004.

Prag, Alexander. "Medinat Yisrael veha-kefar ha-'Arvi." *'Al ha-mishmar*, 1 August 1948.

Rabbi Binyomin (Yehoshua Radler-Feldmann). "Be-shule ha-sefer veha-zeman." *Moznayim* 4 (1935): 76.

Rabkin, Yakov M. *A Threat from Within: A Century of Jewish Opposition to Zionism.* London: Zed Publishing, 2006.

Rabinovitch, Simon. "Simon Dubnov and the Dawn of a New Diaspora." *Leo Baeck Institute Year Book* 50 (2005): 280.

Ratzabi, Shalom. *Between Zionism and Judaism: The Radical Circle in Brith Shalom, 1925–1933.* Leiden: Brill, 2002.

Ravid, Benjamin. "The Human Dimension of *Wissenschaft des Judentums*: Letters from the Rawidowicz Archives." In *Studies in Arabic and Hebrew Letters in Honor of Raymond P. Scheindlin*, edited by Jonathan P. Decter and Michael Rand, 87–128. Piscataway, N.J.: Giorgias Press, 2007.

———. "Le-hayav veli-khetav shel Shimon Rawidowicz." In *'Iyunim be- mahshevet Yisra-'el*, 1: xvii–lxxxii. Jerusalem: Rubin Mass, 1969.

———. "Shimon Rawidowicz u-Vrit 'Ivrit 'Olamit: perek be-yahasim ben tarbut 'Ivrit be-tefutsah le-ide'ologyah ha-Tsiyonit." In *Studies and Essays in Hebrew Language and Literature: Berlin Congress: Proceedings of the 16th Hebrew Scientific European Congress*, 119–54. Jerusalem: Brit Ivrit Olamit, 2004.

Ravitzky, Aviezer. *Messianism, Zionism, and Jewish Religious Radicalism.* Translated by Michael Swirsky and Jonathan Chipman. Chicago: University of Chicago Press, 1996.

Robinson, Jacob, et al. *Were the Minorities Treaties a Failure?* New York: Antin Press, 1943.

Robinson, Shira Nomi. "Occupied Citizens in a Liberal State: Palestinians under Military Rule and the Colonial Formation of Israeli Society, 1948–1956." Ph.D. diss., Stanford University, 2005.

Rose, Jacqueline. *The Question of Zion.* Princeton, N.J.: Princeton University Press, 2005.

Rosenthal, Steven T. *Irreconcilable Differences: The Waning of the American Jewish Love Affair with Israel.* Waltham, Mass.: Brandeis University Press, 2001.

Ross, Dennis. *The Missing Peace: The Inside Story of the Fight for Middle East Peace.* New York: Farrar, Straus, and Giroux, 2005.

Russman Halperin, Liora. "The Arabic Question: Zionism and the Politics of Language in Palestine, 1918–1948." Bachelor's thesis, Harvard University, 2005.

Sachar, Abram L. *Brandeis University: A Host at Last.* Hanover, N.H.: University Press of New England, 1995.

Sanders, Moshe, and Marion Aptroot. *Jewish Books in Whitechapel: A Bibliography of Narodiczky's Press.* London: Duckworth, 1991.

Sarna, Jonathan. *American Judaism: A History.* New Haven, Conn.: Yale University Press, 2004.

Schäfer, Barbara. "Jewish Renaissance and *Tehiyya*: Two that are One?" *Jewish Studies Quarterly* 10 (2003): 322–23.

Schechtman, Joseph B. *The Arab Refugee Problem.* New York: The Philosophical Library, 1952.

———. *Postwar Population Transfers in Europe, 1945–55.* Philadelphia: University of Pennsylvania Press, 1962.

School of Oriental Studies, London Institution. *Report of the Governing Body and Statement of Accounts.* Hertford: Stephen Austin, 1935–47.

Schmitt, Carl. *Political Theology: Four Chapters on the Concept of Sovereignty.* Translated by George Schwab. Cambridge, Mass.: MIT Press, 1985.

Segev, Tom. *1949: The First Israelis.* New York: Free Press, 1986.

――――. *The Seventh Million: The Israelis and the Holocaust.* Translated by Haim Watzman. New York: Hill and Wang, 1973.

Shain, Yossi. *Kinship and Diasporas in International Affairs.* Ann Arbor, Mich.: University of Michigan Press, 2007.

――――. "The Role of Diasporas in Conflict Perpetuation or Resolution." *SAIS Review* 22, no. 2 (Summer–Fall 2002), 115-144.

Shalom, Zaki. *David Ben-Guryon: Medinat Yisra'el veha-'olam ha-'Arvi.* Sde Boker: Hamerkaz le-moreshet Ben-Guryon, 1995.

Shamir, Shimon, and Bruce Maddy-Weitzman, eds. *The Camp David Summit—What Went Wrong? Americans, Israelis, and Palestinians Analyze the Failure of the Boldest Attempt Ever to Resolve the Palestinian-Israeli Conflict.* Brighton: Sussex Academic Press, 2005.

Shapira, Anita. "Hirbet Hiz'ah: Between Remembrance and Forgetting." *Jewish Social Studies* 7, no. 1 (2000): 1–62.

――――. *Land and Power: The Zionist Resort to Force, 1881–1948.* Translated by William Templer. New York: Oxford University Press, 1992.

Sharaby, Linda. "Israel's Economic Growth: Success without Security." *MERIA: Middle East Review of International Affairs* 6, no. 3 (September 2002): http://meria.idc.ac.il /journal/2002/issue3/jv6n3a3.html#Linda%20Sharaby.

Sharon, Avraham. *He'arot shovinistiyot le-'inyan ha-'Arvim.* Tel Aviv: n.p., 1949.

――――. *Torat ha-Tsiyonut ha-akhzarit.* Tel Aviv: Sifriyat De'ot, 1944.

Shatz, Adam, ed. *Prophets Outcast: A Century of Dissident Jewish Writing about Zionism and Israel.* New York: Nation Books, 2004.

Sheffer, Gabriel. *Diaspora Politics: At Home Abroad.* Cambridge: Cambridge University Press, 2003.

――――. *Moshe Sharett: Biography of a Political Moderate.* Oxford: Clarendon Press, 1996.

Shenhav, Yehouda. "Arab-Jews, Population Exchange, and the Palestinian Right of Return." In *Exile and Return: Predicaments of Palestinians and Jews,* edited by Ann M. Lesch and Ian S. Lustick, 225–45. Philadelphia: University of Pennsylvania Press, 2005.

――――. "Hitching a Ride on the Magic Carpet." *Ha-arets,* 15 August 2003.

――――. "What do Palestinians and Arab-Jews Have in Common: Nationalism and Ethnicity Examined through the Compensation Question." http://www.arts.mcgill.ca /MEPP/PRRN/PAPERS/shenhav1.htm.

Shikaki, Khalil. "The Right of Return." *The Wall Street Journal,* 30 July 2003.

Shlaim, Avi. "The Debate about 1948." *International Journal of Middle Eastern Studies* 27 (1993): 289.

――――. "Husni Za'im and the Plan to Resettle Palestinian Refugees in Syria." *Journal of Palestine Studies* 15, no. 4 (Summer 1986): 76.

Soloveitchik, Joseph Dov. *Divre hashkafah.* Jerusalem: Sifriyat Eliner, 1992.

Stanislawski, Michael. *For Whom do I Toil? Judah Leib Gordon and the Crisis of Russian Jewry.* New York: Oxford University Press, 1988.

Sternhell, Zeev. *The Founding Myths of Israel.* Translated by David Meisel. Princeton, N.J.: Princeton University Press, 1997.

Strauss, Lauren B., and Michael Brenner, eds. *Mediating Modernity: Challenges and Trends in the Jewish Encounter with the Modern World: Essays in Honor of Michael A. Meyer.* Detroit, Mich.: Wayne State University Press, 2008.

Sufian, Sandy, and Mark Levine, eds. *Reapproaching Borders: New Perspectives on the Study of Israel-Palestine.* Lanham, Md.: Rowman and Littlefield, 2007.

Tartakower, Aryeh. "Mishtar-demokratyah bi-medinat Yisra'el," *Metsudah* 7 (1954): 77.

Teveth, Shabtai. *Ben-Gurion and the Palestinian Arabs: From Peace to War.* Oxford: Oxford University Press, 1995.

Torres, María de los Angeles. *In the Land of Mirrors: Cuban Exile Politics in the United States.* Ann Arbor, Mich.: The University of Michigan Press, 1999.

Troen, S. Ilan, and Noah Lucas, eds. *Israel: The First Decade of Independence.* Albany, N.Y.: State University of New York Press, 1995.

Tucker, Gordon. "Review of Rawidowicz's *State of Israel* collection and James Diamond's *Homeland or Holy Land? The Canaanite Critique of Israel.*" *Judaism* 37 (Summer 1988): 364–75.

United Jewish Communities. "American Jewish Contributions to Israel." 1948–2004. http://www.jewishvirtuallibrary.org/jsource/US-Israel/ujatab.html.

United Nations Conciliation Commission for Palestine (PCC). "Observations on Some of the Problems Relating to Palestine Refugees." 28 March 1949. http://domino.un .org/UNISPAL.NSF/c25aba03f1e079db85256cf40073bfe6/1c4639213dbdfad985 256cafo0726eec!OpenDocument.

United Nations General Assembly. Resolution 194, 11 December 1948. http://daccessdds. un.org/doc/RESOLUTION/GEN/NR0/043/65/IMG/NR004365.pdf?OpenElement, 22 December 2006.

Van Cleef, Eugene. "Eastern Baltic Waterways and Boundaries with Special Reference to Königsberg." *Geographic Review* 35, no. 2 (April 1945): 266.

*Ve'idat ha-histadrut "Tarbut" be-London: din ve-heshbon.* London: Tarbuth Association, 1938.

Wisse, Ruth R. *Jews and Power.* New York: Shocken, 2007.

Ya'ari, Meir. "Ki tetsu le-milhamah." *'Al ha-mishmar,* 30 July 1948.

Yaron, Kalman, and Paul Mendes-Flohr, eds. *Mordekhai Martin Buber be-mivhan hazeman.* Jerusalem: Magnes Press, 1993.

Yizhar, S. "Hirbet Hiz'ah," *Shiv'ah Sipurim.* Tel Aviv: ha-Kibuts ha-Me'uhad, 1971.

Zertal, Idit. *Israel's Holocaust and the Politics of Nationhood.* Translated by Chaya Galai. Cambridge: Cambridge University Press, 2005.

# ACKNOWLEDGMENTS

Writing a book is, in most cases, a collaborative effort, and surely so in this case. The responsibility for any errors remains wholly mine, but I must acknowledge with deep gratitude those individuals and institutions whose expert assistance and kind support made this book possible. The Lucius N. Littauer Foundation, as it so often has in the field of Jewish studies, enabled the publication of this book through a generous subsidy. I am privileged to work at an institution, UCLA, that values the importance of research. Thanks are due the UCLA Faculty Senate, Humanities Dean Tim Stowell and Social Science Dean Reynaldo F. Macias for their financial support for this book. Much of my time at UCLA over the past four years has been spent directing the Center for Jewish Studies, a challenging and thrilling assignment at once. Managing our very busy schedule, not to mention my life, would simply not be possible without the extraordinary staff of the center: David Wu, Gina White, Mary Pinkerson, and my close colleague of ten years, our wondrously efficient and forbearing assistant director, Vivian Holenbeck.

In the course of researching the book, I made use of the following archives and relied on the kindness of the following individuals: the American Jewish Archives (Kevin Proffitt), the Robert D. Farber Archives and Special Collections at Brandeis University (Karen Abramson), the Central Zionist Archives (Batya Leshem), the Central Archive of the Hebrew University (Etty Alagem), the Chicago Jewish Archives of the Spertus Institute of Jewish Studies (Joy Kingsolver), the Jewish National and University Library Archives (Rivka Plesser), the Universitätsarchiv of Humboldt-Universität in Berlin, and the London Metropolitan Archives. A particularly hearty thanks goes to Ben Ravid who, as noted in the introduction, was unstinting in answering every request, large and small, and in granting me full access to the Rawidowicz Archive located in the basement of his home.

A number of colleagues and friends were kind enough to take time from their busy schedules to read various parts of the manuscript. I thank Andy Apter, Zvi Ben-Dor Benite, David Ellenson, Ruth Gavison, Liora Halperin,

Hagit Lavsky, Nadera Shalhoub Kevorkian, Menachem Lorberbaum, Adam Rubin, David Ruderman, Chaim Seidler-Feller, Nomi Stolzenberg, and Roger Waldinger. Particular thanks go to those who read the entire manuscript and whose critical comments significantly improved its content and style: Michael Berenbaum, David Biale, Ra'anan Boustan, Michael Brenner, Michael A. Meyer, Derek Penslar, Ben Ravid, and Anita Shapira. I also thank Stephanie Chasin, who read every line of the text with her typically keen eye. Jake Cunningham and Hillel Eyal provided outstanding research assistance that was of indispensable value to the completion of this project. As always, David Hirsch provided expert bibliographic help from his perch as Judaica librarian at the Young Research Library.

Colleagues at Brandeis University have been supportive of this project from the beginning. Eugene Sheppard, former student and dear friend, carefully read the book and passed it on for consideration by the Tauber Institute for the Study of European Jewry. The institute's executive director, Sylvia Fuks Fried, is a person of exceptional competence, discernment, and charm who guided the book through to the University Press of New England (UPNE) of which Brandeis University is a constituent member. Thanks are also due Jehuda Reinharz, president of Brandeis University and Tauber series general editor, for consenting to include the book in the series. The Press always seemed to me the most appropriate venue for a book about one of Brandeis' most interesting early faculty members. I thank UPNE's editor-in-chief, Phyllis Deutsch, for her sage advice and willingness to take on a book of this nature, as well as the book's able copyeditor, Betty S. Waterhouse.

To my ongoing marvel, Los Angeles remains a vibrant intellectual, cultural, and social milieu. I gratefully acknowledge the friendship of Steve Aron, Sharon Brous, Adam Rubin, Teo Ruiz, Hilary Schor, Chaim Seidler-Feller, Daniel Sokatch, and, with deep sadness, the late R. B. Kitaj, for adding so much stimulation and spice to life. The anchor of it all, though, is my family. Nomi Stolzenberg remains the love of my life, my best friend, and most careful reader. She manages to balance the competing demands of her own career and our family with great skill and compassion. Our proudest creation is the stupendous trio of daughters with whom we've been blessed: Tali, Noa, and Sara. They are the lights of our life—and have been uppermost in my thoughts throughout the writing of this book. Nomi and I have tried to inculcate in them the values of self-respect and respect for others in equal measure, often with the inextricably entwined fate of Jews and Arabs in mind. It is my hope that they will continue the struggle for peace and justice that remains so urgent in our day.

This book is dedicated to Arnold J. Band. It was a fateful encounter with Arnie as a senior in college that sealed my fate as a Jewish historian. I have had the privilege of knowing him as a teacher, and for the last seventeen years at UCLA, as a colleague and friend. Notwithstanding his famously irascible demeanor, he has seen to this transition with remarkable ease and goodwill; indeed, his example is a powerful inspiration to me. He and his wife Ora have been a font of valuable information about Simon Rawidowicz based on their encounters with him in Boston in the 1950s. Above all, Arnie agreed to join me in translating Rawidowicz's challenging Hebrew text, "Between Jew and Arab." Without his masterful command of Hebrew literary style and history, the chapter would have remained an unreadable mess. Arnie also read every page of this book with his customary acuity. He devoted so much time and energy to this task not because he shares Rawidowicz's (or my) political perspective. Rather, he is ever the teacher, genuinely interested in new approaches while insistent on attending to the wisdom of the past. In the case of this book, he knew when to encourage and when to restrain. He also knew to appreciate Simon Rawidowicz's great strengths, as well as the weak points in his ideological and political project. Arnie's clarity and open-mindedness helped bring this book to life; both qualities strike me as essential in understanding the central issue— the Arab Question—that lies at its core.

## Illustration Credits

Images on pages 21, 22, 25, 26, 27, 38, 42, 43, 55, 56, 67, and 68: Courtesy of the Rawidowicz Archives. Image on page 34: Courtesy of the Central Zionist Archives. Image on page 37: Reprinted from *Atlas Historyczny Polski* (Warsaw: PPWK, 1977). © PPWK S. A. POLAND Prof. Ładogórski T. Images on pages 45, 46, and 48: Courtesy of the Universitätsarchiv, Humboldt-Universität, Berlin. Image on page 65: Courtesy of the London Municipal Archives. Image on page 80: Courtesy of Chicago Jewish Archives, Spertus Institute of Jewish Studies. Image on page 83: Courtesy of the Robert D. Farber University Archives, Brandeis University.

# INDEX